German Memory Contests

Studies in German Literature, Linguistics, and Culture

German Memory Contests

The Quest for Identity in Literature, Film, and Discourse since 1990

Edited by
Anne Fuchs, Mary Cosgrove,
and Georg Grote

CAMDEN HOUSE

First published 2006 by Camden House
Transferred to digital printing 2007

Camden House is an imprint of Boydell & Brewer Inc.
668 Mt. Hope Avenue, Rochester, NY 14620, USA
www.camden-house.com
and of Boydell & Brewer Limited
PO Box 9, Woodbridge, Suffolk IP12 3DF, UK
www.boydellandbrewer.com

ISBN: 1–57113–324–0

Library of Congress Cataloging-in-Publication Data

German memory contests: the quest for identity in literature, film, and
    discourse since 1990 / edited by Anne Fuchs, Mary Cosgrove, and
    Georg Grote.
        p. cm. — (Studies in German literature, linguistics, and culture)
    Includes bibliographical references and index.
    ISBN 1–57113–324–0 (hardcover: alk. paper)
        1. Germany—Civilization—20th century—Psychological aspects.
    2. Memory—Social aspects—Germany. 3. Group identity—Germany—
    History—20th century. 4. Germany—History—1990—Historiography.
    I. Fuchs, Anne. II. Cosgrove, Mary. III. Grote, Georg, 1966–
    IV. Title. V. Series: Studies in German literature, linguistics, and culture
    (Unnumbered)

DD290.26.G465 2006
306.0943—dc22

2006007786

A catalogue record for this title is available from the British Library.

This publication is printed on acid-free paper.
Printed in the United States of America.

Contents

Ethnicity/Hybridity

Memory Politics

Acknowledgments

THIS VOLUME CONSISTS of fourteen selected articles by scholars from Germany, Great Britain, the United States, and Ireland. Engaging in a dialogue on cultural identity in unified Germany, the contributors explore the dynamic of contemporary German memory debates from a range of interlocking positions.

In order to make the volume accessible to non-German speakers, all German quotations have been translated into English. Unless otherwise stated, all translations were made by the author of the respective article.

The publication of this volume was made possible by the generous support of the Humanities Institute of Ireland (HII) at University College Dublin. An international conference on "Memory Contests: Cultural Memory, Hybridity and Identity in German Discourses since 1990" was hosted and funded by the Humanities Institute in June 2004. We gratefully acknowledge the HII's support and further assistance by the Goethe Institute and the German Embassy, which have been staunch supporters of Irish German Studies over the years.

The completion of the volume in autumn 2005 was helped by the Irish Research Council for the Humanities, which awarded a Senior Fellowship to Anne Fuchs. We would like to thank all funders for their support. Special thanks go to Jim Walker at Camden House, who offered invaluable editorial comments, supporting the project enthusiastically to completion.

A. F., M. C., G. G.
Dublin, March 2006

Introduction: Germany's Memory Contests and the Management of the Past

Anne Fuchs and Mary Cosgrove

IN AN ESSAY ENTITLED "The Present as History," the eminent British historian Eric Hobsbawm cites the famous opening lines of L. P. Hartley's novel *The Go-Between* (1953): "The past is another country. They do things differently there."[1] For Hobsbawm, Hartley's aphorism aptly summarizes a key idea that should guide good historical research, namely that historical understanding is premised on the "otherness of the past."[2] When historians fail to keep this insight in mind, they run the risk of producing anachronisms rather than credible historical explanations. And yet, the point of Hobsbawm's essay is to turn this premise precisely on its head by examining how historians' own experiences of history can influence their perceptions of it in a fundamental way. Citing John Charmley's Churchill biography as an example, Hobsbawm argues that the biographer's attempt to reassess Chamberlain's long-discredited appeasement policy was only possible because Charmley was not a member of the war generation who had experienced this period first hand.[3] For Hobsbawm, his generation of historians did not have to go to the archives to know that a deal with Hitler was simply impossible. Of course, Hobsbawm's point is not that only old men write good history but rather that historical research is malleable: the passing of the political generation that had direct experience of the Second World War is a case in point in that it marks "a major, if often silent, shift in that country's politics, as well as in its historical perspective on the war and — as is evident in both France and Italy — Resistance."[4]

In the case of Germany, this shift has not been silent but in the years following unification a rather noisy affair fought out in a series of public debates about how Germans should manage the recent past. Among the most prominent examples are the much-cited Walser-Bubis debate, the debate about the Wehrmacht exhibition, the protracted discussion about the building of the Holocaust memorial in Berlin, the controversy about the relevance of 1968, and, with reference to the GDR past, the debates about the Stasi past, the legacy of Socialism, or — from an eastern perspective — the question of West German cultural hegemony. More recently, the (re)discovery of Germans as victims of war and expulsions from the eastern regions has added a new sentimental tenor to such collective soul-searching. The ferocity of some of these controversies shows that the dates of 1945 and 1989 do not just refer to key moments in the shaping of Germany's postwar political landscape; they are emotionally charged nodes on the gendered and generational memory map that guides the German identity discussions that are the topic of this volume. There are many complex reasons for these memory debates: above all, unification did away with the political underpinnings of the postwar era, foreboding the arrival of the global economy that would swiftly erode the social security of the GDR. Nearly fifteen years later, in the era of the declining welfare state, it has dawned on West Germans that they too are affected by the consequences of globalization. Massive social and economic uncertainty triggered a wave of debates about Germany's past, as if public consensus about the past had to be established before a joined future could be mastered.

In reunified Germany, the past is thus not so much another country where they do things differently, but a hotly contested territory. The idea of memory contests refers to the special features of German memory debates since unification. Several thematic strands dominate these debates: first, unification triggered an investigation of the wider cultural and social divisions between east and west; second, with the ever increasing historical distance to National Socialism, the 1990s saw a notable redisovery of private family memories. Once these entered the public domain, they exposed the limits of Germany's official remembrance culture that for decades sidelined people's private memories of war. Third, against the backdrop of the aging of the generation of the 1968ers, the memory debates of the 1990s were characterized by a huge investment in the idea of generations, along with the scrutiny of generational conflict and transgenerational dialogue. Elsewhere we have argued that

> in contrast to the old paradigm of "Vergangenheitsbewältigung" [coming to terms with the past], the term memory contests puts emphasis on a pluralistic memory culture which does not enshrine a particular normative understanding of the past but embraces the idea that individuals and groups advance and edit competing stories about themselves that forge their changing sense of identity. The notion of memory contests thus gives expression to the fact that memories always offer heavily edited versions of selves, groups and of their worlds.[5]

Memory contests are highly dynamic public engagements with the past that are triggered by an event that is perceived as a massive disturbance of a community's self-understanding. In the case of Germany, this disturbance was of course caused by the period of National Socialism, which fundamentally dislodged Germans' shared self-perception as an exemplary *Kulturnation*. The city of Weimar as the seat of eighteenth-century literature, philosophy, and art had been the very embodiment of Germany's heritage as a *Kulturnation*. The idea of *Kulturnation* was defined on the

one hand by concepts specific to the German culture, such as Herder's
notion of the German language and, on the other, by ideas that transcend
the German culture, such as Goethe's notion of "Weltliteratur" (world literature). After the war, the cultural leadership of the two Germanys tried
to reconnect with this heritage pedagogically: East Germany claimed that
the great German classics were the real precursors of the socialist state and
could be used for re-educating the people for the emerging socialist order.
Inexpensive editions of the classics were printed in the GDR, the so-called
"Bibliothek deutscher Klassiker" (Library of German Classics), to popular-
ize and spread the sense of a cultural heritage that since the eighteenth
century had emphasized notions of freedom, justice, and beauty.[6] West
Germany's cultural leadership also tried to reinvigorate such notions for a
program of re-education. The historian Friedrich Meinecke proposed in
his book *Die deutsche Katastrophe* (The German Catastrophe, 1946) that
the German people should be reminded of the value of a particular version
of German "Innerlichkeit," an inwardness that was culturally defined.
Goethe societies should be founded with the purpose of "die lebendigen
Zeugnisse des großen deutschen Geistes durch den Klang der Stimme den
Hörern ins Herz zu tragen" (carrying the living heritage of the great German cultural tradition by means of the tone of the voice into the hearts of
the audience).[7] The problem was that such programs saw the twelve years
of National Socialism simply in terms of an "Unterbrechung der Überlieferung" (an interruption of tradition), as one contributor to the Christian-
Socialist magazine *Frankfurter Hefte* put it. This disturbance of tradition,
it was felt, could be overcome by realigning the nation with its true
cultural values.[8] The German *Bildungsbürger* of the postwar period sought
consolation in cultural tradition. This explains the success of conservative
Christian or even nationalistic authors and poets who ignored the challenges of the present and sought refuge in escapist poetry that gave expression to conservative ideas in conventional forms.[9]

However, this regression into an unchallenged tradition was relatively
short-lived. The writings of these authors had no impact beyond the
1950s, and they are completely forgotten today. Especially after the highly
publicized Auschwitz trials in the early 1960s in Frankfurt, it had become
evident that Weimar did not just stand for the great German classics from
Goethe and Schiller to Herder but also for the nearby German concentration camp Buchenwald. A new cultural elite emerged that embraced a discourse of critical engagement with the causes of National Socialism. One
should of course emphasize that such attempts to work through the past
were not an invention of the 1960s: the question of German collective
guilt had already been raised in the immediate postwar period by intellectuals such as Thomas Mann, Hannah Arendt, and Karl Jaspers.[10] In 1945,
in his first lecture series after the war, at Heidelberg University, the
philosopher Jaspers addressed the issue of Germans' collective guilt. In

contrast to Mann, who after the war insisted on an insurmountable distance between himself as an emigrant and the German people, Jaspers used the collective pronoun "we" throughout his lectures to indicate that all Germans, even the exiles, had to deal with this issue in a comprehensive fashion.[11] But such concern with the management of the past had little resonance in the wider public, which was, after all, preoccupied with economic survival. The climate of repression was one of the main targets of the students of 1968, who attacked their parents and teachers for their denial of the past.[12] However, the wider public only began to engage with this topic after the screening of the American series *Holocaust* on German TV in 1979.[13]

The example of 1968 demonstrates a second characteristic of memory contests. Memory contests question and investigate established cultural norms and values that have helped to define the nation since the eighteenth century. Memory contests are iconoclastic: they challenge the cultural heritage through which groups of people articulate and sculpt a positive self-image. Even where participants in such memory debates put forward traditional views about national identity and collective memory, they ultimately contribute to a critical investigation of the validity of these norms. Most modern (western) nations have traditionally managed their past through historical research, museums, artistic expression, literature, and the media, all of which feeds into what Benedict Anderson calls "imagined communities."[14] The imagined community of the modern nation employed a relatively homogenous set of cultural practices that created a sense of togetherness. In our globalized era, however, the binding force of high culture has been lessened considerably. The dispersion of culture into a range of alternative lifestyles, self-fashionings, or religious and ethnic sub-groupings that no longer share a set of cultural values makes the "invention of tradition"[15] — a hallmark of the nineteenth-century nation state — a vicarious project of the impoverished cultural imagination. Faced with the fragmentation of society into a set of cultural niches, neoconservatives tend to advocate the proper management of the nation's past. They propose to simply re-instate the delegitimized national narrative as a cure for the ailments of our fragmented reality. Recently, German center-right politicians have suggested that all ethnic minorities in Germany must subscribe to the German "Leitkultur" (dominant culture). On the occasion of the conservative Christian Social Party (CSU) conference in Bavaria, the party leader and Ministerpräsident Edmund Stoiber gave the following definition of German national identity:

> Traditionelle Werte, nationale Identität, Zusammenhalt und Bindungen machen ein Volk stabiler, selbstbewusster, krisenfester gegen Gefährdungen. Das spüren die Menschen im rauen Wind der Globalisierung und der Bedrohungen durch Terror und religiösen Fanatismus. [. . .] Unser Volk ist eine Schicksalsgemeinschaft. Diese Gemeinschaft ist entstanden

aus einer gemeinsamen Geschichte im Schlechten wie im Guten, gemeinsamer Sprache und Kultur, gemeinsamen Traditionen und gemeinsamer
christlicher Religion. Alles zusammen ist Teil unseres geistig kulturellen
Wurzelgeflechts.[16]

[Traditional values, national identity, solidarity, and close ties make a people more stable, more self-aware, and better equipped to deal with crises
and danger. People sense this in the raw wind of globalization and the
threat of terror and religious fanaticism. [. . .] We as a people are a community united by fate. This community has emerged out of a shared history both good and bad, shared traditions and a shared Christian religion.
All of this forms part of our spiritual and cultural roots.]

This highly regressive notion with its emphasis on a "shared fate," Chris-
tianity, and tradition did not go unchallenged. For example, in a lead article in *Die Zeit*, the editor Marion Gräfin Dönhoff dismantled the idea in
the following way:

Als ich das Wort von der "Leitkultur" zum ersten Mal hörte, musste ich
automatisch an den aufreizenden, unverfrorenen, selbstherrlichen wil-
helminischen Satz denken: "Am deutschen Wesen soll die Welt einst noch
genesen." Darum finde ich die Proteste gegen diesen Begriff unter-
stützenswert.
    Wir leben heute in einem sich immer mehr integrierenden Europa. Die
Globalisierung in Wirtschaft und Finanzen hat sich weitgehend durchge-
setzt. Desgleichen der Supranationalismus im politischen Bereich und im
Kommunikationswesen. Die Kultur wird folgen.[17]

[When I first got word of the "Leitkultur" discussion, I automatically
had to think of the provocative, insolent, high-handed Wilhelmine sentence: "One day again the world will heal itself through the essence of
Germany."
    Today we certainly live in an increasingly integrated Europe. Globaliza-
tion in economy and finance has asserted itself extensively. The same goes
for supranationalism in the political arena and in communications. Culture comes next.]

There is consensus among intellectuals that such attempts to reinstate a
heritage culture offer little more than a placebo in the face of the deepen-
ing cracks and rifts within our transnational, multi-cultural societies. However, the idea of a stable and normative *Leitkultur* appealed to those
sections of the wider public that feel threatened by the forces of globalization. Although *Leitkultur* is a regressive concept, it reflects fears that are
also fairly widespread in other Western European nations. Evidence of this
fear is the rise of the Right in the Netherlands and popular doubts about
further European integration as expressed in the rejection of the European
Constitution by the French people in 2005.

And yet, while most nations of Europe are struggling with the global and economic forces that have already eroded a good deal of national sovereignty, the management of the past is less contentious in some western countries than in others. Public discourse in France, for example, regularly invokes the French Revolution as an unquestionable identity marker of Frenchness that affects all French citizens, regardless whether they are of Algerian or domestic French origin. However, the violent street protests in France in the autumn of 2005 show that this national narrative is under jeopardy too: the street battles and fires in the outskirts of the big cities drew attention to widespread discrimination and marginalization of second generation immigrants in France. By contrast to France's colonial legacy, Germany's management of the past is still fraught by the haunting legacy of the Third Reich. It is obvious that the twelve years of National Socialism have caused a massive disturbance in the national narrative. In spite of West Germany's institutionalized pedagogy of *Vergangenheitsbewältigung*, which has indeed managed to establish a discourse of contrition, there remains a nearly imperceptible anxiety of influence that manifests itself in the regular assertion that Germany is a normal democracy.

The notable ferocity of recent German memory contests reflects the deeply personal tenor of these attempts to understand German history. The last decade has witnessed a sharp increase in autobiographies, talk shows, and TV documentaries that engage with the personal experience of eyewitnesses of the Third Reich. The boom in the memory industry voices an awareness of the passing of the last generation of first-hand witnesses of National Socialism, who lived through the period as children and young adults. The personal accounts and stories of the last generation of eyewitnesses have produced a new transgenerational dialogue. In many ways, this dialogue is less antagonistic than when the '68ers confronted their parents with the past in the 1960s. After more than forty years of an institutionalized "discourse of contrition," it has become possible at last to address the floating gap between the subjective experience of history and scholarly historical explanations. Memory contests set the personal and the historical, the private and the public, fact and imagination in dialogue with one another. This dialogue concerns the question of how we can make room for the articulation of the bottom-up experience of history without, however, opening the door to complete historical revisionism. Since the groundbreaking work of Maurice Halbwachs it is generally accepted that personal memories of eyewitnesses that are passed down in family legends are highly malleable and subject to multiple practices of editing and historical revisionism.[18] By contrast, historiography emphasizes a structural or functional perspective on history that takes little interest in personal life stories.

The gap between historical research and the communicative memory of the Third Reich is the subject of a recent study entitled *Opa war kein*

Nazi (Grandpa Was No Nazi): the sociologist Harald Welzer and his researchers analyzed the dialogue about the Nazi past in three generations of forty contemporary German families.[19] Focusing on the transformations of history in the archive of family memories, the sociologists found that even in families in which one or both grandparents were deeply enmeshed with National Socialism, the family narratives tend to be characterized by a high degree of loyalty to the family members. Although the grandchildren showed no signs of sympathizing with National Socialism, and although they regarded the Holocaust as a heinous crime, they tended to represent their grandparents' role during the period in an embellished light. Welzer and his researchers call such editing of family narratives across generational thresholds a process of "kumulative Heroisierung," cumulative heroization, which draws attention to the malleability of family memory.[20]

Although Welzer's study highlights the gap between historical knowledge on the one hand and the production of social memory on the other, his methodology has its clear limits. The study included only families in which the three generations shared stories about the past; it thus lacks a perspective on those significant cases where the generations did not communicate directly about the past.

In contrast to Welzer's concern with overt communication between the generations, Gabriele Rosenthal analyzed the significance of communicative silence about the past in families of Holocaust survivors and perpetrators.[21] Although Rosenthal and her team also found that perpetrator families tend to produce family myths that cover up the underlying hidden family history, they also dealt with families in which the children or grandchildren become delegates of their parents' or grandparents' unmastered guilt.[22] This illuminative study demonstrates that it is not sufficient to analyze only what is being said about the past in postwar families. The unsaid, the *sous-entendues* (ghost-notes), can function as a powerful transmitter of an unmastered inheritance that is silently passed down the generational line. The transmission of family secrets through a generational chain is the concern of a number of contributions in this volume.

At this point it is useful to distinguish between two types of memory contests: first, those that are instigated by public actors, and second, those that are the result of what we will call the "historical uncanny." In the first category belong such controversies as the well-known Walser-Bubis debate.[23] Another more recent example is the debate about Germans as victims of the Allied bombing raids, which was first triggered by W. G. Sebald's lectures titled *Luftkrieg und Literatur* (The Air-Raids and Literature, 1999).[24] Sebald raised the question why there were hardly any credible literary accounts of an experience that had traumatized Germans for generations, a topic that will be examined in more detail in this volume. The publication of Günter Grass's novella *Im Krebsgang* (Crabwalk) in 2002 shows that Sebald had hit a nerve of the times by homing in on feelings that had led an underground existence in postwar German discourse. While Grass's novella explored from an intergenerational perspective and without a hint of historical revisionism the theme of German wartime suffering, the same cannot be said of *Der Brand* (The Fire, 2002) by the historian Jörg Friedrich. This book did not just adopt the perspective of Germans as victims of the carpet bombing campaigns but employed a somewhat inflammatory register that, as Aleida Assmann argues, portrays the Allied bombings as a war against the civilian population and the treasures of German culture.[25] Reaching its tenth edition in the first year of publication, the book is a symptom of a highly popular trend to recast Germans as victims of war and expulsions. This tendency was already apparent in the 1950s, when many Germans considered themselves Hitler's first victims.[26] These examples show that memory contests can be triggered by public figures who intervene in what they perceive to be a too-consensual remembrance culture. In each case, these interventions aim to push the boundaries of Germany's cultural memory beyond the institutionalized discourse of remembrance. Furthermore, these debates do not take place exclusively in a rarified space of intellectual discussion. The German media plays a key role in propelling these debates forward and in disseminating their messages: the televised debate between Martin Walser and Ignatz Bubis on 14 December 1998, arranged by the *Frankfurter Allgemeine Zeitung*, is one such example of the media-fueled visibility of contested memory in Germany today.

The second type of memory contest is not the product of direct discursive intervention but the result of what we will call "the historical uncanny." The significance of the 9th of November in twentieth-century German history is a case in point: it is the date when the Social Democrat Philipp Scheidemann proclaimed the first German Republic in Berlin,[27] the date of the Hitler Putsch in 1923, the date of the pogrom night known as the "Reichskristallnacht" (Night of the Broken Glass) in 1938, and finally the date of the Fall of the Wall in 1989. Clearly, the 9th of November is laden with historical significance. Faced with the ambiguity of the date, the German Bundestag felt that it carried too uncanny a burden to make it Germany's national day. Instead, a completely neutral date, October 3, was chosen as the Day of Unification. In this instance, the historical uncanny is the result of the strange coincidence that historically interrelated events actually did occur on the same date. While the Hitler Putsch and the Reichskristallnacht are haunting signatures of the Third Reich, which caused the division of Germany that was finally overcome on 9 November 1989, Scheidemann's proclamation of the first German Republic is an equally haunting reminder of the failure of democracy. After 1989 no one wanted to be reminded of previous historical failures. The correlation between these dates creates an uncanny repetition effect that historians do not normally deal with since it exceeds a rational framework of analysis.

The historical uncanny is the proper domain of fiction; it suggests that historical change can be motivated by subconscious factors that act across generational thresholds.

The historical uncanny is also a vessel for the expression of the personal experience of history. In recent years, it has become the focal point of a growing number of family narratives that adopt a transgenerational perspective on Germany's past. Among these are Monika Maron's *Pawels Briefe* (Pavel's Letters, 1999), Hans-Ulrich Treichel's *Der Verlorene* (The Lost One, 1999), Günter Grass's *Im Krebsgang*, and Uwe Timm's *Am Beispiel meines Bruders* (On My Brother's Example, 2003), which appeared in English translation under the somewhat misleading title *In My Brother's Shadow* (2005). Other notable examples in this respect are Reinhard Jirgl's *Die Unvollendeten* (The Incomplete Ones, 2003), Stephan Wackwitz's *Ein unsichtbares Land: Ein Familienroman* (An Invisible Country: A Family Romance, 2003), Thomas Medicus's *In den Augen meines Großvaters* (In My Grandfather's Eyes, 2004), and Dagmar Leupold's *Nach den Kriegen* (After the Wars, 2004). The narrators of these stories, who research their families' histories, are as interested in the silences and gaps in the family narrative as they are in the overt family legends that have been passed down through the generations. Tuning into the unsaid that punctures the archive of family legends, these narrators adopt the role of "phantomologists" who explore an unmastered inheritance within the domain of the family. This body of literature is the topic of a number of chapters in this volume.

In the majority of these narratives, the unifying experience of a generation is used as an explicit reference point that either validates or questions a particular set of historical explanations. However, the relationship between a generation and its historical experience is far from clear; it requires urgent critical attention. The common understanding of the concept of a generation is based on membership in an age group, which predisposes individuals to similar historical experiences and cultural influences. Straddling the biological factor of birth and cultural influences that shape a generation, the term thus always carries the risk of explaining historical phenomena with reference to natural processes. In order to avoid this pitfall, the term requires careful handling and historical analysis. Cultural critics have come up with a range of explanations. In the nineteenth century, Wilhelm Dilthey defined the concept in terms of a harmonious relationship between the individual's biography and his times.[28] Dilthey's explanation implicitly presupposed that it is great men who make great history. His concept of a generation did not really encompass the lives of ordinary people; rather it referred to the biographies of great men whose lives provide an age with a mirror of its historical and cultural achievements. In an article entitled "Das Problem der Generationen" (The Problem of Generations) the sociologist Karl Mannheim tried to move away from Dilthey's understanding of a "geistige" (intellectual) bond among members of a generation by analyzing the concept in analogy to class: like class membership, membership in a generation was not a question of choice but one of birth; a generation needs its members' conscious awareness to form a generational bond.[29] Mannheim thus advanced the level of analysis considerably by putting forward a social understanding of the idea of a generation. And yet, in spite of his achievement in this regard, he too ultimately subscribed to the notion that the *Zeitgeist* of a particular age is the product of the intellectual élite that puts its stamp on its times.

Mannheim wrote his article in 1928, that is, in the interwar era when the so-called "lost generation" had returned beaten and demoralized from the war.[30] Deprived of a proper education and job prospects, the former soldiers retreated into a group identity that was largely modeled on their camaraderie during the war. Resentful of the Weimar Republic, this generation channeled its disappointments into a feverish form of nationalism that wanted to tear down class barriers in favor of a community like theirs, which had been forged in the trenches of the First World War. In the discourse of the generation of young men that had participated in the war, the concept was largely used to refer to particularly male forms of bonding in response to national humiliation and defeat. Against this background it is hardly surprising that the concept became increasingly contaminated by proto-fascist notions of the German nation as a "Schicksalsgemeinschaft," a community shaped by fate. From here it was only a step to the idea of a racially defined community that was predestined to change history.

The fascist contamination of the concept of generations explains why the term played a small role in the humanities after the Second World War. Although the generation of defeated soldiers expressed its shared set of experiences within a generational framework, the concept of generations had become too enmeshed in National Socialism to help with the critical analysis of cultural and historical change. While it continued to play a role in everyday life, especially in youth culture, it was written out of academic discourse by the 1960s. Instead, the 1960s saw the upsurge of paradigms that emphasized the structural or functional perspective on historical change. Marxism, structuralism, functionalism, feminism, psychoanalysis, and, finally, deconstructivism swept away the biographical method that had underpinned much of generational discourse; these intellectual movements also challenged the idea that great men change and write history.

So, why is it that the concept of the generation has become such a fashionable idea in contemporary memory debates? Why has it been embraced by popular culture and academics alike? Finding plausible answers to these questions is a main concern of this volume, which, on the one hand, examines recent cultural expressions of generational discourse in literature, film, and political culture, and on the other, offers a range of critical perspectives on the usage of the term itself.[31]

The discourse on the generation in contemporary memory contests is often accompanied by the idea that historical experience is intrinsically traumatic. This is an idea that has gained momentum through the complementary works of Cathy Caruth and Marianne Hirsch.[32] In her work on the relationship between trauma and historical experience, Caruth puts forward the argument that we are always separated from historical experience by the repression inherent in trauma. We can therefore only ever approximate historical experience belatedly through traumatic re-enactment. This is a highly selective, imbalanced, and narrow view of what constitutes history in that it privileges traumatic experience over all other forms of historical experience. It should come as no surprise, therefore, that Caruth's work takes the Holocaust specifically as the defining benchmark of historical experience, a problematic argument that has been analyzed and critiqued by a growing number of scholars.[33] For if the paradigm of historical experience is indeed the feeling-structure of trauma and repression, as Caruth argues, then the Holocaust loses its historical specificity altogether and runs the risk of becoming just another calamitous event in the traumatic history of mankind. This sweeping perspective also implies, somewhat contradictorily, that all of history collapses into the structure of traumatic repression for which the Holocaust is paradigmatic. Caruth does not seem to take into consideration that there might exist other equally valid but non-traumatic kinds of historical experience. Thus, we could say that Caruth does two mutually exclusive things simultaneously: first she introduces a paradigm of valid historical experience that is based on trauma and that prioritizes the Holocaust; second, this very uniform view of history makes the Holocaust indistinguishable from the rest of history, so that it loses any sense of uniqueness.

Hirsch was the first to introduce the concept of postmemory into debates about the memory of the Holocaust. The idea of postmemory attempts to provide theoretical underpinnings for an inevitable development in contemporary Holocaust memory culture: the increased reliance on mediated versions of the past, visual and written, due to the passing away of the generation that experienced the Holocaust and the resulting disappearance of communicative memory. Postmemory describes the increasingly constructed nature of memory for the generations born after the Holocaust. It shows how the descendents of victims and perpetrators invest historical documentation — in the form of family photos, diaries, memoirs — with varying degrees of imaginative fantasy and employ fictional strategies in order to produce a family narrative that bridges the generational gap. While this might provide continuity, tradition, and identity in an otherwise fractured and fragmented family history, the fictionalizing perspective of the belated generation often succumbs to the temptations of sentimentalizing narrative and thus revises history from a subjective perspective. Hirsch's argument concerning the mediation of Holocaust memory thus adds a new angle to the findings of Rosenthal's empirical study, mentioned earlier. The desire to plaster over or rewrite the dark or traumatic family past often expresses itself in transgenerational trauma when the descendents of the first generation repeat unconsciously the repressed trauma of the past. In contrast to Rosenthal's psychoanalytic study, however, Hirsch's notion of postmemory and Caruth's understanding of traumatic history run the risk of universalizing trauma. The present volume on memory contests proposes instead a more differentiated approach to the past that makes room for alternative interpretations of historical experience.

The essays in this volume engage with all of the above themes, covering a wide variety of memory discourses in literature, politics, photography, film, minority culture, and museum culture. Touching upon gender, generations, memory and postmemory, trauma theory, ethnicity, historiography, family narrative alongside many other topics, the contributions engage in a productive dialogue that gives a comprehensive picture of current German memory contests. In his consideration of what the institutionalized official memory discourse of the immediate postwar era — *Vergangenheitsbewältigung* — means, Peter Fritzsche raises a major issue that informs nearly all of the contributions: the tendentious force of narrative when put to the task of establishing a viable national identity in the present. He finds that narratives of the 1950s employed a whole range of strategic techniques in order to find a usable national past. For example, the figure of the Jew was written out of postwar Heimat narratives, historical and literary, so that Germans could more easily understand themselves as victims of the Allied bombings, and so could avoid taking responsibility for the past. However, the temptations of narrative are always accompanied by their uncomfortable doppelgänger: the sense of narrative insufficiency, which for Fritzsche derives from a much wider knowledge in the general population of complicity in Nazi crimes than was admitted by the sentimental 1950s narrative of the nation. Fritzsche suggests that it is time to move away from a normative discourse on what German memory ought to be like. Instead, we should examine the texts that employ narrative strategies of avoidance and repression so that we can understand better the conflicted process of simultaneous denial and critical self-reflection intrinsic to these narratives.

Roger Woods presents an excellent example of such an internally split and self-contradictory narrative around German identity since 1990 in his essay on the problems of the New Right. As a conservative movement that wants to re-establish German identity on the basis of a proud *Volksgemein-schaft*, the New Right is characterized by resurgent nationalism. However, it is unable to produce a clear narrative of identity around the political notions of *Volk* and *Reich* because the movement's cultural component is profoundly aware of the impossibility of achieving this aim. Thus, while on the one hand the political elements of the New Right movement call for a traditional image of the nation, its cultural component sees through this endeavor and, recognizing that the nation cannot be re-introduced as a viable identity base, the movement ends up in a continuing identity crisis. Andrew Plowman's assessment of postunification texts that deal with the memory of the 1950s also touches upon the self-consciously dual discourse of postwar narrative and its insufficiency. These texts are simultaneously nostalgic and critical; written from a personal perspective, they move dialectically between positive identification and criticism.

That the traditional concept of the nation has been exhausted — a main message of memory contests — is reinforced by Jennifer Michaels's essay on Afro-German women's struggle for a cultural space and recognition since unification. Unification is presented by this group of women writers and activists as a strongly negative experience for Germany's minority ethnic groups, immigrants, and refugees. This body of literature challenges white German hegemony by rediscovering the history of blacks in Germany. Thus, it argues for a more pluralistic, multicultural, and tolerant society. Afro-German women writers also draw attention to Germany's problematic colonial past by exposing continuing racist attitudes in postunification Germany. Their contention is that Germany has yet to deal adequately with its role in this episode of European history; the Nazi persecution of blacks is also a submerged chapter of German history that needs to be re-examined.

Dagmar Lorenz and Cathy Gelbin continue the focus on the place of minority groups in postunification Germany and in an increasingly globalized Europe. Lorenz describes the range of textual strategies employed by German- and Austro-Jewish writers who wish to establish themselves as a distinct group after the Holocaust. The search for a viable Jewish identity since the Holocaust often takes the form of reconnecting to prewar Jewish religious and cultural traditions. Lorenz concludes that Jewish identity is cast as a position of insurmountable isolation by most of these writers, ongoing evidence of the reluctance to once again assimilate into German culture. Gelbin makes a similar point in her discussion of the re-emergence of the golem figure in German and Jewish film and literature since unification. In the work of some writers, the golem stands for a vehemently antiassimilationist position. It is also a figure from Jewish tradition, so its reappearance in Jewish works is evidence of the ongoing search for an identity that has its roots in the past. However, the golem is a highly malleable figure and has been used to express anti-Semitic attitudes arising from or fostered by German fears about globalization, a discourse that taps into the fin-de-siècle association of Jews with a destructive modernity. Again, the German nation in combat with an identity crisis produced by international market forces reappears within these anti-Semitic renditions of the golem. Gelbin also adds that this kind of manipulation and selective use of an image steeped in a long literary and cultural tradition often has the self-gratifying effect of converting Germans into victims.

Several articles deal with the concepts of generation, postmemory, and transgenerational trauma. The current plethora of family narratives shows the centrality of the idea of generations and of intergenerational memory in German literature. Fritzsche notes that one tactic of the sentimental narrative of the nation typical for the 1950s is to focus on local historical context, provincial *Heimat*, and the family. Thus, the history of the period is converted into a local history of the family. This emphasis, he points out, forces the uglier national history of recent times into the background and has the added bonus of making it possible for Germans to present themselves as victims of the Allied bombings. In contemporary fiction, family is still a basic institutional structure, but it is viewed in a much more critical way than it was in the willfully blind type of narrative Fritzsche discusses. Where Fritzsche notes that the representation of the catastrophe of the war as a natural disaster facilitated the erasure of political agency from 1950s accounts of the war, Elizabeth Boa shows how this rhetorical strategy has been turned on its head by recent narratives about the legacy of the GDR. Looking at examples of family allegory in literature and film, Boa finds that this kind of narrative, far from eliding the political, imposes a generational structure onto political history. The children of the founder generation are keen to distance themselves from their parents, and these narratives are thus very critical of parental complicity in the running of the GDR state. While the texts discussed all use deliberate misrepresentation — or more plainly put, lying — as a strategy for presenting the past, narrative's insufficiency rears its head as the desire of the second generation for moral simplicity along a clear generational divide is denied through a range of cleverly arranged narrative ambivalences that center on sexuality, desire, and the body. Boa thus examines the second generation's disturbed relationship to the founder generation at a time when the GDR past is becoming normalized. Many of these narratives, however, remain marooned in a discourse of guilt and shame about the past that is expressed through descriptions of the body and that is a reluctant acknowledgement of complicity in the GDR past.

Anne Fuchs's essay on *Väterliteratur* argues that this genre of German literature must be read in awareness of the internal contradictions of the concept of generations. She examines the duality of the term's meaning: on the one hand, since the French Revolution it is associated with the rejection of older generations and the related notions of regeneration, youth, and newness, while on the other, it is linked to the idea of genealogy, of the origins of a race, its history, and its identity. While the *Väterliteratur* of the late 1970s and early 1980s used generational conflict to express rejection of the Nazi family patriarch, the recent versions of this genre are more balanced in their evaluation of the father's role in National

Socialism. This circumspect examination of the interference of the political and the personal is not a feature of the earlier literature. In particular, Uwe Timm's and Dagmar Leupold's texts on this theme epitomize a responsible engagement with the past from the second-hand perspective of the descendent generation.

In many of the contributions in this volume, the tension between the search for affiliation and the rejection of tradition features clearly because contemporary German literature is often caught between divided loyalties. On the one hand, explorations of the family's past express a strong desire for a sense of origin, genealogy, or belonging, but on the other, these excavations of the past involve a sober critique or at times a harsh rejection of the war generation. In this way, the identity struggle of the German New Right as presented by Woods can be understood as the result of the conflict between the desire for roots in a generational tradition and the need to reject this tradition. Thus, the desire for affiliation and identity within a certain tradition of the nation clashes with the insight that this genealogy must be rejected on the grounds that it is not viable in contemporary Germany. Jonathan Long's essay on postmemory in Monika Maron's *Pawels Briefe* shows how Maron's search for genealogical roots in the family narrative is highly selective, as she rejects her mother — representative of the founder generation of the GDR — in favor of identification with her Jewish victim grandfather. Similar to Boa's piece on GDR narratives of wish-fulfillment through misrepresentation, Long reveals the cunning political manipulation at work in such an uneasy mix of genealogical and generational discourse.

Long's contribution is notable also for its excellent appraisal of Hirsch's concept of postmemory. His perceptive analysis of *Pawels Briefe* exposes the many limitations of this academic theory, which has been widely, and for Long uncritically, disseminated since it first appeared in the late 1990s. Other contributions point to the role played by academic inaccuracy and reductionism in the forging of memory contests. In her assessment of the "Crimes of the Wehrmacht" photo exhibitions and a lesser-known exhibition entitled "Fotofeldpost," Chloe Paver shows how reductionist academic scholarship contributed to the highly moralized and mythical figure of the soldier photographer. The intellectual background to the first exhibition isolated the soldier figure from the historical context of photographic practice in the 1930s and 1940s, thus inscribing one of the sentimental strategies mentioned by Fritzsche: the tactic of containment — representing Nazi perpetrators as a small, mythical, and contained group, separate from the rest of the population. Paver draws our attention to the more obscure, but more considered "Fotofeldpost" exhibition, which restored a sense of context and thus a measure of sobriety, to the reception of the phenomenon of the soldier photographer.

In a similar vein, Matthias Fiedler defends film as a productive repository of memory contests. Due to what he terms a reproachful academic discourse that tends to equate commercial success with intellectual vacuity, film has been underestimated as a medium that can tell us much about the ongoing memory contests in contemporary Germany and as a sophisticated narrative form that reflects self-consciously on its own limitations. Fiedler examines the many films made during the 1990s about the Third Reich and its legacy in the present. He rejects claims that films encourage naive identification only, and argues that many of these commercially successful films employ a highly nuanced visual language that emphasizes the idea of memory as a process. Because film reflects on its own narrative insufficiency, film can offer a space for criticism and ethical reflection. Films therefore analyze the function of cinema as a cultural institution within a memory-obsessed culture at a time when reliance on postmemory and mediated images is becoming increasingly prevalent.

A further theme that appears across a number of contributions is gender. A number of articles make the point that generational discourse concerns not only the periodization of history and the transgenerational resurfacing of memories; it is also fundamentally a discourse on gender. Fuchs's piece on *Väterliteratur* shows how the children of Nazi patriarchs unmask the roots of a particular form of German masculinity embodied in the father figure: the cold persona. Boa also points out the highly gendered nature of the attacks by the younger generation on the older GDR generation in her analysis, and Cathy Gelbin highlights the problematic gendering of the golem figure in narratives that equate German suffering with Jewish suffering.

A number of articles deal with the role W. G. Sebald has occupied in memory contests since 1990. Fuchs's reading of Sebald's *Luftkrieg* essay on the Allied bombings finds that the invective it performs against 1950s German writers is evidence of transgenerational traumatization: Sebald is dependent on the very group of writers he so vehemently rejects. Much of the *Luftkrieg* essay expresses surreptitiously the desire for affiliation, belonging, and identity, and for a *Heimat*, ironically in the postwar ruin. At the same time, there is the recognition that *Heimat* is no longer possible because it is tainted by the National Socialist corruption of the concept. Sebald's essay is a further example of narrative insufficiency in postwar German literature: a sentimental and critical discourse on *Heimat* and origin converge and contradict each other in the symbol of the ruin. In a similar vein, Cosgrove argues that Sebald's self-understanding as a writer in the postwar German context is hugely influenced by his rejection of non-Jewish German writers. By the same token, he takes as his role models German- and Austro-Jewish writers of the 1960s who began to engage critically with the victim perspective on the Holocaust. Cosgrove suggests that Sebald's literary identity runs along the same contradictory narrative of genealogical rejection on the one hand, and on the other, the search for affiliation within a tradition of Jewish writing. The power of biography and generational affiliation is undeniable for Sebald's understanding of history and of himself.

Finally, Stefan Willer explores the role of multilingualism in recent German narratives. His analysis of the thematization of exile, multilingualism, and translation in Goldschmidt's and Sebald's novels unearths a preoccupation with the limitations of German discourse on the past. These writers suggest that multilingualism and translation can provide us with a different way of accessing subjective experiences in the past, of articulating and coming to terms with trauma. Willer's concept of multilingualism implies that the act of writing always entails a departure from everyday language and thus from conventional notions of identity. From this perspective, literary language is a kind of "translation" of ordinary language: expressing ideas, thoughts, and the unsaid between two different language registers, its condition could be described as bilingual. As such, it is an excellent vessel for expressing the historical uncanny. Willer thus raises a point of great relevance for the literary language used in several of the texts discussed in the volume, for where else can the uncanny, the highly personal and the repressed side of history — the otherness of history — be voiced effectively, if not in literary language?

To conclude: this volume on German memory contests does not subscribe to a normative ethics of memory; it investigates instead the emerging pluralism of memory cultures. While some critics might view this new pluralism as a problem requiring urgent pedagogic intervention, the contributions to this volume show that Germany has now entered a new phase of historical consciousness. This does not mean that memory of the Third Reich can be abandoned but that other topics are beginning to reclaim their space in public discourse. It is inevitable that this new pluralism makes the memory of the Third Reich a phenomenon that is ever more open to historical revisionism and contestation. But as long as the new pluralism is accompanied by a healthy critical response, this is a sign of the fruits of the pedagogy of remembrance that has informed unified Germany's public discourse since the early 1990s.

Notes

[1] Eric Hobsbawm, "The Present as History," in *On History* (London: Weidenfels & Nicolson, 1997), 228–40; here: 233.

[2] Hobsbawm, "The Present as History," 233.

[3] John Charmley, *Churchill, The End of Glory: A Political Biography* (London: Hodder & Stoughton, 1993).

[4] Hobsbawm, "The Present as History," 233.

[5] Mary Cosgrove and Anne Fuchs, "Introduction," *German Life & Letters* 59/2 (2006), special issue: *Memory Contests*, ed. by Anne Fuchs and Mary Cosgrove, 3–10; here: 4.

[6] See for example the introduction to the two-volume edition of Hölderlin's works: the editor points to the contrast between ideal and reality as a defining tension of Hölderlin's poetry. However, by emphasizing that Hölderlin did not resign himself to this discrepancy but aimed to overcome it, Herbert Greiner-Mai aligns the national pathos of Hölderlin's poetry with the agenda of the GDR. See, "Einführung," in *Hölderlins Werke in zwei Bänden*, ed. and introduced by Herbert Greiner-Mai (Berlin and Weimar: Aufbau-Verlag, 1968), vol. 1, 5–34; here: 19.

[7] Friedrich Meinecke, *Die deutsche Katastrophe: Betrachtungen und Erinnerungen* (Wiesbaden: Brockhaus, 1946), 175.

[8] Clemens Münster, "Zum Aufbau der geistigen Bildung," *Frankfurter Hefte: Zeitschrift für Kultur und Politik*, ed. by Eugen Kogon and Walter Dirks, 8 (1946): 703–14; here: 706.

[9] The majority of these authors had continued to thrive under National Socialism; many had been members of the *Reichsschrifttumskammer* that had organized the alignment of cultural production with National Socialist aims. A good example in this respect is the author of the notorious *Volk ohne Raum* (A People without Space, 1932) Wilhelm Grimm, who founded a center for nationalist-conservative authors after the war, the so-called "Lippoldsberger Dichtertreffen," where a revival of Heimat-Dichtung took place. Another example is the nationalist poet Wilhelm Schäfer, who was highly regarded during National Socialism and whose *Anekdoten* (Anecdotes) of 1943 found their way into the schoolbooks of the postwar period.

[10] See Thomas Mann's 1945 essay, "Warum ich nicht nach Deutschland zurückkehre," in *Essays 6: Meine Zeit 1945–1955*, ed. Hermann Kurze and Stephan Stachorski (Frankfurt am Main: Fischer, 1977), 33–45. With this essay Mann responded to Walter von Molo's invitation to return to Germany to help with the country's moral and political rebuilding. For Mann the gap between the emigrants and those who had stayed in Nazi Germany was so wide that a return seemed impossible. Mann continued to publish essays on Germany and the Germans. In 1945 Hannah Arendt immediately resumed her correspondence with her former teacher, the philosopher Karl Jaspers. Arendt, who became one of the most significant political philosophers of totalitarianism in the twentieth century, commented in detail on Jasper's book *Die Schuldfrage* (The Question of Guilt), published in 1945. See *Hannah Arendt: Karl Jaspers Briefwechsel 1926–1969*, ed. Lotte Köhler and Hans Saner (Munich, Zurich: Piper, 2001), 88–93.

[11] Karl Jaspers, *Die Schuldfrage* (Heidelberg: L. Schneider, 1946).

[12] On the issue of the immediate postwar German memory culture see Aleida Assmann, "Persönliche Erinnerung und kollektives Gedächtnis in Deutschland nach 1945," in Hans Erler, ed., *Erinnerung und Verstehen: Der Völkermord an den Juden im politischen Gedächtnis der Deutschen* (Frankfurt am Main: Campus, 2003), 126–38.

[13] On the development of German memory politics see Bill Niven, *Facing the Nazi Past: United Germany and the Legacy of the Third Reich* (London, New York: Routledge, 2002).

[14] Benedict Anderson, *Imagined Communities: Reflections on the Origin and Spread of Nationalism* (London: Verso, 1983).

[15] Eric Hobsbawm and Terence Ranger, eds., *The Invention of Tradition* (Cambridge: Cambridge UP, 1983).

[16] See Edmund Stoiber, "Für unser Land: Klare Werte, klarer Kurs," speech held on the occasion of the CSU party conference on 20 November 2004. See http://www.csu.de/home/uploadedfiles/Reden/041120_ptrede.pdf

[17] Marion Dönhoff, "Leitkultur gibt es nicht," *Die Zeit* 46 (2000). See http://www.zeit.de/archiv/2000/46/200046_leitkultur.xml

[18] See Maurice Halbwachs, *On Collective Memory*, ed. and trans. by Lewis A. Coser (Chicago: U of Chicago P, 1992).

[19] Harald Welzer, Sabine Moller, Karoline Tschugnall, *"Opa war kein Nazi"* — *Nationalsozialismus und Holocaust im Familiengedächtnis* (Frankfurt am Main: Fischer, 2003).

[20] Harald Welzer, Sabine Moller, Karoline Tschugnall, *"Opa war kein Nazi,"* 79.

[21] Gabriele Rosenthal, ed., *Der Holocaust im Leben von drei Generationen: Familien von Überlebenden der Shoah und von Nazi-Tätern* (Gießen: Psychosozial Verlag, 1997).

[22] In some cases the grandchildren were tormented by the idea that they too might be potential perpetrators and they reacted to this with a tendency to punish themselves for their grandparents' deeds. See Rosenthal, *Der Holocaust im Leben von drei Generationen*, 364–76.

[23] This debate was triggered by Martin Walser's highly controversial speech "Erfahrungen beim Verfassen einer Sonntagsrede" (Experiences When Writing A Sunday Speech) on the occasion of his acceptance of the Peace Prize of the German Book Traders Association on 11 October 1998. Walser used his public address to radically break with the West German discourse of *Vergangenheitsbewältigung* (coming to terms with the past) that had dominated all intellectual engagement with the Nazi past in West Germany since the late 1950s. He explicitly and quite vehemently critiqued the omnipresence of Holocaust images in the media and the creation of a Holocaust industry. Furthermore, he challenged the rationale for building a Holocaust memorial right in the center of Berlin and suggested that the Holocaust was being instrumentalized by various interest groups. See Martin Walser, "Erfahrungen beim Verfassen einer Sonntagsrede," in *Die Walser-Bubis-Debatte: Eine Dokumentation*, ed. Frank Schirrmacher (Frankfurt am Main: Suhrkamp, 1999), 7–29; here: 13. The late Ignatz Bubis, who responded both in his capacity as President of the Jewish Council and as a Holocaust survivor, interpreted this as a barely disguised act of anti-Jewish incitement and insisted on the continued need to remember the victims of the Holocaust through public rites and memorials. See Ignatz Bubis, "Rede des Präsidenten des Zentralrats der Juden in Deutschland am 9. November 1998 in der Synagoge Rykerstrase in Berlin," in *Die Walser-Bubis-Debatte*, 106–13; here: 108. For subsequent academic debates see: Amir Eshel, "Vom eigenen Gewissen: Die Walser-Bubis-Debatte und der Ort des Nationalsozialismus im Selbstbild der Bundesrepublik," *Deutsche Vierteljahresschrift für Literaturwissenschaft und Geistesgeschichte* 2 (2000): 333–60; Anne Fuchs, "Towards an Ethics of Remembering: The Walser-Bubis Debate and the Other of Discourse," *German Quarterly* 75.3 (2002): 235–47.

20 ◆ ANNE FUCHS AND MARY COSGROVE

[24] W. G. Sebald, *Luftkrieg und Literatur. Mit einem Essay über Alfred Andersch* (Munich, Vienna: Hanser, 1999). The English translation appeared under the title: *On the Natural History of Destruction*, trans. by Anthea Bell (London: Hamish Hamilton, 2003).

[25] Jörg Friedrich, *Der Brand: Deutschland im Bombenkrieg* (Munich: Propyläen, 2002). For a critical perspective on Friedrich's book see Aleida Assmann, "On the (In)compatibility of Guilt and Suffering in German Memory," in special issue *Memory Contests, German Life & Letters* 59/2 (2006): 187–200.

[26] On this issue also see Norbert Frei, *1945 und wir: Das Dritte Reich im Bewußtsein der Deutschen* (Munich: Beck, 2005).

[27] Two hours later communist Karl Liebknecht proclaimed the first "freie sozialistische Republik" (Free Socialist Republic). The so-called November Revolution had been started by the seamen of the German navy on 29 October 1918; their strike quickly spread to other German cities. On 7 November the house of Wittelbach was toppled in Bavaria; on 9 November Prince Max von Baden announced the resignation of Kaiser Wilhelm II, which was followed by Scheidemann's proclamation of the first German Republic. Effectively this was the beginning of the Weimar Republic.

[28] Wilhelm Dilthey, "Uber das Studium der Geschichte der Wissenschaften vom Menschen, der Geschichte und dem Staat," in *Die geistige Welt, Einleitung in die Philosophie des Lebens. Erste Hälfte: Abhandlungen zur Grundlegung der Geisteswissenschaften. Gesammelte Schriften V*, ed. Georg Misch (Leipzig, Berlin: B. G. Teubner, 1924), 31–73.

[29] Karl Mannheim, "Das Problem der Generationen," in *Wissenssoziologie*, ed. by Kurt H. Wolff (Soziologische Texte 28) (Berlin, Neuwied: Luchterhand, 1964), 509–65. For an English translation see K. Mannheim, "The Problem of Generations," in *Essays on the Sociology of Knowledge*, ed. by Paul Kecskemeti (London: Routledge, 1964), 276–322.

[30] On this issue see Alexander Honold, " 'Verlorene Generation': Die Suggestivität eines Deutungsmusters zwischen Fin de siècle und Erstem Weltkrieg," in Sigrid Weigel, Ohad Parnes, Ulrike Vedder, Stefan Willer, eds., *Generation: Zur Genealogie des Konzepts — Konzepte von Genealogie* (Munich: Fink, 2005), 31–56.

[31] A recent publication deals primarily with material expressions of contemporary German memory culture. Entitled *Memory Traces*, the book evokes an archaeological image of cultural remembrance in the tradition of Benjamin. By contrast, our volume provides theoretical reflection on new and developing concepts in this field, such as trauma and generation. See Silke Arnold-de Simine, ed., *Memory Traces: 1989 and the Question of German Cultural Identity* (Oxford, Bern, Berlin: Lang, 2005).

[32] Marianne Hirsch, *Family Frames. Photography, Narrative and Postmemory* (Cambridge, MA, London: Harvard UP, 1997); Cathy Caruth, *Unclaimed Experience: Trauma, Narrative, and History* (Baltimore, London: Johns Hopkins UP, 1996).

[33] For an incisive critique see Dominick LaCapra's book, *Writing History, Writing Trauma* (Baltimore, London: Johns Hopkins UP, 2001); Sigrid Weigel, "Téléscopage

im Unbewußten: Zum Verhältnis von Trauma, Geschichtsbegriff und Literatur," in *Trauma: Zwischen Psychoanalyse und kulturellem Deutungsmuster*, ed. Elisabeth Bronfen, Birgit Erdle, and Sigrid Weigel (Cologne, Weimar, Vienna: Böhlau, 1999), 51–76. Anne Fuchs, "Trauma or History? The End of World War II in Margret Boveri's *Tage des Überlebens*," in *Schreiben gegen Krieg und Gewalt: Ingeborg Bachmann und die deutschsprachige Literatur*, ed. by Dirk Goettsche, Franziska Meyer et al., Krieg und Literatur X (Göttingen: V&R unipress, 2006), 103–18.

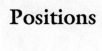

Positions

1: What Exactly is *Vergangenheitsbewältigung?* Narrative and Its Insufficiency in Postwar Germany

Peter Fritzsche

O NE YEAR AFTER STALINGRAD, Victor Klemperer imagined how the war would be represented once it had ended. He transcribed into his diary the story of Horst-Siegfried Weigmann, whose death had been announced in the local paper on 19 January 1944, with a swastika inside the Iron Cross at the side of the notice. The announcement read: "Ordained by fate, my only dear son, student of chemistry, Lance Corporal Horst-Siegfried Weigmann, volunteer, holder of the Iron Cross, Second Class, participant in the Polish and French campaigns, was suddenly and unexpectedly taken from this life in the midst of his studies at only twenty-four years of age." The death notice is signed "in deep sorrow" by his father, Bruno Weigmann, a musician from Munich. Klemperer continues in his diary to explain that some of Klemperer's friends knew the family and recalled that the mother was divorced from the father, and was Jewish. She had been among the Jews arrested in what Klemperer refers to as Dresden's "letzter *Aktion*" (last action). The son found out, posed as a Gestapo officer, and managed to speak to his mother in order to smuggle her out of prison and into hiding. Klemperer adds that there are said to be many Jews in hiding, particularly in Berlin. At the entrance of the prison, however, mother and son ran into a Gestapo officer who knew Weigmann and thus discovered the ruse. The mother was sent to Theresienstadt, and the son hanged himself in his prison cell. Klemperer heaves this tragedy onto a more purposeful plain, juxtaposing the suicide with the iron cross and commenting that Weigmann "ist wirklich auf dem Feld der Ehre gefallen und hat mehr Tapferkeit bewiesen als irgendein Soldat in der Schlacht" (he really fell on the field of honor and demonstrated more courage than any soldier in battle). The story of his brave actions — Klemperer continues to ennoble this incident — "wird fraglos in die Literaturgeschichte eingehen" (will undoubtedly go down in literary history). The young Weigmann will be the hero of plays and novels.[1]

Klemperer's vignette is extraordinary. First and foremost, it introduces the problem of representation of genocide after the war even as Klemperer remains worried about his own survival to the end of the war. He wonders how plays and novels will deal with the Third Reich, the eastern front, and the fate of Germany's Jews. As his diaries reveal, Klemperer was not at all clear about the nature of Nazism's hold over the Germans, but with Weigmann he projected lines of continuity with the pre-Nazi past just as he opened up lines of discontinuity in order to resolve the question. What Klemperer proposed, even after the vast majority of Dresden's and Germany's Jews had been rounded up and killed, is nothing less than a drama of national reconciliation. What follows is my extrapolation, based on signals in the diary account, of what Klemperer most likely had in mind.

The "Mischling" son is placed at the center of newly negotiated German-Jewish relations, which restores the heritage of mixed Jewish-Christian marriages even if the mother cannot be saved, while repudiating the father, who, we can safely assume, divorced his Jewish wife out of sheer opportunism. That both the hero and the Jewish mother die, whereas the patriotic, "Aryan" father survives, is an equation consistent with wartime realities: the number of deportations and the vast numbers killed. Nonetheless, with his sacrifice, the son holds out the possibility that the damage inflicted on Germany's Jews can be healed; the "Mischling" son stands out as the hero, applauded and honored by the German public. Even as the story turns on the awful coincidence of recognition at the entrance to the prison, it also gestures toward other places — hiding places — overseen by other people, who help the Jews, indicating the existence of a genuinely non-Nazi Germany. The price of reconciliation, however, is the repudiation of the father, representative of the older generation, who lacks his son's courage and attempts to veil his son's anti-Nazi action with his German military service. In the end, the drama that Klemperer imagines works by sacrificing the mother to underscore the complicity of the father. At war's end, thousands of German Jews are dead, but so is Germany's militaristic nationalism.

It is important that war service itself is not rejected. To work as a reconciliationist drama, the story does not challenge the honor of German soldiers in France or Poland, but rather shames the one-sided representation of events by the father. It is not the soldier-son who is the hypocrite, but the civilian father who misplaces the swastika inside the iron cross. Indeed, the "iron cross" and the son's sacrifice at home reinforce each other dramatically. The postwar audiences that Klemperer implicitly assembles in this literary success story are brought together through the successful combination of the iron cross and Jewish valor. It is the German-Jewish *Mischling*, Lance Corporal Horst-Siegfried Weigmann, who becomes the symbol of the new Germany.

What does it mean that Klemperer could outline this classical story of national reconciliation, a German *Antigone*, in January 1944? In spite of the often quoted diary entry of 16 April 1941, in which Klemperer concedes,

"Jetzt: Doch, ich urteile als Jude" (Now: Yes, I judge as a Jew), Klemperer embellished a literary plot in which Germany's cultural heritage is left intact and Germans and Jews have reconciled.[2] Despite all the killings that had transpired by early 1944, including the wholesale evacuation of Dresden's Jews, Klemperer imagines reconciliation, and he does so in a format that relies on a national narrative and a cohesive cultural history — Weigmann's story will "go down in history."[3] There is no mistaking the relentless brutality of the Nazis. Yet in my reading, Klemperer's rendition also opens up new spaces, the hiding spaces in Berlin, for example, and it depends on the mutual interaction of the heroism of Jews and the heroism of soldiers. It is a rehabilitative national drama. Moreover, the despicable behavior of the father serves as a lightning rod. Larger questions about the overall complicity of ordinary Germans are not raised; the father's evil contains them. Klemperer's readiness, as I am simulating it here, to imagine the German public embracing Weigmann's actions further underscores the basic good character of the majority. In Klemperer's version, postwar Germans will readily know Weigmann as a hero, and they will disqualify the father from the nation. And finally, while the story talks about arrests, "last actions," and Theresienstadt, these elements are in the background, secondary to the characters of mother, father, and son. The story takes place in a German city, with its newspaper, its medical school, and its prisons, but does not imagine the newly built assembly points, concentration camps, or work details in the occupied territories. It is not about the Holocaust, but German identity. Both the son and the mother are dead. But if they were alive, the drama presumes that they would not only be accepted by postwar audiences but would feel comfortable in their midst.

To be sure, Klemperer did not know the full scope of the Holocaust, even in January 1944, although a few days earlier he had scornfully thrown the evidence of "die Morde in Kiew . . . Und, und, und" (the murders in Kiev . . . And, and, and) in the face of German propaganda and a few days later reiterated his "ständige Lebensgefahr als Jude" (constant danger of death as a Jew).[4] His own imaginative realm, like the Weigmann drama, is very much defined by the limitations of his freedom that come with his mixed marriage to his wife Eva, a non-Jew. There were many things that Klemperer would come to learn only later. But I do not think the precise knowledge of the Shoah is the key issue. Klemperer's retelling of the Weigmann story indicates just how tempting the continuities of narrative are even for an estranged German such as Klemperer and how vexing the problem of representation appears. What does the Weigmann incident suggest about what the memory of the war will be?

First, Klemperer immediately poses the anecdote as a problem. Klemperer was plainly thinking about the challenge of mastering the past, assembling stories, finding the right dramatic register. Indeed Klemperer's company continued to mull over the problem: "Katz sagte: 'Ich kannte ihn

. . . ich koennte in vierzehn Tagen ein Drehbuch seines Falles schreiben' "
(Katz said: "I knew him . . . I could write a script about his case in a fort-
night"). He admits both the necessity and the plausibility of representing
the disaster that has taken place.

Second, though he may have "judged as a Jew," Klemperer did not
approach the deportations and murders of Dresden's Jews as a civilizational
break that definitively separated the fate of Jewish survivors from that of
German onlookers and perpetrators. On the contrary, just as the last waves
of arrests take place, the Jews are brought back into view. The actions of the
son are intended to return the mother to Berlin and, in Klemperer's
account, return the Jews to the German stage and restore them to German
history. The assumption that Germans and Jews can resume life among one
another is very strong. Third, this desire for resumption or retrieval is
related to the fact that the drama that Klemperer believes will go down in
history is not about German actions against the Jews; it is not about the
Jewish struggle to maintain dignity and ward off despair; it is about the re-
integration of both Jews and Germans in a morally righted postwar society.
The Holocaust does not cripple the nation.

Fourth, the Weigmann story achieves its effects by associating moral
action with national service. The son is introduced as a soldier first. That
he returns home to study medicine is probably because of wounds he has
suffered at the front. Only then does he attempt to save his mother. Germany's national traditions are not undermined, and it is the national frame
that gives the heroic actions their pathos. Klemperer's desire for a redemptive national story seems strong. Moreover, the drama is centered around
the active subjectivity of the son. Tenses and verbs are arranged so that
audiences can identify and respond to morally righteous action. The active
verbs of the son are contrasted with the father's version of the death which
was, as he said, "ordained by fate."

Fifth, alongside morally righteous action, Klemperer upholds both the
possibility and the desirability of a national cultural tradition. The Weigmann
story goes "down into history and literature," thereby joining earlier plays
and novels to augment an identifiable cultural tradition. Klemperer's hero
joins a cast of preceding heroes that constitutes German history.

And finally, sixth, the Nazis are projected onto the figure of the father
and are thereby represented as a duplicitous minority. There is no thematization of general complicity or collective guilt. Indeed, the murder of the
Jews is partially redeemed in the rejection of the nationalism and racism of
the father in favor of a bona fide Jewish-German symbiosis. In the end, the
overall continuity that Klemperer invokes with the phrase "going down in
history" does allow for changes in direction. Postwar Germany will have a
different future, not the father's, but the son's, the *Mischling*'s.

My reading of Klemperer's account as a sentimental, even kitschy
drama points to striking similarities with the contemporary history that

Germans narrated and recited after the war. I make this comparison not to excuse or justify the production of self-serving versions of the Nazi past, or to tar Klemperer with the apologist's brush, but rather to underscore how strong conventional narratives remain, how tempting the search for a usable national past was, and how important the nation remained as a nexus of memory. While scholars have long lamented the way Germans in the first decades after the war tendentiously remembered the Nazis, the war, and the Holocaust, they have not adequately understood how and why those memories have taken the form they have. They have assumed that memories can and should be used as critical tools of self-reflection in a process of *Vergangenheitsbewältigung*. I want to turn the question around and ask: given the tendentious nature of memory work, what can we learn about the pattern of remembering and the possibility of critical reflection? Rather than measure German recollections against some normative standard, I propose to examine memory as the work of continually selecting and thereby maintaining some control over the past. Collective memories are neither accurate nor critical, but rather function in self-serving narratives that preserve active, meaningful subjects — in this case, Germany. Yet in the German example it is also possible to see the ways in which collective memory continuously reflected on the conditions of its own production. Most of the conventional histories written by Germans after the war are self-conscious, searching for the right dramatic effect just as were Klemperer and his friend Katz. From the very beginning, the challenges of representation, the problem of too much or too little history, were part of the process of mastering the past. I suggest that one key to understanding the dynamic of *Vergangenheitsbewältigung* is the recognition that the concept, and eventually the word itself, was always part of the post-1945 German process of historicization. The self-conscious quality of the effort to assemble usable narratives ended up creating a measure of critical distance to the narratives themselves that was then available to readers.

Klemperer's account of Weigmann is atypical of postwar historiography in one crucial way. At the center of Klemperer's drama is the figure of the Jewish German who, as we know, did not come back and who does not reappear in any recognizable form in postwar German literature — at least not until the publication of Klemperer's own diaries. But many of the other features by which Klemperer describes Weigmann's fate are helpful in thinking about the construction of German pasts.

First of all there was an extraordinary production of plays and novels in the postwar period. Far from suppressing the past, which has been the conventional interpretation of everyday historical discourse in the 1950s and 1960s, Germans selectively embellished it and even obsessed over it. Over "Stammtische" and around "Skatspiele," and in popular novels and television documentaries, veterans, war widows, "Ostdeutsche," and their families shared stories that centered on the wartime suffering of German individuals and gradually constructed a story of Germany's national ordeal seen through the prism of its catastrophic end in 1945.[5] Throughout the 1950s, *Dorfchroniken* and *Familienchroniken*, composed by local historians and families, detailed the broken legacies of collective lives in the former German East. To the picture books of the 1950s and 1960s were added television programs which documented the end of the war, the bombings and evacuations which for most Germans constituted their firsthand experience of the war. Popular novelists such as Jürgen Thorwald achieved bestseller status as they thematized German suffering in the East.[6] Beginning with Theodor Plevier, novels of Stalingrad were extremely popular as well. By the late 1950s, weekly editions of fictionalized war stories sold up to 60,000 copies.[7] Throughout this period, novels, magazines, photo collections, and other documentations about German losses in the Second World War were produced by a huge if self-absorbed publication industry that historians have simply ignored. The popular fascination with Stalingrad or the lost territories in the East, renewed since 1989 with the proliferation of pastoral images of East Germany, continues to this day.

It is clear that this archive is extremely selective, focusing as it does on particular themes of the suffering of German soldiers ("Stalingrad"); around the bombing and destruction of German cities ("Dresden"); and around the expulsion of some twelve million Germans from eastern Europe ("Vertreibung"). It focuses on Germans as victims, not on the victims of the Germans, and it does not come close to describing the variety of experiences that Germans had during the Third Reich. But what gave the stories about Stalingrad, Dresden, and the expulsions their coherence and durability is that they fashioned a narrative of Germany's national ordeal that recognized the suffering of individuals, promoted social empathy and social solidarity, and blurred questions of political complicity. In the first postwar decades, collective memories could not recreate the German subject in the grand style by producing "good actions" and "recognizable heroes," but they did rebuild German subjectivity in a minimally acceptable way by providing Germans the status of victims.

The sentimental narrative of the suffering nation came into sharper focus when the Nazis were talked about. As was the case in the First World War, betrayal is a theme that stands out in the collective memory of the Second World War. But unlike the "stab-in-the-back" legend in which the divide between the home front and the battlefront placed Germans into opposing, highly partisan camps, the accusation of betrayal during and after the Second World War worked to promote the unity and homogeneity of the nation. The most fundamental treason imagined was that of the Nazi inner circle, which allegedly betrayed the national cause by waging a racist war: Germans were betrayed by their Führer. This version of events is obviously misleading, but to a great extent it forestalled internal divisiveness which was the result of the charges of widespread treason after the

First World War. The articulation of victimhood kept intact the idea of the German nation and probably facilitated the transition to democracy.

In postwar narratives, the number of real Nazis gets smaller and smaller, and the responsibility they bear for misleading the nation, exterminating the Jews, and invading Russia grows larger and larger. This is well known, and Klemperer too used this strategy of containment with the duplicitous figure of the father. At the same time, as the diminished number of Nazis became more menacing, Germany itself became more and more an old-fashioned space of small towns, filled with hardworking inhabitants who saw themselves as inheritors of a long if somewhat blurry historical tradition. In this sense, the Holocaust made *Heimat* possible.[8] Throughout postwar Germany, rebuilt historic architectural ensembles produced a new coziness around churches, town halls, and market squares. History had to be indistinct to work as heritage, so sites with political specificity, such as synagogues destroyed in 1938, were neither restored nor remembered. History linked the postwar present to long cultural continuities that anchored Germany in a common and ancient European past. Contemporaries came to see the evidence of historical continuity everywhere; the preservationist movement boomed in a period when Germans regarded, according to one survey, most buildings that surrounded them as historic.[9]

What is interesting is that this rendering of historicity resisted what had been the Nazi stress on German particularism and German racial destiny as much as it resisted confrontation with German complicity in the Nazi past. This serves as a reminder that the efforts of collective remembering are not intended to be accurate, precise, or critical. On the contrary, they produce the effect of collective belonging and historical continuity, of national survival and cultural richness. Collective memory produces what Ulla Hahn has called "unscharfe Bilder" (blurred images) because it is a feeling, not a naturalistic representation of the past; it provides the means of mutual recognition, not the arguments of causality.[10]

This imprecise but widespread rehistoricization of the natural and social landscape allowed West Germans at least to think of their communities as historically rooted, but politically innocent. Things were as they always had been (this is the effect of historical rootedness) until politics crashed in from the outside in the form of "Nazis" or, more commonly, the war, which arrived in 1943 with aerial bombings, then refugees, and finally Allied soldiers. Klaus Naumann refers to a "suddenness" by which the intrusion of the war was remembered.[11] To this day, memories of the war are composed in ways that create local and domestic normalcy and that exoticize world history. The political connections that had linked the community to the political nation, the aim of the insurgent grass-roots mobilization of the nationalist Right in the 1920s, are forgotten in the effort to produce normalcy. The *Vertriebene* (expellees) from the German East, in particular, describe idyllic, self-contained rural settings from which they were expelled in a ruthless manner. The beginning of the Federal Republic is choreographed with the long treks of homeless Germans, a rebirth that does not inquire about the origins of homelessness and expulsion.

The emphasis on *Heimat* permitted the political nation to disappear, the mass support for the Nazis to fade from consciousness, and local inhabitants to gradually come to be seen as victims. This is the reason why it is local history — that of Dresden, Hamburg, Hildesheim — rather than national history that tends to articulate the memories of victims of the bombing campaigns. This means that disasters of the war are seen as natural catastrophes, which are what befall local places. Even the Holocaust is put into this existential domain, out of the reach of local subjects and out of the reach of even the historical imagination. The contexts of history and the judgments of morality are covered up in what Helmut Dubiel describes as a three-way process of "Abspaltung," the separation of the perpetrators who are represented in terms of a very few outsiders; "Opferhaltung," the designation of Germans as victims; and the existentialization of collaborative political projects such as the war and the destruction of the Jews.[12] If war is regarded as part of natural history, politics ceases to be a useful category of analysis.

Historical continuities formulated around local places and normal if injured Germans constituted a sentimentalized narrative of the nation that was selective and self-serving, and one that has also been surprisingly durable, although not unanimously subscribed to. This sentimentalization achieves a representation of the past that resonated with the difficult experiences of non-Jewish Germans in the years 1943 to approximately 1947. However, this vernacular narrative worked by avoiding much discussion of the Jews, the primary victims of the Nazis. In other words, while the narrative rejects the Nazis, it rests uneasily on their policies. It quietly reproduces the elimination of Jewish life in Germany and upholds the feeling of being "unter uns" — "it is just us."[13] As Norbert Frei argues, the identification of Germans as victims is nothing less than the postwar survival of the Nazi-era *Volksgemeinschaft*.[14] Therefore, the sentimental narrative of the suffering nation cannot achieve the German-Jewish symbiosis that Klemperer's drama created. But other elements on which Klemperer's story relied are in place: the strong desire for a meaningful national narrative, the vague and indistinct reconstruction of the past to facilitate a broad reconciliation with cultural tradition, the honorable service of Germany's soldiers, the isolation and diminishment of the Nazi perpetrators, and the creation in popular consciousness of non-Nazi spaces such as *Heimat*. All this is testimony to the strength of national narratives and their ability to displace other perspectives and other stories in order to create a recognizable national whole. In my view, this has been the primary function of history in postwar Germany. According to Harald Welzer and his team of researchers, even today when Germans explicitly acknowledge the extent of the crimes of the Nazis and the ways in which Nazi policy was interwoven into German society in the 1930s and 1940s, the stories they tell each other at home about the period are fuzzy accounts of non-Nazi actions that feature active, morally upright grandparents rather than critical, self-reflective insights into the family past.[15]

It is the desire for narrative coherence, and for the grammatical coherence and activism of the subject, the stability of the "we," that largely determines what elements of the past are remembered. Looked at the other way, it is precisely the inability to gratify the desire for meaningful, coherent narratives that leaves individuals traumatized and perplexed and their memories fragmented and isolated, as was often the case among the surviving victims of the Nazis. But, as Lawrence Langer argues, even in the case of Holocaust testimonies, particularly those that are written down and thus more carefully crafted, the value placed on fashioning an active subject and constructing a redemptive plot persisted.[16]

Today, the Holocaust is at the very center of the history of the twentieth century. It stands out as a disaster of the first magnitude and we find it difficult to imagine ourselves without knowledge of it. But the post-Holocaust world is itself a historical construction, the origins of which need to be examined and not simply held out as the standard for judging memory. In fact, for many decades, the Holocaust was not the focus of much scholarly inquiry or civic remembering in Germany or elsewhere. Among the survivors in the years after 1945, Peter Novick argues, the recognition of the specific Nazi aim to exterminate the European Jews was offset by the desire not to reproduce the Nazis' insistence on the difference of the Jews and to participate in the general anti-fascist consensus. Throughout Europe, former occupied nations such as France, Holland, and Belgium recognized the hero or victim status of the majority of their citizens and thereby avoided making potentially bitter distinctions between collaborators, bystanders, and active resisters, or between volunteer workers and labor conscripts in the Reich.[17] Repatriation of thousands of non-German workers, former prisoners, and concentration-camp survivors was at once a physical return and a narrative inclusion in what Pieter Lagrou refers to as a "national epic" of resistance. What this meant was the subordination of the particular *milieux de mémoire* of the different groups, whether they had been active in resisting the Nazis or eager to collaborate with the occupiers, or whether they had been the targets of Nazi racial policy.[18] Neither the rhetoric of anti-fascism nor of anti-totalitarianism made much use of the evidence of the death camps, the mass shootings in the Soviet Union, or the death marches.

In the United States and Israel, the Holocaust was not central to historical consciousness either. Well into the 1970s, U.S. history textbooks did not discuss what the meaning of the murder of six-million Jews might be. Historical narratives that described the confrontation of the Soviet Union and the United States as a global struggle between Communism and the liberal West or that took satisfaction in the military stability finally achieved in the North Atlantic by the two world wars did not need to pass through Auschwitz or Birkenau, sites that were widely known but undertheorized. "Even the numerals *One* and *Two*" indicate "a mode of perception based on mere continuity," argues Dan Diner.[19] Whatever special mention Auschwitz received in the 1950s and 1960s was usually in conjunction with Hiroshima, a twinning that dehistoricized the Shoah into a looming existential threat that was invoked without reference to specific historical situations. In these versions, Auschwitz was more about the perilous future than the awful past.

The sentimental narrative of the German nation worked in other more positive ways as well. It did largely repudiate the father. In my view, the localized nature of the production of normality in the postwar years resisted the obsessive concern with the mortal body of the nation that is so plain to see after the First World War. After all, it was in the 1920s that Germans were anything but silent or evasive about their past. This too represented a way of mastering the past, but one in which Germans immersed themselves in world history and set about creating a national consciousness of survival, vigilance, and battle-readiness. Contrary to what happened after the Second World War, local places after the First World War avidly sought connections to national history in the tumultuous political mobilizations of paramilitary groups, political parties, and anti-Versailles campaigns. If Ernst Glaeser, the Weimar-era novelist, described himself as the "last civilian" amidst the permanent political campaigns of the 1920s, his counterparts in the 1950s would have found "only civilians." German narratives after the Second World War are thus much closer to the "communities of suffering" that Omer Bartov finds in France and Britain after the First World War.[20] At the same time, the sentimental narrative of the nation also resisted revanchist politics. Political offensives to revise Germany's borders or undo the postwar order could gain little traction — the organized politics of right-wing expellee groups notwithstanding. The provincial coziness of postwar Germany stifled such endeavors. Increasingly the present was regarded as the best place in time to inhabit. This was not altogether a bad thing.

Historians would condemn the sentimental version as bad history. Yet it is striking to see just how much critical historiography in West Germany followed collective memory. I do not want to push this argument too far, but I want to suggest ways in which even the structural social histories of progressive historians produced some of the same effects as the sentimental memories they condemned. In the first place, there was extraordinary investment in finding a useable, honorable German past, which the traditions of the German labor movement and the Social Democratic Party provided. Even in East Germany, the celebration of socialist tradition did not culminate in a massive indictment of the middle classes, who were regarded in mostly passive terms, as victims of modernization and the manipulations of elites. Post-1945 history thus did not re-enact the partisan divisions of the time after 1918. When it comes to the Nazis, historians for a long time unwittingly cast them in the role of aliens on the social margins, arriving from outside. National Socialists achieve breakthroughs, they prey on voters, they push desperate Germans over the edge. Thus when the time comes to analyze the Third Reich, the Nazis disappear. There is the small group around Hitler, but otherwise Germans are not really enthusiastic supporters. The Third Reich is regarded as a nation of opportunists, grumblers, and bystanders, not ideological collaborators.[21]

To parse the (mostly unintentional) rhetoric of even the best scholarship would seem to reveal that it was a small minority of Nazis who wielded the active verbs, as if National Socialism had been an alien force that arrived to immobilize the larger population. Peter Steinbach, for example, concludes that those Germans who did not resist "willig dem nationalsozialistischen Meinungsdruck unterwarfen" (willingly subjected themselves to the pressure of Nazi opinion).[22] Here "subjected" and "pressure of opinion" are muscular, physical terms that array Germans and Nazis into two distinct camps and leave the Germans without real conviction or ability to act. In a similar vein, Hans Mommsen maintains that the middle classes "völlig dem Sog der nationalsozialistischen Propaganda erlegen war" (completely succumbed to the pressure of National Socialist propaganda).[23] Again physical terms serve to separate the middle classes from the Nazis. Even Martin Broszat's concept of "Resistenz," borrowed from medicine, accents the foreign nature of Nazism, which attempted to attach itself to the German body.[24] This sort of rhetoric does not directly deny that many thousands of Germans were Nazis. But it does fashion "Nazis" and "Germans" into collective nouns whose syntactical use side by side suggests mutual exclusion rather than kinds of equivalence. And for many years, the Holocaust itself was analyzed in terms of bureaucratic and structural processes that detached perpetrators from the genocidal aim. General indifference rather than willful complicity was the harsh moral lesson.

What is unsatisfying about an analysis of why the narrative of the sentimental nation has been so durable is that it seems to freeze German perspectives on the past and to withhold the possibility of new, critical thought on the matter. The emphasis I place on the power of satisfying narratives also seems complacent because it does not realize the responsibility of scholars to get the wider community to see through kitsch and to acknowledge measures of responsibility. I am not sure how plausible it is to do this, since collective memories do not work by seeing clearly, and while people acknowledge the importance of critical reflection, they generally avoid scrutinizing their own histories, which is why Welzer's informants today all tell anti-Nazi stories. As a pedagogical undertaking, critical *Vergangenheitsbewältigung* may well be an illusion. But it is also ahistorical to simply leave the domineering national narrative in place. Moreover, just about any observer of the German scene feels that understandings of the Nazi past have become more critical, certainly in official culture, but also in the social exchanges of everyday life and in the recent spate of family memoirs and family novels. How far and how deep does this go? And is it countermanded by recent texts such as Jörg Friedrich's study of the air war, *Der Brand* (The Fire, 2002) which recall Germans primarily as victims?

What strikes me about recent commentaries on the public engagement with the Nazi past is the speed with which the discussion moves from specific histories of victimization and complicity to the general protocols about having a discussion about the German past. From one side, the insistence that finally critical perspectives are possible; from another, relief that the sons' fierce indictments have yielded to the more nuanced reappraisals of the granddaughters; from another quarter, the bittersweet realization that now, finally, our story can be told: the story of surviving air raids, the Russian counter-offensive, the expulsions from the East; and from yet others, the renewed demand that one finally draw a line, a "Schlußstrich," under all this examination of the past. All of these responses could be heard in the last years, from the Goldhagen debate to the frenzied arguments about the Wehrmacht exhibit to reviews of Friedrich's *Der Brand*. It is significant that these reflections on narrative have themselves been the echoes of numerous heated debates since 1945 about how to talk about German history. The sentimental narrative of the nation has always been accompanied by reflection on how this narrative arises or is constructed. Such reflection is both a result of knowledge about complicity and the means by which more critical inquiries have been introduced.

I would argue that the sentimental narrative reveals its own insufficiency by continuously slipping into a self-reflective mode in order to justify itself, reassert its adequacy, insist on its own necessity, and legitimate itself by comparing itself to other narratives. One can see this from the very beginning: the denunciation of the "victor's justice" at Nuremberg was not just about particular criminal actions, but the larger moral frame that gave German crimes their specificity; the insistence on the honor of the "clean" Wehrmacht is an implicit answer to a nagging question concerning the army's fundamental complicity in the dirty killing of civilians; the reference to Germany's "six million" lost in the prisoner-of-war camps in the Soviet Union makes explicit reference to the Holocaust; and the alacrity with which high-ranking Nazis were granted amnesty by the first session of the Bundestag was accompanied by the demands that the nation be allowed to compose its own history. Clearly, important media events such as the Eichmann trial, the extensively reported 1965 Frankfurt trials, and the television screening of the movie "Holocaust" (1979) propelled the discussion forward, but the debate about the terms for discussing German history has, in fact, been around since 1945. The huge success of Alexander and Margarete Mitscherlich's book *Die Unfähigkeit zu trauern* (The Inability to Mourn, 1967), as a result of which the title became a household phrase, stands as a partial refutation of its thesis.[25] The anguished concern with the fate of German history after the catastrophe of the Second World War, something already expressed by Friedrich Meinecke in *The German Catastrophe*, and the more popular and self-serving suspicion that the world would never forgive the German people for the crimes committed by the Nazis, reveal a striking self-absorption with one's own problems at the expense of the victims; they also reveal an attentiveness to the problems of narrative posed by war and genocide. While this attentiveness is generally expressed in unappetizing ways, it repeatedly undermined the self-sufficiency that the sentimental narrative of the nation tried so hard to produce. Put simply, *Vergangenheitsbewältigung* is not an abstract description, a set of expectations, but has always been an openly contested discussion about narrative, something Klemperer had already started to think about in 1944.

Moreover, German discussions of Nazi crimes were always conducted with the knowledge that third parties were listening. I think this is quite important. Concern for international appearances — Germany vis-à-vis the Americans, the former occupied countries in Europe, and finally Israel — was not always welcomed, but it was unavoidable. It meant that the strategies of narrating German history became as important as the elements of the history itself. This, too, allowed former Nazis and other Germans to begin to imagine the perspectives of their military enemies and racial victims. The internationalization of German history was already apparent in the turbulent debates about the causes of the First World War, and became much more insistent after the Second World War, precisely because the world wars meant that German history did not just belong to Germans. As a result, foreign interlocutors are tolerated in German debates and are prominent in German scholarship to a far greater extent than elsewhere in Europe. French and British history are much more self-contained.

Indeed, I get the sense that the sentimental narrative of German history takes the form of a response to an implicit question posed by an outsider about the complicity of ordinary Germans in Nazi crimes and thus about collective guilt. The narrative is in the form of an answer. The reply is usually in the negative — "no, the Germans were not collectively guilty" — but the reply rests on the knowledge that such an indictment exists, that such a question can be posed.[26] And I would go a step further: the desire to master the past and the difficulty in doing so, the endurance of the sentimental narrative and the persisting evidence of its own insufficiency are symptoms of the general suspicion that the Nazi seizure of power was a total seizure of German history and of German hearts and minds. Norbert Frei has come right out and said it: the willingness to support a general amnesty in the early 1950s was a sign of collective guilt.[27] It is precisely the general nature of the mobilization *for* National Socialism, the involvement of so many Germans in an obviously ideological project, and also the displacement of millions of Germans in the years after 1945, that makes for difficulties in finding a resolution of the German past. Self-serving narratives of victimization always remained incomplete, not least because they never could produce the heroic, morally upright actions that filled out the epic narratives of anti-fascism elsewhere in Europe. The insufficiency of the German narrative, and particularly its defensiveness, repeatedly exposed the traces of the secret knowledge of complicity. This insufficiency has also invited debates about the nature of collective memory, about the ways in which to compose German history, and about the nature of *Vergangenheitsbewältigung*. The word itself has become woven into the historical narratives. There is a general acceptance of the idea that German history cannot rest, and this, I think, creates the basis for a self-reflective and critical appraisal of the past, one that is dramatically missing in other places around the world.

The anguish over narrative — Klemperer's imagined "plays and novels," the effort to claim victim status, the insistence on a "Schlußstrich," the persistent feeling that not everything has been told — all this both encouraged a sentimentalization of the national narrative and exposed its insufficiency. The energetic production of lines of continuity with the period before the Nazis came to power, the relativisms of Hitler versus Stalin, and the spaces of normality were all bad history; but they exposed both the collective investment in a rehabilitative national story and the impossibility of achieving it. The outspoken desire for narrative coherence revealed the traces of more complicated stories that have prevented the fulfillment of that desire. Suspicion that there was too little history — or the frustration that there was too much — were signs of restlessness and disquiet, which are the aftermath of catastrophe and mass death, complicity and victimization. In the end, the sentimental narratives of collective memory concluded in the conditional tense, ended in question marks, and offered no resolution. They failed to master the past and thereby remained open to re-interpretation, open to Martin Walser but also to Ignaz Bubis, open to Jörg Friedrich but also to W. G. Sebald. This restlessness is now part of the story.

Notes

[1] Victor Klemperer, *Ich will Zeugnis ablegen bis zum letzten: Tagebücher 1942–1945* (Berlin: Aufbau-Verlag, 1995), 477–78. Entry for 23 January 1944.

[2] Klemperer, *Ich will Zeugnis ablegen*, 588. Entry for 16 April 1941.

[3] Klemperer, *Ich will Zeugnis ablegen*, 447. Entry for 23 January 1944.

[4] Klemperer, *Ich will Zeugnis ablegen*, 474, 479. Entries for 17 and 27 January 1944.

[5] See Peter Fritzsche, "Volkstümliche Erinnerung und deutsche Identität nach dem Zweiten Weltkrieg," in Konrad H. Jarausch and Martin Sabrow, eds., *Verletztes Gedaechtnis: Erinnerungskultur und Zeitgeschichte im Konflikt* (Frankfurt: Campus, 2002), 75–97.

[6] Examples are Thorwald's novels *Es begann an der Weichsel* (It Began On The River Weichsel, 1948) and *Das Ende an der Elbe* (The End At the Elbe, 1950).

[7] See Joe Perry, "The Madonna of Stalingrad: The (Christmas) Past and West German National Identity after World War II," *Radical History Review* 83 (2002): 7–27; Michael Schornstheimer, *Die leuchtenden Augen der Frontsoldaten: Nationalsozialismus und Krieg in den Illustriertenromanen der fünfziger Jahre* (Berlin: Metropol, 1995); and Jörg Bernig, *Eingekesselt: die Schlacht von Stalingrad im deutschsprachigen Romanen nach 1945* (New York: Peter Lang, 1997); and, comprehensively, Robert G. Moeller, *War Stories: The Search for a Usable Past in the Federal Republic of Germany* (Berkeley: U of California P, 2001).

[8] See Michael Geyer, "The Place of the Second World War in German Memory and History," *New German Critique* 71 (1997): 5–40; here: 20.

[9] See Rudy Koshar, *Germany's Transient Pasts: Preservation and National Memory in the Twentieth Century* (Chapel Hill: U of North Carolina P, 1998), 243–47.

[10] Ulla Hahn, *Unscharfe Bilder* (Munich: Deutsche Verlagsanstalt, 2003).

[11] Klaus Naumann, *Der Krieg als Text: Das Jahr 1945 im kulturellen Gedächtnis der Presse* (Hamburg: Hamburger Edition, 1998), 44–45.

[12] Helmut Dubiel, *Niemand ist frei von der Geschichte: Die nationalsozialistische Herrschaft in den Debatten des Deutschen Bundestages* (Munich: Carl Hanser, 1999), 69.

[13] Victor Klemperer, *I Will Bear Witness, 1933–1941* (New York: Randon House, 1998), 233. Entry for 17 August 1937.

[14] Norbert Frei, *Adenauer's Germany and the Nazi Past: The Politics of Amnesty and Integration* (New York: Columbia UP, 2002), 231–32.

[15] Harald Welzer et al., eds., *"Opa war kein Nazi": Nationalsozialismus und Holocaust im Familiengedächtnis* (Frankfurt: Fischer Verlag, 2002); and also Harald Welzer, "Der Holocaust im deutschen Familiengedächtnis," in Volkhard Knigge and Norbert Frei, eds., *Verbrechen erinnern: Die Auseinandersetzung mit Holocaust und Völkermord* (Munich: Beck, 2002), 342–58.

[16] Lawrence L. Langer, *Holocaust Testimonies: The Ruins of Memory* (New Haven: Yale UP, 1991). See also Peter Fritzsche, "The Case of Modern Memory," *The Journal of Modern History* 73 (March 2001): 87–117.

[17] Peter Novick, *The Holocaust in American Life* (New York: Houghton Mifflin, 1999); Pieter Lagrou, *The Legacy of Nazi Occupation: Patriotic Memory and National Recovery in Western Europe, 1945–1965* (New York: Cambridge UP, 2000).

[18] Lagrou, *The Legacy of Nazi Occupation,* 36.

[19] Dan Diner, "The Destruction of Narrativity: The Holocaust in Historical Discourse," in Moishe Postone and Eric Santner, eds., *Catastrophe and Meaning: The*

Holocaust and the Twentieth Century (Chicago: U of Chicago P, 2003), 67–80; here: 69, 72.

[20] Ernst Glaeser, *The Last Civilian*, trans. Gwenda David and Eric Mosbacher (New York: Robert M. McBridge and Co, 1935); Omer Bartov, " 'Fields of Glory': War, Genocide, and the Glorification of Violence," in Postone and Santner, eds., *Catastrophe and Meaning*, 117–35; here: 123.

[21] See my argument in "Where Did All the Nazis Go? Reflections on Collaboration and Resistance," *Tel Aviver Jahrbuch fuer deutsche Geschichte* 23 (1994): 191–214.

[22] Peter Steinbach, "Der Widerstand als Thema der politischen Zeitgeschichte," in Gerhard Besier and Gerhard Ringshausen, eds., *Bekenntnis, Widerstand, Martyrium: Von Barmen 1934 bis Plötzensee 1944* (Göttingen: Vandenhoeck & Ruprecht, 1986), 11–74; here: 53.

[23] Hans Mommsen, "Der Widerstand gegen Hitler und die deutsche Gesellschaft," in Jürgen Schmädeke and Peter Steinbach, eds., *Der Widerstand gegen den Nationalsozialismus: Die deutsche Gesellschaft und der Widerstand gegen Hitler* (Munich: R. Piper, 1985), 3–24; here: 14.

[24] Martin Broszat, "Resistenz und Widerstand," in Broszat and Elke Fröhlich, eds., *Bayern in der NS-Zeit*, vol. 4 (Munich: Oldenbourg, 1983), 691–709.

[25] Alexander and Margarete Mitscherlich, *The Inability to Mourn: Principles in Collective Behavior*, trans. Beverley R. Placzek (New York: Grove Press, 1975 [1967]).

[26] Karl Jaspers, *The Question of German Guilt*, trans. E. B. Ashton (New York: Dial Press, 1948).

[27] Frei, *Adenauer's Germany*, 305.

2: The Tinderbox of Memory: Generation and Masculinity in *Väterliteratur* by Christoph Meckel, Uwe Timm, Ulla Hahn, and Dagmar Leupold

Anne Fuchs

Väterliteratur and the Language of Silence

VÄTERLITERATUR (FATHERS' LITERATURE) could be considered a late byproduct of the student movement of 1968 in that some of its former members embarked on a literary exploration of postwar German family life in the late 1970s.[1] Concerned with the authoritarian father figures that, according to these authors, dominated the family dynamics of the postwar period, these novels attempt to show how the National Socialist past of the war generation infiltrated postwar family life. Wavering between a whimsical style on the one hand and outright aggression towards the domineering father figure on the other, these narratives have been dismissed by some critics for their apparent lack of critical distance and the shrillness of their tone.

A case in point is Ernestine Schlant, who discusses the genre in her 1999 study *The Language of Silence* and notes that the majority of these narratives share so many substantive, linguistic, and structural similarities that they are "virtually formula novels."[2] For Schlant, the genre largely fails to make the important connection between family life and political practice. This narrative insufficiency is further compounded by the genre's failure to come to terms with the Holocaust. Although she concedes that many of the narratives "approach the Holocaust subjectively, through the narrator's attempt at conversations with their elders," she deplores the peripheral role of Jews in this literature: "In narratives that are full of one specific sort of affect — anger against the parent and rage at the mistreatment of the child — there is a curious lack of affect when it comes to the Holocaust" (Schlant, 92–93).

Schlant's dismissal of the genre reflects the normative approach underpinning her entire book, which posits that all German narratives about National Socialism must also foreground the Holocaust and its victims. In clear contrast to Schlant's view this chapter argues that *Väterliteratur* made a valid contribution to German memory contests by exposing the

intergenerational dynamic that shaped postwar family life. Notwithstanding the emotional style of many of these narratives, the best examples of
the genre helped to deconstruct a particular notion of masculinity, which
has its bedrock in the *völkisch* ideology of the early twentieth century.

Using Christoph Meckel's *Suchbild: Über meinen Vater* as a point of
departure that exemplifies many of the original characteristics of the genre,
I will move on to a discussion of three recent versions of the genre, Uwe
Timm's *Am Beispiel meines Bruders* (On The Example of My Brother,
2002), Ulla Hahn's *Unscharfe Bilder* (Blurred Images, 2003), and Dagmar
Leupold's *Nach den Kriegen* (After the Wars, 2004). With the exception of
Hahn's work these narratives aim to create a high degree of authenticity:
they are not works of fiction but autobiographical narratives written in an
analytical-discursive style that embeds family history in the history of the
German nation. Timm, Meckel, and Leupold build their own biographies
into their narratives to ensure that their analyses of postwar family life are
read in terms of a psychological diagnosis of a collective condition. The
continuities and discontinuities between Meckel's father book and the contemporary examples of the genre will be examined with reference to their
respective treatments of the intergenerational dynamic and, in particular,
the theme of masculinity. Before discussing these narratives in some detail,
it is, however, necessary to reflect on the concept of "generation."

Between Rupture and Continuity:
Generational Discourse

"It is difficult to think of a notion that has become more commonplace yet
at the same time more opaque than that of 'generation.'"[3] The opening
sentence of Pierre Nora's analysis of the establishment of the concept of
generations through the French Revolution summarizes well the semantic
ubiquity and elasticity of the term. From a contemporary German point of
view the business of talking about generational experience appears to have
become particularly fashionable in the last decade, that is, precisely at the
historical juncture when the aging 1968ers began to examine critically their
youthful protest in the 1960s and the long-term effect this had on society.[4]
While this already points to a crucial link between the modern usage of the
term "generation" and youthful revolutionary zest, in the postwar landscape the term had of course wide currency among other social cohorts,
above all the war generation, whose first-hand involvement with and experience of National Socialism and of the Second World War was a constant
reference point for its self-understanding. Born around 1905, this generation
had actively supported National Socialism and, after the war, adopted a position that the historian Norbert Frei describes as "reflexartige Schuldabwehr".

(reflexive denial of guilt) and "Auskunftsverweigerung" (refusal to communicate).[5] It was precisely this generation's self-understanding that triggered
the intergenerational contest between fathers and sons and fathers and
daughters in the wake of 1968. Sandwiched between the war generation
and the 1968ers are members of the so-called "skeptical generation." Born
between 1925 and 1930, its members, including Günter Grass, Martin
Walser, and Hans Magnus Enzensberger, were socialized during the Nazi
period but emphatically embraced the project of a critical engagement with
Germany's past in the postwar period.[6]

As Sigrid Weigel observes, such counting of generations can be
observed in disciplines where history is interpreted with reference to a massive historical caesura, above all in German historiography since 1945, in
Holocaust studies, and also in postcolonial studies. A generational genealogy appears to have the dual advantage of providing us with a clear model of
periodization and of anchoring these periods in the collective memory.
However, Weigel rightly points out that our modern, largely synchronic
usage of the term generation as membership in a given age group with a
shared experiential horizon has taken the place of a much older semantics
that encompasses the idea of genesis and genealogy. Etymologically the
term goes back to Greek *genos* and Latin *generatio*, which connote genealogy, reproduction, lineage, and thus the historical continuity of a people,
race, or species. Clearly, genealogy and lineage are diachronic ideas spanning
several generations and thereby establishing the continuity of history by
means of the genealogical ordering of origin and sequence. The notion of
generation is thus rooted in biological meaning, but at the same time it regu-
lates legal, social, and cultural issues of affiliation, such as inheritance laws.[7]

As Pierre Nora shows, a shift away from genealogy occurred during
the French Revolution. With the revolution of 1789, youth burst onto the
political scene, eradicating the *ancien regime*'s hereditary rule in favor of
democratic principles of free individuals, unburdened by lineage and heritage. It is therefore not coincidental that the Declaration of the Rights of
Man of 1793 proclaims that "a generation has no right to subject any
future generation to its laws."[8] This implies that generations as a social and
political force are bound up with the idea of constant regeneration and
thus the notion of youth. What Nora terms the "eschatology of rupture"
makes the revolution an intrinsically generational phenomenon that gives
birth to an egalitarian world in which historical change accelerates (Nora,
502). However, in clear contrast to the real caesura of 1789, the rupture of
1968 is merely symbolic: Nora reads 1968 in terms of "a revolutionary
mime" in which nothing really happened other than "a violent affirmation
of horizontal identity that suddenly dominates and transcends all forms of
vertical solidarity" (Nora, 503–4). Blasting away older forms of solidarity,
such as family or class, the idea of generation took the place of other social
allegiances. "In a world of constant change," writes Nora, "in which every

individual has occasion to become his or her own historian, the generation is the most instinctive way of converting memory into history. Ultimately that is what a generation is: the spontaneous horizon of individual historical objectification" (Nora, 528).

With its emphasis on regeneration through rupture, Nora's analysis highlights the revolutionary evolution of the modern meaning of the term generation; however, he also draws attention to the concept's underside, namely a sense of lack and mourning about those moments of historical grandeur that later generations have not experienced. His reading is firmly embedded in French historiography in that it posits that the Romantics had a melancholy relationship to the French Revolution, revealed in their reflections in their historical writings on their own sense of belatedness. The lack of participation in the formative moment of the nation's history becomes a source of melancholy reflection. The same sense of being born in history's aftermath informs the postwar generation's perspective on the Second World War as a further momentous historical event. Nora's reflection on melancholy as the underside of generational renewal shows that in spite of the French Revolution the concept remains ultimately entangled in a discourse about origins and heritage.

It is precisely this ambiguity that characterizes German *Väterliteratur*. On the one hand *Väterliteratur* refutes the importance of tradition and lineage in quite an aggressive fashion; on the other, many of these narratives also express a melancholy longing for the very ideas that they attack so vehemently, namely family heritage and tradition. However, since the rejection of tradition is the main ideological force behind *Väterliteratur*, this longing for lineage is never properly addressed in these texts; it only finds indirect expression on the level of subtext. The need for tradition and heritage thus remains an unresolved issue in the first wave of *Väterliteratur*. This helps to explain why a new version of the genre has become popular in German literature since the late 1990s: the repressed longing for tradition now resurfaces in terms of a transgenerational legacy that requires further working through. In today's Germany what Pierre Nora calls "the tinderbox of memory" has ignited a generational blaze.[9] Analyzing the genre's characteristic oscillation between rupture and continuity, I will demonstrate that many of these narratives locate the need for a break with the past in a particular form of masculinity.

Of Damaged Fathers and Ruined Families: Christoph Meckel and Uwe Timm

Väterliteratur is of course not an invention of the 1968ers. Its paradigmatic precursor is Franz Kafka's *Brief an den Vater* (Letter to My Father,

1919), which, with its accusatory style, sets the tone for the genre. Referring to his deep-seated fear of his father Hermann in the opening sentences, Kafka paints a picture of a physically and mentally domineering father, whose greatest failing, however, is assimilation. Focusing on the lack of Jewish rites and traditions in the family's life, Kafka's text thus makes the disturbance of genealogy and tradition one of its main concerns.

While the patriarch in Kafka's narrative is a powerful ogre of sorts, in Christoph Meckel's *Suchbild* the father is portrayed simultaneously as a despot and as a helpless figure.[10] Opening with the happy memory of a ride in the father's car, a significant moment that the narrator associates with a "Gefühl von Sicherheit und blindem Vertrauen, eine wunderbare Gewißheit in seiner Nähe" (feeling of safety and blind trust, a wonderful sense of reassurance in his proximity, *S*, 9), the narrative then sets out to dismantle this image. Christoph's father, Eberhard Meckel (born in 1907), was a traditionalist poet and literary critic who, throughout the 1930s, continued to write poetry and stories untouched by the times. For Meckel, his father's lyrical escapism is a signature of an entire generation of intellectuals, who unlike the émigrés Brecht, Döblin, and Mann relied on a depoliticized belief in universal values:

> Allerlei Literaten seiner Generation (eine ganze Phalanx der jüngsten Intelligenz) lebten erstaunlich zeitfremd weiter. Man kapselte sich in Naturgedichten ab, verkroch sich in die Jahreszeiten, im Ewigen, Immergültigen, Überzeitlichen, in das Naturschöne und Kunstschöne, in Vorstellung von Trost und in den Glauben an die Hinfälligkeit zeitbedingter Miseren. (*S*, 22)

> [All sorts of writers of his generation (a whole phalanx of the youngest intelligentsia) continued to live a life untouched by the politics of the day. They shut themselves away into their nature poetry, seeking refuge in the seasons, the everlasting and eternal and transcendental spheres, in nature and art's beauty, in notions of comfort and the belief that the wretched state of things was a temporary affair.][11]

This generation's subscription to a catalogue of humanistic values goes hand in hand with a strong belief in the Prussian military tradition that is seen in opposition to the vulgarity of National Socialism. For Meckel it is highly significant that the father abhors National Socialism not so much for its ideology but for its lack of style (*S*, 34). He shows that the father's snobbish disinterest in politics only disguises his support for brutalized forms of violence that National Socialism legitimized. Interspersing the biographical narrative about the father with quotations from the father's war diaries, the narrator draws out the father's growing collusion with National Socialism. A collage of quotations reveals the extent to which the father had embraced NS ideology during the war. An entry of 24 January 1944 mentions Auschwitz in the following way:

Im Abteil eine Frau, in Lemberg zivilangestellt; sie erzählt von einem Frühstück in einem Warschauer Lokal, das 4000 Zloty gekostet hat, von den Schiebereien und Geschäftsmethoden der Deutschen allenthalben in der Verwaltung. Bestechungen Überpreise und dergleichen mehr, vom KZ in Auschwitz usw. — Als Soldat ist man doch so fern all dieser Dinge, die einen im Grunde auch gar nicht interessieren; man steht für ein ganz anderes Deutschland draußen und will später im Kriege sich nicht bereichert haben, sondern ein sauberes Empfinden besitzen. Ich habe nur Verachtung für diesen zivilen Unrat. (*S*, 43)

[In my train compartment was a woman who was employed as a civilian in Lemberg; she talks about a breakfast in a café in Warsaw that cost her 4000 Zloty, the racketeering of the Germans everywhere in the administration. Bribes, higher charges, and things like that, she also mentioned the KZ in Auschwitz etc. — As a soldier one is quite removed from all this stuff, things that don't really interest one; one stands for quite a different Germany in the field and after the war one does not wish to have profited from the war but one wants to come back with a clean conscience. I can only despise such civilian vermin.]

The laconic reference to Auschwitz and the ensuing reflection on the soldier's emotional distance from the reality of war and persecution brings into relief the image of the cold persona, detached from all empathy and emotional involvement. The entry of 27 January 1944 reinforces this image drastically:

Auf einem Umweg zum Mittagessen Zeuge der Erschießung von 28 Polen, die öffentlich an der Böschung eines Sportplatzes vor sich geht. Ein wüster Leichenhaufen, in allem Schauerlichen und Unschönen jedoch ein Anblick der mich äußerst kalt läßt. Die Erschossenen hatten zwei Soldaten und einen Reichsdeutschen überfallen und erschlagen. Muster eines Volksschauspiels der neuen Zeit. (*S*, 43–44)

[On a detour on my way to lunch I witness the execution of 28 Poles, which is done publicly on the embankment of a games pitch. A horrible pile of corpses, but in spite of all the ghastliness and unsightliness this scene leaves me completely untouched. The executed Poles had robbed and killed two soldiers and a German from the Reich. This is an example of the popular drama of our new times.]

It is precisely the shocking coldness of these diary entries that motivates this investigation of the father's life: having read the war diary he can no longer treat his relationship with his father merely as a personal affair. The diary turns the seemingly private into a case study of an entire generation. What follows is an anatomy of this generation's value system, which with its deep-seated authoritarianism relied on the military code of honor, conformity, and duty to the fatherland to sidestep the notion of individual responsibility and conscience. Taking over the "Toilettenjargon der

Herrenmenschen" (the pissoir jargon of the superior race, *S*, 50), the father is shown to also adopt the eliminatory racism and anti-Semitism of Nazism.

Meckel's anatomy of a generation thus goes far beyond a mere accounting of personal childhood injuries. His portrait of a father makes an important connection between National Socialism and a code of honor that goes back to Wilhelmine society and fully flourished during the First World War. As Helmut Lethen has shown in his brilliant study of the German anthropology of the interwar period, the loss of the First World War mobilized a culture of heroic shame.[12] In contrast to a culture of guilt, which operates on the basis of introspection, a culture of shame employs social fears and conventions to produce a functionalized notion of selfhood that is built on appearance and image rather than on subjectivity and self-expression (Lethen, 36). Against the backdrop of defeat in the First World War and in the face of the massive social transformations of the Weimar Republic, the figure of the cold persona emerged in the 1920s, advocating the masking of pain and emotion behind a protective shield. The experience of the First World War had already produced what Lethen calls the "Kältepanzer von Ehre, Tapferkeit, Ruhm und Härte" (the cold armor of honor, courage, fame and hardness, *S*, 115), the paradigmatic expression of which is the figure of Jünger's steel warrior, a point to which I return later. As Lethen shows, the cult of coldness emphasizes techniques of mimicry and masking in order to disguise the subject's vulnerability; with its code of honor it reflects specifically male fears of exposure and maps out a masculine notion of selfhood.

The total exclusion of woman from this arena of self-construction is exemplified by Helmuth Plessner's anthropology of the interwar period: according to Plessner, the self must only enter the public arena equipped with a knight's armor. He writes: "Alles Psychische, das sich nackt hervorwagt, trägt das Risiko der Lächerlichkeit" (everything psychological that shows itself in its nakedness runs the risk of being ridiculous).[13] Without his protective shield the self is reduced to the powerlessness of the creature. Bereft of social status, membership in a class, and the protective shield of social conventions, the creature leads a pariah existence at the bottom of the social pile.[14] The creature is the unmasked self, the self without protection, human existence as "organische[s] Bündel in Todesnot" (terrified organism in fear of death; Lethen, 256), or, in the words of Georgio Agamben, it is bare life.[15] The anthropology of the 1920s thus reacted to the perceived risk of social degradation by formulating a theory of social self-constitution based on the idea of the social mask and a hard masculinity. Only in the safety of the private home can the cold persona drop his mask. Plessner's male subject is thus an extremely guarded self that can only find temporary relief from the demands of constant self-control through a woman's gift of love. As Lethen comments, woman is thus excluded from this "Fechtsaal der Subjektkonstitution" (fencing arena of the subject's constitution; Lethen, 94).

In Meckel's *Suchbild*, the extracts from the narrator's father's war diaries display how, in the course of the war, he adopts the cold persona, turning himself into a steel warrior who remains untouched by the suffering of the Polish and Jewish civilian population around him. Far more than a settling of old scores, the book aims to deconstruct precisely this notion of masculinity that spans the two world wars and reaches into the postwar period. After his imprisonment as a prisoner of war, the father returns a dethroned, helpless despot, wavering between sudden outbursts of rage and moments of tearful sentimentality. Although the father is shown to accept the idea of German collective guilt, according to his son he ultimately fails to deal with the far more pressing question of his personal responsibility. His anecdotal stories about the cruelty of war gloss over his own involvement and engage in a settlement of guilt, based on a "Punktsiegstrategie" (*S*, 86), a scoring of moral brownie points that utilizes precisely the same code of honor that had fueled National Socialist ideology. A good example of this is the father's insistence that his behavior during the war was always "TADELLOS"[16] (irreproachble, *S*, 86); it betrays a breathtaking clouding of conscience that, according to Frei, is the signature of the war generation's attitude to the past. The total ruination of Germany's infrastructure is reflected in the ruination of the German family:

> Der Krieg hatte die Familien zugrunde gerichtet. Die Väter taumelten nach Hause, lernten ihre Kinder kennen und wurden als Eindringlinge abgewehrt. Sie waren fürs erste verbraucht und hatten nichts Gutes zu sagen. Der für den Vater freigehaltene Platz wurde von einem Menschen besetzt, der fremd und feindlich oder zerrüttet war und Position als Erzieher bezog — das war nicht glaubhaft. Beschädigte Ehen und verstörte Gefühle, Ruinen, Hunger und schlechte Aussichten auf Zukunft, zehnmal geflickte Strümpfe und kalte Öfen — wie sollte da Freude in den Familien sein. (*S*, 95)

> [The war had ruined the families. The fathers staggered back home, meeting their children who rejected them as intruders. They were exhausted and had nothing positive to communicate. The place that had been reserved for the father was now taken by a person who was alien and hostile or deranged and who assumed the position of educator — that was hardly credible. Damaged marriages and disturbed feelings, ruins, hunger, and bad prospects, socks ten times darned and cold heaters — how could there have been any sense of joy in the families?]

Meckel's narrative is scathing, but offers a highly analytical reading of the problem of masculinity in the postwar period. Entitling his narrative "Suchbild" (in search of/an attempt at a portrait), Meckel draws attention to the fact that, as a narrative combining the selection and evaluation of the biographical data of his father's life, his portrait necessarily entails a degree of fictionalization: "Die Erfindung offenbart und verbirgt den Menschen" (invention always reveals and disguises a human being, *S*, 55).

The title of Uwe Timm's *Am Beispiel meines Bruders* seems to suggest a significant shift of emphasis: instead of homing in on the father, the narrative is triggered by the figure of Timm's older brother Karl-Heinz, who joined the Waffen-SS at the age of eighteen and was killed on the Eastern front on 16 October 1943.[17] Timm's narrative analyzes how after his death the older brother assumed an iconic status in the family's collective memory of itself; representing the notion of "der tapfere Junge" (*AB*, 16), the brave boy who never lied and was always obedient (*AB*, 21). The family legend turned the figure of the brother into an exemplary icon, embodying precisely those problematic male virtues that ignited the conflict between father and sons and fathers and daughters in the postwar period. Unlike Meckel, who erases his mother and siblings from his account[18] in order to accentuate the father-son conflict, Timm includes all family members: the story about his brother is primarily a story about the brother's phantomlike existence in the postwar family. Notwithstanding this important widening of scope, the book can be read as a variant of *Väterliteratur* because it too unmasks the patriarchal underpinnings of postwar German society.

However, Timm's narrative investigation of postwar German family dynamics can only take place on the basis of historical distance: only after his mother and older sister have died is he at liberty to scrutinize the family legend (*AB*, 12). As in Meckel's *Suchbild*, it is a diary, in this case the brother's shocking war diary, that necessitates the narrator's inquiry. Beginning on 14 February 1943, the diary records every day at the front until it suddenly terminates on 7 August of the same year. Devoid of any emotional involvement or subjective reflections, the diary makes highly disturbing reading: "75m raucht Iwan Zigaretten, ein Fressen für mein MG" (*AB*, 19; 75m away Ivan smoking cigarettes, fodder for my MG).[19] As in Meckel's case, the narrative opens with a happy and emotionally charged childhood memory:

> Erhoben werden — Lachen, Jubel, eine unbändige Freude — diese Empfindung begleitet die Erinnerung an ein Erlebnis, ein Bild, das erste, das sich mir eingeprägt hat, mit ihm beginnt für mich das Wissen von mir selbst, das Gedächtnis [. . .]. (*AB*, 9)

> [Lifted up into the air — laughter, jubilation, boisterous delight — that sensation accompanies my recollection of an experience, an image, the first to make a lasting impression on me, and with it begins my self-awareness, my memory [. . .]. (*MB*, 1)]

Describing a hide-and-seek game between the toddler and his older brother, the narrative begins with a Proustian scene, a unique moment of exuberant re-unification. However, for all of its uplifting symbolism, this iconic moment of togetherness will remain isolated. Instead of insisting on the depoliticized innocence of one's childhood memories, as Martin Walser has done, Timm shows how deeply the personal is affected by the political. The complete absence of any dreams, desires, and hopes from the brother's war diary exemplifies this; with its exclusive focus on the war, the technical preparation of the attacks, target practice, and war technology, it bars access to the brother's inner self: "Um die eigene Geschichte und um die Erfahrbarkeit eigener Gefühle betrogen, bleibt nur die Reduktion auf Haltung und Tapferkeit" (*AB*, 31; Cheated of his own story, of a chance to experience his own feelings, he was reduced to putting a brave face on things, *MB*, 22). What comes into focus here is how the military code of courage that masks the brutality of the war also erases the self's sense of subjectivity and self-expression to a point where it makes little sense to speak of selfhood.

The postwar family legend does not reflect on the brother's reduction to a functionalized soldier during the war; his name continues to be shorthand for the still unquestioned masculine code of honor that was carried into the postwar period by the war generation that was born around the turn of the twentieth century. Like Meckel, Timm analyzes how this generation of fathers responded to its degradation at the end of the war by exercising its deeply ingrained authoritarianism within the four walls of the family unit: "Die Kommandogewalt hatten sie im öffentlichen Leben verloren, und so konnten sie nur noch zu Hause, in den vier Wänden, herumkommandieren" (*AB*, 69; Our fathers had lost the power of command in public life and could exercise it only at home, within their own four walls, *MB*, 59). Politically, militarily, and mentally dethroned, this generation is also shown to be morally and emotionally obtuse: its inability to mourn is paradigmatically reflected in conversations of the "Kameraden" (fellow soldiers), which routinely revolve around missed opportunities to win the war:

Sie kamen abends, saßen zusammen, tranken Cognac und Kaffee und redeten über den Kriegsverlauf. Suchten Erklärungen, warum der Krieg verloren gegangen war. Es wurden noch einmal Schlachten geschlagen, Befehle korrigiert, unfähige Generäle abgesetzt, Hitler die militärische Befehlsgewalt entzogen. Kaum vorstellbar, daß das abendfüllende Themen für diese Generation waren. (*AB*, 78)

[They came round in the evening, sat together, drank coffee and cognac and talked about the war. They tried to find explanations for why it had been lost. Battles were fought all over again, wrong orders put right, incompetent generals dismissed, Hitler deprived of his command of the army. It is hardly imaginable now to think of that generation discussing such subjects all evening. (*MB*, 67)]

This moral obtuseness, which turns the war into an adventure park of sorts, goes hand in hand with massive linguistic deformations that affect the discourse of the postwar period. Dodging the question of individual moral responsibility, the parental generation hides behind linguistic stereo-types that allow the construction of a victim identity: "Hitler der Verbrecher. Die Sprache wurde nicht nur von den Tätern öffentlich mißbraucht, sondern auch von denen, die von sich selbst sagten, *wir sind noch einmal davon gekommen*. Sie erschlichen sich eine Opferrolle" (*AB*, 106–7; Hitler the criminal. Language was publicly misused not just by the killers but by those who said of themselves, *well we got off again*. They slipped into the victim's role under false pretenses, *MB*, 95). Peppered with the Nazi jargon of the *Endlösung* and the *Untermensch* or the countless abbreviations of the Nazi apparatus, the war stories of these war comrades display a far-reaching mutilation of the German language and mentality (*AB*, 101). The physical expression of this generation's moral deformation is the ubiquitous image of the damaged male body:

> Die Kommißsprache, die Sprachverstümmelungen, die ihre Entsprechun-gen in körperlicher Versehrtheit fanden; die Hinkenden, an Krücken Gehenden, die mit einer Sicherheitsnadel hochgesteckten leeren Jack-enärmel, die umgeschlagenen Hosenbeine, die quietschenden Prothesen. (*AB*, 101)

> [Army terminology, linguistic mutilations that found their counterpart in physical injury: men limping on crutches, an empty jacket sleeve fastened with a safety pin, trouser legs turned up, squeaking artificial limbs. (*MB*, 90)]

In contrast to W. G. Sebald, who in his essay on *Luftkrieg und Literatur* (Air Raids and Literature, 1999)[20] had argued that the bombing and flat-tening of the German cities was repressed in the postwar period, Timm draws attention to the fact that the German war narrative always included stories of the bombing raids. Referring to the bombing of his family's home on 25 July 1943, Timm traces the slow conversion of the traumatic experience into an entertaining anecdote in the family legend: the repeti-tive re-telling of the family's flight through the burning streets of Ham-burg produces eventually a formulaic narrative that disguises the original trauma: "Das Eigentümliche war, wie der Schock, der Schreck, das Entset-zen durch das wiederholte Erzählen langsam faßlich wurde, wie das Erlebte langsam in seinen Sprachformeln verblaßte" (*AB*, 41–42; it was strange the way in which shock, alarm, horror gradually became compre-hensible through repeated telling, the way experiences slowly faded when put into words, *MB*, 31).

Like Meckel's father, Timm's father subscribes to a code of behavior that aims to mask the self's vulnerability. A polished host and gifted after-dinner speaker, the father lives in permanent status anxiety. With a constant eye on what people might think of him, he embodies the culture of shame that Lethen's book analyzes. Fearing ridicule and public exposure, the father evaluates himself only in terms of his public appearance: "Was die Leute denken, das war die immerwährende Sorge um die eigene Geltung. Nicht in der oberflächlichen Bedeutung, was die anderen von einem halten, sondern als Spiegel dessen, was man selbst von sich halten kann, was ist man, als was erscheint man" (*AB*, 82; What would people think? He was constantly anxious about his status. Not in the superficial sense of what others thought of him, but as reflecting his own idea of himself, of what he was and what kind of figure he cut, *MB*, 72). This fear of embarrassment, which again has its historical roots in the Wilhelmine code of honor and the experience of defeat in the First World War, internalizes the gaze of the onlooker, the social other. Lethen suggests that the cold persona's refusal to mourn after the Second World War points to the repetition of an attitude that, after the end of the First World War, had great resonance in the public.[21] An important example in this respect is Carl Schmitt, who in 1947 described his imprisonment as an American POW in terms of a degrading nakedness.[22]

Entangled in their code of honor, this generation of fathers also re-enacts the erasure of women, which had already characterized the anthropology of the interwar period. For the father girls simply don't count: Timm's father's chauvinistic desire to be a father of sons leads to the complete marginalization of Timm's older sister, who as the first-born child with the wrong gender is shunned by the father: "Tatsächlich zeigt ihn keines der Fotos mit der Schwester in körperlichem Kontakt, nicht auf dem Arm, nicht an der Hand, nicht auf dem Schoß" (*AB*, 51; And indeed none of the photographs show my father in physical contact with my sister, she is never in his arms, or holding hands, or on his lap, *MB*, 41). Dismantling the enshrined status of the absent dead brother, Timm also questions the gender politics of the postwar period. His reading of the family dynamic is a counter-reading that investigates the place of the female actors in the postwar family. The book therefore gives detailed portraits of the mother and the older sister: carefully restoring the place of the sister in the family romance, Timm shows how she lived under the shadow of the idealized dead brother.

Timm portrays his mother as a realist, a breadwinner, and a loving caregiver who adjusts to the harsh conditions of 1945 and who continues to run the family business into old age. Unlike Meckel, who in his *Suchbild: Meine Mutter* launches a shrill attack on his mother, Timm is careful to respect the integrity of his mother's life. Although she is a member of the war generation and ultimately shares its value system, her realism is shown to be an important counterpoint to the ideological rigidity of the *pater familias*. Timm empathizes with this generation of mothers and daughters who, subordinating their own needs, saw their families through the postwar period.

Timm's dialogic investigation of the past marks a significant shift away from the antagonistic examination of the parental generation in the father books of the late 1970s and 1980s. It would be a mistake, however, to suggest that this indicates the neat transition from the 1968er paradigm of rupture towards a new paradigm of transgenerational continuity and understanding. Although Timm demonstrates a heightened self-awareness and the ability to empathize with his family members, like Meckel he too distances himself from the male protagonists with their cold persona and false code of honor. And although Meckel's first impulse is the desire for rupture, the force of his antagonism points to a latent desire for a family life that would be unaffected by the war and National Socialism. Motivated by the anxiety of influence he engages in a narrative exorcism that aims to destroy all traditional forms of transgenerational solidarity. And yet, the flipside of such monologic gestures of self-proclamation and conflict is an underlying sense of loss of meaningful traditions and models of lineage. The violent affirmation of renewal through a generational break remains willy-nilly wedded to the concept's genealogical dimension.

Between Sentimental Empathy and Historical Analysis: Fathers as Soldiers in Ulla Hahn and Dagmar Leupold

In contrast to Timm's inclusion of the females in his narrative, Ulla Hahn and Dagmar Leupold return to a more narrow focus on the father-daughter relationship, a precursor of which is Elisabeth Plessen's *Mitteilung an den Adel* (Message for the Nobility, 1979). Hahn's *Unscharfe Bilder*, the only text discussed here that is not autobiographical but a novel, exploits one of the most significant memory contests of the 1990s: namely the debate around the controversial exhibition *Vernichtungskrieg: Verbrechen der Wehrmacht 1941–1945*, which documented the large-scale involvement of so-called ordinary soldiers in war crimes.[23]

In Hahn's novel, the exhibition is used as a ploy that ignites a conflict between father and daughter.[24] The protagonists are Hans Musbach, a retired high school teacher, and his daughter Katja, who has followed in her father's footsteps and embarked on a teaching career. Musbach is introduced as a refined and enlightened person who embraces the same belief in education and humanism that features in Meckel's *Suchbild*. But unlike Meckel, Hahn's Katja maintains a cordial and warm relationship with her father until she visits the Wehrmacht exhibition, where she believes to recognize her father in one of the photographs. However, this revelation comes only at the end of the novel: at the beginning Katja gives a copy of the exhibition catalogue to her father to jog his memory, an unwanted gift that in his view he does not need because as a teacher he has done his bit by analyzing and discussing the past with his students for decades (*UB*, 18). Employing the structure of the detective novel, the story records the daughter's intermittent interrogation of her father.

Forcing the father to confront the past, Katja seeks an admission of personal guilt. The narrative uses a quotation from Wittgenstein's *Philosophische Untersuchungen* (Philosophical Investigations, posthumously published in 1953) as a recurring leitmotiv: "Ist eine unscharfe Fotografie überhaupt ein Bild eines Menschen? Ja, kann man ein unscharfes Bild immer mit Vorteil durch ein scharfes ersetzen? Ist das unscharfe nicht oft gerade das, was wir brauchen?" (Is a blurred photograph really an image of a person? Indeed, is it always in our interest to replace a blurred image with a sharp one? Isn't the blurred image often exactly what we need?). In the dialogue between father and daughter, the notion of the blurred image is a contested issue: while Katja insists on "sharp images," that is, the need for historical objectivity and documentation, her father emphasizes the truth of his subjective memories. Nevertheless, he accepts his daughter's challenge to immerse himself once more in the past and narrates a series of war stories that include all the formulaic elements of war narratives, such as the soldiers' plight at the Russian front, the experience of hunger, coldness, camaraderie, cruelty, and the loss of a best friend. Another important ingredient in this cocktail of youthful innocence and suffering is his love story about his time with Wera, a Russian partisan whose life he claims to have saved. Seeing through this story as a screen memory,[25] the daughter eventually musters up her courage and asks him directly whether he was the soldier in the Wehrmacht exhibition photo who is shown to execute someone. The father now tells a new story about how an SS soldier who knew him from school had forced him to kill a Russian civilian. The execution is described thus:

> Ich hörte, wie er seine Pistole entsicherte, hinter mich trat und zischte: "Auf der Flucht erschossen!," bevor er Abstand nahm. So viel von mir wie ich von meinem Opfer. Ich tat wie mir befohlen. Hielt in die Richtung, wo der Mann stand. Zog ab. Der Schuß ging los. Da stand Hugo! Vor mir stand seine schmächtige Gestalt, bleigrau gefroren mit verrutschten Unterhosen, und eine warme rote Rose wuchs ihm aus der Brust. Ich sackte zusammen. "Verdammter Idiot," hörte ich noch. Dann verlor ich das Bewußtsein. Eine gnädige Ohnmacht. (*UB*, 268–69)

> [I heard how he took the safety off his pistol; he stepped behind me and hissed: "Shot as a fugitive!" before he took position. Exactly the same distance from me that I had to my victim. I did as I was told. Pointed the gun in the man's direction, pulled the trigger. A shot went off. There was Hugo! Right in front of me there was his frail figure, frozen blue and grey with his underpants hanging off him and a warm red rose growing out of his breast. I collapsed. "Damned idiot," I heard someone say before I lost consciousness. A merciful blackout.]

With its trivializing and kitschy register, this scene converts the perpetrator into a victim of sorts and reintroduces the dubious notion of "Befehlsnotstand" (following orders) into the debate: the father portrays himself here as an ordinary soldier who was forced to carry out a war crime against his will. Although Hahn appears to subject this scene to historical scrutiny by having Katja discover that in the photograph nobody was standing behind the soldier (*UB*, 274), the narrative ends on a highly ambivalent and ultimately unsatisfactory note: when in a final twist the broken father admits that nobody had forced him to shoot, the daughter absolves him from her charge because the date of the photo does not coincide with the father's purported biography:

> "Aber," stammelte Katja, "du bist nicht der Mann auf dem Foto! Du kannst es gar nicht sein. Du bist es nicht gewesen! Das Foto ist von dreiundvierzig. Winter. Da warst du doch bei den Partisanen! Du warst es nicht. Du hast nicht geschossen!"
> "Doch! Ich hätte nein sagen können, hörst du: nein! Ich habe geschossen. Das Foto ist von dreiundvierzig im Winter? Was tut das zur Sache? Ich bin es nicht auf diesem Foto? Spielt das denn eine Rolle? Ich weiß doch, was war. Dieses Foto oder nicht. Ein Foto oder keines. Verzeih mir — wenn du kannst." (*UB*, 275)

> ["But," Katja muttered, "you are not the man in the photo! It couldn't have been you. It wasn't you! The photo is from winter 1943. That's when you were with the partisans! It wasn't you. You didn't shoot!"
> "Yes I did! I could have said no, do you hear me: no! But I shot. The picture is dated winter 1943? What does that change? I'm not the one in the photo? Does that make a difference? I know what happened. This photo or that, a photo or no photo. Forgive me — if you can."]

This is not just a piece of bad writing but also an example of bad memory politics: the novel ends with the tearful reunion of father and daughter and the daughter's sense of guilt for having subjected the father to the terror of historical investigation. The sociologist Harald Welzer rightly observes that with this novel Hahn legitimizes precisely the blurred images that make up much of the reservoir of German transgenerational family memories.[26] Shifting focus from the question of the parents' guilt to their children's lack of empathy for their plight, the novel, according to Welzer, constructs the convenient notion of a guiltless guilt.[27]

Hahn's novel presses nearly all the buttons of contemporary memory contests: in addition to the context of the Wehrmacht exhibition, there is an implied allusion to the Walser debate when Musbach, like Walser in *Der springende Brunnen* (A Springing Fountain, 1998), reminds Katja that the era of National Socialism was not just characterized by Hitler's speeches, Nazi parades, terror, and military drill, but also by his youthful preoccupations outside the political frame (*UB*, 58). A little earlier, the novel directly refers to the victim-perpetrator debate as triggered by Günter Grass's *Im Krebs-gang* (Crabwalk, 2002) (*UB*, 27); this is followed by Musbach's reflection on generational dialogue (*UB*, 52, 54), two episodes that recall the generation of 1968 and its members' antagonism towards their parents (*UB*, 64, 255), a brief discussion of Peter Weiss's seminal *Ästhetik des Widerstandes* (Aesthetics of Resistance, 1975–1981) (*UB*, 70) and two references to Ernst Jünger's contested notions of the steel soldier and of sacrifice (*UB*, 119, 172). With its superficial inventory of current memory contests the novel resolves the dialectic of the desire for a complete break with the family heritage on the one hand and the longing for genealogy and tradition on the other, a hallmark of *Väterliteratur*, in favor of a one-sided and forced harmonization. At the conclusion of the novel transgenerational empathy overrides crucial historical disctinctions: in the end the father appears as just another victim of history's cruelty.

In contrast to Hahn's narrative, Dagmar Leupold's *Nach den Kriegen* ignites the tinderbox of memory once more.[28] As in Meckel, it is the death of the father that triggers the daughter's investigation of his life story. Framed by the daughter's journey from the United States back to Germany to attend her father's funeral — which she misses due to her flight being delayed — the daughter remembers her final visit to her father when he was gravely ill in hospital. The memory of seeing his naked body in its raw physicality before death is an uncanny reminder of a shared lineage and genealogy:

> Daß ich von ihm abstammte — eine Abzweigung, ein Ausschnitt war —, schien mir im Zustand der Nacktheit auf die wörtlichste Bedeutung reduziert, alles Potentielle war gelöscht zugunsten einer fest berechneten Summe. In den Anzügen, die er trug, war er im Auftrag unterwegs: Zum Bridgeturnier, auf Klassenfahrt, zu Symposien, Kleidung war etwas Öffentliches, war Lebensssstoff, Kleidung erzählte vom Vater und wies nicht auf die Tochter zurück. Im nackten Körper dagegen war der Vater — auf dem Kind unheimliche Weise — ohne Vorwände zu Hause und ähnelte darin allen anderen Menschen. Also auch der Tochter. (*NK*, 19)

> [That I descended from him — that I was a branch of his, an extract of sorts — seemed to me to gain a literal meaning when I saw his nakedness, everything that had been a potential dimension was now erased in favor of a sum total that was calculated in an exact manner. Wearing his suits he was always after some official assignment: the bridge competition, a school trip, symposia; clothes were of a public nature, the material of life, his clothes represented the father without pointing back to his daughter. However, in his naked body the father suddenly seemed to be at home without reservations, which the child found uncanny. He resembled all other human beings. And this also included his daughter.]

Without the protective shield of his well-groomed public persona, the father in his illness appears as precisely the unmasked self, the helpless creature that the cold persona had tried to fend off. This exposed nakedness is uncanny because it brings to the fore an existential semblance and relatedness that makes it impossible for the daughter to draw a line between herself and her father. In many ways, this hospital scene with its imagery of the dying father and the daughter's recognition of the inevitability of familial affiliation signifies the return of the repressed by pointing to her own mortality. It also highlights the interdependence of genealogy and generational renewal: while the daughter's move to the United States and the start of her own family exemplifies her desire for a new beginning; the death of her father forces her to see herself as a daughter and thus as part of an unwanted genealogy, the symbolic expression of which is a wax stamp that the father had made in order to vouch for the life story that he always wanted to write but never managed to put on paper (*NK*, 7). Inheriting this wax stamp, the daughter sees it as a posthumous assignment to give shape to his damaged life and to their damaged relationship:

> Im Roman hätte sein Leben eine Form und ein Format erhalten, da er ungeschrieben blieb, schien es ihm vergeblicher und ungestalter. Auch mir geht es hier um diese vermißte Gestalt, eine Gestalt, deren Beschädigung durch den Krieg geschah. Der Krieg geht mitten durch die Familien, ein Graben. (*NK*, 7)

> [A novel would have given his life a definite form and meaning, however, since it was never written his life seemed to him more pointless and without shape. I too am interested in that missing shape, a shape that had been damaged by the war. The war runs through the families, a trench.]

This task of giving shape to the father's life through narration entails the unmasking of the family legends that, according to the daughter, are the product of the type of familial co-fabulation that inevitably constructs a sense of familial togetherness (*NK*, 33–34). And yet, although the daughter's narrative is a counter-reading to the father's self-image, she views her enterprise in terms of a self-imagining that assigns to the fragmentary selves of father and daughter the dignity of a wholeness that only the written word can provide (*NK*, 34). It is precisely this dialectic between a need for *Gestalt* (form) and the realization that the gaps and ruptures of life cannot be healed that make this a particularly compelling example of *Väterliteratur*.

Like Timm's book, Leupold's *Nach den Kriegen* offers an analysis of postwar family life, which appears, with its emphasis on economic reconstruction and the accumulation of status symbols, in a phrase coined by F. C. Delius, as the "Steinzeit der Demokratie" (the stone age of democracy).[29] The narrator juxtaposes memories of her childhood, such as the image of herself roller-skating in the streets, with the critical analysis of the ideology of the "Aufschwung" (economic boom, *NK*, 76). But in spite of the parental focus on the future and the "Verwaltung der Wohlstandsträume" (the administration of their dreams of prosperity, *NK*, 77), the war still haunts the present.

The father, who in the course of the war lost three fingers, continues to fight various imaginary wars at the dinner table so that eating and conducting warfare become intertwined in the child's imagination. In order to understand the deep-seated failure of communication between father and daughter, the daughter reconstructs his biography. Family photographs, the father's war diary, his postwar literary writings, as well as other historical documents are used to reconstruct the formative stages in the father's biography: we learn that he was born as a member of the German minority in Polish Bielsko in 1913, and that after finishing secondary school and his father's suicide he studied mathematics and physics in Lemberg supported by his sister. His Germanness, or rather his status as a member of the German minority, becomes the touchstone of his identity as well as a career choice (*NK*, 116). Refusing to accept a Polish teaching post, the father moves to Vienna until he becomes a "Kreisschulrat," a school inspector, in the German occupied territory known as the Generalgouvernement. He joins the NSDAP in 1941, is drafted into the Wehrmacht in 1942, which he spends in Russia until he is wounded; recovering in Stettin he begins to keep a diary, which is composed, according to his daughter, with an eye on the posthumous reader. Interspersing quotations from the war diary with her personal reflections and historical documents such as quotations from the notorious Generalgouverneur of the occupied Polish territory, Hans Frank, or from the party program of the German *Jungdeutsche Partei* in Poland, the narrative adopts a variety of angles to give form to the father's life.

The resulting hybridity of this narrative must, however, not be read in terms of a polyphony that gives voice to the relativity of all historical interpretations but rather as a documentary technique that ensures a high degree of historical objectification. By placing the father's diary in a wider historical context, the narrative shows that the emotional and psychological makeup of his generation was steeped in *völkisch* ideology and its core idea that the alleged superiority of the German people necessitated the colonial subjugation of Eastern Europe. Citing various passages from her father's diary that record conversations between Frank and the founder of the *Jungdeutsche Partei*, Rudolf Ernst Wiesner, about the imminent extermination of the Jews, the daughter highlights the father's complete emotional detachment from the subject of these conversations (*NK*, 127). As in Meckel and Timm, the self's stylization in terms of the cold persona is the focal point of the daughter's analysis. In her eyes the complete absence of empathy with the suffering of the Jews and Poles draws attention to the double vision of the diary writer: on the one hand he adopts the mask of the cold strategist who only registers the civilian population's suffering in terms of collateral damage; on the other he is shown to be fired up by his ideological mission (*NK*, 129). After the war the father views neither his own life nor history in terms of the sum of individual and collective deeds but rather "als eine nach eigenen Gesetzen sich vollziehende, periodisch wiederholende Dynamik, die sich die Geschichte unterwirft" (in terms of a periodically repetitive dynamic that subjects history to its own laws, *NK*, 167).

The great role model for this generation's characteristic attitude to the war was Ernst Jünger. His name crops up in Meckel, Timm, and Hahn: while Meckel mentions his father's admiration of Jünger (*S*, 28), Hahn has Hans Musbach distance himself from the Jünger cult of his generation and from the notion of sacrifice (*UB*, 172). Timm also comments on Jünger's pervasive influence: he highlights his father's generation's failure to make the connection between the absolute values of courage in the face of death, duty, and sacrifice as paradigmatically expressed in Jünger's *In Stahlgewittern* (The Storm of Steel, 1920), and the later application of these values to even more deadly purposes in the Nazi era (*AB*, 153). But it is Leupold's narrative that offers an in-depth analysis of Jünger's formative influence on this generation of males. Drawing out stylistic similarities between her father's postwar diaries and Jünger's *Strahlungen* (Radiation, 1949), she shows to what extent the father adopts the Jüngerian pose of the cool observer who scans the world unemotionally with a scientific eye. Jünger's modernist interest in the surface of appearances, in a world free of cause and effect, has been analyzed as an example of a modernist aesthetic that realizes the dream of man's synchronization with modern technology.[30] In Jünger's work the anthropology of the cold persona is fetishized in the figure of the steel warrior, who in the death zones of war immunizes himself against the experience of pain. Encountering the first soldier with a steel helmet, Jünger describes this significant moment in terms of the erasure of subjectivity as symbolized in the leveling of a man's personal voice:

> Er war der erste deutsche Soldat, den ich im Stahlhelm sah, und erschien mir sogleich als Bewohner einer fremden und härteren Welt. [. . .] Das vom stählernen Helmrand umrahmte unbewegliche Gesicht und die eintönige, vom Lärm der Front begleitete Stimme machten einen gespenstischen Eindruck auf uns. [. . .] Nichts war in dieser Stimme zurückgeblieben als ein großer Gleichmut. Mit solchen Männern kann man kämpfen.[31]

> [He was the first German soldier who I saw wearing a steel helmet; and he immediately appeared to me like the inhabitant of an alien and tougher world. [. . .] Framed by the steel-rim of the helmet, his immobile face and his monotonous voice, which was accompanied by the noise of the front had an uncanny effect on us. [. . .] This voice retained nothing but a great indifference. One can fight with such men.]

As Lethen comments, readers of the right-wing camp tend to feel attracted to this iconic steel warrior but repelled by the modernity of Jünger's analysis of the modern type; in contrast, readers of a left-liberal persuasion tend to

focus on Jünger's quasi-Marxist concept of the modern worker, but they
reject his iconography of the warrior (Lethen, 206). Leupold's interest lies
squarely with the ethical consequences of this modernist separation of the
aesthetic from the moral domain. Applied to the political sphere, this
sidelining of the moral produces the Fascist ideology with which so many
intellectuals, including her father, identified. As Jünger's disciple and
epigone, the father in his diary mimics Jünger's language down to the level
of style. Dagmar Leupold describes Jünger in terms of the first observer
who surveys the surface of objects without any interest in cause and effect
(*NK*, 169). For Leupold an episode in *Strahlungen I*, Jünger's war diary, a
copy of which she inherited from her father, illustrates paradigmatically the
moral consequences of such a studied and sterile objectivity. Jünger's diary
entry of 29 May 1941 relates how he had been asked to witness the execution of a deserter. Leupold cites the opening passage, in which Jünger
refers to this as one of a "Flut von widrigen Dingen" (a flood of inoppor-
tune things) that he has to attend to; but in the end he accepts the assignment because he is driven by a "higher curiosity":

> Im Grunde war es höhere Neugier, die den Ausschlag gab. Ich sah schon
> viele sterben, doch keinen im bestimmten Augenblick. Wie stellt sich die
> Lage dar, die heute jeden von uns bedroht und seine Existenz schattiert?
> Und wie verhält man sich in ihr?[32]

> [It was really a higher curiosity that made me decide. I have seen many
> people die but nobody at a predetermined moment. What is this situation
> that threatens all of us, shadowing our existence? And how does one
> behave in it?]

Jünger's amoral observation of the world goes hand in hand with a meta-
physical leap that turns man into a being that is driven by higher forces. In
the postwar era, this notion of a higher determinism allowed the convenient move from the troubling question "who am I?" to "who are we?";
a shift from the individual to the collective, from introspection to external
factors (*NK*, 173). While Jünger's detached observation of the world
might be an aesthetically interesting experiment, for Leupold it produces a
highly reductive notion of the intellectual who merely takes note of the
phenomena of the world without judgment:

> Wir werden bewegt, von außen, eben von den Stürmen, und ihre Kraft,
> ihre Richtung verändert uns — auch innerlich. Aber wir bleiben Zuschauer,
> Getriebene. Die Aufgabe des aufmerksamen (Selbst-)Beobachters — also
> nach Jüngers Auffassung des Intellektuellen — ist folglich die eines Pro-
> tokollführers. Er muß genau verzeichnen, was vorfällt; er macht die
> Bestandsaufnahme, er inventarisiert die Welt. Den Käfern, der Liebe, dem
> Massenmord und der Hauptmahlzeit wird dasselbe, genau abgewogene

Interesse gewidmet. Das Sichtbare und das Ereignishafte haben immer Vorrang vor dem Inneren. (*NK*, 174)

[An external force is moving us, the storms, and their force and direction changes us — even on the inside. But we remain spectators who are tossed around. The task of the alert observer (of his own self) — that is according to Jünger the intellectual — is that of a scribe. He must note down precisely what happens; taking stock he produces an inventory of the world. He dedicates exactly the same calculated attention to beetles, to love, to mass murders or the main dish of the day. That which is visible and eventful always has priority over introspection.]

Leupold's analysis of the iconic status that Jünger occupied in this generation of men thus helps to explain the causes of their disastrous moral blindness. Jünger appealed to a man like Leupold's father because Jünger's aesthetic perspective on all the phenomena of this world justified the generation's profound lack of moral judgment and, furthermore, he provided them with a metaphysical determinism that allowed them to avoid the painful business of introspection.

However, in spite of her astute critique of the generation's ideological makeup, Leupold's book does not close on an acrimonious note. Having worked through her father's diaries and other writings by him, she visits his grave and remembers another family legend. But this time it is one that concerns her own birth: according to her father, he nurtured her after she and her twin sister were prematurely born:

Frühgeburt im Niederlahnsteiner Krankenhaus ohne Brutkasten, da sei er es gewesen, der mich gefüttert habe, ebenso habe er, zwei Monate später, nach unserem Einzug zu Hause, in der Nachtschicht mich übernommen, in seinen Schoß gebettet, den großen Glatzkopf in der Armbeuge — das machte er pantomimisch vor —, habe gestaunt über das häßliche Kind, dem Wimpern, Haare und Nägel fehlten. Grottenmolch, sagte er, du sahst aus wie ein Grottenmolch. Bei einem Ausflug von Kärnten nach Slowenien besuchten wir eine Tropfsteinhöhle; in den Tümpeln darin zeigte er mir die transparenten, nachtschattigen Molche und wiederholte: So hast du ausgesehen. Ich habe dich trotzdem gefüttert.

Im Grunde spielt es keine Rolle, ob es so war oder nicht. Es ist der Anfang einer Geschichte. (*NK*, 221)

[Premature birth in the hospital of Niederlahnstein, without an incubator. So it was he who fed me, and two months later after we had moved into our house — it was he who took me over during the night shifts, placing me in his lap, my big bald head in the crook of his arm — he mimicked this for me — surprised about this ugly child who had no eye lashes, hair or nails. A water newt, you looked just like a water newt, he said. On a trip from Carinthia to Slovenia we visited a cave full of stalagmites; in one of the puddles he showed me a water newt, transparent and with a

night-shady appearance. And he repeated: that's what you looked like.
But I fed you anyway.
   It doesn't really matter, whether it's true or not. It is the beginning of
a story.]

By reinstating a family legend, at the center of which is an image of unconditional love and care, Leupold also reinstates the notion of genealogy and
affiliation, and of a lineage that engenders stories. The final conciliatory
gesture of putting a bunch of flowers (the highly delicate mimosa) on his
grave does not, however, in any way negate her previous critique of a particular version of Germanness and German maleness. But now that she has
given the missing shape to her father's life, distance and affection, generational renewal and the recognition of her own familial lineage are poised
in a delicate balance.

   To conclude: All four narratives discussed in this chapter adopt a
bottom-up, specifically inner-familial perspective on major historical events.
The privatization of history is thus one of the main signatures of this literature, in that it views the political, social, and economic factors that motivated National Socialism through the lens of family history. This conflation
of history with personal memory can be used to very different effects:
Hahn's novel resolves the complex dialectic between rupture and continuity, a defining characteristic of *Väterliteratur*, in favor of a rather forced
harmonization that is at the expense of historical analysis and objectification. In contrast to the sentimental denouement of *Unscharfe Bilder*,
Meckel, Timm, and Leupold provide an anatomy of the paternal generation in order to lay bare the ideological underpinnings that continued to
influence the postwar period well into the 1950s. All three narratives identify a specifically masculine code of honor as one of the main reasons for
the breakdown of communication in German postwar families. While all
three narratives aim to dismantle those family legends that have produced
negative legacies haunting the sons and daughters, Uwe Timm adopts a
highly self-reflexive and dialogic stance that takes account of the narrator's
own affective position and leaves the integrity of his siblings and parents
intact. By contrast Meckel's book offers a far more scathing and unrelent-
ing account of the long-term damage caused by a generation of helpless
despots in the postwar family. However, Leupold's analytical investigation
of the paternal generation's Jünger cult shows that contemporary *Väterliteratur* cannot be simply read in terms of a new investment in transgenerational understanding and solidarity. To varying degrees, the narratives by
Meckel, Timm, and Leupold maintain the dialectic between continuity and
rupture, between the desire for a generational break and affiliation, between
historical analysis and subjective memory. If this dialectic is abandoned,
as in Hahn's case, the genre runs into the danger of a sentimentalized
harmonization of memory, which ultimately downplays the factuality of

history. Only when and if this transgenerational literature manages to negotiate the potential gaps between history and memory does it avoid the pitfall of a historical revisionism that abandons the notion of personal responsibility.

This privatization of history thus also results in a significant rediscovery of autobiographical modes of writing about the past and a new investment in authorship: abandoning the 1960s' declaration of the death of the author and the analysis of the social and linguistic structures that precede individual agency, these intergenerational authors emphatically embrace autobiographical forms of writing in order to restore the notion of individual historical agency and responsibility. Furthermore, these family narratives shift focus from the question of what happened in the past to how these repressed events have disturbed postwar familial relations. They often investigate personal diaries, letters, and photographs in order to exorcise the family's negative legacy. As meta-narratives, they examine the belatedness of their own engagement with this topic and explore the function of deferral and transference as a latent but nevertheless crucial means of communication across generational thresholds.

Notes

I would like to thank the Irish Research Council for the Humanities and Social Sciences, whose generous funding in 2005/6 enabled me to write this essay.

[1] Prominent examples of *Väterliteratur* are Elisabeth Plessen's *Mitteilung an den Adel* (Message for the Nobility, 1979); Hermann Kinder's *Im Schleiftrog* (The Grinding Trough, 1977); Ruth Rehmann's *Der Mann auf der Kanzel: Fragen an einen Vater* (The Man in the Pulpit: Questions for a Father, 1979); Bernward Vesper's *Die Reise* (The Trip, 1977); Peter Härtling's *Nachgetragene Liebe* (Belated Love, 1980) and Christoph Meckel's *Suchbild: Über meinen Vater* (In Search of a Portrait: About My Father). A late example of this first wave of father books is Peter Schneider's novella *Vati* (Daddy, 1989), which relates the one and only encounter between the concentration-camp doctor Josef Mengele and his son Rolf.

[2] Ernestine Schlant, "Autobiographical Novels — Generational Discourse," in *The Language of Silence. West German Literature and the Holocaust* (New York: Routledge, 1999), 80–98; here: 85. Also see Jochen Vogt's more sympathetic reading of the genre: "Er fehlte, er fehlte, er hat gefehlt . . . Ein Rückblick auf die sogenannten Väterbücher," in *Deutsche Nachkriegsliteratur und der Holocaust*, eds. Stephan Braese, Holger Gehle, Doron Kiesel, Hanno Lowey (Frankfurt am Main, New York: Campus, 1998), 385–99; and Claudia Mauelshagen, *Der Schatten des Vaters: deutschsprachige Väterliteratur der siebziger und achtziger Jahre* (Frankfurt am Main, Berlin: Lang, 1995).

[3] Pierre Nora, "Generation," in *Realms of Memory: Rethinking the French Past*. Vol. 1: *Conflicts and Divisions*, translated from the French by Arthur Goldhammer (New York: Columbia UP, 1996), 499–531; here: 499.

[4] Two prominent examples stand out in this respect: Uwe Timm's novel *Rot* (Red, 2001) and Friedrich Christian Delius's *Mein Jahr als Mörder* (My Year as an Assassin, 2004). Both novels attempt a retrospective and personal evaluation of 1968.

[5] Norbert Frei, *1945 und Wir: Das Dritte Reich im Bewußtsein der Deutschen* (Munich: Beck, 2005), 12, 37.

[6] One has to caution, however, that the counting of generations and the attempt to map generational affiliation onto a history of mentality is fraught with pitfalls: while Frei's model implies that the generation born around 1900 also made up the first generation after the Second World War with many of its members shaping policy in education, politics, and the judiciary, Sigrid Weigel views the "Flakhelfer" generation as the first, albeit concealed postwar generation. See Sigrid Weigel, " 'Generation' as a Symbolic Form: On the Genealogical Discourse of Memory since 1945," *The Germanic Review* 77 (2002): 264–77; here: 273. Also see: Norbert Frei, ed., *Hitlers Eliten nach 1945* (Munich: dtv, 2003). Heinrich Böll, a key actor in the postwar period, fits neither model: born in 1917 he was neither a member of the generation born around 1900 nor did he qualify for membership of the "Flakhelfer" generation. His critical engagement with Germany's moral responsibility shows that the notion of generation must not be viewed in a deterministic manner.

[7] Weigel, " 'Generation' as a Symbolic Form," 163. For a comprehensive analysis of the genealogy of the concept see the essays in Sigrid Weigel, Ohad Parmes, Ulrike Vedder, and Stefan Willer eds., *Generation. Zur Genealogie des Konzepts — Konzepte von Genealogie* (Munich: Fink, 2005).

[8] Cit. in Pierre Nora, "Generation," 502.

[9] This is in contrast to Nora's claim that generation as a *lieu de mémoire* is a particularly French phenomenon. Nora writes: "There are indeed 'French' generations. If, moreover, a generation is a *lieu de mémoire*, it is not at all in the simple sense that shared experiences imply shared memories. It is rather as a result of the simple yet subtle interplay of memory and history, of the eternally re-emerging dialectic of a past that remains present, of actors who become their own witnesses, and of new witnesses in turn transformed into actors. When all three elements are present, a mere spark can ignite a blaze. It is their presence in today's France, that tinderbox of memory, that fuels the 'generational' blaze" (Nora, "Generation," 530–31). I would argue that the legacy of two World Wars and National Socialism has indeed ignited such a generational blaze in Germany.

[10] Christoph Meckel, *Suchbild: Über meinen Vater* (Frankfurt am Main: Fischer, 1983). Further references appear in the text as *S* followed by the page number.

[11] All translations are mine unless otherwise indicated.

[12] Helmut Lethen, *Verhaltenslehre der Kälte: Lebensversuche zwischen den Kriegen* (Frankfurt am Main: Suhrkamp 1994), 35.

[13] Cit. in Lethen, *Verhaltenslehre der Kälte*, 85.

[14] A poignant example of the creature is the soldiers who returned from the war so badly injured and disfigured that they were locked up in special institutions since their appearance in the public was deemed not to be acceptable.

[15] See Giorgio Agamben, *Homo Sacer: Sovereign Power and Bare Life*. Translated from the Italian by Daniel Heller-Rozen (Stanford: Stanford UP, 1998).

[16] Meckel uses capitals whenever he wants to emphasize the father's insistent tone of voice.

[17] Uwe Timm, *Am Beispiel meines Bruders* (Cologne: Kiepenheuer & Witsch, 2003). All subsequent references appear in the text as *AB* followed by the page number.

[18] In 2002 Meckel published a complementary and equally scathing portrait of his mother, entitled *Suchbild: Meine Mutter* (Munich, Vienna: Hanser, 2002).

[19] All English quotations follow the translation by Anthea Bell. See Uwe Timm, *In My Brother's Shadow*. Translated from the German by Anthea Bell (London: Bloomsbury, 2005). Cited as *MB* followed by page number. Here: 10.

[20] Translated as *On the Natural History of Destruction*. Translated from the German by Anthea Bell (London: Hamish Hamilton, 2003).

[21] Lethen, *Verhaltenslehre*, 215.

[22] See Carl Schmitt, *Ex Captivitate Salus. Erfahrungen der Zeit 1945/47* (Berlin: Duncker & Humblot, 1950), 79. On Schmitt's culture of shame see Lethen, *Verhaltenslehre*, 219–31.

[23] When some of the captions of the photos were proven to be historically inaccurate, the exhibition was withdrawn and relaunched after the necessary corrections were made. Some 850,000 visitors saw the exhibition in Germany and Austria, with many visitors looking at the photos with magnifying glasses to identify family members. On this issue see Chloe Paver's article in this volume.

[24] Ulla Hahn, *Unscharfe Bilder: Roman* (Munich: dtv, 2005). All further references appear in the text as *UB* followed by the page number.

[25] See Sigmund Freud, "Über die Deckerinnerung," in *Gesammelte Werke*, ed. Anna Freud et al., vol. 1 (Frankfurt am Main: Fischer, 1999), 529–54.

[26] Harald Welzer, "Schön unscharf. Über die Konjunktur der Familien- und Generationenromane," *Mittelweg 36* 1 (2004): 53–65. Here: 56. Also see Harald Welzer, Sabine Moller, and Karoline Tschugnall, *"Opa war kein Nazi": Nationalsozialismus und Holocaust im Familiengedächtnis* (Frankfurt am Main: Fischer, 2002).

[27] Welzer, "Schön unscharf," 57.

[28] Dagmar Leupold, *Nach den Kriegen* (Munich: Beck, 2004). All subsequent references appear in the text as *NK* followed by the page number.

[29] Friedrich Christian Delius, *Mein Jahr als Mörder* (Berlin: Rowohlt, 2004), 126.

[30] See Lethen on this, *Verhaltenslehre*, 198–215.

[31] Ernst Jünger, *In Stahlgewittern* (Stuttgart: Klett-Cotta, 1978), 104.

[32] Ernst Jünger, *Strahlungen I* (Stuttgart: Klett-Cotta, 1988), 242. Leupold cites a slightly different version: "Auch will ich mir gestehen, daß ein Akt höherer Neugier den Ausschlag gab" (170).

3: Telling It How It Wasn't: Familial Allegories of Wish-Fulfillment in Postunification Germany

Elizabeth Boa

GDR LITERATURE WAS HIGHLY DIALOGIC. Given the level of state control over journalism and film, the literary field offered an arena of coded debate for the discerning reader to decipher. Literature mattered; it was politically significant. In postunification times state intervention has receded, but leitmotivic echoes and aesthetic stratagems still wander from text to text as vehicles of political and moral argument feeding on and into the often bitter polemics in the journalistic media. The polemics frequently turn on competing historical paradigms, taking the form of memory contests. As Mary Fulbrook notes, a sense of acceptable national identity is often constructed by singing tales of heroes and martyrs.[1] GDR orthodoxy celebrated the heroes and martyrs of the communist resistance and the survivors who, together with workers by hand and brain, built up the new socialist state: "Auferstanden aus Ruinen" (Arisen from Ruins), as the national anthem put it. But now that the orthodox song sheet has been torn up, how is a sense of national identity to be constructed in the Berlin Republic that will be acceptable to citizens of the former GDR and help to close the mental gap between east and west Germans?

Obvious heroes in popular accounts of unification are the people who poured through the Wall on 9 November 1989. The protesters in Leipzig or Berlin and the intellectuals who spoke to the masses in Alexanderplatz also figure, if more ambiguously, as critics of the GDR state but not necessarily heroes of unification, since many of them looked to a Third Way. And who are the villains in the tales of heroism? Can the heroes of the founding generation be transmuted into villains without turning much of the population into colluding fellow travelers? In analogy with postcolonial discourse, Gisela Brinker-Gabler coined the term "dis/re/location" to designate the collective and individual sense of rupture followed by repositioning, but the analogy breaks down somewhat when it comes to the land the dis/re/located East Germans have left behind.[2] For in contrast to the postcolonial search for roots, German postunification polemics sometimes seem aimed less at discovering than at cutting off roots.

This essay will compare two novels and a film, with a brief postscript on one further novel. The texts have been chosen for three common features: first, they self-reflexively engage both with the past and with the difficulties of such engagement in postunification Germany; second, they allegorize family relations to tell histories of the GDR; and finally they deal in stories that are evidently false. Perversely, they tell it how it was through telling it how it wasn't. Since Plato's Republic, tellers of tales have been denigrated as liars. One aim will be to explore the purposes explicit lying may have in uprooting the self from an unwanted past, while retaining enough of a root system from which to cultivate a livable identity.

Monika Maron's *Stille Zeile sechs* (Quiet Row Number Six, 1991) centers on a father/daughter relationship. Thomas Brussig's *Helden wie wir* (Heroes Like Us, 1996) also conveys a son's relationship with his father, but centers on mother and son. The film *Good Bye Lenin* (2003), so I shall argue, engages with *Helden wie wir* in a memory contest by way of a massive revaluation of the mother/son relationship. As a structure persisting yet changing through time, the family serves as a controlled but quite complex prism, bringing together the more remote, parental past history as communicated to the younger generation and the more immediate remembered history of the child/parent relations. At the same time, cultural and social memory, mediated in many ways, feeds into and modifies the familial and personal memory stores, so that remembering is a constantly evolving process subject to revaluation under the impact of current events.[3] The familial allegories discussed here all foreground that last element in memory formation — or memory invention. Generations in families mark a clear divide between parents and children, though the gap in years can vary greatly. Historical generations, measured as forty years or so, are a more slippery matter, being defined relative to significant historical events or epochal concepts. The confrontations between old and young that structure the texts may turn out differently depending on differences in the ages of both characters and authors. As a genre within the field of memory culture, familial allegories differ from subtle explorations of memory in biographical writing. They superimpose a familial binary of old and young upon political history to dramatic effect, turning history into a confrontation between opposing blocks. And they transport gendered relations within the family into the political domain to rhetorical effect. In the texts at issue here, the younger generation defines its identity over against the other of the older generation. Crucial to their position in postunification polemics is how the confrontation is shaped. Does an agonistic contest evolve into reconciliatory dialogue? Does the younger subject move on or remain in thrall? Does filial monologue silence the parental voice? Or do all differentiating boundaries between older other and younger complicit self threaten to collapse? Important too is whether it remains a family quarrel, or whether, alongside the internal battles, there is any meeting between an East German or socialist subject and a West German or capitalist other.

A Historians' Quarrel:
Monika Maron's *Stille Zeile sechs*

The historians' quarrel in the West and the fictional shouting matches around the same time in *Stille Zeile sechs* had at least one issue in common, namely whether National Socialism and Stalinism are comparable.[4] When she asserts that "Siberien liegt bei Ravensbrück" (Siberia is next to Ravensbrück), the enraged Rosalind Polkowski undoes a difference her enemy Beerenbaum insists upon.[5] Yet Rosalind's rage perhaps masks an unacknowledged likeness between the older and the younger generation within the GDR, so that the attack turns against her too. The quarrel, played out in the mid-1980s, pits seventy-eight-year-old Professor Herbert Beerenbaum, formerly responsible for ideological matters at Berlin University, against the narrator, forty-two-year-old former historian Rosalind Polkowski. Beerenbaum, who has a nervous tremor in his right hand, employs Rosalind as his literal handmaiden or right-hand woman, dictating to her his memoirs, an *apologia pro vita sua*. Beerenbaum is a self-proclaimed representative of the GDR founding generation, the men and women who returned from concentration camps or exile and set up a new state in 1949. His memoirs instantiate the orthodox historical paradigm, beginning with his proletarian origins in the Rhineland, through the ordeals during the Third Reich and exile, and now as chronicler of the historical triumph of communism, a victim who became a victor. Beerenbaum holds up his victim status during the Third Reich as a guarantee of permanent innocence, a shield against attack that Rosalind seeks to puncture by probing questions about internecine struggles, unexplained deaths in Moscow and the Gulag, the imprisonment by the GDR leadership of dissidents from among their own ranks in the 1950s, the building of the wall in 1961, the orders to shoot those engaged in the crime of *Republikflucht* (fleeing the Republic), attacks on intellectuals who did not toe the line. Thus two histories stand opposed.

In their struggle for mastery, the combatants deploy different narrative strategies. Beerenbaum follows a linear chronology in tracking his own part in the historical triumph of communism. But interposed between Beerenbaum and the reader is Rosalind. From her position of narrative control she disrupts Beerenbaum's story by starting at the end with Beerenbaum's funeral in the early spring of 1986 and zigzagging backwards and forwards, mixing accounts of their meetings beginning in the summer of 1985 with other encounters and fragmentary memories of her own, the earliest references being Beerenbaum's birth in 1907 and war-baby Rosalind's first meeting at the age of seven with her father on his return from a prisoner-of-war camp. Rosalind's non-linear montage awkwardly juxtaposes the personal and the political. Against Beerenbaum's narrative flow she sets discontinuous chunks. Her method has something of the materialist approach advocated by Walter Benjamin in blasting details out of embeddedness in narrative.[6] The estranged detail becomes a chisel to crack open received ideas. Rosalind refuses the interpretative mastery of orthodox history, but rather tests the master narrative on its own ground and against quotidian details of domestic life. In raising the matter of a daughter cooking lemon cream for a father so taken up with world history that he fails to notice, Rosalind echoes the famous faux naive question in Brecht's "Fragen eines lesenden Arbeiters" (Questions from a Worker Who Reads): on hearing that Caesar conquered Gaul, the worker asks if he did not even have a cook with him.[7] As a female child, young Rosalind is even more absent from world history than Caesar's cook. Her complaint seems not just naive but infantile, yet it offers an insight into the subliminal workings of power.

Begun before the wall opened, but published in 1991, the novel contains many hints that the victor in the Marxist grand narrative is doomed posthumously to become one of history's losers. To that extent, Rosalind's disruptive strategy succeeds and she wins the memory contest. Her key weapon is to puncture Beerenbaum's claim to speak for the working class as the collective subject of history. Her questions about Stalinist persecution of comrade-communists fatally undermine the vision of proletarian unity. She launches an empiricist attack, as she calls it, on idealist historicism: there is no underlying logic of history; communism is just what communists do; when Beerenbaum denounced her friend the count, who then spent three years in prison, he was not acting out of historical necessity but out of unacknowledged resentment against the educated. Her analysis echoes Nietzsche rather than Marx, and turns Beerenbaum from the agent of history into a social type full of hidden resentment. (As we shall see, Rosalind has her own creeping resentments.) Another devastating question is why the proletariat, if they are the agents of historical progress, failed to prevent the rise of National Socialism. Rosalind asks this question not of Beerenbaum, but of her father, many years earlier as a little girl trying to please him by coming up with clever questions. But it comes at a key moment of textual splicing between a meeting with Beerenbaum and memories of her father, creating an allegorical equivalence between the two men, a whole generation, and the ideology of a regime. Thus even as Rosalind punctures Beerenbaum's representative claims to historical agency based on class, she herself lends him representative status as an embodiment of patriarchal power.

The text signals in many ways Beerenbaum's uncanny power over Rosalind as a revenant or ghost of her dead father. Rosalind's key complaint is her father's indifference to his child, so taken up is he with world history. The jarring juxtapositions of the personal and the political convey this bitterness. Polkowski père as schoolmaster and Beerenbaum in the university subordinate young people to an abstract purpose. Patriarchal and political power are mutually reinforcing systems working through institutions such as the family and hierarchical bureaucracies. Abstract idealism is a mask disguising lust for power. The emptiness of the ideal comes out in the emptiness of Beerenbaum's clichéd language, which Rosalind disconcertingly parrots in advance, having heard it all before from her father. The primitive lust for power breaks through when the dying Beerenbaum's claw-like hand clutches at Rosalind's breast — or is it at her heart? Yet by this point Beerenbaum is at death's door and is all along a doddering old fellow in a cardigan and claret-colored slippers. So where does his power come from? Seen as a simple allegory of the state, Beerenbaum's power comes from external geopolitical sources and from internal institutions such as the army or the Stasi, personified in his sinister son Michael. But Maron's primary interest is not the threat of force underpinning state power, but the psychic processes that bring people to accede to their own subordination. Rosalind's infantile rages, her often involuntary mimicry of Beerenbaum, her fantasy of a murderous attack suggest a Lacanian analysis. According to Lacan infants pass through what he terms the mirror phase on first seeing their own reflection. When the infantile "hommelette" (little man) sees how its image in the mirror moves in response to its own movements, the baby (in a baby-bouncer) in turn mimicks the movements in the mirror, identifying with its own mirror image in a fantasy of omnipotence. This is the first, so Lacan suggests, of many identifications with the Other, starting with the imagined Father.[8] Beerenbaum's power over Rosalind is largely imaginary; he mirrors back at her the illusory power she projects upon him and in so doing disempowers herself, subjecting herself to an illusion. The layout of his room, the desk he sits behind, the play of light exposing her to his gaze but leaving his eyes unseen position her as the object of the internalized paternal gaze she imagines Beerenbaum directing at her. Lacan's mirror stage is a psychoanalytic appropriation of Hegel's Master/Slave dialectic.[9] The novel invokes a present struggle unto death for mastery over the past with the future as prize. In Hegel's account, the self seeks to wrest recognition from the other with no answering recognition. Rosalind suffers under the traumatic memory of her father's refusal of recognition and now tries in turn to force Beerenbaum to recognize her way of seeing while denying recognition for his view. But Beerenbaum's aging body triggers the hallucinatory return of the imagined Father, and Rosalind descends into infantile rage.

Another model is Mozart/Da Ponte's *Don Giovanni*. Rosalind toys with the idea of translating into German Da Ponte's brilliant but supposedly untranslatable recitatives, a project that, like taking notes to Beerenbaum's dictation, again involves the transmission of another's words. "E non voglio più servir" (*SZ*, 176; I no longer wish to serve), "no, no, no, no, no, no," the servant Leporello insists in the opening aria. Yet he does go on serving to the bitter end. Volker Braun's *Hinze Kunze Roman*, which came out in 1985 just as Rosalind and Beerenbaum were quarrelling, satirizes collusion between regime and people in a master/servant duo reminiscent of the Don and Leporello. Leporello keeps threatening to leave his master, but stays for money. Rosalind refuses to think for money, but goes on taking 500 marks a month as Beerenbaum's handmaiden. Leporello and his master imitate one another. Like a puppet, Leporello mimes the gestures of passion as his master sings the words (act 2). In transcribing Beerenbaum's words, Rosalind acts as a puppet or instrument of his will. Her mimicry of his language seems satirical at first, but she finds herself involuntarily imitating his words and his grimaces. As Andrew Webber comments on the doppelgänger: "It echoes, reiterates, distorts, parodies, dictates, impedes, dumbfounds."[10] Rosalind seems possessed by Beerenbaum as by a doppelgänger who speaks from her mouth in a drastic collapsing of the boundaries between generation and gender.

The memory contest pits Beerenbaum's memoirs against Rosalind's devastating questions, which, backed by public historiographic knowledge, undermine her adversary's testimony as a participant and witness. But postunification GDR intellectuals in their turn faced devastating questions derived from hitherto secret but now public sources and the accusation that critical engagement with the regime had merely bolstered it. This was the nub of the so-called *Literaturstreit* (literature quarrel), a memory contest that hinged on whether Christa Wolf was a prime critic or prime stooge of the GDR regime. Rosalind's encounters with Beerenbaum mark the latest phase in a paradoxical history of critique and complicity that begins with a little girl's efforts to please her father by asking him questions that will displease him, but force him to acknowledge her. In a bitter paradox, her critical thinking often employs Marxist argument to question the practice of socialism as it existed. Her resignation from the Barabas Historical Institute is a different strategy, one of disengagement, and might have offered her a niche in Prenzlauer Berg. 1985 saw the publication of the anthology *Berührung ist nur eine Randerscheinung* (Contact Is a Merely Peripheral Phenomenon), edited by Elke Erb and Sascha Anderson. The title signals the disengagement from politics practiced by the Prenzlauer Berg poets.[11] But Rosalind renews the face-to-face contact. Engaging on Beerenbaum's territory draws her into power games that she cannot control. Her critical questioning is perhaps merely a foil against which men like Beerenbaum and her father can hone their power by refusing her recognition or infantilizing her, by pinioning her as a woman in the male gaze, finally clutching at her even at death's door, like the Stone Guest's icy grip at the end of *Don Giovanni*.

Rosalind is a critical intellectual, then, but with an only intermittent history of merely verbal opposition. Fear of having passively colluded awakens in Rosalind the longing to take action. Yet she quotes Ernst Toller's question "Muß der Handelnde immer schuldig werden?" (*SZ*, 41; must he who acts always incur guilt?), for the deed she longs for is obscenely violent, like the killing of scapegoats by oedipally as much as politically driven terrorists in the West. Guilty through action, guilty of inaction? Telling how it wasn't is Rosalind's response to the double bind. She at once acts but cancels out her action by telling two different versions of what happened, one imagined and one actual. Chloe Paver uses the term "overt fictionalization" to pinpoint a feature in 1960s novels confronting the unmasterable Nazi past, and there is Derrida's device of placing terms "sous rature," under erasure, by crossing them out, but leaving the crossed-out words in the text.[12] Material under erasure is often sensationalistic in the manner of horror, pornography, or melodrama.[13] Peter Brooks defines melodrama as the genre that, in post-revolutionary France and in post-sacred culture, made the universe morally legible again and celebrated the sign of virtue, pitting innocence against villainy in a Manichean universe.[14] Rosalind longs for such clarity; her grimaces and shrieks, the spittle flying as she attacks Beerenbaum, evoke the gamut of melodramatic acting. But the bipolar energy flow in melodrama can switch to turn victim into villain, so rendering the universe absurd rather than morally legible. The erasure in *Stille Zeile sechs* of the melodramatic encounter between victim and villain does not expunge its effect, but leaves the postunification reader oscillating between desire and disappointment, desiring but denied stark moral simplicities.

Rosalind divides herself into three: a first-person narrator, a third-person observer-narrator who wants to act, and the Rosalind who does act (*SZ*, 207–9). The violent excess as Rosalind III punches an old man, knocks out his false teeth, kicks his testicles, jumps on his chest, suggests rage against something more and beyond what the text tells. Given what we now know about Maron's involvement with the state security in the 1970s, Andrew Plowman rightly comments that we cannot read Rosalind's assault on the gaps in Beerenbaum's memoirs without irony.[15] But we can read her assault on his balls, if I may be so crude, with more understanding. Writing under erasure gives vent to the corrosive resentment Maron must have felt at allowing herself to be manipulated into complicity, resentment that her critical opposition could be ignored, or that it might have merely strengthened the regime, resentment that she could not just turn aside, do her own thing, go away, so that even on leaving the GDR in 1988 on a three-year visa she was writing *Stille Zeile sechs* and still trying in 1989 to get *Flugasche* (Fly Ash, 1981) published in the GDR, so that even her writerly biography has been dictated by a regime she could not break free of mentally: "Hirneigenschaft statt Leibeigenschaft" (*SZ*, 206; mental, not physical servitude) as Rosalind shrieks.[16] Telling it how it wasn't expresses desire for and at the same time destroys the black-and-white Manichean division between villain and victim.

A last word about allegorical bodies. Rosalind calls herself an empiricist. She denies the reality of the idea: there are only people and their actions. Yet Beerenbaum at times loses his reality as an old man to become power incarnate. Like the senile yet infantile giant father in Kafka's *Das Urteil* (The Judgment), Beerenbaum is an uncanny emanation. Metonymic details such as his cardigan and slippers, funny yet sinister in their harmlessness, are like the father's nightshirt in Kafka's story. They take on a nightmarish hyperrealism as vessels of repressed memory. A screen for Rosalind's memories of her father, Beerenbaum's body is also an archaeological site. Rosalind reads physical traces of his life history in his body; and in silhouette against the light his body becomes an icon for power in the abstract — the idea. "Corpus nos veritatem cognoscere docet . . ." (*SZ*, 66; the body tells us the truth). But the different signifying systems at play within the body as text offer competing truths. For example, Rosalind's father had scurvy as a prisoner of war and lost all his teeth. Her infantile triumph when she imagines knocking Beerenbaum's dental plate from his mouth means one thing if she is overthrowing an icon, but quite another if she is punishing an old man for being ruined by wartime experiences that those born later cannot quite imagine. Rosalind accuses Beerenbaum of telling it how it wasn't by omission and as an authorial alter ego is herself open to the same charge. But Maron does offer a pretty big hint in Rosalind's vengeful female gaze as it anatomizes an old man's body and in her iconoclastic trampling on the power that has held her in thrall. At the same time a more rational, fairer woman, Rosalind I we might call her, does not after all tear out Beerenbaum's tongue and even permits him direct speech to say something of the history of a generation that survived the depression and exile, or, like Beerenbaum's wife, imprisonment in Ravensbrück, or returned toothless from years of rotting in labor camps. In the end, the heroine and the novel do acknowledge differences between the Third Reich, Stalinism, and the GDR.

Sons and Mothers: *Helden wie wir*

The title of *Helden wie wir* signals from the start an exercise in telling it how it wasn't: for "we" are not heroes. The euphoric aftermath of 9 November 1989 encouraged the comforting view that heroic popular action, rather than the waning of Soviet power, brought the GDR to an end at the very moment of its fortieth anniversary. But what is needed, Brussig's hero suggests, is for people to face up to their failure over decades to resist an authoritarian regime: "Solange sich Millionen Versager ihrem Versagen nicht stellen, werden sie Versager bleiben" (as long as millions of failures do not face up to their failure, they will remain failures).[17] This is one of many passages where the satirical mask slips to give voice to a critical persona different from the servile yet triumphalist hero Klaus Uhltzscht, or where the same sentence is double-voiced and readable in different ways. Like Maron, then, Brussig is concerned with the self-subordination that enabled society to go on functioning under an authoritarian regime so that force was rarely necessary. The difference between Nazi times and the GDR, Klaus wryly notes, is that nobody got shot fleeing unless they were fleeing the Republic (*HWW*, 280). The novel is cast as a grotesque contest between memoirist Klaus Uhltzscht and all other historians. Rosalind may have killed off the Marxist-Leninist grand narrative, but Klaus boasts not only of ending the division of Germany, the postwar European settlement, the short twentieth century, the Modern Age, and the Cold War. He has also brought about the End of Ideology and the End of History (*HWW*, 293). But in a triumphalist memoir worthy of a Beerenbaum, Klaus reinstates history and his place in it: "Ich entdeckte, daß ich eine *Vergangenheit* habe und daß diese Vergangenheit eine *Bedeutung* hat" (*HWW*, 293; I discovered that I have a *past* and that this past has a *meaning*). Both novels, then, tell it how it wasn't to counter the shame of self-subordination, for Rosalind did not kill Beerenbaum just as Klaus did not bring down the wall single-handedly, though of course his hand is not the organ he did not use to not bring down the wall.

In *Stille Zeile sechs*, the male genitalia do not make an appearance until page 208, but in *Helden wie wir* they pop up already on page three. Both novels pit infantile protagonists against the fathers' generation, both have hospital scenes, and in both the offspring attack the paternal genitalia. Klaus messes up his own organ pretty nastily as well in an accidental almost-unmanning. Conversely, Rosalind almost unwomans herself in shifting from feminine communing with flowers to thuggishness. But both revert safely to gender type, Rosalind with her bouquet of freesias at Beerenbaum's graveside, Klaus as his mighty organ changes the course of history. If Rosalind is a Leporello, Klaus is a "kleiner Trompeter" (little trumpeter): in donating his life's blood for an operation supposedly to save Erich Honecker, General Secretary of the SED, Klaus replays the role of the legendary little trumpeter who in 1925 fell to an assassin's bullet meant for the communist leader Ernst Thälmann, so saving the communist leader's life at the cost of his own.[18] Like Rosalind's sense of herself as a puppet robbed of her biography, Klaus complains that he always did what others wanted, never what he wanted (*HWW*, 282). Rosalind experiences out-of-body self-division and imagines unmanning the imaginary Father, though she prays afterwards that the actual man, Beerenbaum, will not die. Klaus, by contrast, asserts that he really did twist his dead father's testicles and has never regretted it. Klaus's out-of-body experience comes at the moment of his own near death during the blood donation, when he realizes that he is indifferent to death because he has not lived his life. In both novels, a father or his doppelgänger becomes an icon. But the uncanny paternal body in *Stille Zeile sechs* modulates in *Helden wie wir* into scatological satire: "Da lag sie, die Scheiße in Menschengestalt" (*HW*, 267; there it [the father's corpse] lay, a turd in human shape). One can just see the newspaper cartoon.

Myriad further similarities and pointed contrasts suggest a wider discursive field that both novels inhabit. For example, a key episode in *Stille Zeile sechs* is the Graf's dismissal from his university post. In *Helden wie wir* the physics teacher Küfer is dismissed. But where Maron attacks the authorities and the failure of intellectuals to show solidarity, Brussig focuses on the failure of ordinary people, parents, and pupils. Klaus's mighty organ is a fantasy compensation for a mass collusion that expunges any difference between regime and people. The biggest contrast, however, is the arrival alongside the paternal turd in human shape of the maternal wiper of bottoms. There is no equivalent in *Stille Zeile sechs* of Klaus's phallic mother, the hygiene expert. Rosalind's father ignored a daughter's domestic labor of love to concentrate on world history. Klaus's greatest humiliations are inflicted by a mother's labors of love in the service of world history. Whereas Rosalind complains of her father's absence for the first seven years of her life, Klaus suffers under his mother's eight-year presence throughout his early childhood. If Rosalind's father devotes himself to his teaching career, ignoring his daughter, Klaus's mother sacrifices her career as a doctor, submitting her son to intimate, unceasing surveillance. Of course traditional symbolism equates fathers and the state. But hand-in-hand with the paternal police state, the maternal nanny state delivers childcare and education, public health, and libraries. The satire continues a long German tradition of intellectual hostility to the bourgeois family as the basis of authoritarian social order, whether in Wilhelmine Germany or the GDR. A sub-dominant domestic matriarchy sustains the patriarchal state; the mood is reminiscent of Heinrich Mann's *Der Untertan* (The Underling, 1918). School, youth organizations, summer camps and such like provide a link between family and wider society.

For both Maron and Brussig complicity is a central theme, and in both novels the authors' attack on complicity is highly gendered. Klaus is not a reliable narrator, of course, but the satire of failed manhood implicitly posits proper manhood as the prime value crushed by the GDR. A satirical monster, Klaus is both the primary butt and the prime joker, thus leaving unclear when his attitudes are being ridiculed, when they are to be taken straight, or when they are under erasure, ambiguously true and not true, giving voice to resentments that often have less to do with socialism than with sexism. His laddish opinions appeal to an implied male audience personified in Mr. Kitzelstein. Like Rosalind's physical disgust at old men with false teeth and scurvy, Klaus's attack on a whole postwar generation of older women makes for uncomfortable reading. Both novels evoke the oppressive weight on the younger generation of their parents' suffering, which disarms the children and holds them in thrall. Just as Beerenbaum becomes the Father, so Klaus's mother is heightened into a castrating phallic Mother, while the *Übermutter* Christa Wolf overshadows Honecker as a butt of satire to become the iconic embodiment of her generation. These were the women, Klaus says, who crawled from the ruins of the Third Reich and for the first time felt proud of themselves, but their pride as they drank from the bottle labeled socialism was really just campfire feelings: "Ich meine das nicht überheblich" (I'm not just being arrogant), he unconvincingly concludes, "Es wäre mir genauso gegangen" (*HWW*, 287–88; I'd have been just the same). Rosalind makes a similar admission that under the conditions of her father's generation she too might have become a communist (*SZ*, 162). But whereas Beerenbaum's tirade in *Stille Zeile sechs* about growing up in poverty, children with rickets, damp houses, and class war is reported in direct speech, in the passage just cited from *Helden wie wir* maternal history is subsumed into the filial monologue. Klaus can, of course, counter that he has included verbatim Christa Wolf's Alexanderplatz speech, delivered to the gathered multitudes on 4 November 1989. Given that Klaus initially thinks he is listening to the women's national ice skating coach, the effect, as even fans of Christa Wolf admit, is wickedly funny, rather like the scene in the Monty Python film, *The Life of Brian*, when the line from the Sermon on the Mount comes across as "Blessed are the cheese makers." But the satirical point of Klaus's comments on Anne Frank's diary or his comparison of the death of fifty million people in the Second World War with the death of fifty million spermatozoa when he masturbates is harder to discern. Then there is masturbation while fantasizing over Simone de Beauvoir or a bit from Wolf's *Nachdenken über Christa T.* (The Quest for Christa T., 1968) as stimulus. As with the British TV show "Men Behaving Badly," it is not clear whether we are supposed to laugh at or with Klaus. The satire is directed primarily against fantasy compensation for failed manhood through ludicrously puffed up super-manhood. But it works by defining proper manhood in opposition to social or moral values, figured as maternal, that limit the freedoms of angry young men and are not peculiar to the GDR. Some issues are common to both Germanies, for example remembering the Nazi past, some to any modern society, for example women's double burden, public welfare, funding for libraries, even hygiene. As globalization proceeds, some readers may fear not the nanny welfare state, but its disappearance. On the literary front, it is a matter of taste whether Brussig's broad satire comes as a relief from Wolf's always subtle but sometimes precious manner. It may be a matter of generation or gender how far readers identify with Klaus's more outrageous squibs or whether they side with Simone de Beauvoir, with the women who crept from the ruins and brought up the children, and with mothers torn between childcare and professional fulfillment.

And So Farewell to the GDR Heimat:
Good Bye Lenin

The seventh tape of Klaus's dictated memoirs mockingly celebrates the "geheilter Pimmel" (the sick prick saved) in a rhyming jibe at Christa Wolf's first novel *Der geteilte Himmel* (The Divided Sky, 1963). Just as "Himmel" means both heaven and sky, so "geheilt" means both saved and cured. Thus Brussig's punning subtitle parodies the modes of redemptive or therapeutic history that aim at closure or cure. At the end of *Good Bye Lenin*, fireworks explode across the once divided sky, scattering the ashes of a beloved mother who embodied the GDR; a father long absent in the West is reunited with his children and bids farewell to the wife who remained behind; a Russian nurse and a young German protester, his sister and her new Wessi fellow find love in united Berlin, united Germany, and united Europe and mourn the passing of socialist ideals that the GDR state did not realize but which informed much of the everyday lives of ordinary people. This redemptive happy ending may be the last, but it is not the only word in a film in which Coca Cola, West cigarettes, Burger King, growing unemployment, and neo-Nazi graffiti signal victorious global capitalism and a still unmastered German past. *Good Bye Lenin* is not victors' history, then, but a melancholy and witty lament for the losers. The shift to young east Germans facing the capitalist future as well as the socialist past contrasts with *Stille Zeile sechs*, where the West does not figure, and with *Helden wie wir*, where Mr. Kitzelstein is an empty cipher. Yet the film and *Helden wie wir* have many motifs in common. School and youth summer camp fare better in the film. Both have hospital scenes and sexy young nurses with good motherly qualities — "Mütterlichkeit" — rather than the bossy "Bemutterung" under which young men fret. In the film the nurse nurses the mother, however, and accuses the son of over-mothering his mother in a comical deconstruction of gender stereotypes. Klaus's mother wipes her son's bottom; in *Good Bye Lenin* the bed-bound mother complains that she cannot even go to the bathroom alone, implying intimate filial services. Alex boasts of his "männliche Ausstrahlungskraft" (male charisma) in Klausian terms, but is otherwise a model new man and loving son, proud of his mother's success in her career, unlike Klaus's sour resentment of his sourly resentful mother.[19] Brussig attacks Klaus's complicity; the film celebrates Alex's protest, signaled in his name, which echoes the popular shortened name of the Berlin square where the protesters gathered in 1989. As his mother travels in a taxi to be honored by the regime her son is protesting against, we recognize that the son's protest against socialism as it really exists is fueled by the mother's everyday socialist practice. This is, then, a huge re-evaluation of mother and son compared with Klaus's awful mother and his servile collusion.

There are comparisons to be drawn too with *Stille Zeile sechs*. Rosalind Polkowski dreams of killing a father-figure by jumping on his chest; Alex learns how to keep a mother alive by delivering thumps on her chest to keep her heart going. The film draws the patriarch out of the Lacanian imaginary, so robbing him of his power. In Rosalind's imagination, a doddery old man in red slippers and cardigan uncannily transmutes into power incarnate. The film, by contrast, makes a clear division between a doddery old woman in blue slippers and nightgown and a statue passing grotesquely across a once divided sky, as down below the woman gazes in dawning recognition of a change whose import she cannot yet grasp. Iconoclasm here makes do literally with an icon, a statue. Cut off at the waist, the statue lacks phallic power; an admonitory hand is no compensation. The intimate, inner-German confrontation between Rosalind and Beerenbaum takes place indoors. In the film the mother steps out of doors, into the street, and the disappearing icon leaves a European-wide theater, marking the end of an era in world history. The shift between the novel and the film from Stalin and Stalinism to Lenin is a further distancing effect, for the goodbyes to Lenin began long ago, before the worst chapters in twentieth-century history had been written.

Yet if the patriarch is diminished, the matriarch still has power over her son. For like Rosalind's or Klaus's hatred, so Alex's love threatens to entangle him in the past. *Good Bye Lenin* draws ironically on the Heimat mode as a vehicle enabling the work of mourning and negotiation of historical change. Heimat plots often deploy familial allegory, a leading motif being the rite of passage as the son's attachment to the maternal Heimat loosens, enabling him to move on and lead his life. The discourse of Heimat — meaning homeland — dates back to the decades following the first unification of Germany, when it mediated between older local loyalties and the new Reich.[20] Here the mediation is between East German loyalties and a unified Germany. The GDR initially banned local history societies and *Heimatkunde* (home studies) as taught in schools during the Third Reich. But by the mid-1950s Heimat discourse was reappropriated in socialist guise with a view to encouraging loyalty to the GDR in young people. Socialist Heimat songs punctuate the sound track of *Good Bye Lenin*. In the West, 1950s Heimat films were a popular genre. Part escapist, they also negotiated solutions to social problems: fathers returning from the war had to find a way back to their children; divorce was an issue — here we briefly glimpse the second wife; new partners must care for children not their own, as Rainer does here for Paula. The lost childhood Heimat is remembered in sepia tones in shaky hand-held video. The videos and Alex's memories in voice-over tell it both how it was and how it wasn't. For there is the revelation of the mother's regret that she did not follow her husband and her guilt at withholding his letters; yet the mother's greatest achievement was to make daily life in the GDR homely.

The most spectacular examples of telling it how it wasn't are the imaginary news reports Alex and his friend concoct to shield the mother, who was in a coma when the wall came down, from the shock of a discovery that might kill her. Their efforts culminate in a video re-configuration of the unification process showing a flood of people moving from West to East rather than vice versa. A look-alike of the cosmonaut Sigmund Jähn, a boyhood hero for fatherless Alex, announces the imminent unification. The benign taxi driver who plays the iconic national hero Jähn shows no uncanny tendencies to turn into power incarnate.[21] Counterfactual history is an extended exercise in writing under erasure: it is always crossed out by what actually happened, while disputing that it had to happen. A recent example is Michael Kleeberg's *Ein Garten im Norden* (A Garden in the North, 1998), which imagines an early twentieth century that would not lead into the Third Reich, only for the dream to fail in the end. Such failed wish-fulfillment is rather like that practiced by the schoolteacher Küfer in *Helden wie wir,* who runs films backwards, thus putting the Spanish Civil War or the Great Depression under erasure and canceling for a moment the German bombing of Guernica. Crucial to counterfactual history is less the light it throws on the past than its agenda in the present. Debates about Kleeberg's novel turned on whether it belongs within right-wing revisionist discourse or offers a left-liberal plea for open debate in a democratic Germany.[22] In context, Küfer's dream is subversive because it would have erased the GDR in advance. Thematically closer to *Helden wie wir* is Christian v. Ditfurth's *Die Mauer steht am Rhein: Deutschland nach dem Sieg des Sozialismus* (The Wall at the Rhine: Germany after the Victory of Socialism, 1999), which imagines the GDR triumphant and a unified socialist Germany stretching to the Rhine. In contrast to this anti-socialist awful warning, however, the mood in *Good Bye Lenin* is reconciliatory: "Schaut euch das an," Alex's deluded mother exclaims, "die Menschen wollen in unser Land" (*GL*, 104; just look at that, people want to come to our country). "Stell dir vor," Christa Wolf exclaims, as quoted in *Helden wie wir*, "es ist Sozialismus und keiner geht weg!" (*HWW*, 285; just imagine, it is socialism and nobody is leaving). Given the historical moment, both exclamations of socialist success come across as absurd. But whereas the novel is unremitting in its mockery, that the dream in the film is under erasure does not expunge the desire that socialist values might somehow survive the onslaught of capitalist consumerism and competition. The concocted videos, films within the film, self-reflexively assert the value of sentimentality in enabling people to look back yet move on, as this sentimental film advocates.

Postscript

Rosalind's inheritance of Beerenbaum's memoirs, passed on to her by his sinister son, suggests that the memory contest will continue even after the death of the GDR. Maron's latest novel *Endmoränen* (Glacial Moraines, 2002) is in anti-Heimat mode. It depicts with naturalist gloom and wry self-irony everyday life in provincial Brandenburg: a stony landscape left behind after the passing of a glacier. Perversely, the narrator mourns the passing of state interference, which at least made literature meaningful as the vessel of hidden messages: where are the meanings now? The mood lightens towards the end, however, and the narrator sensibly returns to Berlin. Maron has since published *Geburtsort Berlin* (Birthplace Berlin, 2003), a comically critical and affectionate homage to the titular city of the new republic that is also her birthplace. That the photographs are by her photographer son, Jonas Maron, suggest good postunification relations between the generations. It is to be hoped too that Klaus will stop beating himself up and recognize, as his author has, that life in the Sonnenallee was not all bad. As for *Good Bye Lenin*, its reconciliation of practical socialism and youthful protest was especially successful with West European audiences; in France, for example, it drew the biggest public for a German film since 1945. Written and directed by West Germans, the film appeals to those who loathe western triumphalism and hope that socialist aspirations may survive, but who did not experience socialism as it really existed.

The novels give voice to daughters and sons and set up the older generation as butts; even the affectionately pictured mother in *Good Bye Lenin* spends a lot of the time unconscious or deceived. To redress the balance and give voice to the mother, where better to look than Christa Wolf's *Medea: Stimmen* (Medea: Voices) published head to head with *Helden wie wir* in 1996. This might seem to be the ultimate telling it how it wasn't, since everyone has known for millennia that Medea killed her children. But Wolf's novel belongs to a diametrically opposite genre: it asserts how it was, in correction of a mythical how it wasn't. That traduced Medea is absolved can be seen in part as the author's self-justification in face of unjust media attack. The mode is tragic, conveying a bleak sense of exile from both Germanies. *Stille Zeile sechs*, by contrast, is a grotesque comedy, *Helden wie wir* a satirical comedy, and *Good Bye Lenin* a sentimental comedy. A culture of guilt and a culture of shame, it has been suggested, structure German dealings with the past.[23] Wolf's novel, with its central symbol of a dead child, belongs squarely in the former. *Stille Zeile sechs* and *Helden wie wir*, by contrast, belong in the latter, though in Maron's text shame is more heavily shadowed by guilt than in Brussig's. When Kafka's Josef K. dies at the end of *Der Prozeß* (The Trial) it was as if the shame would outlive him. To voice shame and rage while staying alive is a step forwards. In turning away from both cultures, *Good Bye Lenin* comes closest to advocating normalization, not in forgetting the past, but in looking to the survival into the future of maternalist social values as a counterweight to global capital. In that, the film and *Medea: Stimmen*, modally at opposite extremes of the comic and the tragic, paradoxically are ideologically closer. They are more outwards-directed than the other two texts, which probe shamefully intimate memories internal to the GDR. All these works, however, exemplify in their different ways productive literary engagement in German memory contests.

Notes

[1] Mary Fulbrook, "Re-presenting the Nation: History and Identity in East and West Germany," in *Representing the German Nation: History and Identity in Twentieth-Century Germany*, ed. Mary Fulbrook and Martin Swales (Manchester: Manchester UP, 2000), 172–92; here: 177.

[2] Gisela Brinker-Gabler, "Exile, Immigrant, Re/Unified: Writing (East) Postunification Identity in Germany," in *Writing New Identities: Gender, Nation, and Immigration in Contemporary Europe*, ed. Gisela Brinker-Gabler, Sidonie Smith (Minneapolis: U of Minnesota P, 1997), 264–92; here: 265.

[3] See Aleida Assmann, "1998 — zwischen Geschichte und Gedächnis" in Aleida Assmann, Ute Frevert, *Geschichtsvergessenheit Geschichtsversessenheit: Vom Umgang mit deutschen Vergangenheiten nach 1945* (Stuttgart: Deutsche Verlags-Anstalt, 1999), 21–52 for an excellent introduction to postunification debates on memory and history.

[4] Rudolf Augstein et al., eds., "*Historikerstreit*": *Die Dokumentation der Kontroverse um die Einzigartigkeit der nationalsozialistischen Judenvernichtung* (Munich, Zurich: Piper, 1987) documents the historians' quarrel.

[5] Monika Maron, *Stille Zeile sechs* (Frankfurt am Main: S. Fischer, 2001), 142. Page numbers for subsequent references will be given in brackets in the text preceded by the letters *SZ*.

[6] Walter Benjamin, "Das Passagen-Werk. Aufzeichnungen und Materialien," in *Gesammelte Schriften*, vol. 1, ed. Rolf Tiedemann (Frankfurt am Main: Suhrkamp, 1982), 79–81.

[7] Bertolt Brecht, "Fragen eines lesenden Arbeiters," in *Gedichte 2: Sammlungen 1938–1956*, vol. 12 of *Werke*, Große kommentierte Berliner und Frankfurter Ausgabe, eds. Werner Hecht, Jan Knopf, Werner Mittenzwei, Klaus-Detlev Müller (Berlin, Weimar: Aufbau; Frankfurt am Main: Suhrkamp, 1988), 29; "Questions from a worker who reads," in Bertolt Brecht, *Poems 1913–1956*, ed. by John Willett and Ralph Manheim with the cooperation of Erich Fried (London: Eyre Methuen, 1976), 252–53.

[8] Jacques Lacan, "Le stade du miroir comme formateur de la fonction du Je," in *Écrits* (Paris: Éditions du Seuil, 1966), 93–100.

[9] Georg Wilhelm Friedrich Hegel, "Herrschaft und Knechtschaft," in *Phänomenologie des Geistes* (Hamburg: Felix Meiner, 1952), 146–50.

[10] Andrew Webber, *The Doppelgänger: Double Visions in German Literature* (Oxford: Clarendon Press, 1996), 3.

[11] Sascha Anderson and other "disengaged" intellectuals were later shown to have had Stasi involvement.

[12] Chloe E. M. Paver, *Narrative and Fantasy in the Post-War German Novel* (Oxford: Clarendon Press, 1999), 15–16; Jacques Derrida, *De la grammatologie* (Paris: Minuit, 1967), 31.

[13] Brian McHale, *Postmodernist Fiction* (London, New York: Routledge, 1987), 102.

[14] Peter Brooks, *The Melodramatic Imagination: Balzac, Henry James, Melodrama, and the Mode of Excess* (New York: Columbia UP, 1984), 43.

[15] Andrew Plowman, "History, Identity and the Writer: Helga Königsdorf and Monika Maron since 1990," in *Legacies and Identity: East and West German Responses to Unification*, ed. Martin Kane (Oxford: Peter Lang, 2002), 81–96.

[16] Maron's first novel *Flugasche* attacking environmental damage and press censorship in the GDR was published in the West in 1981.

[17] Thomas Brussig, *Helden wie wir* (Berlin: Volk & Welt, 1996), 312. Page numbers for all subsequent references will be given brackets in the text preceded by the letters *HWW*.

[18] Fritz Weineck, a horn player with the Red Front, was one of eleven comrades shot at an election meeting in Halle in 1925 where the communist leader Ernst Thälmann had just spoken. The song, text by W. Wallroth, appropriated the melody of a nationalist song of 1915, "Von allen Kamaraden." In the 1930s, a Nazi version celebrating Horst Wessel became popular. Such appropriations and reappropriations exemplify memory contests in the medium of popular song. See http://ingeb.org/Lieder/vonallenu.html and http://www.blueplane.de//DDRlieder/Lieder/Trompeter.htm, visited 11 February 2005.

[19] Michael Toteberg, ed. *Good Bye Lenin*. Ein Film von Wolfgang Becker, Drehbuch von Bernd Lichtenberg, Co-Autor Wolfgang Becker (Berlin: Schwarzkopf & Schwarzkopf, 2003), 17. Page numbers for subsequent references will be given in brackets the text preceded by the letters *GL*. The film is available in video and DVD.

[20] On Heimat, see Elizabeth Boa and Rachel Palfreyman, *Heimat — A German Dream: Regional Loyalties and National Identity in German Culture 1890–1990* (Oxford: Oxford UP, 2000).

[21] This benign deception contrasts with Victor Pelevin's *Omon Ra* (1992). In Pelevin's best-selling satire, telling it how it wasn't takes the form of an elaborate deception the Soviet authorities practice upon the naive hero, causing him to believe he is a cosmonaut in outer space, when he is actually shut up in a phony spaceship in the Moscow metro; until the end, the deception is repeated upon the reader. Thanks to Morven Creagh for drawing this Russian example to my notice.

[22] Jessica Amann, "The Fantastic in the Post-Wende German Novel," Ph.D. dissertation, University of Nottingham, 2003, Chapter 5.

[23] Aleida Assmann, "Die Schlagworte der Debatte," in Assmann, Frevert, *Geschichtsvergessenheit Geschichtsversessenheit*, 53–96; here: 88–96.

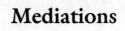

Mediations

4: Being Translated: Exile, Childhood, and Multilingualism in G.-A. Goldschmidt and W. G. Sebald

Stefan Willer

CURRENT GERMAN LITERATURE is marked by a new tone in the representation of scenes, events, and figures of the National Socialist period and the Shoah: it diverges from previous ways of coming to terms with the past. This is true not only for younger writers who — like Norbert Gstrein in *Die englischen Jahre* (The English Years, 1999) or *Selbstporträt mit einer Toten* (Self-Portait with a Dead Woman, 2000), Marcel Beyer in *Spione* (Spies, 2000) and Katharina Hacker in *Eine Art Liebe* (A Form of Love, 2003) — work on a narrative dialectics of memory and imagination, but also for writers of the postwar generation and even for some contemporaries of the events in question. These writers generate literary discourses on cultural memory that focus on the secret, uncanny, and barely accessible parts of history, exposing identity, collective or individual, as a fictional construct. This development in German literature is connected to the way the discourses themselves unfold. I will argue that in certain German literary discourses it is the "Germanness" of the discourse itself that is at stake. In pursuing this line of thought, I will examine texts written during the 1990s by Georges-Arthur Goldschmidt and W. G. Sebald. While these two authors write about completely different experiences and life circumstances (determined by their years of birth, 1928 and 1944), they nevertheless treat the same subject: emigration and exile. In both cases, the treatment of this subject affects the very diction of the texts. Sebald's and Goldschmidt's writings tend to multilingualism — each in their own way — thus displaying the limitations of "German discourses" as such. They problematize the nationality of discourse by touching, testing, and transgressing the borders and boundaries of monolingualism.

The process of emigration is essentially connected to problems of language reorientation: the process of adapting to another language. However, in the research on German emigration between 1933 and 1945 the reality of language reorientation has been regarded mostly as just an aspect of acculturation. According to this view, language is just one of the many skills emigrants had to develop in order to assimilate into their new environment.[1] The actual importance of language acquisition and of the concrete problems of bi- and multilingualism has not yet been examined thoroughly in German exile scholarship.[2] Even in the field of exile literature, the forced reorientation of the exiled individual within a new language has long been regarded as the loss of competence in any single language: the loss of monolingualism. For decades, scholarship has been dominated by the supposedly self-evident connection between one's native tongue and one's identity, as expressed in Alfred Döblin's retrospective formulation that abandoning one's language was even worse than being skinned alive, disemboweled, and committing suicide.[3] While a handful of critical readings of exile literature investigated the impact of exile on language and style in the 1970s and 1980s,[4] it was commonplace to reavow statements like Döblin's, affirming that the change from one language to another equaled a loss of identity.[5] By the 1990s, however, this perception had changed somewhat: in an innovative article from 1995, Dieter Lamping argued that the issue of bilingualism in exile literature was still unexplored. He suggested that the forced language reorientation of exiled writers be interpreted against the background of modern transnationality, which would reveal the linguistic dimension of current trends of cultural globalization and would re-envision "world literature" from a more contemporary perspective.[6]

This more positive view of language reorientation introduces the idea that linguistic deracination must not always be experienced as catastrophe. Emigrant writers need no longer be regarded as if they were merely subjected to language change, the objects of a process over which they have little control. Instead, many such writers have developed complex and varying attitudes towards the way in which they had to learn and use a newly acquired language and towards their loyalty to, or indeed forgetfulness of, their native tongue, as can be seen in Susanne Utsch's analysis of Klaus Mann's reflections on the language problem.[7] When it comes to literary memory, however, the problem of linguistic transition presents itself in yet another way. Both Goldschmidt and Sebald deal with childhood memories, the former in terms of an autobiographical retrospective, the latter in terms of fictional reconstruction. Multilingualism has a performative quality in their respective texts that allows them to do two things at once. On the one hand, the presence of multilingualism points to the protagonists' language and identity confusion. This linguistic evocation of disorientation exposes the limited sense of liberation that follows on from the enforced acquisition of another tongue. On the other hand, however, the performative dimension of multilingualism in Sebald's and Goldschmidt's texts enables them to produce a genuinely literary attitude towards language.

G.-A. Goldschmidt:
Bilingualism as Experience and Ability

Among contemporary authors, French-German writer Georges-Arthur
Goldschmidt represents an exemplary case of bilingualism. Born in Reinbek
near Hamburg in 1928, he had to leave Germany at the age of ten because
of his Jewish ancestry. He attended a boarding school in the French Alps,
grew up in France, and was naturalized as a French citizen after the war.
He then became a German teacher at a French *lycée* and began translating
German literature into French. Goldschmidt's initial essayistic and literary
production appeared first in French in the late 1960s. It was only with considerable delay, in the 1990s, that he commenced writing literary prose in
German.

In his autobiographical work, Goldschmidt repeatedly recapitulates
the exile experience of his childhood: his transport from Germany to
France without his parents, his contact with an unknown language, his tor-
ment at the hands of his French boarding school companions and the
headmistress. The earlier of these texts were written in French: *Le miroir
quotidien* (The Daily Mirror, 1981), *Un jardin en Allemagne* (A Garden in
Germany, 1986), and *La forêt interrompue* (The Interrupted Forest,
1991). All have been translated into German, by Peter Handke among
others. When writing *La forêt interrompue*, Goldschmidt started to work
on a book in German, *Die Absonderung* (The Separation, 1991). The following book, *Die Aussetzung* (The Suspension, 1996), was also written in
German, but the next one, *La traversée des fleuves* (Crossing the Rivers,
1999), was written in French. The latter was to be the first of his own
books that Goldschmidt translated: the German version, *Über die Flüsse*,
appeared in 2001. This inventory of his work does not just provide biblio-
graphical detail, but also points to the transitions between the languages
that are at the center of Goldschmidt's writing. All these prose works —
which are internally linked, reflecting and repeating each other in many
ways — deal with translation as life experience, as a transformation affecting identity. It is the youth himself who is, as it were, translated. Being
transferred to a foreign country, he undergoes a kind of metamorphosis,
both linguistic and personal, that coincides with his first bodily and emotional experiences of puberty. It is thus a more or less common boyhood
impression of internal dissociation that here contributes to the extremely
difficult and painful transformation from one language to another. This
complex of identity disruption is reflected through a specific way of narrating: a nameless third person (referred to as "he" or "one") narrates these
personal experiences and, in taking over the voice of the "I," marks the distance between first-hand experience and the narration of this experience.
Regarding this distance and the kind of uncertainty it produces in the

reader's mind, it seems appropriate to designate Goldschmidt's texts as "auto-fictions," a term that describes the literary surplus and poetic creativity of his autobiographical writing, as has been suggested by Martin Rector.[8] It is only in *La traversée des fleuves/Über die Flüsse* — explicitly designated as "autobiography" — that a memorizing and authenticating "I" is introduced.

In Goldschmidt's narratives, exile causes a monstrous guilt complex in the boy, connected to the imposed sudden self-consciousness of being Jewish. Growing up in a secularized Protestant family, he was not only ignorant of his Jewish descent, but he never knew what "being a Jew" actually meant. Now this attribution — historically imposed by the National-Socialist ideology of "race" and "blood," which is nevertheless not overt in Goldschmidt's text — is strangely converted into a confession of masturbation: "Ich habe an mir selber herumgefummelt"[9] (I was playing around with myself). Thus, the confession is an acknowledgment of the "shame" attached to being Jewish at this particular historical juncture; this shame is articulated through an image of adolescent sexuality. Since this confession must never be said out loud, the ten-year-old protagonist of *Die Absonderung* keeps it secret alongside the complex of affirming and denying his Jewish identity, which in his mind is inseparable from the sexual taboo: "Wäre er wirklich ein Jude gewesen, er hätte es nie sagen dürfen, wie er auch das *andere* nie sagen durfte" (*Ab*, 17; if he had really been a Jew, he would have never been allowed to say it, just as he was not allowed to say the *other* thing).

Accordingly, the child's body is the sphere in which the new foreign language becomes concrete, as the following excerpt shows. After some time at the boarding school, the boy suddenly recognizes "mit einem Schlag" (in a flash) that he is able to speak French without really knowing how. His language epiphany takes place on a winter's day when a schoolmate, on seeing the first snowflakes, exclaims, "les premiers flocons" (the first snowflakes).

> Es war, als ströme alles bisher Gehörte in dieses einzige Wort "flocons" ein, als verwirkliche sich auf einmal die ganze Sprache, es hatte sich die neue Sprache um ihn herum wie eine Raumbeschaffenheit entwickelt. (*Ab*, 50)

> [It was as if all that he had heard so far was streaming into this single word "flocons," as if suddenly the complete language was being realized, the new language having developed around him like a quality of space.]

The spatial and bodily dimension of language experience generates hard physical images in Goldschmidt's text, as can be seen in the following passage where the boy is ordered by the headmistress to cut himself a rod for his own punishment:

"Je veux une bonne badine de coudrier," war ihm gesagt worden: Ich brauche eine gute Haselgerte. Das Wort "coudrier" hörte er zum erstenmal, und doch wußte er sofort, welche Baumart gemeint war, als hätte sein Auge im voraus schon alles um ihn selber gewußt. [. . .] Sorgfältig brach er die Haselgerte — sie hatte die passende Länge, damit konnte man ausholen, sie würde sich um seine Hüften winden, und er würde sich unter ihr vor Schmerz aufbäumen. (*Ab*, 124/126)

["Je veux une bonne badine de coudrier," he had been told: I need a good hazel switch. He heard the word "coudrier" for the first time, and yet he knew at once which kind of tree was meant, as if his eye had known everything about himself in advance. [. . .] He plucked the hazel switch carefully — its length was appropriate, you could really swing with this, it would wind around his hips, and he would rear up with pain.]

In this extract, the intuitive and successful translation of "coudrier" immediately evokes what it means in the boy's mind: the word is associated with pain and punishment. This pattern of association continues as one day the boy happens to find a picture emblematic for this interrelation of translation, pain, and masturbation. Skimming through the Latin textbook from which he has to do a translation (as a punishment), he sees an illustration that fascinates him: a half-naked Roman boy being punished by his teacher:

Neben dem Jungen stand der Magister, die Rute schwingend; auf dem prallen Gesäß des nackten Schülers waren schon Striemen zu sehen. Der Junge hielt den Kopf zum Zuschauer gewendet. (*Ab*, 137–38)

[Beside the boy there was the schoolmaster, wielding the rod; on the naked pupil's taut bottom one could already see the welts. The boy's head was turned to the spectator.]

In light of this discovery, the protagonist comes to terms with his own fate in the belief that it is part of a great chain of tradition. That night, his joy in suffering culminates in a scene of identification that is at once a scene of masturbation:

Am Abend dann im Bett schloß er die Augen und wurde dieser Jüngling [. . .]. Ganz langsam ließ er die Finger die Vorhaut hinauf- und hinuntergleiten, bis er sich vor Wollust aufbäumte. [. . .] Er wand sich unter der Strafe, wie der junge Römer. Noch nie hatte er eine derartige gotthafte Schärfe empfunden, er schrie auf, jubelte in sich hinein. (*Ab*, 138–39)

[That evening in bed he closed his eyes and he became this youth. [. . .] Quite slowly he made his fingers slide up and down the foreskin, until he reared with lust. [. . .] He writhed under the punishment, just like the young Roman. Never before had he sensed such god-like sharpness, he cried out, rejoiced into himself.]

What Goldschmidt performs here is a drastic and yet intricate application of the concept of *translatio studii*, meaning the transfer of classical culture and knowledge into non-classical epochs. The protagonist of *Die Absonderung* identifies with the Roman youth in an intuitive and bodily way, but this enthusiastic moment of blurred identities is a direct consequence of his studying and translating the classical Latin language — a study that is linked to punishment and thus reveals the threatening power of the institutions in which such translations take place.

Translation is a key element throughout Goldschmidt's narratives. It is not just one motif among many others but rather the origin of poetic generation, as can be seen in the way these texts are linked. As previously mentioned, *Die Absonderung* and *La forêt interrompue* were written roughly at the same time in different languages. Moreover, they are based on more or less the same material, which renders them almost parallel texts. Regarding Goldschmidt's bilingual production process of that time, one might speculate that the texts are even more closely related than parallel texts, that *Die Absonderung* translates itself into *La forêt* and vice versa — which would make each a copy of the other. If we read Goldschmidt's oeuvre in this way, we end up viewing the individual books as different versions of one extensive *texte général* with the same passages and sentences appearing time and again in several versions. To highlight this literary method, I shall now offer a cross-reading of a scene that strikingly recurs in *La forêt interrompue*, in *Die Absonderung*, and then again in *La traversée des fleuves*. In this passage the exiled boy comes across some German soldiers who have occupied the village in the Alps. As it is imperative that the boy not reveal that he himself is German, he must not let it be known that he understands the soldiers' language.[10]

La forêt interrompue:

Au débouché du chemin, encore pris dans la pente, stationnait une voiture militaire allemande, deux autres soldats y étaient assis et ils parlaient sa langue, ils avaient la voix forte et lui il comprenait tout ce qu'ils disaient, il aurait volontiers parlé avec eux.[11]

At the top of the path, still on the slope, stood a German military vehicle, another two German soldiers were sitting there, and they spoke his language, their voices were loud and he understood everything they said, he would have liked to talk to them.

Die Absonderung:

Als er am Spähwagen vorbeikam und so tat, als ginge ihn das alles nichts an, hörte er zwei Soldaten über ihn sprechen. Gierig beinahe hörte er nach dem Klang seiner Muttersprache. Jahrelang hatte er ihn nicht mehr gehört, und doch verstand er jedes Wort. (*Ab*, 173)

When he passed by the scout car pretending that this was not his concern at all, he heard two soldiers talking about him. Almost greedily he listened to the sound of his mother tongue. He had not heard it for years, and still he understood every word.

La traversée des fleuves:

Au débouché du sentier stationnait un véhicule de la Wehrmacht et les deux soldats qui y étaient assis trouvèrent que j'étais bien bouclé et bien blond, qu'il y avait de jolis enfants en Savoie. J'étais si fier de tout comprendre qu'il me fallut me mordre les lèvres pour ne pas engager la conversation avec eux.[12]

At the top of the trail stood a Wehrmacht vehicle and the two soldiers sitting inside found that my hair was neatly curled and blond and that there were pretty boys in Savoy. I was so proud of understanding everything that I had to bite my lips not to start a conversation with them.[14]

Über die Flüsse:

Am Wegansatz stand ein Spähwagen der Wehrmacht, und die beiden Soldaten, die darin saßen, fanden, daß ich schöne blonde Locken hatte und daß es in Savoyen hübsche Knaben gäbe. Ich war so stolz, alles zu verstehen, daß ich mir auf die Lippen beißen mußte, um nicht mit ihnen eine Unterhaltung anzufangen.[13]

The deviations can be identified in detail, starting with the most obvious phenomenon that "He" is turned into "I" in the autobiography (French and German). Other alterations are more particularized: only in the first version are the soldiers' voices described as "loud"; the "chemin" in *La forêt interrompue* becomes a "sentier" in *La traversée des fleuves;* only *Die Absonderung* speaks of "Muttersprache" and mentions that the boy has not heard it for years. Generally speaking, the autobiographical versions somehow seem more narcissistic, as the boy's pride about his ability to understand is stressed and we learn that the soldiers speak about his beauty. It nonetheless remains difficult to determine decisively the significance of each deviation. Reading the texts so closely, one sees that perhaps the more idiomatic translation of the common French expression "me mordre les lèvres" would have been "mir auf die Zunge beißen," whereas "mir auf die Lippen beißen" in German sounds a little more "literary." But it is all the more evident that the significance of these deviations and modifications only reveals itself by virtue of comparison *in between* the versions: that is, in the gray zone between languages where meaning is no longer fixed but ambivalent. The very act of translation thus uncovers linguistic and semantic operations that are always in force when we use any given language: the reality that language is not a stable and unchanging phenomenon, but an ongoing process that continually produces new meanings. This echoes one of Goldschmidt's findings in his poetological essay *Une chaise à deux dossiers* (A Chair with Two Backs), published in 1991 at the beginning of his bilingual writing career.[15] It is the nature of language, Goldschmidt states, that none can say exactly what another says, that there is no speaking "in place of" another language, but that nonetheless all languages say "the same thing" — from which the "temptation to translate" arises (74). But why say that translation is a "temptation"?

The uncanny recognition of the native tongue in the above passages from *La forêt interrompue* and *Die Absonderung,* as well as the torments linked to the acquisition of the new French language may justly be called traumatic experiences. Hence it follows, one might argue, that Goldschmidt's protagonist suffers from a kind of language compulsion neurosis. If on the one hand, idiomatic recognition is a threatening temptation, while on the other, translation is linked to punishment — and this, again, *is* a temptation for Goldschmidt's youthful *alter ego* — then indeed there seems to be no way out of the uneasiness of existence in between the languages. Moreover, Goldschmidt's reiteration and re-translation of his own story could in itself be regarded as another reflection of that compulsion and thus, above all, as a document of traumatic experience. His self-interpretation, however, goes against this reading. He does not emphasize trauma, but liberation from it. And it is in bilingualism that he finds the way to liberate himself from trauma and constraint.

Goldschmidt experimented with this idea in two books on Freud and the German language, written in French: *Quand Freud voit la mer* (When Freud Beholds the Sea, 1988) and *Quand Freud attend le verbe* (When Freud Anticipates the Verb, 1996).[16] Here he argues that psychoanalysis is fundamentally based on the German language; for him, German is the true language of the unconscious. Most of the examples given for this rather bold thesis are drawn from Freud's psychoanalytical terminology itself, contrasting the German notions with their French equivalents. While these French terms were "invented," mostly using Greek or Latin roots so that they form a specific academic language, Goldschmidt maintains that Freud's terms are current German expressions that always refer to physical reality: *Trieb* (drive), *Zwang* (force), *Ausdruck* (expression), *Verdrängung* (repression). As a result of this link to physicality, the German language comes across as an archive of original meanings for psychoanalytic discourse, characterized above all by the "perceptibility of etymologies" (*Fr,* 27). In short: the German language as the founding language of psychoanalysis automatically gives the unconscious in clear text. This is an open contradiction, of course, for how can the unconscious speak directly and with clarity?

Again, Goldschmidt suggests translation as the way out of this complex. By translating the German language of the body, complete with its neurotic tendencies, into the French language of spirit and freedom, the compulsion neurosis of German might be cured, because in French, Freud's project of turning the "it" into the "I" is realized to the utmost extent. At first glance, this thesis seems but a repetition of, say, Johann Gottlieb Fichte's polemical comparison between corrupt, latinized French and natural, vigorous German:[17] the evaluation is merely reversed. As a typology of languages, this is obviously nonsense in terms of modern linguistics. But as a poetological self-assertion, Goldschmidt's idea is quite telling. It is not focused on the different *types* of languages but on the *act* of comparing them, that is: making them similar *and* dissimilar at the same time. He stages what he calls "das kleine Vergleichsspiel der beiden Sprachen miteinander"[18] (the little game of parallel the two languages play with each other). In the texture of his essay, this leads to interesting performative contradictions in the general thesis of the fundamental difference between German and French. In drawing parallel after parallel, Goldschimdt opens up a new space "entre-deux-langues" (*Fr*, 59). French is no longer the analyzing meta-language here, but takes part in a creative playfulness in which linguistic objects and linguistic operations become intertwined — revealing the poetic substrata of every etymological analysis.[19]

Thus Goldschmidt's achievement in his books on Freud is not a complete anamnesis — or even a therapy — of the neurotic German language, but the recognition that in the space between the languages "it is all there, and you always come from one point to another" (*Fr*, 61). Goldschmidt's vision of translation as it is developed in these books is the faculty of association put to its extreme, meaning the capacity to reach every possible point — word, expression — of one language from any given point of the other. Practically speaking, this is the ability of every "real" bilingual speaker. On a poetological level, however, this versatility aims at a zone where bilingualism and narrative memory converge. Because "it is all there," every story is a repetition — and, *in that*, a translation — of a story that has been told before. As Goldschmidt puts it, following the passage from *Über die Flüsse* quoted above: "Das habe ich schon alles in früheren Büchern erzählt"[20] (All of this I have already told in former books).

He who is able to speak in several tongues may consider bilingualism, as Goldschmidt does, incredible good fortune; a means through which one can close the cultural breach of exile and destruction. In an interview with Hans-Ulrich Treichel he claimed:

> Nein, für mich hat es nie eine schizoide Selbstwahrnehmung gegeben, ich habe mich immer in beiden Sprachen unglaublich glücklich gefühlt. [. . .] Ich glaube, daß das Zweisprachige eine Erlösung ist und kein Hindernis.[21]

> [No, there has never been a schizoid self-perception for me, I always felt incredibly happy in both languages. [. . .] I believe that bilingualism is a redemption and not an impediment.]

W. G. Sebald:
Multilingualism as Speech Impediment

On this point my analysis turns to W. G. Sebald's *Austerlitz* (2001). Similar to Goldschmidt's positive evaluation of multilingualism discussed above, there is a moment in *Austerlitz* when someone seems "incredibly happy" in between two — or even three — languages.[22] In this passage, Austerlitz, the main protagonist, has finally succeeded in finding not only the house in Prague in which he spent the first years of his childhood, but also his former nurse Věra, who is still living there. Austerlitz, who is in fact looking for his mother and does not at first recognize Věra, "stammers out" a sentence in Czech that he has, as he claims, "laboriously learnt by heart":

> Promiňte, prosím, že Vás obtěžuji. Hledám paní Agátu Austerlitzovou, která zde možná v roce devatenáct set třicet osm bydlela. Ich suche eine Frau Agáta Austerlitzova, die möglicherweise hier 1938 noch gewohnt hat. Věra bedeckte in einer Schreckensgeste ihr Gesicht mit ihren beiden, wie es mich durchfuhr, unendlich vertrauten Händen, starrte mich über ihre gespreizten Fingerspitzen hinweg an und sagte nur, sehr leise, aber mit einer für mich wahrhaft wundervollen Deutlichkeit, diese französischen Worte: Jacquot, so sagte sie, est-ce que c'est vraiment toi? (*Au*, 223–24)

> [*Promiňte, prosím, že Vás obtěžuji. Hledám paní Agátu Austerlitzovou, která zde možná v roce devatenáct set třicet osm bydlela.* I am looking for a Mrs Agáta Austerlitzová who may have been living here in 1938. With a gesture of alarm, Věra covered her face with both hands, hands which, it flashed through my mind, were endlessly familiar to me, stared at me over her spread fingertips, and very quietly but with what to me was a quite singular clarity spoke these words in French: *Jacquot*, she said, *dis, est-ce que c'est vraiment toi?* (215–16)][23]

The "stammering" Czech and the nursery French mingle with the German of the narration — thus giving rise to a "quite singular clarity" within a scene that is utterly strange and even spooky. The protagonist, Austerlitz, is a specimen of the living dead. Věra's gesture of horror on recognizing him conveys the fact that she is seeing a ghost before her. Freud's concept of "das Unheimliche" (the uncanny) is evoked here, precisely in the sense in which Sebald used the term in his essays on Austrian literature entitled *Unheimliche Heimat*.[24] The "Unheimlich" in this sense does not lie in something unknown or foreign, but at the core of familiar things and of familiar language.

The highly complex scene I have quoted is a crystalization of linguistic familiarity and strangeness in Sebald. The French and Czech languages intrude into the German language of the narration. However, the narrator of this scene, Austerlitz himself, is not the narrator of the novel as a whole, who remains nameless but is strikingly reminiscent of the author W. G. Sebald.[25] Just like Sebald, he has emigrated as a young man in the 1960s, and of his own free will, from a small town in southern Germany. Unable to tolerate what he experiences as the never-ending afterlife of National Socialism, he seeks a tolerable way of living in a country that is referred to as England, but which seems somehow extraterritorial and impalpable. From there, he repeatedly travels to Belgium, where, several times, spread out over many years, and under mysterious circumstances, he meets Auster-litz, usually in transitory spaces like waiting rooms and hotel bars. As a nar-rator, he repeats and translates what he has been told by his protagonist, who speaks alternately French and English. However, Austerlitz's native tongue is Czech, which he has to learn again "laboriously" because he has completely forgotten it, just like everything else concerning his early child-hood, due to his emigration from Prague to Wales as a four-year-old child. Austerlitz learns that he is actually named "Austerlitz" only years later when all other traces of his earlier life have vanished. It is exactly at that point in the novel that the reader learns about the *wrong* name Austerlitz had to use for the time being, his alias, which is, paronomastically, Elias.[26] This occurs in another multilingual scene while the multilinguality vanishes in the English translation:

> Vorderhand allerdings sei er [Austerlitz's headmaster, Penrith-Smith] verpflichtet, mir zu eröffnen, daß ich auf meine Examenspapiere nicht Dafydd Elias, sondern Jacques Austerlitz schreiben müsse. It appears, sagte Penrith-Smith, that this is your real name. (*Au*, 101)

> [First, however, it was his duty to tell me that I must put not Dafydd Elias but Jacques Austerlitz on my exam papers. It appears, said Penrith-Smith, that this is your real name. (93)]

The story told in *Austerlitz* is quite similar to that of Goldschmidt's alter ego: a boy of Jewish descent escapes the Nazis by emigrating without his parents, where he is exiled and "translated." Sebald's protagonist, how-ever, is hardly capable of freeing himself from the trauma of his childhood exile and the loss of his parents. Consequently, his multilingualism is nei-ther a realized communicative utopia, nor can it be controlled by means of accomplished translation. It is rather a calamity that troubles his every attempt at communication. He not only "stammers" his forgotten Czech, but also suffers from "Sprachfehler" and "Stotteranfälle" (*Au*, 50; a slight speech impediment and occasional fits of stammering, 42) when he speaks English, the language he had to learn as an exiled child. Moreover, this state of exile is described as being influenced by several phenomena of lin-guistic alienation. Austerlitz's foster father, a Calvinist preacher, is, like his wife, mostly incapable of communication, but undergoes a change every Sunday in church, becoming a highly eloquent speaker who tells of the Last Days in the transcendent language of the prophets. Nevertheless, learning the idiom of the Holy Writ turns out to be an extremely difficult task for the little boy Austerlitz. Significantly, his greatest success in lan-guage acquisition lies in memorizing the biblical account of language con-fusion: he manages to learn the chapter from the first book of Moses by heart and succeeds in reciting it "fehlerfrei und mit schöner Betonung" (*Au*, 84; correctly and with good expression, 76).

The extreme disorientation of language and memory that Austerlitz experiences is manifested through an image that combines language with the architectural topography of an old town, a common allegory of memory:[27]

> Wenn man die Sprache ansehen kann als eine alte Stadt, mit einem Gewinkel von Gassen und Plätzen, mit Quartieren, die weit zurückreichen in die Zeit, mit abgerissenen, assanierten und neuerbauten Vierteln und immer weiter ins Vorfeld hinauswachsenden Außenbezirken, so glich ich selbst einem Menschen, der sich, aufgrund einer langen Abwesenheit, in dieser Agglomeration nicht mehr zurechtfindet, der nicht mehr weiß, wozu eine Haltestelle dient, was ein Hinterhof, eine Straßenkreuzung, ein Boulevard oder eine Brücke ist. *(Au,* 183)

> [If language may be regarded as an old city full of streets and squares, nooks and crannies, with some quarters dating from far back in time while others have been torn down, cleaned up and rebuilt, and with suburbs reaching further and further into the surrounding country, then I was like a man who has been abroad a long time and cannot find his way through this urban sprawl any more, no longer knows what a bus stop is for, or what a back yard is, or a street junction, an avenue or a bridge. (174–75)]

Likewise, Austerlitz's language disorientation indicates his loss of consciousness and recollection. When he is hospitalized due to mental disorder, all of the languages residing in him create a Babylonic confusion for which he can only serve as a medium. As he reports later, this confusion coincides with complete memory loss. He speaks of the time "in der Salpêtrière, als ich mich weder an mich, noch an meine Vorgeschichte, noch sonst irgend etwas erinnern konnte und, wie man mir später berichtete, in diversen Sprachen zusammenhanglose Dinge redete" (*Au*, 383–84; in the Salpêtrière, when I could remember nothing about myself, or my own previous history, or anything else whatsoever, and as I was told later I kept babbling disconnectedly in various languages, 377). On the other hand, the mingling of languages is also essential for Austerlitz's memory. Until he remembers his childhood self, he cannot embark on a search for the past. Thus, he is haunted by his multilingual memories, which means that he literally sees ghosts who talk to him in a language confusion that hovers between unintelligibility and ultimate understanding:

> Es war in Momenten besonderer Schwäche, wenn ich glaubte, nicht mehr weiterzukönnen, daß mir dergleichen Sinnestäuschungen widerfuhren. [. . .] Auch hörte ich, wie hinter meinem Rücken über mich geredet wurde in einer fremden Sprache, Litauisch, Ungarisch oder sonst etwas sehr Ausländisches, dachte ich mir, sagte Austerlitz. *(Au,* 188)

> [It was at moments of particular weakness, when I thought I could not go any longer, that my senses played these tricks on me. [. . .] And I would

hear people behind my back speaking in a foreign tongue, Lithuanian, Hungarian, or something else with a very alien note to it, or so I thought, said Austerlitz. (180)]

The phrase of "something with a very alien note to it" could be taken as an indirect reference to the relationship between Austerlitz and the narrator: between the traumatized multilingual speaker and the person giving his narrative voice to him and thus allowing him to speak in the first place. The German language of this narrator is unknown to Austerlitz, like all things German, which, as he notes one day, form a blind spot within his otherwise encyclopedic knowledge. Significantly, German is also the language of those who are responsible for the "Absterben der Muttersprache" (*Au*, 203; the dying away of my native tongue, 195). Considering this link between the German language and a buried past, and the further connection between a German narrator-translator and the traumatized individual who avoids all things German, one could also use the phrase "something with a very alien note to it" to characterize the narrative as a whole. In its elaborate, quasi-nineteenth-century German, Sebald's novel thematizes the shame surrounding German as the language of the perpetrators. That is why the text is always interrupted, affected by communication difficulties, and haunted by languages other than its own.

The function of multilingualism thus comes close to Sebald's technique of inserting photos in his text. These enigmatic and intriguing pictures can only be interpreted as illustrations at first glance. As soon as one takes a closer look at them, it becomes ultimately puzzling what they illustrate and what can be seen in them.[28] Just as Sebald's photos are not the ornamentation of his words, his use of several languages does not just add local color, but is an essential component of the way in which all of his prose works are written. Thus, it is surprising that multilingualism has not been much investigated within the expanding scholarship on Sebald: Heinrich Detering is alone when he remarks in his review of *Die Ausgewanderten* that Sebald's strange stylization and abrupt shifts from German to English betray the author's resistance to writing in German at all.[29]

For Sebald, the use of several languages certainly was an indispensable tool in making his elaborate German prose appropriate for his stories: multilingualism gave him the chance to emphasize and unsettle "Germanness" at the same time. By contrast, for Goldschmidt multilingualism arises through the very constitution of his French-German *texte général* and is not aimed at unsettling Germanness specifically, but shows the positive side to being in translation: being liberated between languages and identities. Sebald, however, does not share Goldschmidt's optimistic view of liberation from the compulsions of language by means of translation: in his narratives, the mixture of languages works instead as an indicator of the linguistic unconscious. Nonetheless there are functional and structural correspondences between Sebald's and Goldschmidt's multilingualism. In both cases the use of language in the texts points to a different way of speaking that questions the idea of the mastery of language. Despite Goldschmidt's evident bilingual ability and Sebald's stylistic proficiency, the utopia suggested in their writing departs from a vision of language mastery and instead evokes a linguistic space of otherness that goes beyond the confines of the monolingual norm. In his poetological reflections on bilingualism, Goldschmidt draws a conclusion that would be an equally valid statement about Sebald's poetics of multilingualism. Speaking about the language unconscious and about the "failles" and "défaillances" (gaps and feints) of language, Goldschmidt claims that writing commences exactly at the point where language ceases to work and where languages "open up" ("En réalité, c'est sur le même inconscient linguistique, sur les mêmes failles, les mêmes défaillances que s'ouvrent les langues et c'est là que l'écriture commence. C'est là où la langue ne marche pas"[30]).

Conclusion

In his 1813 essay *Über die verschiedenen Methoden des Uebersezens* (On the Different Methods of Translation), the Protestant theologian, Romantic philosopher, and translator of Plato Friedrich Schleiermacher characterized bilingual speakers as "wunderbare Männer [. . .], wie sie die Natur bisweilen hervorzubringen pflegt" (miraculous men that nature sometimes produces), but seemed to regard them ultimately as supernatural beings. Bilingualism, he stated, should be regarded as "eine frevelhafte und magische Kunst" (a wicked and magical art) and those practicing it as quasi-doubles who intend to mock the laws of nature.[31] Thinking of Sebald's ghosts, Schleiermacher's anxious fascination with speaking in several tongues seems quite pertinent. As a poetological argument, however, the exclusion of this "miraculous" phenomenon would prove restrictive. In light of Goldschmidt's and Sebald's multilingualism, one could even argue that writing can and must commence where language ceases to work. In other words, the space of writing, as a space of translation — the translation of experience into narrative — is the in-between space outside and beyond language where meaning is never fixed or stable. As soon as the writing subject translates his or her experience into the medium of the written word, there is a sense in which they give up the self as known in the previous language medium. From this perspective, the idea of writing in a native tongue, with all its connotations of ownership, belonging, and certain identity, is suddenly on shaky ground. In this way, literature can be regarded as a kind of second language, one that no matter how hard we try to "acquire" constantly evades us, producing excesses of meaning in some places, deficits in others. If we accept this view, then everything in literature can be seen as an effect of this existential multilingualism, understood as exophony — the idea that all literature exists outside of the *phoné* of the mother language.[32] This is what Goldschmidt seems to have in mind when he generalizes, "Jeder Schriftsteller ist zweisprachig"[33] (every writer is bilingual). As a sweeping generalization Goldschmidt's statement is of course questionable, but interesting. The following concluding remarks outline the extent to which this link between writing and multilingualism contributes to a poetics of memory.

The fact that there has always been multilingual literature and that the mingling of languages has a specific function in literary texts[34] attests to the centrality of multilingualism for the study of literature. Today, it seems more evident than ever that national boundaries of culture must be questioned. This does not mean that one should or even could do away with them altogether. But theories and works of postcolonial literature[35] have justly emphasized that the rather generalizing concept of monolingual national literatures is not an accurate reflection of what is going on in world literature. Following Lamping's above mentioned suggestions, the ability of many literary authors to move between different languages challenges the homogenizing idea of national literary canons that try to organize literary works according to one language and one nation. In this respect, authors of the twentieth century who wrote in more than one language (like Vladimir Nabokov and Samuel Beckett[36]) or authors who extensively thematized their multilingualism (like Elias Canetti[37]) can be regarded as exemplary figures.

Given recent concepts of comparative literature, it becomes more and more evident that multilingualism can indeed open up a new space for case studies as well as for general theories of literature, transgressing the norm of monolingualism and achieving a more refined practice of differentiating the plurality of idioms in a single author or text.[38] Moreover, such a research program could lead to a rapprochement of literary criticism and linguistics: after all, phenomena of multilingualism have gained considerable attention in linguistics for decades. Since Uriel Weinreich's *Languages in Contact* (1953), language shift and language maintenance have been explored in manifold ways. In this field of study, the empirical observation that people shift from one language to another for different reasons, or that they maintain their original language under circumstances in which normally they would be likely to give it up, has given rise to the psychological and sociological analysis of "language attitudes" in populations and individuals, that is, of the ideas and practices that motivate speakers to use or not use a certain language or language variety in certain domains.[39] These inquiries all question the presumption that monolinguism is an intrinsic and implicit human characteristic and have led to axiomatic formulations like, "Le plurilinguisme est la règle, l'unilinguisme l'exception"[40] (multilingualism is the rule, monolingualism is the exception), and even to somewhat speculative generalizations on the multilingualism of human beings as such.[41]

It is obvious that bilingual acquisition in childhood especially is of importance within the linguistic context. Indeed, given the extensive case-studies on bilingual children from the first half of the twentieth century, the primary acquisition of more than one language can be regarded as a model of multilingualism, while language shift has been thoroughly studied in cases of childhood migration.[42] All of these studies focus on the orality of language acquisition. This is precisely where literary research begins to be relevant — meaning not only academic scholarship, but in a much wider sense of the term the findings of analytical thought that literary texts contain and reveal by virtue of a carefully crafted literary discourse. If we understand literature as a medium capable of exposing to us the space of translation, the in-between zone of language, then literary analysis can show to what extent the supposedly immediate, illiterate, and primary language experience can only be conceptualized as a mediated one. With Goldschmidt and Sebald, this experience is suggested through the process of remembrance and reconstruction both protagonists engage in. Goldschmidt's auto-fictions as well as Sebald's *Austerlitz* are case studies in multilingualism that produce a kind of knowledge about language that could not have been yielded in the realm of linguistics or psychology. In that sense, multilingualism is an exemplary site of literature.

Notes

[1] See Christhard Hoffmann, "Zum Begriff der Akkulturation," *Handbuch der deutschsprachigen Emigration 1933–1945*, ed. Claus-Dieter Krohn et al. (Darmstadt: Primus, 1998), col. 117–28.

[2] See Claus-Dieter Krohn, "Einleitung," *Handbuch der deutschsprachigen Emigration 1933–1945*, col. 1–4.

[3] Döblin writes: "Sich davon ablösen? Aber das heißt mehr, als sich die Haut abziehen, das heißt sich ausweiden, Selbstmord begehen." Alfred Döblin, "Als ich wiederkam . . . ," *Schriften zu Leben und Werk* (Olten: Walter, 1986), 267–72; here: 270.

[4] See Wulf Köpke, "Die Wirkung des Exils auf Sprache und Stil. Ein Vorschlag zur Forschung," *Exilforschung* 3 (1985): 225–37.

[5] See Manfred Durzak, "Laokoons Söhne. Zur Sprachproblematik im Exil," *Akzente* 21 (1974): 53–63.

[6] Dieter Lamping, " 'Linguistische Metamorphosen.' Aspekte des Sprachwechsels in der Exilliteratur," *Germanistik und Komparatistik: DFG-Symposion 1993*, ed. Hendrik Birus (Stuttgart: Metzler, 1995), 528–40; here: 539. For recent linguistic concepts of language reorientation and language shift, see *Methodological and Analytical Issues in Language Maintenance and Language Shift Studies*, ed. Maya Khemlani David (Frankfurt: Lang, 2002); *Creoles, Contact, and Language Change.*

Linguistics and Social Implications, ed. Geneviève Escure (Amsterdam: Benjamins, 2004); *Mehrsprachigkeit, Minderheiten und Sprachwandel/Multilingualism, Minorities and Language Change*, ed. Peter H. Nelde (St. Augustin: Asgard, 2004).

[7] See Susanne Utsch, " 'Vergnügen und Qual des englisch-Schreibens': An Approach to the Literary Language Shift of Klaus Mann," in *Die Alchemie des Exils: Exil als schöpferischer Impuls*, ed. Helga Schreckenberger (Vienna: edition präsens, 2005).

[8] See Martin Rector, "Frühe Absonderung, später Abschied. Adoleszenz und Faschismus in den autobiographischen Erzählungen von Georges-Arthur Goldschmidt und Peter Weiss," *Peter Weiss Jahrbuch* 4 (1995): 122–39. See also Michaela Holdenried, "Das Ende der Aufrichtigkeit? Zum Wandel autobiographischer Dispositive am Beispiel von Georges-Arthur Goldschmidt," *Archiv für das Studium der neueren Sprachen und Literaturen* 149 (1997): 1–18; Alfred Bodenheimer, "Kenntlichkeit und Schuld. Zur literarischen Jugendautobiographie G.-A. Goldschmidts," in *In der Sprache der Täter: Neue Lektüren deutschsprachiger Nachkriegs- und Gegenwartsliteratur*, ed. Stephan Braese (Opladen: Westdeutscher Verlag, 1998), 149–66; Hans-Jürgen Heinrichs, "Die Überquerung der Flüsse. Das autobiographische Schreiben von Jorge Semprun und Georges-Arthur Goldschmidt," *Merkur* 54/6 (2000): 487–99.

[9] Georges-Arthur Goldschmidt, *Die Absonderung: Erzählung* (Zurich: Ammann, 1991), 19. Subsequent references to this work are cited in the text using the abbreviation *Ab* and page number.

[10] This seems to echo a passage in Jean Améry where the refugee has to summon all his "Angst und Vernunftkontrolle" (fear and rational control) not to talk to an SS-man in their mutual native dialect, but instead to stammer some phrases in his "under cover" French. Jean Améry, "Wieviel Heimat braucht der Mensch," in *Jenseits von Schuld und Sühne: Bewältigungsversuche eines Überwältigten* (Stuttgart: Klett-Cotta, 1988), 67–68.

[11] Georges-Arthur Goldschmidt, *La forêt interrompue. Récit* (Paris: Seuil, 1991), 36.

[12] Georges-Arthur Goldschmidt, *La traversée des fleuves. Autobiographie* (Paris: Seuil, 1999), 170.

[13] Georges-Arthur Goldschmidt, *Über die Flüsse. Autobiographie* (Zürich: Ammann, 2001), 205.

[14] The English translation from the German is identical except that "Spähwagen der Wehrmacht" translates as "Wehrmacht scout car" as opposed to "vehicle."

[15] Georges-Arthur Goldschmidt, "Une chaise à deux dossiers/Ein Stuhl mit zwei Lehnen" [German translation by Michael von Killisch-Horn], *Sirene* 4/8 (1991), 68–99; here: 74.

[16] Georges-Arthur Goldschmidt, *Quand Freud voit la mer: Freud et la langue allemande* (Paris: Buchet/Chastel, 1988), 27. Subsequent references to this work are cited in the text using the abbreviation *Fr* and page number.

[17] Johann Gottlieb Fichte, *Reden an die deutsche Nation* (1807/1808, Hamburg: Meiner, 1978), 72.

[18] Georges-Arthur Goldschmidt, "Vorwort zur deutschen Ausgabe," *Als Freud das Meer sah: Freud und die deutsche Sprache*, trans. Brigitte Große (Zurich: Ammann, 1999), 11.

[19] See Stefan Willer, *Poetik der Etymologie: Texturen sprachlichen Wissens in der Romantik* (Berlin: Akademie, 2003), 14–26.

[20] Goldschmidt, *Über die Flüsse*, 205.

[21] Georges-Arthur Goldschmidt/Hans-Ulrich Treichel, "Jeder Schriftsteller ist zweisprachig. Ein Gespräch," *Sprache im technischen Zeitalter* 32/131 (1994): 273–85; here: 285.

[22] W. G. Sebald, *Austerlitz* (Frankfurt am Main: Fischer, 2003). Subsequent references to this work and the English translation by Anthea Bell (London: Penguin, 2002) are cited in the text using the abbreviation *Au* and page numbers for the German and English editions respectively.

[23] Just note the slight differences in the wording of the "other" languages: Czech and French are in italics only in the English translation; an accent appears on the last vowel of Vera's surname; a "dis" ("say") is added to her words.

[24] W. G. Sebald, *Unheimliche Heimat: Essays zur österreichischen Literatur* (Salzburg: Residenz, 1991).

[25] Mark R. McCulloh, *Understanding W. G. Sebald* (Columbia, SC: U of South Carolina P, 2003), 110.

[26] For the use of names in Sebald, see Iris Denneler, *Von Namen und Dingen. Erkundungen zur Rolle des Ich in der Literatur* (Würzburg: Königshausen & Neumann, 2001), 133–58.

[27] See Anne Fuchs, *"Die Schmerzensspuren der Geschichte": Zur Poetik der Erinnerung in W. G. Sebalds Prosa* (Cologne: Böhlau, 2004), 41–67, especially 47–54 ("Topografische Netzwerke in 'Austerlitz'"); R. J. A. Kilbourn, "Architecture and Cinema: The Representation of Memory in W. G. Sebald's 'Austerlitz,'" in *W. G. Sebald: A Critical Companion*, ed. J. J. Long and Anne Whitehead (Edinburgh: Edinburgh UP, 2004), 140–54.

[28] See Heiner Boehncke, "Clair obscur. W. G. Sebalds Bilder," *Text + Kritik* 158: *W. G. Sebald* (2003), 43–62; Markus R. Weber, "Die fantastische befragt die pedantische Genauigkeit. Zu den Abbildungen in W. G. Sebalds Werken," *Text + Kritik*, 63–74.

[29] Heinrich Detering, "Große Literatur für kleine Zeiten. Ein Meisterwerk: W. G. Sebalds 'Die Ausgewanderten,'" *Frankfurter Allgemeine Zeitung*, 17 November, 1992, reprinted in *W. G. Sebald*, ed. Franz Loquai (Eggingen: Isele, 1997), 82–87; here: 86.

[30] Goldschmidt, "Une chaise à deux dossiers," 78.

[31] Friedrich Daniel Ernst Schleiermacher, "Ueber die verschiedenen Methoden des Uebersezens," *Das Problem des Übersetzens*, ed. Hans Joachim Störig (Darmstadt: Wissenschaftliche Buchgesellschaft, 1963), 38–70; here: 50, 64.

[32] See *Exo-Phonie: Anders-Sprachigkeit (in) der Literatur*, ed. Susan Arndt, Dirk Naguschewski, Robert Stockhammer (in press).

[33] Goldschmidt/Treichel, "Jeder Schriftsteller ist zweisprachig," 284.

[34] See Leonard W. Forster, *The Poet's Tongues: Multilingualism in Literature* (London: Cambridge UP, 1970); András Horn, "Ästhetische Funktion der Sprachmischung in der Literatur," *Arcadia* 16 (1981): 225–41.

[35] See *Hybridity and Postcolonialism: Twentieth-Century Indian Literature*, ed. Monika Fludernik (Tübingen: Stauffenburg, 1998); *Multiculturalism & Hybridity in African Literatures*, ed. Hal Wylie (Trenton, NJ: Africa World Press, 2000); Patsy J. Daniels, *The Voice of the Oppressed in the Language of the Oppressor: A Discussion of Selected Postcolonial Literature from Ireland, Africa, and America* (New York: Routledge, 2001); *Beyond the Borders: American Literature and Post-Colonial Theory*, ed. Deborah L. Madsen (London: Pluto Press, 2003).

[36] See Antonina Filonov Gove, "Multilingualism and Ranges of Tone in Nabokov's 'Bend Sinister,' " *Slavic Review* 32 (1973): 79–90; Ann Beer, " 'Watt,' Knott and Beckett's Bilingualism," *Journal of Beckett Studies* 10 (1985): 37–75.

[37] See Anne Fuchs, " 'The Deeper Nature of My German': Mother Tongue, Subjectivity, and the Voice of the Other in Elias Canetti's Autobiography," in *A Companion to the Works of Elias Canetti*, ed. Dagmar C. G. Lorenz (Rochester, NY: Camden House, 2004), 45–60.

[38] See *Multilinguale Literatur im 20. Jahrhundert*, ed. Manfred Schmeling, Monika Schmitz-Emans (Würzburg: Königshausen & Neumann, 2002).

[39] See Uriel Weinreich, *Languages in Contact: Findings and Problems* (The Hague: Mouton, 1953); Joshua A. Fishman, "Language Maintenance and Language Shift as a Field of Inquiry," *Linguistics* 9 (1964): 32–70; Robert C. Gardner, *Social Psychology and Second Language Learning: The Role of Attitudes and Motivation* (London: Arnold, 1985); Atilla Yakut, *Cultural Linguistics and Bilingualism: A Bibliography* (Frankfurt: Landeck, 1994); Peter Garrett, Nikolas Coupland, Angie Williams, *Investigating Language Attitudes: Social Meanings of Dialect, Ethnicity and Performance* (Cardiff: University of Wales Press, 2003); *Plurilinguisme — Mehrsprachigkeit — Plurilingualism: Enjeux identitaires, socio-culturels et éducatifs*, ed. Lorenza Mondada and Simona Pekarek Doehler (Tübingen: Francke, 2003).

[40] Georges Lüdi/Bernard Py, *Être bilingue* (Bern: Lang, 2003), 1.

[41] See Mario Wandruszka, *Interlinguistik: Umrisse einer neuen Sprachwissenschaft* (Munich: Piper, 1971); *Die Mehrsprachigkeit des Menschen* (Munich: Piper, 1979).

[42] See Jules Ronjat, *Le développement du langage observé chez un enfant bilingue* (Paris: Champion, 1913); Werner F. Leopold, *Speech Development of a Bilingual Child: A Linguist's Record* (Evanston, IL: Northwestern UP, 1939–1949); Donald C. Porsché, *Die Zweisprachigkeit während des primären Spracherwerbs* (Tübingen: Narr, 1983); Rosemarie Tracy, "Vom Ganzen und seinen Teilen. Überlegungen zum doppelten Erstspracherwerb," *Sprache und Kognition* 15/1–2 (1996), 70–92; Annette Kracht, *Migration und kindliche Zweisprachigkeit: Interdisziplinarität und Professionalität sprachpädagogischer und sprachbehindertenpädagogischer Praxis* (Münster: Waxmann, 2000); Stefan Schneider, "Frühkindliche Mehrsprachigkeit aus sprachwissenschaftlicher Sicht," in *Vielerlei Zungen: Mehrsprachigkeit + Spracherwerb + Pädagogik + Psychologie + Literatur + Medien*, ed. Allan James (Klagenfurt: Drava, 2003), 11–48.

5: "Ein Stück langweiliger als die Wehrmachtsausstellung, aber dafür repräsentativer": The Exhibition *Fotofeldpost* as Riposte to the "Wehrmacht Exhibition"

Chloe E. M. Paver

THIS ESSAY EXAMINES DIVERGENT approaches to the scholarly analysis and public exhibition of a particular corpus of photographic images: photographs taken by, or of, Wehrmacht soldiers during the Second World War. Though my title refers to the two exhibitions whose competing approaches are my central concern, properly speaking the exhibitions in question numbered three: two related but distinct exhibitions organized by the Hamburger Institut für Sozialforschung (hereafter HIS) on the subject of the crimes of the Wehrmacht, which ran from 1995–1999 and from 2001–2004 respectively;[1] and, sandwiched between them in the year 2000, the exhibition *Fotofeldpost: Geknipste Kriegserlebnisse 1939–1945*, mounted by the Deutsch-Russisches Museum Berlin-Karlshorst (hereafter DRM) and concerned with the practice of amateur photography among soldiers on the Eastern Front.[2] After some preliminary considerations, my essay addresses two interrelated issues: how *Fotofeldpost* diverged in its approaches from the first of the so-called Wehrmacht Exhibitions;[3] and how the photo-historical scholarship that fed into, built on, or ran parallel to the exhibitions constructs the figure of the soldier-photographer.

There is a fine line between analyzing a memory contest that took place in reality and staging one in retrospect, in the process of writing cultural history. As evidence that this particular contest is not of my own imagining I could cite early reviewers of *Fotofeldpost*, who labeled the exhibition "eine Art Gegenausstellung" (a kind of counter-exhibition) and "die andere Wehrmachtsausstellung" (the other Wehrmacht exhibition).[4] However, Peter Jahn, curator of the DRM, told a press conference that the exhibition was not to be understood as a commentary on, let alone as a corrective to, *Verbrechen der Wehrmacht*.[5] Jahn also refrained from taking direct aim at *Verbrechen der Wehrmacht* in his exhibition, mentioning it on none of the display boards, and only once, in passing, in the more discursive catalogue. Indeed, since the catalogue's bibliography cites none of the HIS's publications and only two very general texts that were also cited by the organizers of the first Wehrmacht Exhibition, all signs are that the makers of *Fotofeldpost* simply overlooked *Verbrechen der Wehrmacht*. Certainly, given its expertise in photographic history and the history of the war in the East, the DRM had no great need of the HIS. *Fotofeldpost* was based on an archive of amateur photographs built up during the 1990s and drew on exhibition practice at the DRM and its fellow Berlin museum Topographie des Terrors, both of which had experience of displaying photographs taken by, or of, Wehrmacht soldiers. There is therefore no reason to doubt Jahn's assertion (in a letter to the author) that the *Fotofeldpost* exhibition would have been mounted, Wehrmacht Exhibition or no.[6]

It would thus be possible to dismiss the notion of a "Gegenausstellung" (counter exhibition) as media spin, were it not that, even as he was diverting the press from the enticing prospect of institutional rivalry, Jahn also pinpointed the differences between his exhibition and *Verbrechen der Wehrmacht*: "Eine solche Thesenausstellung," he said of the HIS's exhibition,

> muss undifferenziert sein — das ist zugleich ihre Stärke und ihre Schwäche. Unsere Schau ist ein Stück langweiliger als die Wehrmachtsausstellung, aber dafür repräsentativer für das Geschehen an und hinter der Front. [. . .] Wir stellen unsere Bilder viel stärker in ihren Kontext.[7]
>
> [A polemical exhibition like that is bound to be overgeneralized: that is both its strength and its weakness. While our exhibition is a bit more boring than the Wehrmacht Exhibition, it is also more representative of events at and behind the front. [. . .] We place our images more firmly in their context.]

Thus, while the organizers sensibly resisted the temptation to court short-term media attention by styling their exhibition a riposte to *Verbrechen der Wehrmacht*, *Fotofeldpost* did, *de facto*, contest the methods and meanings of the HIS exhibition thanks to its quite different methodological premises. Indeed, as my analysis will show, certain aspects of the exhibition only make sense against the background of the first Wehrmacht Exhibition. But before I proceed to that analysis I need to say both something specific about the contrasting material circumstances of the exhibitions and something general about how the ideas propagated by exhibitions achieve longevity in the public realm and in scholarly study.

If the relationship between these exhibitions can be read as a memory contest, then it is a contest that pitted David against Goliath. The first Wehrmacht Exhibition attracted some 800,000 visitors, the second 420,000; *Fotofeldpost* about 6,000.[8] The *Fotofeldpost* catalogue had a print run of about 2,200, of which fewer than 2,000 had sold at the time of writing; though the HIS has declined to release its sales figures, both its

catalogues ran to more than one edition, and even if we assume a less generous ratio of visitors to sales than for *Fotofeldpost*, it is likely that sales of
each reached six figures. There is also a temporal and a spatial dimension to
the unequal status of the exhibitions. Together, the two Wehrmacht Exhibitions ran for a total of 278 weeks spread over a period of seven years;
Fotofeldpost, by contrast, ran for a mere ten weeks; and while the traveling
Wehrmacht Exhibitions were able to reach a geographically diverse public,
Fotofeldpost's reach was limited by its immobility at the DRM. Though the
Bündnis der Grünen showed an interest in hiring out the exhibition, the
plans came to nothing.

What I acknowledge from the outset, then, is that while the deployment of photographic images in *Fotofeldpost* might, in intellectual terms,
be considered a corrective to the first Wehrmacht Exhibition, that corrective is likely to have had a limited effect outside academic circles, given that
for every person who visited *Fotofeldpost* another 132 had seen the
Wehrmacht Exhibition. Though there is insufficient space to present it
here, there is evidence that the scholarly approaches of the *Fotofeldpost*
team informed the much more circumspect but also quite imaginative
analysis of photographic evidence displayed in the second Wehrmacht
Exhibition, so that, in the public sphere at least, the work of *Fotofeldpost*
has probably been disseminated more through this secondary process than
through the original exhibit.

This narrative of the transmission of ideas is further complicated by the
uneven efforts of the three exhibitions' organizers to preserve evidence of
their work for posterity. To demonstrate this, it is necessary to work backwards from the second Wehrmacht Exhibition, which, thanks to the unexpected success of the first, had a sizeable budget, sufficient to fund an
extensive website,[9] to underwrite the production costs of a DVD,[10] and to
subsidize a substantial printed catalogue.[11] This great door-stop of a book
records the exhibits in almost exhaustive detail: only the contents of the
exhibition's PC and audio stations are (of necessity) omitted, but these are
captured on the truly exhaustive DVD. The website contains, in addition,
all the press releases about the second exhibition, together with a broad
selection of press reviews. Moreover, because the HIS granted the website
ongoing funding and because the DVD was released just before the exhibition finally closed its doors (itself a sign of the HIS's confidence in its
Verbrechen der Wehrmacht brand) both website and DVD have been able
to document the second exhibition in its three-dimensional form as a public presentation, capturing at least three venues through still photographs,
360-degree digital panoramas and a guided tour. In its "slide-show" of
stills from the exhibition rooms in Berlin, the website even glosses the
exhibition's methods of display.

The HIS had not always been so self-reflective: the catalogue of the first
Wehrmacht Exhibition was neither a complete record of the exhibits nor

did it contain any indication of how those exhibits had been displayed (though for its own purposes the HIS archived a complete record of the display boards). Only once the exhibition became a byword for controversy did the HIS publish a series of volumes analyzing intellectual, public, and media responses to it, illustrated by a small number of photographs of the exhibition space and the display boards. Further textual and photographic evidence was collected for inclusion in the PC stations, catalogue, and DVD of the second exhibition, which chronicled the history of the first.

Taken together, all these strategies have rescued the spatial and social experience of the two Wehrmacht Exhibitions from the oblivion that conventionally attends an ephemeral public performance. By contrast, the spatial and social experience of *Fotofeldpost* is threatened with just such oblivion because anybody wanting information about such matters as its visitor numbers, its reception in the press, and the distribution of the material around the exhibition space has to trespass on the valuable time of the museum's curator. Even then, the records he is generous enough to send one — press reviews and still photographs of the exhibition room — are much less comprehensive than the HIS's lavish published records of *its* two exhibitions. All this means that the HIS has been able to memorialize its two exhibitions (as distinct from the historical documents contained in them) much more effectively than the DRM. While the DRM would doubtless, and quite rightly, counter that it has better things on which to spend its money than immortalizing its exhibition aesthetics, this laudable lack of institutional vanity nonetheless makes the two Wehrmacht Exhibitions decidedly more attractive as objects of study than *Fotofeldpost*. Accordingly, they are likely to be the subject of university seminars for years to come. While this self-selection is not entirely unjust, given that the controversies provoked by the Wehrmacht Exhibitions deserve analysis, this essay is in part an attempt to ensure that such seminars must also take account of *Fotofeldpost*, which, for all its lack of sensation, made a serious contribution both to the study of German photographic history and to exhibition practice.

Imagining the Soldier-Photographer

The small number of falsely attributed photographs and the more general carelessness about sourcing that led to the withdrawal of the first Wehrmacht Exhibition have been analyzed by others;[12] my concern lies with the deployment of the photographic material in the exhibition space and in particular with the exhibitors' unspoken attitudes towards amateur photographers in the Wehrmacht (whom I will call soldier-photographers to distinguish them from their professional counterparts in the propaganda corps). This might seem an odd point of departure given that the first

Wehrmacht Exhibition was characterized by its *lack* of interest in photographers, amateur *or* professional. Despite relying heavily on photographs to document the crimes named in its title, the exhibition said nothing about the men who took the photographs or the circumstances under which they took them. In the minds of visitors and commentators, however, the figure of the photographer seems to have appeared unbidden like a specter. Defying the normal tendency of photographs to efface the photographer, the images in *Verbrechen der Wehrmacht* seemed to draw attention to him, for if someone had snapped the scenes of firing squads, gallows, round-ups, and mass graves, then someone had also seen them. And in the popular imagination this witness was emphatically *not* a propaganda-corps photographer, whose job it was to document military activity (even though professionals were responsible for at least twenty percent of the images at the exhibition), but rather an amateur photographer who could choose what he did and did not photograph. This, at least, is how Bill Niven, drawing on media reports and on readers' letters to newspapers, describes the public's response to the images. The exhibition, he says, conjured up the figure of a soldier-photographer who "observes, registers, knows, indeed objectifies his knowledge, but does not intervene. He comes to symbolize the position of those many German soldiers who observed crimes, or knew of them, yet did not protest."[13]

While Niven implies that this public response is part of the positive legacy of the exhibition, one could read it more skeptically, for the fact that the mythicized figure of the soldier-photographer can be used in the service of a liberal morality (to express righteous indignation at the widespread passive acquiescence in crimes) does not make it any less mythical. Arguably it was precisely the HIS's silence about the photographers that produced this effect, whereby a large and extremely heterogeneous group of men coalesced into a single symbolic embodiment of moral cowardice. I have written elsewhere about the way in which the Jewish-Austrian filmmaker Ruth Beckermann, in her response to a particular photograph in the first Wehrmacht Exhibition, somewhat willfully constructs an imaginary soldier-photographer who casually exercises his power over a group of Jewish victims by taking a snapshot of them (I say "willfully" because the photograph in question was part of a series taken by a propaganda-corps photographer and because it ought to have been possible to recognize it as such).[14] Beckermann's description of this act suggests that the imagined figure of the soldier-photographer, whose defining characteristic is his readiness to photograph the suffering of others without intervening on their behalf, was already sufficiently common currency by the late 1990s for her to conjure him up in a few brief words.

Corresponding as it does to what Marianne Hirsch calls "postmemory,"[15] Beckermann's imaginative reanimation of this photograph of a young Jewish woman can be judged positively, as a creative response by a second-generation survivor to the unresolved trauma of her parents' suffering; the treatment of soldier-photographers in scholarly writing is more open to question. A companion publication to the first Wehrmacht Exhibition, edited for the HIS by Hannes Heer and Klaus Naumann, reprinted one article and commissioned another exploring the motivations of those soldier-photographers who took pictures of persecution and crimes.[16] Thus, while the exhibition itself remained silent about photography in the Wehrmacht, the HIS's wider academic project took account of it. The articles in question, one by Dieter Reifarth and Viktoria Schmidt-Linsenhoff, the other by Bernd Hüppauf, take what one might call the What-were-they-thinking-of? approach, attempting to fathom, in a more or less systematic and theorized way, what could have gone through the mind of a man who pressed a camera shutter moments after another human being had died of asphyxiation on the gallows or had been shot in the head. The two articles come to different conclusions, but while both concede a range of possible motives for photographing persecution and execution, within the framework of the articles a soldier is defined as one who photographs persecution and execution: the authors cite no instances of soldiers who did not photograph persecution and execution; they barely acknowledge that soldiers who photographed persecution and execution took photographs of other subjects as well; and they blank out those aspects of soldiers' lives that were unrelated to photography or to the witnessing of persecution and execution. Reifarth and Schmidt-Linsenhoff's designations "der Amateurfotograf des Terrors" and "der Nazi als Amateurfotograf"[17] (the amateur photographer of acts of terror; the Nazi as amateur photographer) indicate this reductive tendency (though Hüppauf does take issue with the more extreme implications of the latter).

Two later articles, written outside the context of the HIS exhibition, one by Judith Levin and Daniel Uzel, the other by Alexander Rossino, challenge what they regard as a universalizing tendency by Reifarth and Schmidt-Linsenhoff and Hüppauf, arguing that they fail to consider the empirical context of individual photographs or, indeed, the difficulty of establishing that context in most cases.[18] Yet even these scholars concur with their predecessors that photographs that document racial or political persecution and murder form a discrete body of images that are to be understood largely with reference to one another rather than with reference to images of other subjects or to things other than images. Even where, as in Hüppauf's article, the photographs are compared with images produced under quite different circumstances, the purpose is still to situate them within an iconographical tradition of atrocity images, so that like is still being compared with like. This privileging of the diachronic over the synchronic obscures the contemporary contexts of photographic practice in the 1930s and 1940s; the act of isolating atrocity photographs from photographs of other subjects artificially constructs a soldier-photographer whose defining activity is, to borrow Susan Sontag's phrase, regarding the pain of others.

Something analogous happened when one of the very few photographs to show Wehrmacht soldiers in the act of photographing dead bodies was cropped to provide a cover illustration for the English-language edition of Heer and Naumann's volume of essays (an abridged version that reproduces Hüppauf's article but not Reifarth and Schmidt-Linsenhoff's, which was perhaps felt by then to have been superseded).[19] It is apparent from the full image, reproduced in the *Fotofeldpost* exhibition,[20] that the picture is of two bodies on a gallows. Beyond the two bodies, which we see from behind, is a bank of about twenty Wehrmacht soldiers, of whom at least four are aiming cameras at the front view of the bodies, while at least a further two hold cameras loosely in their hands. Although the *Fotofeldpost* catalogue provides no contextual information, the fact that at least one of the two hanged bodies has a placard tied around its neck strongly suggests that these are men or women who, having been adjudged partisans, have been hanged publicly as a deterrent; this is also implied by their lack of uniform and by the presence of a boy or girl of about twelve, who is highly unlikely to have been admitted to an execution in a military setting.

In the cropped version on the cover of *War of Extermination* we see the more completely framed of the two bodies and, beyond it, a selection of the assembled soldiers, including three who are holding cameras prominently. By cutting out the second, only partly framed body, the figure of the child, and at least eight soldiers who are not, or not visibly, in possession of a camera, and by foreshortening the perspective of the original so that the observing presence of the photographer is no longer clearly felt, the cropped image creates an undiluted, bilateral relationship between the soldier-photographers and the hanged man, and in doing so focuses attention on the soldiers' gaze, with its contradictory mixture of intense curiosity (since the hanged man is obviously the object of their photographic interest) and indifference (the moment of first photographing him having evidently just passed). The cropped image is outlined in white, forming a box that also contains the book title, and this box is pasted over a slightly larger, but also cropped reproduction of the photograph, positioned so that three of the soldiers' cameras appear prominently in the border around the smaller image.

The choice and treatment of this photograph to illustrate a volume that is only peripherally concerned with soldier-photographers may suggest that by the year 2000 the Wehrmacht Exhibition had come to be associated not so much with the crimes of the Wehrmacht as with the moral issues involved in the witnessing, photographing, and photographic reproduction of those crimes. By contrast, no onlookers, with or without cameras, feature in the small clip from a photograph of an execution that was used on the cover of the original, German-language edition (even though the full photograph, reproduced on the inside cover, shows that soldiers did view the dead bodies). My argument is not that the editors had a part in the decision to crop or even to select the cover photograph of the English-language edition; nor indeed that the cropped image will have any measurable effect on the volume's small number of readers (not least because a monochrome green tint all but obscures the figures); my argument is rather that the operation of choosing and cropping the photograph is analogous to the way in which, in some scholarly writing, the soldier as photographer is first stripped of his other professional and private roles and then isolated further from his non-violent contexts in order to distill a purer form of a morally questionable gaze — "der Blick auf die Massenmorde"; "kalte Augen," "heiße Augen"[21] (the gaze that looks upon mass murders; cold eyes, hot eyes) — that lends itself to psychological analysis.

A further step in this process of "cropping" in scholarly writing is the sometimes explicit, sometimes silent construction of a soldier who keeps atrocity photographs in his wallet, side by side with photographs of his loved ones. The idea is first mentioned by Reifarth and Schmidt-Linsenhoff, who write of execution photographs:

> Die meisten Fotografien dieser Art wurden in den Brieftaschen von toten oder gefangenen Soldaten oder SS-Männern gefunden, häufig zusammen mit einem Bild ihrer Mutter, ihrer Verlobten, ihrer Familie.[22]

> [Most of the photographs of this type were found in the wallets of dead or captured soldiers or SS-men, often together with a picture of the man's mother, his fiancée, his family.]

No source is given for this information, and the writers do not claim that any of the photographs reproduced and analyzed in their article came from a soldier's wallet, whereas they do acknowledge that some of them came from photograph albums (which is not to say that those photographs could not previously have been kept in a wallet, simply that we cannot know whether they were or not). Yet because this statement is made early on, and in such a generalized form, it colors our reading of the images subsequently discussed.

The historians of the first Wehrmacht Exhibition corroborate the existence of the wallet phenomenon, if not its extent. The captions of twenty-one of the several hundred photographs displayed in the controversial Iron Cross installation (a set of display boards in the shape of a military medal) identify the source of the photograph as a soldier's wallet. Since many of the Iron Cross photographs are uncaptioned, it is unclear whether we are to understand that all the other photographs were definitely *not* found in soldiers' wallets or whether in some cases their provenance cannot be established. Whatever the case, Reifarth and Schmidt-Linsenhoff's generalization about "most" atrocity photographs is relativized by the Iron Cross, not only because photographs from soldier's wallets are in the minority, but also because only nine of the twenty-one photographs definitely retrieved from wallets depict the corpses of (putative or certain) victims of crimes. By silently narrowing their focus to two categories of photograph, Reifarth and Schmidt-Linsenhoff obscure the obvious but nevertheless significant fact that soldiers carried a variety of images in their wallets, not just family photographs and photographs of the dying or dead.

Kathrin Hoffmann-Curtius makes the photograph-in-the-wallet central to her programmatically titled article "Trophäen und Amulette. Die Fotografien von Wehrmachts- und SS-Verbrechen in den Brieftaschen der Soldaten" (Trophies and Amulets: Photographs of Wehrmacht and SS Crimes in the Wallets of Soldiers). Like other scholars writing at the turn of the millennium, she attempts to distance herself from Reifarth and Schmidt-Linsenhoff and Hüppauf.[23] In particular, she puts the atrocity photographs into both diachronic *and* synchronic contexts (on the one hand, pictorial traditions of the human body; on the other, prevailing conceptions of a soldierly death). She nevertheless follows the lead of earlier scholars in her exclusive focus on images of racial and political persecution and murder, narrowing her focus further to those retrieved from soldiers' wallets. On closer inspection this proves to be an argumentative construct rather than a statement of empirical fact, since she concedes that the Red Army, to whose endeavors we owe the largest archive of such photographs, collected material both from soldiers' wallets and from their packs, and, in addition, that photographs found their way back from the front in albums. She can therefore have no way of knowing which of the photographs she has viewed were found in a soldier's wallet rather than elsewhere among his belongings (certainly the images she reproduces that also appear in the first Wehrmacht Exhibition are not among those that the HIS identifies as coming from a wallet). Nevertheless, the wallet is a key to her thesis that atrocity photographs served as a protective charm: photographs of death carried on the body to ward off death.

Later scholars appear to take the wallet phenomenon for granted. In her thoughtful article about the failings of the two Wehrmacht Exhibitions, Miriam Arani writes

dass [. . .] die privaten Kriegsfotos aus den Brieftaschen deutscher Soldaten die physische Gewaltanwendung der deutschen Exekutive gegen die Zivilbevölkerung in den Kriegsgebieten sehr viel deutlicher zeigen als PK-Fotografien.[24]

[that [. . .] private war photographs from the wallets of German soldiers give a much clearer picture of the violence used by German soldiers against the civilian population in the war zones than do propaganda-corps photographs.]

This sentence is structured around a contrast between amateur and professional photography. Thus, the key word in the description of the soldiers' photographs is "privat," whereas the phrase "aus den Brieftaschen deutscher Soldaten" (from the wallets of German soldiers) is a superfluous descriptive detail, but all the more telling for that, suggesting as it does that the atrocity-photograph-in-the-wallet is an uncontroversial fact that the reader will readily assimilate into an already established scheme of information. A similar logical elision appears in an otherwise well-argued article by Helmut Lethen, in which he suggests that the first Wehrmacht Exhibition provoked emotional responses that the second did not:

> Der größte Stein des Anstoßes des alten Katalogs — die Fundstücke aus den Brieftaschen, in denen Familienfotos der Landser und Bilder Erhängter oder Erschossener nebeneinander lagen — ist in dem neuen entfernt. Die Präsentation dieser Mischung überließ den Betrachter der Frage, wie sich die Morde in die Privatheit der Familiengeschichten einmischen konnten.[25]

> [The biggest bone of contention in the old catalogue — the items retrieved from wallets, in which soldiers' family photographs were found next to pictures of people who had been hanged or shot — has been removed in the new catalogue. The way in which this mixture was presented left the viewer to ponder the question of how it was possible for the murders to intrude into the private sphere of family stories.]

In fact, the catalogue of the first Wehrmacht Exhibition at no point claims that the photographs retrieved from wallets were found alongside family snaps, let alone represents that juxtaposition visually.[26] That the wallet is a rhetorical shorthand becomes clear as Lethen proceeds to use it to evoke a second image, that of the rubbish heap of history (the place to which non-archived objects are consigned), whereas in the following, more discursive, sentence he speaks in the plural of the various places in which photographs were kept, of the "Tornister, Uniformjacken und Brieftaschen" (knapsacks, uniform jackets, and wallets). In these places, he says, soldiers ordered their photographs according to principles that remain little understood. That Bernd Boll later cites Lethen's concept of the "Ordnung der Brieftaschen" (ordering system of wallets), placing this expression in quotation marks though it is not used by Lethen, who writes rather of the "Ordnung der privaten Erinnerungsspeicher" (ordering system of private memory stores), only confirms the appeal of the image.[27]

I am not quarrelling with the fact that an unknown proportion of atrocity photographs were placed alongside family photographs, whether in wallets or in albums, nor that this phenomenon is deserving of analysis; but I am interested in what draws scholars to generalize the phenomenon and to give it prominence in their argumentation. Evidently the juxtaposition of the sacred and the profane promises the scholar access to an abnormal mentality that might yield information about how the crimes of the Nazi era could have happened. The question is whether one can understand that abnormality in isolation, without reference to the complex web of norms in which it was embedded.

Of course, the HIS can no more be held responsible for the work of those photo-historians writing after the first Wehrmacht Exhibition than it can for those — like Reifarth and Schmidt-Linsenhoff — writing before it, and in any case much of their work is very good. Nevertheless, it is possible to see a correspondence between the approaches of this group of scholars to the soldier-photographer and the approach of the HIS to its exhibition material. It would be wrong, however, to paint too black-and-white a picture in which the HIS lacks all photo-critical common sense and the DRM possesses it in abundance. In 1999 Petra Bopp, one of the organizers of the first Wehrmacht Exhibition, looked back at that exhibition's deployment of photographs, and while the tone of her article is perhaps unduly defensive, it offers evidence that the organizers' attitudes towards photographic display were more thoughtful than they have been given credit for and acknowledges the need for more research into the conditions under which photographs were produced.[28] In doing so it anticipates the role that *Fotofeldpost* would play a year later.

Photography and Normality

Fotofeldpost counters the reductive tendency in earlier work on Wehrmacht photography through two main arguments, one quantitative and one qualitative. The quantitative argument states that the overwhelming majority of photographs taken by soldiers were not of atrocities or scenes of persecution; that many soldier-photographers took no pictures at all of dead bodies; and that pictures of executions are no more common than pictures of those killed in battle.[29] The qualitative argument insists on understanding photography as a social practice, rather than as the sum of the images that result from it. Admittedly, Reifarth and Schmidt-Linsenhoff *had* hinted that the way in which images of persecution were framed depended partly on socially transmitted and regulated bodily practices (such as the conventions governing posing for a group photograph), but *Fotofeldpost* goes a great deal further, setting the proportionally tiny corpus of atrocity photographs squarely into a series of explanatory contexts that together constitute the norms of contemporary photographic practice. These include peacetime family photography, journalistic war photography, photography clubs, the regimental photographic culture, the *Feldpostbriefe* in which many photographs were sent home, the market for books and albums of military photographs, and advertising campaigns used by rival manufacturers to compete for the soldier-photographer's business. About half the

photographs reproduced in the *Fotofeldpost* catalogue take the form of fac-
similes of leaves from photograph albums, so that as many photographs as
possible remain embedded in the context in which the photographer
placed them; this means that the viewer is at least aware of the context that
is missing when photographs are reproduced singly.

The DRM's insistence on the limits of what we can ascertain from
photographs and on the impossibility, in most cases, of knowing what was
going on in the mind of the photographer can only really be understood as
a response to the speculative What-were-they-thinking-of? methodology of
earlier scholarship.[30] In particular, *Fotofeldpost* avoids assuming the worst
about the soldier-photographer, or, to put it another way, avoids constructing an immoral gaze in order then to analyze it. Reifarth and
Schmidt-Linsenhoff had speculated, without reference to evidence, that
soldier photographers were not just passive bystanders but executioners,
thus suggestively conflating witnessing with perpetration.[31] By contrast,
Jahn argues in the *Fotofeldpost* catalogue that executioners were not at
leisure to take photographs any more than soldiers in the thick of battle
were at leisure to photograph the action; execution photographs were
therefore generally taken by bystanders or by those who came across the
results of an execution some time after the event.[32] That does not, of
course, rule out the possibility that a given photographer may have committed equivalent excesses at other times, but it does uncouple the act of
photography from the act of violence in the absence of clear evidence of
their connection (and certainly, though it does not serve Jahn's argument
to mention it here, photographs do exist that implicate the photographer
very strongly in the crime depicted).

The ordering of the photographic material in *Fotofeldpost* counters
Verbrechen der Wehrmacht by suggestion rather than explicit argument.
The organizers of the HIS exhibition had not only isolated atrocity photographs from other subjects but also created sub-categories of atrocity:
the Iron Cross installation contained six collages of photographs with very
little explanatory text, each on a different theme, including "Juden-
quälen," "Galgen," and "Genickschüsse" (maltreatment of Jews, gallows,
and shots through the head). The repetition of similar shapes — of hanged
bodies, aimed guns, and dead bodies in ditches — worked suggestively,
creating the shocking impression of murder on a large scale and of the
photography of murder on a large scale, without giving the viewer any
fixed statistical scale by which to judge their extent. *Fotofeldpost* counters
this in two ways, but no less suggestively than the HIS. First, it subsumes
execution photographs under the double heading "Getötete — Ermordete"
(The Dead — The Murdered) and makes no distinction, on the exhibition
boards, between these categories, so that images of men and women killed
on the battlefield are interspersed with images of men and women killed
in non-combat operations. Thus, while the DRM acknowledges that

soldier-photographers did sometimes take photographs of the dying and the dead, it reminds the viewer that the context in which the person in the photograph died cannot always be reconstructed and suggests that, even where it can, to separate one category of dead from another is an artificial exercise (a position with which not everyone will agree).

Secondly, the handful of atrocity photographs is placed almost at the end of *Fotofeldpost*. Of course, the exhibition visitor is not obliged to stick to the prescribed order, but unlike the first Wehrmacht Exhibition, which had no "beginning" and was designed to adapt its shape to different exhibition spaces,[33] *Fotofeldpost* used a simple rectangular layout, running continuously around three sides of a room, with the longer sides divided into bays; only a row of display cases in the central space tempted the viewer to stray from a path around the room. Thus, regardless of whether visitors took up the invitation to it, a linear sequence was on offer, in the exhibition room as much as in the catalogue. In this sequence, the photographs of corpses are preceded by extensive contextual information about photographic practice in the 1930s and 1940s and by a much larger number of photographs that are not of dead bodies: images of the soldiers' military environment, of foreign landscapes, of local people, of destroyed towns and villages, and of prisoners of war. A single subsection follows, and provides a clear counterpoint: sanitized photographs of the German war dead. Given that no historical chronology underlies this order (soldiers did not photograph dead bodies at a later period in the war than they photographed destroyed houses, for instance) and given that the exhibition argues explicitly that executions were just one subject among many for the soldier-photographer, there is no reason why the execution photographs should *not* appear earlier on the display boards, unless the exhibition is deliberately responding to their perceived over-exposure in the Wehrmacht Exhibition. There is a similar sequence in Ulrike Schmiegelt's essay in the catalogue, which only arrives at the subject of atrocity photographs in the last few paragraphs.[34] The danger that the viewer will, out of habit, read a chronology into this order is illustrated by a review:

> Erst allmählich verwandelte sich diese nationale Fotosafari in einem wirklichen Krieg. Auf den kleinen Bildchen mit gezacktem Rahmen brennen Dörfer. Städte liegen in Ruinen. Zerschossene Panzer am Straßenrand. Der Feind: gefangen oder tot.[35]

> [Only gradually did this national photo-safari transform into a real war. In the little photographs with their saw-toothed edges, villages are burning. Towns lie in ruins. Burnt-out tanks on the side of the road. The enemy: captive or dead.]

An exhibition that concerns itself with the normalities of the Third Reich is inevitably going to be open to accusations that it engages in the wrong the kind of "normalization." My view is that this is not the case here, because despite the fact that *Fotofeldpost* insists that soldiers who photographed persecution or murder were the rare exception to the unsensational rule, it also states clearly that many of the photographs that the soldiers did take bear the traces of their socialization in Nazi Germany, particularly in their attitudes towards the populations of the occupied territories; and equally that almost no soldier-photographers betray either an obviously critical perspective of the Wehrmacht's endeavors or an obviously sympathetic view of the occupied population.[36]

Perhaps surprisingly, given the exhibition's studied empiricism, the essay with which Jahn introduces the catalogue invokes the "atrocity photograph in the wallet." His wording, however, hints at a shift in emphasis. Of execution photographs, he writes, "sie waren für viele eher Brieftaschenphotos, ähnlich der Pornografie"[37] (for many men they were more like the sort of photograph that one keeps in one's wallet, similar to pornography). Whereas other scholars cite the atrocity photograph in the wallet, with its explicit or implicit proximity to family photographs, as proof of a pathological depravity (the transgression of a boundary between the sacred and the profane), Jahn's comment implies that to begin to understand this depravity one would have to come at it from the side of normality, considering how a normal transgression of the boundary between the sacred and the profane (keeping pornography in a wallet alongside family photographs) shades into abnormality (treating pictures of dead bodies in ways that echo the treatment of pornography). While the empirical research that might illuminate the norms of photo storage in the Second World War is now all but impossible to carry out, there is nevertheless a value in envisaging its parameters. This, I think, is also Lethen's view when he cautions against privileging the historian's methods of ordering photographs over those of the original owner, which may be mistakenly dismissed as a lack of order simply because the system of ordering can no longer be reconstructed.

In the wake of *Fotofeldpost* there has been further empirical research into the practicalities of photography in the Wehrmacht, notably two articles by one of the organizers of the first Wehrmacht Exhibition, Bernd Boll, who both uses *Fotofeldpost* as a source and adopts its working methods. Among other things, Boll demonstrates that the dividing line between propaganda photography and amateur photography was surprisingly porous: that the army often used soldier-photographers to do the work of the propaganda corps and that the propaganda corps regularly sold photographs to the troops. He also argues that the well-documented prohibitions against taking photographs of executions, so important to psychoanalytical constructions of the soldier-photographer because they support the notion of a taboo, should be understood as one element in a wider institutionalization of amateur photography in the Wehrmacht, whose aim was to produce for posterity the "right" kind of photographic heritage. This is not to say that such institutional censorship was not oppressive; nor to play down the atrocious dishonesty that underlay the project of self-glorification; nevertheless, soldier-photographers are likely to have associated the regimental photographic culture as much with license as with prohibition. In an article on a related theme, Bopp is rather grudging in her recognition of *Fotofeldpost* (which, she implies, built on the foundations of *Verbrechen der Wehrmacht*), but nevertheless adopts the kind of cautious empirical reasoning exemplified by *Fotofeldpost*. She also carefully contextualizes the few atrocity photographs that she analyzes (revealing, for instance, what other scenes the soldier photographed before and after the dead bodies) and selects innocuous images for reproduction in preference to the scenes of death.[38]

While it is in the nature of the material that little is known of the context of the photographs shown in *Fotofeldpost*, and while this problem is acknowledged in the accompanying essays, the sparse and uneven captioning nevertheless sometimes leaves the viewer or reader disoriented. The photographic exhibition *Vor aller Augen*, shown in 2002–2003 by the museum Topographie des Terrors, works rather harder to contextualize its photographs and, where only limited information can be gleaned from them, to delineate precisely the contours and consequences of our ignorance.[39] It unites some of the best aspects of the two exhibitions that I have analyzed here: like the first Wehrmacht Exhibition it sets out to show that many ordinary people must have known about the inhumanities committed during the Third Reich because they photographed them and were photographed watching them, but it takes on board the lesson of *Fotofeldpost* that photographs of the crimes of the Third Reich cannot be displayed without an explanatory context that includes empirical data about the contemporary practice of photography.

Ulla Hahn's novel *Unscharfe Bilder*[40] (Blurred Images) can be read as a less successful bridge between the competing exhibitions than *Vor Aller Augen*. During the first Wehrmacht Exhibition the public's imagination was caught by several stories of people who recognized their fathers in photographs on display.[41] Hahn's novel is an imaginative elaboration of one such news item, exploring the effects on a father-daughter relationship of the sudden revelation of the father's complicity in a war crime. Though the plot revolves around the first Wehrmacht Exhibition, thinly disguised with the title *Verbrechen im Osten* (Crimes in the East), and though Hahn acknowledges as one of her sources the Heer and Naumann volume, the first and warmest note of thanks in her acknowledgments goes to the DRM, without whose friendly support, she says, she could not have written the work.[42] While Hahn may have seen earlier exhibitions by the DRM, her concern with the everyday life of the Wehrmacht soldier and with photographic images (though not, curiously, with the photographer) suggests that she has drawn on *Fotofeldpost*.

Unscharfe Bilder is therefore a novel set at the time of the first Wehrmacht Exhibition that views that exhibition, anachronistically, through the lens of subsequent work by the DRM. It will come as no surprise, therefore, that its plot involves a memory contest. The contest between the approaches of the HIS and the DRM is recast as a generational conflict and, in the process, somewhat caricatured. The daughter is aligned with the HIS inasmuch as she adopts an accusatory stance, insisting that her father account for the atrocity photographs and brooking no exculpatory diversions into the norms of war; her father is aligned with DRM inasmuch as he insists on understanding the context in which the ordinary soldier found himself. As the novel's title hints, the contest is styled as a struggle between two sets of images: the images in *Verbrechen im Osten* and the father's mental images of his own and his fellow soldiers' suffering. Thus, after describing the horrors of the battlefield, the father rejects the visual record constructed by the exhibition catalogue: "Siehst du! Von solchen Bildern, von meinen Toten, von meinen Freunden und Kameraden habe ich in deinem Buch kein Bild gesehen"[43] (There you are, you see! I haven't seen a single picture in your book of images like that, of the dead people that I knew, of my friends). The daughter, on the other hand, fears that if she adopts her father's visual perspective the war will become so normalized that she will lose her moral bearings:

> Die Bilder, die sie dem Vater gebracht hatte, waren nun auch in ihr überschattet von den seinen, den blutigen Bildern seiner Erinnerung. Sie durfte das nicht zulassen. Wo waren die Mörder geblieben?[44]

> [The pictures she had brought for her father were now overshadowed by his pictures, the bloody pictures in his memory. She mustn't allow that to happen. Where had all the murderers gone?]

Hahn's novel thus constructs a polarized conflict between an absolute moral stance and a relativizing one. The DRM did relativize, in the positive sense of putting atrocity photographs into a series of contextual frames, but not in the crude way envisaged by Hahn, which attempts to set German suffering against the suffering of the victims of systematized murder. My contention here is not that Hahn has misunderstood *Fotofeldpost* but that one can use her text to throw into relief the more nuanced relativization attempted by the exhibition.

In her review for *Frankfurter Rundschau*, Ute Frings imagines the effect that *Fotofeldpost* will have on war veterans and, much like Hahn, attributes to these imaginary veterans a defensive, apologist response which results in a struggle between two competing sets of images:

> Gegen die bohrenden Fragen, die auf ihr Gewissen zielen, werden sie die Leichen der toten Kameraden mobilisieren, die sie im blinden Fleck ihrer fotographisch fixierten Kriegserinnerungen versteckt hatten. Die Bilder

kommen zurück. Die als Papierbildchen veröffentlichten und die unveröffentlichten, die nur der individuellen Erinnerung angehören. Dass sich die Bilder der Erinnerung zuletzt als die eindrücklicheren erweisen, ist die späte Rache der Toten an den Lebenden.[45]

[Faced with probing questions that prick their conscience they will mobilize the corpses of their dead comrades, which they had hidden in the blind spot of their photographically fixed war memories. The images return. Those that have been published in the papers and the unpublished ones, which belong solely to individual memory. The fact that the pictures stored in memory prove ultimately to be the more forceful represents the belated revenge of the dead on the living.]

I cannot help feeling that this fantasy, which simultaneously puts veterans in the wrong for weighing the crimes of the Third Reich against German suffering and punishes them by condemning them to the haunting presence of the undead, is not so much the belated revenge of the dead on the living as the revenge of a left-leaning journalist on a social group from whom she feels compelled to distance herself. This brings me back to my uneasy feeling that avowedly liberal academic research may help to construct or validate mythical images of the German amateur soldier-photographer, who, once reduced to the act of taking atrocity photographs, is transformed into an iconic, culpable bystander and a warning example to all right-thinking Germans. While I claim no special immunity from such simplifications, my argument has been that the achievement of the DRM exhibition *Fotofeldpost* is to avoid this tendency towards mythicization while simultaneously avoiding the construction of an alternative myth of the "normal" soldier.

Notes

[1] *Vernichtungskrieg: Verbrechen der Wehrmacht 1941 bis 1944* (Hamburg: Hamburger Edition, 1996); *Verbrechen der Wehrmacht: Dimensionen des Vernichtungskrieges 1941–1944* (Hamburg: Hamburger Edition, 2002).

[2] *Fotofeldpost: Geknipste Kriegserlebnisse 1939–1945* (Berlin: Elefanten, 2000).

[3] For ease of reference I use the popular shorthand "the first Wehrmacht Exhibition" and "the second Wehrmacht Exhibition" while acknowledging that these designations are not entirely satisfactory, since they might be taken to imply that the exhibitions dealt with the Wehrmacht as a whole rather than one aspect of Wehrmacht policy and practice.

[4] Anonymous, "Landser auf dem Donnerbalken," *Der Spiegel*, 27 March 2000; Philipp Gessler, "Die andere Wehrmachtsausstellung," *Tageszeitung*, 2 April 2000.

[5] Jahn's view was reported by several journalists, among them Sven Felix Kellerhoff, "Heile Kriegswelt," *Berliner Morgenpost*, 30 March 2000.

[6] Peter Jahn to Chloe Paver, 17 May 2004.

[7] Kellerhoff, "Heile Kriegswelt."

[8] I am grateful to Peter Jahn for this last figure and for information in the rest of this paragraph. No count was kept of visitors to *Fotofeldpost*: the estimate is based on the total of 40,000 visitors to the museum in 2000 and assumes that during the exhibition's ten-week run visitor numbers were higher than in weeks when no special exhibition was showing at the museum.

[9] http://www.verbrechen-der-wehrmacht.de

[10] Hamburger Institut für Sozialforschung, ed., *Verbrechen der Wehrmacht: Dimensionen des Vernichtungskrieges 1941–1944*, DVD (Hamburg: Hamburger Edition, 2004).

[11] Regine Klose-Wolf to Chloe Paver, 1 June 2004.

[12] For instance Miriam Y. Arani, " 'Und an den Fotos entzündete sich die Kritik': Die 'Wehrmachtsausstellung,' deren Kritik und die Neukonzeption. Ein Beitrag aus fotohistorisch-quellenkritischer Sicht," *Fotogeschichte* 85/86 (2002): 97–124.

[13] Bill Niven, *Facing the Nazi Past: United Germany and the Legacy of the Third Reich* (London and New York: Routledge, 2002), 154.

[14] Chloe Paver, *Refractions of the Third Reich in German and Austrian Fiction and Film* (Oxford: Oxford UP, forthcoming).

[15] Marianne Hirsch, *Family Frames: Photography, Narratives and Postmemory* (Cambridge, MA & London: Harvard UP, 1997).

[16] Dieter Reifarth and Viktoria Schmidt-Linsenhoff, "Die Kamera der Täter," in Hannes Heer & Klaus Naumann, eds., *Vernichtungskrieg: Verbrechen der Wehrmacht 1941 bis 1944*, 475–503 (first published 1983) and Bernd Hüppauf, "Der entleerte Blick hinter der Kamera," in Heer and Naumann, 504–27.

[17] Reifarth and Schmidt-Linsenhoff, "Die Kamera der Täter," 486.

[18] Judith Levin and Daniel Uzel, "Ordinary Men, Extraordinary Photos," *Yad Vashem Studies* 26 (1998): 265–93; Alexander B. Rossino, "Eastern Europe through German Eyes. Soldiers' Photographs 1939–42," *History of Photography* 23 (1999): 313–21.

[19] Hannes Heer and Klaus Naumann, eds., *War of Extermination: The German Military in World War II 1941–1944* (Oxford: Berghahn, 2000). The cover image can be viewed online at Amazon or another bookseller.

[20] *Fotofeldpost*, 45.

[21] Hüppauf, "Der entleerte Blick," 504; Reifarth & Schmidt-Linsenhoff, "Die Kamera der Täter," 500.

[22] Reifarth & Schmidt-Linsenhoff, "Die Kamera der Täter," 481.

[23] Kathrin Hoffmann-Curtius, "Trophäen und Amulette. Die Fotografien von Wehrmachts- und SS-Verbrechen in den Brieftaschen der Soldaten," *Fotogeschichte* 78 (2000): 63–76.

[24] Arani, " 'Und an den Fotos entzündete sich die Kritik,' " 118.

[25] Helmut Lethen, "Der Text der Historiografie und der Wunsch nach einer physikalischen Spur. Das Problem der Fotografie in den beiden Wehrmachtsaustellungen," *Zeitgeschichte* 29 (2002): 76–86; here: 84.

26 Possibly Lethen is thinking of Heer and Naumann, who reproduce a small selection of photographs (418–25) that includes two family photographs and photographs of an execution, though the information about their origins and transmission is so exasperatingly vague that it is impossible to conclude anything concrete from this juxtaposition.

27 Bernd Boll, "Vom Album ins Archiv. Zur Überlieferung privater Fotografien aus dem Zweiten Weltkrieg," in Anton Holzer, ed., *Mit der Kamera bewaffnet: Krieg und Fotografie* (Marburg: Jonas, 2003), 167–78; here: 174.

28 Petra Bopp, " 'Wo sind die Augenzeugen, wo ihre Fotos?,' " in *Eine Ausstellung und ihre Folgen*, 198–229.

29 *Fotofeldpost*, 10, 30.

30 *Fotofeldpost*, 10, 11, 118.

31 "Es ist möglich, daß der Amateurfotograf, wenn er selbst einem 'Partisanen' die Schlinge um den Hals legt oder den Genickschuß vollzieht, einen Kameraden bittet, an seiner Stelle auf den Auslöser zu drücken, damit er selbst und sein 'Höhepunkt' mit ins Bild kommen" (It is possible that the amateur photographer, when he's the one who is putting a noose around the neck of a 'partisan' or delivering the shot to the head, asks another soldier to press the shutter in his place, so that he and his 'special moment' feature in the picture.) (Reifarth & Schmidt-Linsenhoff, 479).

32 *Fotofeldpost*, 10.

33 Klose-Wolf to Chloe Paver, 1 June 2004.

34 Ulrike Schmiegelt, " 'Macht euch um mich keine Sorgen . . .,' " *Fotofeldpost*, 23–31; here: 30.

35 Ute Frings, "Bilder der Erinnerung," *Frankfurter Rundschau* 14 April 2000.

36 *Fotofeldpost*, 10, 118, 134.

37 *Fotofeldpost*, 10.

38 Petra Bopp, "Fremde im Visier. Private Fotografien von Wehrmachtssoldaten," in Holzer, *Mit der Kamera bewaffnet*, 97–117.

39 Klaus Hesse & Philipp Springer, eds., *Vor aller Augen: Fotodokumente des nationalsozialistischen Terrors in der Provinz* (Essen: Klartext, 2002).

40 Ulla Hahn, *Unscharfe Bilder* (Munich: Deutsche Verlags-Anstalt, 2003).

41 Niven, *Facing the Nazi Past*, 159; Bopp claims that such incidents happened at every station on the exhibition's journey, though the evidence appears to be anecdotal ("'Wo sind die Augenzeugen?,' " 202).

42 Since the curator of the museum has no knowledge of this support, Hahn was perhaps assisted by staff in the exhibition rooms.

43 Hahn, *Unscharfe Bilder*, 40.

44 Hahn, *Unscharfe Bilder*, 43.

45 Frings, "Bilder der Erinnerung."

6: German Crossroads: Visions of the Past in German Cinema after Reunification

Matthias Fiedler

> Der Strom der Geschichte floß. Zuweilen trat der Strom über die
> Ufer. Er überschwemmte das Land mit Geschichte.
> — Wolfgang Koeppen, *Tauben im Gras*
>
> [The stream of history was flowing. Now and then, it burst its banks
> and flooded the country with history.]

IF ONE SUBSTITUTES THE TERM "memory" for "history" in the above quotation from Wolfgang Koeppen's 1951 novel *Tauben im Gras* (Pigeons
in the Grass), an accurate description of the intellectual atmosphere in postunification Germany emerges. For at least two decades now almost every
public utterance about the Third Reich — political, cultural, or artistic —
has ignited fierce and passionate memory contests. The inaugural ceremony of the *Neue Wache* in Berlin, Martin Walser's speech in the *Frankfurter Paulskirche*, the erection of a Holocaust memorial in Berlin, the
Crimes of the Wehrmacht exhibition, all these are examples of the ferocity of
public memory contests. Additionally, publications by Daniel Goldhagen,
Jörg Friedrich, and most recently Götz Aly, as well as renegotiations of the
National Socialist past in German literature (most recently in the form of
autobiographical and family narratives) show that Germany is flooded by a
constant stream of contentious memory texts, and that this proliferation
has found its echo in the academic world.

Interesting to note, however, is the fact that the abundance of German
films about the Third Reich made since 1990 has been all but ignored by
academic critics.[1] The following essay suggests two closely interrelated
explanations of why this development in German film has not been dealt
with sufficiently by academics in the same way as other memory contests
surrounding the Third Reich. Furthermore, the very thematization of the
Third Reich in German films since 1990 needs to be reconsidered; in contrast to academic indifference, it suggests that cinema is more than a mere
theme park for modern entertainment and diversion.

The German Predicament in Film Studies

In the academic field of German Studies it seems as if all films about Germany's National Socialist past are evaluated as trivial, commercial, and historically inaccurate. What is striking about this discourse is the reproachful tone it adopts when assessing these films. Peter Reichel's latest study *Erfundene Erinnerung: Weltkrieg und Judenmord in Film und Theater* (Invented Memory: World War and the Jewish Genocide in Film and Theater) proves this point in excess.[2] It repeatedly shows that since 1945 feature films about the Third Reich have been criticized either for trivial or commercial exploitation of the past or for not being true to historical facts. Labeled as nostalgic or biased in their approach to history, none of these "visions of the past" seem to have met the critics' standards. And yet, despite the broadness of Reichel's study, he ultimately fails to question the viability of his own standards. Ironically, his findings reinforce the impression that academic discourse marginalizes cinematic approaches to history; this effectively undermines the premise of his own study. Why should we continue to study films if the outcome of our analysis is from the outset poised to dismiss what we examine and if all that interests us is the question whether a film trivializes or commercializes the past? Reichel's study shows that what I call the reproachful discourse is in danger of becoming a vicious and self-perpetuating circle of analysis. I propose that if we do not want to lose sight of what feature films have to contribute to current debates on memory, a renegotiation of the very standards that guide the analysis of historical films is indispensable.

Even the briefest attempt at such a renegotiation has to look at what underpins and guides the analysis, and in retrospect it appears as if a distinct and influential intellectual tradition in Germany has somehow promoted reservations about the artistic, aesthetic, and cultural value of historical feature films in general. As a phenomenon of popular or mass culture they have been met, observed, and judged from the very beginning with a suspicious eye. In the founding era of film theory, scholars like Rudolf Arnheim, Walter Benjamin, and others negotiated the cinema's position within the larger framework of art. And, as so often, it was Benjamin who set the tone for the following discussion: even though he praises film in *Das Kunstwerk im Zeitalter seiner technischen Reproduzierbarkeit*[3] (The Work of Art in the Age of Mechanical Reproduction, 1935) as a facilitator of a modern mode of perception, he is highly ambivalent about feature films. The key word Benjamin uses in relation to the emerging cinema culture is "Zerstreuung" (distraction), a notion that in opposition to "Sammlung" (concentration) is central to his assessment of modern film.[4] As the new paradigm for the modern perception of art, distraction for Benjamin does not necessarily entail passivity. On the contrary, echoing the values of Bertolt Brecht's epic theater with its anti-illusionist stance as the ideal of how art should guide perception, he points out that the shock effect of montage in film has the potential to animate the masses for revolutionary change.[5] However, the state of distraction in which the audience is held by this new form of art also carries a potential danger. One should bear in mind, of course, that Benjamin's essay seeks to analyze the exploitation of art by fascism in the 1930s, and he claims that modern art, instead of being based on ritual, is based on a different practice: that of politics. It is furthermore the commercial exploitation of film by a capitalist film industry that poses the biggest threat by voluntarily distracting the audience for its own means. And this is where Benjamin's initially positive evaluation of cinema becomes ambivalent. Aimed at mass distribution and high consumption, cinema is seen not only as a new form of modern perception, but also as a threat to the aesthetic standards of "high culture." In its tendency to create a standardized and homogenous cultural product that ensures economic success, it trivializes art by turning it into a commodity. The audience as modern *flâneurs* — a figure described by Benjamin as the paradigm of modern men held in a state of distraction by the cultural industry — is easily seduced by the capitalist film industry on its stroll between the trivialization and commodification of art.[6] The latter became one of the main targets of the *Frankfurt School*. In Max Horkheimer's and Theodor W. Adorno's *Die Dialektik der Aufklärung* (Dialectic of Enlightenment, 1947) the cinéaste — somewhat resentfully — reads: "Autos, Bomben und Film halten so lange das Ganze zusammen, bis ihr nivellierendes Element am Unrecht selbst, dem es dient, seine Kraft erweist"[7] (Automobiles, bombs, and movies keep the whole thing together until their leveling element shows its strength in the very wrong it furthers). Considering the huge impact of the Frankfurt School and Walter Benjamin on subsequent generations of German academics and particularly on theories of mass culture, it is not surprising that cinema as the modern representative par excellence of popular culture encountered an often disapproving reception after 1945. Especially in the early stages of mass culture theory, popular culture with its focus on entertainment and the mass audience was discussed as a key player in processes of cultural decline, and with its appeal to the less educated masses cinema was considered a cornerstone of growing popular culture. And yet, the critical assessments of film and cinema by Adorno and Horkheimer, and to a lesser extent by Benjamin, must be understood and placed within the historical background of their writings: the rise of fascism in Germany.

This contextual perspective on film also arises in the works of the most influential German scholar in the field of film studies: Siegfried Kracauer. The third formative aspect of the reproachful discourse in German film studies crystallizes in his writing. Kracauer's strong preference for realism and historical accuracy in cinematic depictions of the outside world, as put forward in his *Theory of Film*,[8] clearly reflects a suspicion of feature films conditioned by the abuse of visual media during the Third Reich. Thus, looking at subsequent generations of film critics and filmmakers it becomes obvious that the manipulation of moving pictures for propaganda means left its mark on how German historical films were produced and perceived. In 1976, however, the German filmmaker Wim Wenders suggested a more circumspect view of feature films about the German past, stating once and for all that a certain degree of suspicion was inevitable in Germany after the National Socialist era, because "niemals zuvor und in keinem anderen Land ist so gewissenlos mit Bildern und der Sprache umgegangen worden wie hier, nie zuvor und nirgendwo sind diese so sehr zum Transport von Lügen erniedrigt worden"[9] (never before and in no other country have images and language been abused so unscrupulously as here, never before and nowhere else have they been debased so deeply as vehicles to transmit lies).

The large quantity of commercially successful films about the Third Reich that has been produced in Germany after reunification signals a departure from such reservations among German filmmakers. And as I will argue in the following, this new departure in German cinema asks the film critic and analyst to question his or her analytic standards.

The National Socialist Past in German Cinema after Reunification

Postunification German feature films about the National Socialist past, I argue, can be divided into two groups. Historical films like *Stalingrad* (Joseph Vilsmaier, 1992), *Viehjud Levi* (Jew-Boy Levi, Didi Danquart, 1999), *Comedian Harmonists* (Joseph Vilsmaier, 1997), *Aimée & Jaguar* (Max Färberböck, 1999), *Rosenstraße* (Margarethe von Trotta, 2003), and most recently *Der Untergang* (Downfall, Oliver Hirschbiegel, 2004), *Napola* (Dennis Gansel, 2004), and *Der neunte Tag* (The Ninth Day, Volker Schlöndorff, 2004) try to recreate or reframe on screen a certain time and place in the historical period of Nazism. Common features of most of these films are the importance of production design and a narrative that — in its concentration on character and linear narration — follows more or less the classical pattern of Hollywood cinema. Lutz Koepnick has categorized these cinematic depictions of the past as *heritage films*, which "present historical epochs from the perspective of post-memory" because they "address viewers whose entire knowledge of these events is based on various media of cultural transmission."[10] In his attempt to evaluate "the heritage films' representation of history," he argues that "we must develop terms which bring into relief how these films try to revive the past and bridge the discontinuities of history" (77). The outcome of his analysis, however, once again reiterates the common view that "most of the German heritage films articulate nostalgia for the aesthetic pleasure and symbolic inventories of modern German mass culture" (80). Koepnick therefore fails to explain how those representations contribute to current debates from the "perspective of postmemory." Postmemory is a recent concept in the field of memory theory. It was developed by Marianne Hirsch in an attempt to theorize the transmission of memory between parents who had suffered through and survived the Holocaust and their children who had to live with the consequences of their parents' trauma.[11] Hirsch also argues, however, that, beyond the Holocaust, postmemory can mean more generally the constructed memory of an event that one did not experience oneself but that has been passed on or mediated to a younger generation through a series of narratives and images. Postmemory is what happens when this non-experiential generation tries to reconstruct the memory of an event that they did not live through. Thus, while postmemory often takes a documentary approach to the past, relying on photographs, diaries, letters, and memoirs, it also tends towards fictionalization and imaginative investment on the part of the individual who attempts to construct an image of the past.

The notion of postmemory could also be applied to the second group of films I discuss later in this essay. These include: *Nichts als die Wahrheit* (Nothing but the Truth, Roland Suso Richter, 1999), *Die blinde Kuh* (The Blind Cow, Nikolaus Schilling, 1994), and *Die Spur des Bernsteinzimmers* (Trail of the Amber Room, Roland Gräf, 1992). These films form a distinct second category. Set in 1990s Germany, they assess and negotiate the significance of certain aspects of the past for the present. Even though very different in style, genre, and target audience, all these films have a specific narrative structure in common: something from the past reappears in the present and initiates a kind of quest that explores and negotiates the past, thereby establishing its importance for the present. Thus, this second group of films deals with memory processes more overtly than historical films that are primarily set in the past.

In the following, I will analyze a selection of films from both groups — historical films and those films that negotiate the past from a clear vantage point in the present — with a view to showing that there is a need to modify the conventional analytic framework through which feature films are often perceived. According to Anton Kaes, "films signify something not in *abstracto*, but concretely at a certain moment in time, at a certain place, and for a certain audience."[12] If this is true, critical analysis has to reflect on cinema as an important cultural practice of our time that accumulates and circulates symbolic representations and contributes to public debates to a considerable degree.[13]

Visions of the Past

In her study *German National Cinema*, Sabine Hake summarizes her view of historical German films of the 1990s by claiming:

As if to confirm the diagnosis by postmodern theoreticians of the gradual disappearance of history into simulation and spectacle, the new attempts at coming to terms with the past seemed at once more conventional in their reliance on the identificatory effects of classical narrative and more conservative in the validation of the personal in opposition to the political.[14]

The strategy of argumentation that follows on from this claim in Hake's study clearly reveals the pitfalls of the reproachful discourse discussed earlier. Focusing on the films of Joseph Vilsmaier — according to her, "the most successful [German] director-producer-cinematographer of the 1990s" — Hake labels his work "revisionist" by stating that his "films contribute further to the normalisation of German history by reducing the recent past to a visual spectacle" (187). The equation of commercial success with trivialization, or, even worse, revision of the past through the reduction of history to spectacle seems to justify her refusal to analyze these films critically. Hake's study, therefore, is a fine example of how basic presumption (commercial success equals historical simplification) preempts evaluation and analysis in the reproachful discourse. That these historical films of the 1990s have attracted a mass audience, however, makes it all the more relevant to analyze their cinematic visions of the past.

To begin with, the term "historical film" needs further specification. According to the historian Robert A. Rosenstone, historical films can be divided into three categories: "History as drama, history as document, and history as experiment."[15] While films of the first two categories differ in form (documentary vs. feature film), they are, according to Rosenstone, "linked by [the] notion of the screen as a window onto a realistic world" (54). Both forms have in common that they tell "history as a story of a closed, completed, and simple past" that often "emotionalizes, personalizes, and dramatizes" the "story of individuals" (55–56). Historical films presenting history as an experiment on the other hand differ, as Rosenstone points out, in their construction of the historical world: they do "not make the same claim on us as [. . .] the realist film. Rather than opening a window directly onto the past [they] open a window onto a different way of thinking about the past" (58). Drawing on Rosenstone's categories, most of the films discussed in this first section represent history as drama. My analysis of *Rosenstraße* and *Der Untergang* will show, however, that a further distinction of this category is necessary because even though these films present history as drama, I would argue that they employ certain narrative strategies that shift the focus to a representation of history primarily as memory.

From the outset Joseph Vilsmaier's highly successful film *Stalingrad* claims its place in Rosenstone's first category. To a German audience in particular, the single word of the title refers to a defining moment of German military history in the Second World War and furthermore evokes a myth that is highly significant for German cultural memory: the battle of the Sixth Army in Stalingrad. The historicity of the film is reiterated by opening credits that read like an introduction to a history book. This not only confirms what Rosenstone has described as the "opening of a window directly onto the past"; it also communicates this opening as an obliteration of the temporal gap between now and then. The effect is further stressed by the realism of a mise-en-scène that in its usage of color and setting naturalizes the pastness of the events on screen. In other words, the film's production values combine to create the impression that what is dramatized before our eyes is in fact what actually happened. Vilsmaier's naturalization of the past thus carries an implicit truth claim regarding the authenticity of the events depicted. And it is this cinematic emphasis on the naturalization of the past with its implicit claim to authenticity that leaves most Vilsmaier films open to the accusation of revisionism. In the totalizing cinematic world of his movies there is very little space left for the audience to recognize that the events presented on screen are nothing more than one possible reading of the past.

Let us ascertain more closely exactly what reading of the past is conveyed in *Stalingrad*. From the establishing shot that shows the soldiers on their *Fronturlaub* (leave from the front, in this case in Italy), to the last shot, where the camera zooms in on two of the main characters dying in the snow, the film leaves no doubt that its focus is the "ordinary soldier" of the German *Wehrmacht*. Equally, there is no doubt about how these "ordinary soldiers" should be perceived by the audience: in one of the key scenes the protagonists take part in the execution of Russian civilians. The recurring line "Was kann ich tun?" (What am I to do?) and close-ups of the hesitant and terrified faces of the soldiers are juxtaposed with the dominant figure of their superior officer and with the fearful expressions on the faces of the Russian civilians. Thus, long before the sound of bullets puts a final end to the increasing tension of this scene the soldiers are represented as individuals who are forced against their will to commit a crime that betrays the very humanity — the ordinariness of these soldiers — that the film has highlighted up to this point. Many previous scenes, for example, portray the importance of comradeship, honesty, and bravery among the soldiers. In establishing the humanity of the main characters and representing the ordinary German soldier as the victim of an unjust system, *Stalingrad* not only takes sides but invites the audience to sympathize with its anti-heroes. This cinematic attempt to create empathy with the protagonists on screen is further enhanced in the film's battle scenes. The camera position and angle used in the final scene in particular draw the audience behind the German front line; the visual language employed here is clearly reminiscent of the perspective used by the weekly newsreels from the front during the Second World War. Consequently, all that can be seen of the enemy is their tanks, as camera perspective reduces them to an anonymous and de-individualized mass; by contrast, the audience can easily identify the individual faces and distinct figures of the German soldiers.

The most telling effect in this scene, however, is created by the use of cinematic techniques that manipulate the viewer into identification with the German soldiers. The entire agonizing episode is shot in a way that makes it almost unbearable to watch. Edited in a swift and staccato pace, the whole scene is permeated by intense sounds of combat and horrifying images of dying soldiers. At the very end of the scene the sound level reaches its crescendo just as we see one of the protagonists desperately attempting to put on a pair of boots he has taken from a dying soldier. Suddenly there is silence and all we hear is his deeply satisfied comment: "Passt!" (They fit!). The audience too must share the soldier's sense of relief, if for reasons different to him; after more than ten minutes exposure to an onslaught of images and a level of noise that is physically hard to endure, it is gratifying to have the scene end on this manageable note. There is also the shared sense of righteousness around the boot-theft; after a sequence of events that is filmed in such a way as to emphasize the German soldiers' plight and individuality, the audience somehow feels that this individual soldier's opportunism is utterly justified.

The film's attempt to lure the audience into a feeling of solidarity and identification with the ordinary German soldiers does more than present a war fought by German soldiers as a historical spectacle. It can also be seen as a voice in the ongoing debate about the memory of the German soldier. In its effort to establish German soldiers as betrayed national heroes, it explicitly challenges the controversial way they were portrayed in the *Crimes of the Wehrmacht* exhibition.[16] Thus, as a cultural practice that aims at a large audience, the contribution of films like *Stalingrad* to current debates on cultural memory should not be underestimated. For *Stalingrad*'s highly problematic approach to the past is not determined by the debate on the "ordinary German soldiers" nor by efforts to normalize German history. The film's problems arise through its highly selective postmemory perspective that has dispensed with the need to critique cultural memory processes at a juncture when we are increasingly reliant on mediated images of the past. Instead, the film's postmemory reconstruction opts to whitewash the German war effort by focusing on the individual soldier.

Thus, as a highly effective disseminator of such controversial, ethically questionable yet tempting versions of history, popular film should be taken seriously. It is an influential and far-reaching cultural practice, and this is what makes Vilsmaier's persuasive depiction of the German soldier potentially dangerous. The film's visual language seeks to make empathetic identification possible for an audience that can no longer confirm its viewpoint through engagement with eyewitnesses. By opening a window onto the past without questioning this process, *Stalingrad* represents the drama of the German soldiers in the Second World War as authentic event, thus obliterating the fact that what is being presented on screen is only a mediated vision of the past. In other words, the filmic representation of the past is at least twice removed from the historical event it claims to portray so accurately. First, as a film it is a fictional reconstruction of an event in the past, and second, it is doubly fictional when we consider that it relies on media such as history books, memoirs, and other documents for information about this event. At no point in this process of postmemory reconstruction can the authentic event feature as an authentic event, even if it attempts to strike this chord. The truth is that the event is represented to the audience at the end of a process of necessary mediation: the more the narration of the event gets passed on from one medium to the next — from document to history book, from book to film script, from film script to film itself — the more it is likely to become distorted into an interpretation of sources as opposed to an interpretation of the event, thereby becoming a fictional and potentially tendentious account of history.

That this is not true for every historical film that presents history as drama can be observed in films like Max Färberböck's *Aimée & Jaguar* or Margarethe von Trotta's *Rosenstraße*, which, despite their concentration on personal stories, avoid creating a totalizing cinematic past. Set in 1990s Germany, both films establish a narrative perspective that confirms the subjective view of history that is presented retrospectively on screen. And yet, even though films like *Aimée & Jaguar* and *Rosenstraße* employ a melodramatic narrative, they do not present history primarily as drama or document but as memory. While the narrative structure of these films prevents them from qualifying as representations of history as experiment, nevertheless they do something to the representation of history not captured by any of Rosenstone's categories. For this reason I expand his theory to include a fourth category of historical film: films that represent history as memory.

Rosenstraße is the most remarkable cinematic depiction of this interrelation between history and memory among recent historical films; thus my analysis focuses on this particular film. The film begins in 1990s New York, where the audience is confronted by the silent face of Ruth Weinstein (Jutta Lampe), a Jewish woman who has just lost her husband. The first scene, in which we see Ruth preparing for a Jewish mourning ceremony, leaves no doubt that her silence is due not only to her bereavement but also to her experiences in the past. As the camera zooms in to a close-up of her silent and grieving face, a short historical flashback appears showing the face of another woman. This technique of switching from the present to the past, using Ruth's face as a cinematic gateway, is repeated twice in the first scene and is followed by a discussion with her daughter Hannah (Maria Schrader), who tries unsuccessfully to break her mother's silence. Knowing that whatever happened to her mother still affects the whole family, and having met an old friend of her mother's who indicated that the mother's secret is to be discovered only in Germany, Hannah decides to leave for Berlin to find Lena Fischer (Doris Schade), who adopted her mother after her family was deported to the death camps. Disguised as an American journalist, Hannah frequently visits the ninety-year-old Fischer, who tells her the story of a group of "Aryan" women who in 1943 successfully protested against the imprisonment of their Jewish husbands. From Lena she also learns that Ruth's "Aryan" father did not show the same bravery as the women portrayed in the film but deserted her mother and therefore exposed her to deportation.

Although the historical narrative presented in *Rosenstraße* reveals noteworthy aspects of resistance against the National Socialist regime, it is the film's cinematographic reconstruction of the past that is most remarkable. For the audience the first two historical flashbacks are obscured by the fact that no explanation or context is given other than the close-up of Ruth's face before the cut. Thus, we can assume that what we see is a traumatic memory of her childhood. Instead of granting access to the past, the flashbacks are therefore explicitly marked as personal memories unattainable for anyone but Ruth. When Hannah, through her mother's rejection of her marriage to a non-Jewish man, realizes that her mother's bottled-up memories are affecting her present life, she decides to try to unlock these memories. At first glance, the interview scenes in Lena Fischer's flat emphasize the similarities between the two older women through mise-en-scène. Lit by candles and decorated with photographs and mirrors, the corresponding interiors of Lena's and Ruth's flats generate a strong visual link between the two women. Hannah's interviews reveal, however, that in Lena she has found what she was looking for: an eyewitness who is not only willing to talk about the past but who believes in the importance of passing on her experiences to the next generation. From this moment in the film the historical flashbacks become more frequent, longer, and more meaningful. The inaccessibility of suppressed memory contrasts with the openness of memories that are freely transmitted from one medium to the next, a difference that is further emphasized by the film's gradual replacement of close-ups of faces with close-ups of recording machines or other modern technological devices.

By making this cinematic distinction between suppressed and related memories, *Rosenstraße* claims its place in current memory contests where the question of transgenerational memory and silence — the internalization of war memories in the individual — becomes increasingly important. The utopian ending of the film further asserts the importance of intergenerational dialogue for unlocking a traumatic past that will continue to disrupt the present unless it is made accessible to subsequent generations. Hannah's successful excavation of her mother's suppressed memories mirrors the successful resistance of the women in the historical narrative.

Through this parallel a case is made for the importance of working through the past rather than suppressing it. From this perspective, the film's opening sequence, which juxtaposes shots of modern architecture with those of Jewish cemeteries, can be seen as a visual metaphor for the film's underlying proposition: that the fundamental link between past atrocities and the present is to be understood only through dialogue. Thus, in presenting history as memory *Rosenstraße* highlights the fact that for the younger generation the past is accessible only through related and shared memories. And yet, unlike films like *Stalingrad*, it implicitly questions the power of cinema to act as "immediate mediator" of past memories, since it draws attention to the vital importance of the eyewitness who functions as a relay in such a process. Hence, within the world of the film Lena's willingness to satisfy Hannah's curiosity is presented as an important condition for any kind of intergenerational dialogue, while this crucial function is accentuated by an editing style that establishes the face of the eyewitness as the cinematic gateway to those memories.

Thus, while the historical narrative in *Rosenstraße* presents history as drama, I argue that the self-conscious reflection of memory I have outlined necessitates a new category of how historical films present the past on screen: history as memory. Like with Rosenstone's first category screen memories also open a "window onto a realistic world" (54). However, in contrast to films that represent history as drama, these films conceptualize this opening as an act of remembering from the individual perspective of the eyewitness.

This kind of reflection on the role of the eyewitness and on the function of cinema within this context becomes increasingly important in a period where the generation who experienced the war is now gradually disappearing. It is more and more the case that first-hand accounts of this era are no longer available to the generations born after the war. In this respect Oliver Hirschbiegel's controversial film *Der Untergang* offers an interesting viewpoint on the vital yet limited role of eyewitnesses. Quite radical in its cinematic approach, the film retells the last days in the *Führerbunker* mainly from the perspective of Hitler's private secretary Traudl Junge. It would be unfair, however, to accuse the film of historical inaccuracy or to criticize it for its concentration on historical characters whose roles during the Third Reich have not been fully explored. The film aims to present the last days of the National Socialist regime precisely from the claustrophobic viewpoint of those people who still believed in the *Führer*. By taking on the cinematic perspective of the eyewitnesses, *Der Untergang* negotiates the cinema's debatable ability to give insight into the mindsets of historical figures. Yet, at the same time it questions the reliability of eyewitnesses by displaying their limited and uncontextualized viewpoints. The latter is confirmed in the documentary footage of an interview with Traudl Junge that establishes the narrative frame of the film, and in which she authenticates the film's portrayal of her limited viewpoint while she was still a dedicated follower of Hitler.[17] The fact that the film displays rather than judges this viewpoint is, in my view, not an attempt to dissuade the audience from critically evaluating historical figures but a challenge to viewers to investigate their own perceptions and mindsets.

Negotiating the Past

Thus far I have shown not only how historical films can take the shape of manipulative reconstruction (*Stalingrad*) but also that dramatic reconstructions of the past do not necessarily exclude a critical and self-reflective meta-commentary on the filmic reconstruction of history (*Rosenstraße*). I now turn to the second group of films about the past that I mentioned earlier. Set in the 1990s, such films are characterized by a common narrative structure around a quest that leads to exploration and negotiation of the past. This quest, however, can take on very different forms: in Roland Suso Richter's *Nichts als die Wahrheit* (Nothing but the Truth), for instance, it is the fictitious reappearance of Josef Mengele (Götz George) in postunification Germany and his request to be put on trial that initiates the negotiation of the past. Mengele chooses Peter Rohm (Kai Wiesinger) as his lawyer; Rohm is in his thirties and has just finished a book on Mengele, entitled *Einer von Uns* (One of Us). Thus, from the outset the question of generations is introduced by the fact that Rohm, as a representative of the generation of the grandchildren, is asked to defend one of the most vicious perpetrators of the Third Reich. The transgenerational dynamic is further complicated when Rohm, who initially declined to defend Mengele, learns from his mother that as a nurse during the Third Reich she was forced to take part in an act of euthanasia. The revelation of his mother's suppressed memory draws Rohm into the court case, where a search for the truth begins.

The same pattern of the reappearance of and search for the past is present in Roland Gräf's *Die Spur des Bernsteinzimmers* and Nikolaus Schilling's *Die blinde Kuh*. I will discuss these two films in more detail because they offer a particularly interesting perspective on current memory contests by designating the GDR as prime location of this quest. The reappearance of the past is structurally similar in both films. In *Die Spur des Bernsteinzimmers*, the famous Amber Room, a legendary treasure that mysteriously disappeared during the Second World War, attracts the attention of the characters in the film for different reasons. In the establishing shot, we see documentary-like archive images of the Amber Room and a voice-over commentary gives us information about the history of the room and its disappearance during the war. Thus, the film introduces its main theme, the treasure hunt, right at the beginning. For spectators who are familiar with German cinema after 1945 a second theme arises in the following scene: the question of German guilt and perpetration. In this sequence the audience is introduced to the main character Lisa (Corinna Harfouch), whose viewing of the opera *Rheingold* is juxtaposed with scenes showing an old man being threatened by another man. It is only later that the audience learns that one of the men is Lisa's father, while the other man's identity is not revealed. The murder of the father is shot in a way that is reminiscent of one of the most famous German *Trümmerfilme*, or rubble films, Wolfgang Staudte's *Die Mörder sind unter uns* (The Murderers Are Among Us, 1946). Gräf's enhancement of the murderer's shadow on the wall through lighting and camera angle clearly references the famous scene from Staudte's film in which Dr. Mertens calls to account the former Nazi General Brückner for the murder of Polish citizens. Thus, from the beginning the spectator is given a clue as to what Lisa will discover during her treasure hunt: the fact that her beloved father was a white-collar Nazi, or *Schreibtischtäter*. Except for this clue the murder of Lisa's father is at first mysterious for both herself and the audience. After her visit to the opera she discovers her dead father and is made to believe by the police that his death was caused by heart failure. Going through her father's personal belongings, however, she finds information that as an art historian he was involved in the treasure hunt for the Amber Room and a note written by him confirming that he felt his life was threatened. As a result of this discovery, she becomes entangled in the mysterious quest for the remains of the legendary Amber Room to prove that her father was indeed murdered.

The recurrence that triggers the quest in *Die blinde Kuh* also introduces the main theme of the film, although with different cinematic techniques. The first shot presents us with images of a satellite in its orbit around the earth, while a voice-over commentary informs us about strange interferences that were detected by the ASTRA satellite control center in April 1994. On 20 April 1994, Hitler's birthday, the center observed in certain transmission areas flickering images of Hitler and the swastika and located the source of these interferences somewhere near Berlin in Brandenburg. A young engineer is subsequently sent out to research the phenomenon.

Both films share the structure of cryptic event followed by a quest to solve the mystery. However, the past reappears in a very different way in the two films. In *Die blinde Kuh* the recurrence of the past is portrayed by the film as a mediated event: the focus on satellites in the first shot introduces the idea that film and television are under investigation. Ironically, it is the film itself that makes this statement. This self-reflective approach through what could be called "double mediation" is enhanced by the film's cinematography, which clearly presents the film as a film (digital subtitles with dates, specification in subtitles of certain lenses that are used, voice-over that runs almost through the whole film etc.).

The reappearance of the past in both films establishes a link between the National Socialist past and the present, which at the same time highlights the significance of the temporal gap between the two. In clear contrast to *Stalingrad*, which tries to obliterate the gap by reframing the past on screen, the films in question create a strong awareness of the difficulty of bridging the temporal gap. The past in these films is no longer easily accessible, and their cinematography suggests that in the age of postmemory, great care, caution, and critical awareness are necessary for a successful working-through of the past.

The difficulties of such a task are expressed through different cinematic techniques. First, maps and old documents feature prominently in both films as the characters set out on their quests. Second, the way in which the two films are edited expresses the intense concentration and care needed for deciphering these documents accurately. The film thus suggests that reliance on mediated material is a demanding task that requires responsibility. This idea is given visual expression in the close-ups of maps and documents that alternate with close-ups of facial expressions. All close-ups highlight the fact that the past is accessible only through a close reading of already mediated material.

Each film employs a central visual metaphor to express the challenge of the characters' missions. In *Die Spur des Bernsteinzimmers* an old, monumental-styled, multiple-arch railway bridge in an otherwise empty and vast landscape conveys the image of an almost inaccessible past. Shot against the rising sun, the arches seem to be doors, and the dialogue in these scenes suggests that the way to the Amber Room is to be found at the bottom of one of the arches. Thus, the bridge in *Die Spur des Bernsteinzimmers* is a powerful yet enigmatic metaphor that makes visible the theme of access to the past and the attempt to bridge the temporal gap between the present and the past through a determined quest. The same structure of enigma and access is implied in the central visual metaphor of *Die blinde Kuh*: the underground labyrinth of old air raid shelters that the characters enter on their search for evidence of the legendary *Fernsehzug* (TV train). In so doing, they want to prove that by the end of the war the Nazis had achieved such an advanced technological level that they were ready to launch the first-ever television transmission, which was to be used for propaganda purposes.

In their concentration on their protagonists' quests, both films could be read as cinematic depictions of attempts to come to terms with the past: the quest itself as the main theme of both films portrays the difficulty of finding access to a period of the past that still bears a huge amount of meaning for the present. Images of a vast and empty landscape and the almost inscrutable darkness of underground labyrinths cinematically support the spatial impression of the past as a territory yet to be discovered.

Even though both films emphasize their protagonists' quests as an ongoing process, thereby refusing to grant easy closure on a past still deemed to be problematic, what is discovered in the end is still quite significant. In *Die Spur des Bernsteinzimmers* Lisa finds no treasure at the end of the tunnel but discovers instead the rather dark secret that her father was a Nazi perpetrator. Thus, the reappearance of the past that initiated her quest, the murderer of her father, turns out to be the ultimate personal tie between herself and the past. In *Die blinde Kuh* the three main characters find an apparatus that first of all clarifies the rather unusual title of the film. A *blinde Kuh* is a device that according to media historians was invented in the late 1940s and could be described as the prototype of a modern video camera that records images and is able to release them at any time. The discovery of the *blinde Kuh* in the film is therefore significant insofar as this technology would have enabled the Nazi regime to manipulate pictures in an easy and unprecedented manner. As the other central metaphor of the film, the apparatus is somehow the crystallization of different, yet related issues. First, it is a strong representation of the notion of the *nichtvergehende Vergangenheit*, the past that will not end. Created by the Nazi regime, the apparatus still releases images from the past that interfere with modern transmissions. Second, because of its openness to manipulation, the *blinde Kuh* also figures as a reminder that the beginnings of television might not have been as innocent as historians of modern television technology imply when they link the medium of television to the democratic postwar era. What the film introduces cinematographically is crystallized in the central visual and thematic metaphors of the film: a self-reflective investigation and assessment of the medium through the medium itself.

As mentioned before, the quest in both films takes place explicitly in the former GDR, a further point to consider in terms of postunification Germany's memory of the GDR. In *Die Spur des Bernsteinzimmers* the East German landscape is framed as a vast and empty space. Therefore, the film conveys an image of East Germany after reunification as a country yet to be discovered. At the same time, the film is edited in a way that enhances the "Germanness" of this landscape by inserting Wagnerian music in these shots. The same tension between East German territory and "Germanness" can also be found in *Die blinde Kuh*. The underground labyrinth where the search takes place and where the mysterious apparatus is eventually found spreads out underneath the territory of the former GDR. Again, the audience is confronted with a picture of East Germany as a territory that literally suppresses "dark secrets" yet to be discovered. In the final scene the strange interferences are aimed at the *Tagesschau*, the main eight o'clock evening news on German television. In an attempt to prove the superiority of Nazi technology, a conspiracy of former members of the Nazi television unit tries to transmit images of Hitler, the swastika, and the logo of the *Großdeutschen Rundfunk* at exactly eight o'clock, a time when the Germans, referring to Benedict Anderson, could be seen as an *imagined community*.[18]

If we regard the characters' search for the past in both films as a model for *Vergangenheitsbewältigung*, then this tension between East Germany and the re-unified Germany becomes very significant. The search for the past is charged with motifs of discovery and exploration of an imaginary East German space. The representation of East Germany as a blank space can be seen as a critical comment on the GDR's ideologically driven neglect of *Vergangenheitsbewältigung*, as opposed to the "obsession with history" evident in West Germany. By leaving the beaten track of West German issues in favor of the emptiness and darkness of the East German territory, both films draw a critical comparison between the two German states' approaches to the memory of the National Socialist past and assert the necessity of further investigations of the suppressed and hidden past.

Conclusion

Considering the insights of my analysis, it seems appropriate to adjust the lens through which German feature films about the Third Reich are commonly perceived. Earlier I introduced the reproachful discourse of film analysis within German Studies, which has its roots in a specific tradition that increasingly came to judge commercially successful films as intrinsically trivial. The modern usage of the word "trivial" conceals an interesting tension, particularly when it is used as a pejorative term to analyze art. In common sense understanding, "trivial" denotes something that is of little importance, a petty thing of negligible value. However, a glimpse at the Latin root reveals another dimension: deriving from Latin *trivia*, literally meaning crossroad; the adjective *trivialis* translates into "belonging to the public streets." Considering this semantic tension, the question arises which of the two denotations is meant when critics accuse a film of trivializing the past. Is the film of little importance or did it bring the topic to where it belongs? Or should there be a causal connection saying it is unimportant *because* it belongs to the public streets? Clearly, film critics are using the term in its modern pejorative sense when they dismiss commercially successful films on the past. I wish to turn this perspective around, however, by arguing that cinema, as an important part of modern popular culture and the public sphere, is in the best sense of the word a truly trivial art. Cinematic representations carry, accumulate, and circulate a considerable amount of what Stephen Greenblatt has termed the inherent "social energy" of art.[19] My analysis of postunification German feature films about the Third Reich shows that most of them engage closely with currently debated issues, and that they also offer important insights about the manner in which the past is being negotiated. Most decisively perhaps, many of the films discussed examine the function of cinema at a time when the reliance on mediated memories is increasingly important. Yet, many of the films reject the rather naive notion, exemplified by Joseph Vilsmaier's *Stalingrad*, that feature films should reliably bear direct witness to the past and reconcile the audience with its national history. On the contrary, instead of affirming the suggestive power of cinema, a number of German feature films after 1990 negotiate cinematic approaches to the past in a much more subtle manner.

And yet, despite their critical approach, historical films like *Rosenstraße, Aimée & Jaguar*, and most recently *Der Untergang* do not present history as an experiment, as Rosenstone's third category of historical films is meant to. Reaching out to a larger audience, they generally employ a narrative that is linear and a plot that is melodramatic, following the cause-and-effect-driven structure of popular mainstream cinema. The perception among critics, however, that commercial success is almost always an indication of a somewhat naive and uncritical representation needs to be reevaluated as I have suggested above: by revising the view of popular cinema as, in the worst sense of the word, trivial.

The commercial success of films like *Rosenstraße* and *Der Untergang* and others discussed in this essay reflects, apart from their high levels of cinematic quality, a thriving cinema culture in Germany.[20] Furthermore, the success of such productions demonstrates that their negotiations of the past are still relevant to a German society that is increasingly separated from first-hand experiences of the National Socialist past. I would argue that it is not so much the entertainment they provide, but the way in which some films approach the historical period that makes them so attractive to a larger audience. Filmmakers and their audiences seem to understand that a film is something very different from a history book. While we expect the latter to be true to historical facts, we do not have the same expectation of historical feature films. An analysis that gauges the artistic value of a feature film by its historical accuracy therefore fails to notice that both filmmakers and their audiences have moved on. Even though a critical evaluation of historical films has to take into account the question of accuracy, more attention should be paid to the way in which feature films negotiate the past. This seems more and more relevant at a time when we are coming to rely increasingly on mediated memories of the National Socialist period. By critically examining the accessibility of the past or presenting it as memory, many of the films discussed take part in a process that could be described as representative of a general shift within German society. The memories of the Third Reich that were once contained in the private, individual consciousnesses of witnesses are now being reassigned to the public sphere. And it seems as if cinema is an appropriate place for such a shift to take place: as a cultural institution it reflects the tension between public and private, the public act of going to the cinema and watching a movie with strangers while still isolated in the darkness of the theater and in one's private, individual reception of the film.

Notes

[1] Even though he does not establish a link to current memory debates Lutz Koepnick has worked on cinematic representations of the Third Reich: Lutz Koepnick, "Reframing the Past: Heritage Cinema and Holocaust in the 1990s," in *New German Critique* 87 (2002): 47–82. See by the same author: "Honour Your German Master. History, Memory, and Identity in Joseph Vilsmaier's Comedian Harmonists (1997)," in *Light Motives. German Popular Film in Perspective*, eds. Randall Halle and Margaret McCarthy (Detroit: Wayne State UP, 2003), 349–75.

[2] Peter Reichel, *Erfundene Erinnerung: Weltkrieg und Judenmord in Film und Theater* (Munich: Hanser, 2004).

[3] All references to this work cite the later edition: Walter Benjamin, *Das Kunstwerk im Zeitalter seiner technischen Reproduzierbarkeit* (Frankfurt am Main: Suhrkamp, 1963).

[4] "Zerstreuung und Sammlung," Benjamin writes, "stehen in einem Gegensatz, der folgende Formulierung erlaubt: Der vor dem Kunstwerk sich Sammelnde versenkt sich darein; [. . .]. Dagegen versenkt die zerstreute Masse ihrerseits das Kunstwerk in sich" (Benjamin, 40; Distraction and concentration form polar opposites which may be stated as follows: A man who concentrates before a work of art is absorbed by it. [. . .] In contrast, the distracted mass absorbs the work of art).

[5] "Die Rezeption in der Zerstreuung, die sich mit wachsendem Nachdruck auf allen Gebieten der Kunst bemerkbar macht und das Symptom von tiefgreifenden Veränderungen der Apperzeption ist, hat am Film ihr eigentliches Übungsinstrument" (Benjamin, 41; Reception in a state of distraction, which is increasing noticeably in all fields of art and is symptomatic of profound changes in apperception, finds in the film its true means of exercise).

[6] For a discussion of the flâneur, see Benjamin, *Charles Baudelaire: Ein Lyriker im Zeitalter des Hochkapitalismus*, ed. Rolf Tiedemann (Frankfurt am Main: Suhrkamp, 1969).

[7] I refer here to the later edition: Horkheimer and Adorno, *Dialektik der Aufklärung: Philosophische Fragmente* (Frankfurt am Main: Fischer, 1979), 129.

[8] Siegfried Kracauer, *Theory of Film: The Redemption of Physical Reality* (New York: Oxford UP, 1960). The German translation was published four years later: Siegfried Kracauer, *Theorie des Film: Die Errettung der äußeren Wirklichkeit*, revised edition translated from the English by Friedrich Walter und Ruth Zellschan (Frankfurt am Main: Suhrkamp, 1964).

[9] Wim Wenders, "*That's Entertainment: Hitler*," in *Emotion Pictures: Essays und Filmkritiken* (Frankfurt am Main: Verlag der Autoren, 1986), 115.

[10] Koepnick, "Reframing," 76.

[11] Hirsch, *Family Frames: Photography, Narrative and Postmemory* (Cambridge Massachusetts, London: Harvard UP, 1997). See also J. J. Long's contribution on this theme in the present volume.

[12] Anton Kaes, "German Cultural History and the Study of Film: Ten Theses and a Postscript," in *New German Critique* 65 (1995): 47–58.

[13] This is an argument that has also been put forward by Gill Branston in *Cinema and Cultural Modernity* (Buckingham, Philadelphia: Open UP, 2000).

[14] Sabine Hake, *German National Cinema* (London and New York: Routledge, 2002), 186–87.

[15] Robert A. Rosenstone, "The Historical Film: Looking at the Past in a Postliterate Age," in *The Historical Film: History and Memory in Media*, ed. Marcia Landy (London: Athlone Press, 2001), 50–66; here: 52.

[16] For a discussion of the *Wehrmacht* soldier photographer and the exhibitions on this theme, see Chloe Paver's essay in the present volume.

[17] The interview is taken from André Heller's and Othmar Schmiderer's documentary: *Im toten Winkel: Hitlers Sekretärin* (Blind Spot: Hitler's Secretary, 2002).

[18] Benedict Anderson, *Imagined Communities: Reflections on the Origin and Spread of Nationalism* (London: Verso, 1983).

[19] Stephen Greenblatt, *Shakespearian Negotiations: The Circulation of Social Energy in Renaissance* (Oxford: Clarendon, 1988).

[20] According to the official internet portal to German Cinema which was launched at the *Berlinale* 2004, the number of national productions increased in 2004 from fifty-four to sixty. And even more important: the national market share of German films showed in Germany has reached 23.8%, the highest level in fifteen years (see: http://www.filmportal.de).

7: Monika Maron's *Pawels Briefe*: Photography, Narrative, and the Claims of Postmemory

J. J. Long

MONIKA MARON'S *PAWELS BRIEFE* (Pavel's Letters, 1999) is one of numerous recent German-language texts that thematize the efforts of the so-called second generation, sons and daughters of Holocaust survivors and perpetrators, to uncover, reconstruct, and represent events that happened before they were born. The narrator of this autobiographical text seeks to piece together the biography of her grandfather, Pawel Iglarz, a Polish Jew who had converted to Baptism and emigrated with his wife Josefa to Berlin, where he worked as a tailor until the Nazi rise to power. In 1938 he was expelled from Germany. Offered the choice between divorce and expulsion, Josefa joined him the following year, and they settled in Kurow, Poland. In early 1942, he was deported to the Belchatow ghetto and thence to the concentration camp at Kulmhof (Chelmno), where he died, Josefa having predeceased him. While in Belchatow, Pawel exchanged a large number of letters with his family, and the discovery of these letters in 1994 triggers the process of reconstruction.

As Maron peruses the aforementioned letters, she realizes that she has never experienced her mother as somebody else's daughter. Her son Jonas, she adds, knows her both as a mother and as the child of his grandmother, but Maron herself has been denied this dialectic of familial continuity. As a result, she has no memories of her grandparents and creates an image of them retrospectively.[1] As Friedericke Eigler notes, the continuity of family memory was destroyed literally by the murder of millions, but also figuratively through the forgetting and repression that — though for different reasons — affect perpetrators, victims, and their descendants.[2] A plethora of fictional and autobiographical texts have, over the past two decades or so, sought to thematize this discontinuity, and to explore the possibility of bridging the generational gaps opened up by the historical caesura of the Holocaust. Maron's retrospective reconstruction of her grandfather's life situates her narrative project firmly within this wider trend.

One of the most important attempts to theorize this cultural current is provided by Marianne Hirsch, whose concept of postmemory has become immensely influential in recent discussions of Holocaust representation and the literature of transgenerational transmission. Its wide application, however, brings its own problems. As Edward W. Said points out in his essay "Traveling Theory": "once an idea gains currency because it is clearly effective and powerful, there is every likelihood that during its peregrinations it will be reduced, codified, and institutionalized."[3] If, as Said goes on to claim, it is the critic's job to challenge theory, to "point up those concrete instances [. . .] that lie outside or just beyond the interpretive area necessarily designated in advance and thereafter circumscribed by every theory" (242), then postmemory must be tested critically against texts that fall just outside its immediate purview.

Pawels Briefe is one such text. I have not selected it randomly, but because it evinces many of the characteristics of "postmemorial" narrative, while also possessing elements that resist the application of postmemory as an analytical or descriptive category.[4] In what follows, I offer an account of postmemory that dwells on some of the problems inherent in the concept, before exploring some of these problems through a reading of *Pawels Briefe*. My purpose is not to demolish or dismiss the notion of postmemory, but to find out what it might have to tell us about *Pawels Briefe* — and, indeed, what *Pawels Briefe* might have to tell us about postmemory — in the spirit of what Said calls "critical consciousness" (242).

The Claims of Postmemory

Here are two definitions of postmemory that sum up its essential features:

> Postmemory characterizes the experience of those who [. . .] have grown up dominated by narratives that preceded their birth, whose own belated stories are displaced by the powerful stories of the previous generation, shaped by monumental traumatic events that resist understanding and integration.[5]

> Postmemory is distinguished from memory by generational distance and from history by a deep personal connection. Postmemory is a powerful and very particular form of memory precisely because its connection to its object or its source is mediated not through recollection but through imaginative investment and creation. (*Family Frames*, 22)

In the opening chapters of Hirsch's book *Family Frames* and also in her essay "Surviving Images," postmemory emerges both as a structure of transgenerational transmission and as the subject-position occupied by the children of Holocaust survivors.[6] Indeed, since traumatic memory is by its very nature belated and is recognizable only through its aftereffects, Hirsch conjectures that members of the second generation may occupy a privileged position with respect to their parents:

> Perhaps it is *only* in subsequent generations that trauma can be witnessed and worked through, by those who were not there to live it but who received its effects, belatedly, through the narratives, actions, and symptoms of the previous generation. ("Surviving Images," 222)

As such, postmemory establishes the second generation as the heroic subject in a narrative of belated recuperation or, as Hirsch herself puts it, "reconstitution and repair" ("Surviving Images," 222). This shifts epistemological authority from first to second generation, which implicitly devalues the first generation's experience, while also hollowing out ("evacuating," "displacing," "crowding out," to use Hirsch's terms) the subjectivity of the second generation and replacing it with the effects of the previous generation's trauma. This in turn undermines Hirsch's contention that postmemory is an ethical mode of transgenerational identification that resists the incorporative and appropriative emphases in classic psychoanalytic accounts of identification:[7] the notion of a largely passive subject "dominated" and "shaped" by an unknown past implies a degree of unconscious identification that leaves little scope for ethical reflection. For the ethical, as Kaja Silverman stresses, "becomes operative not at the moment when unconscious desires and phobias assume possession of our look, but in a subsequent moment."[8]

And yet, as Marita Grimwood has pointed out, postmemory undergoes a significant shift of emphasis as this passive subject gives way to an agent capable of *choosing* a postmemorial position.[9] Hirsch states that she does not wish to restrict the notion of postmemory to the remembrance of the Holocaust ("Surviving Images," 221), and also opens up the possibility of a kind of elective postmemory, according to which one can occupy the postmemorial position through a process of willed identification, a kind of "*retrospective witnessing by adoption*."[10] The privileged position of the second generation here becomes infinitely extensible, in the double sense of applying to potentially any historical event and being potentially available to any subject. If postmemory does indeed designate a structure of transmission and a subject-position, then its relevance clearly exceeds the historical specificity of the Holocaust and the family. But such a loss of specificity once again problematizes Hirsch's claim that the practice of inscribing the traumatic experiences of others into one's own life story provides a model of "an *ethical* relation to the oppressed or persecuted other."[11] The universal availability of the postmemorial position carries the potential for distinctly unethical exploitation. Inscribing another's life story into one's own biography is by no means necessarily ethical, as the cases of Karin Mylius or Binjamin Wilkomirski demonstrate.[12]

Furthermore, an "*ethical* relation to the oppressed or persecuted other" sits uneasily with the notion of "imaginative investment and creation" that Hirsch sees as a defining feature of postmemory. Imagination and creation, after all, contain the possibility of unregulated fantasy that need pay no attention at all either to historical accuracy or to the otherness of the other. The question is: how can this imaginative investment and creation be policed in order to prevent appropriation or even usurpation of the other's experiences?

One solution to these ethical dilemmas that emerges in Hirsch's discussion is the necessity of documentation. Postmemory is textually mediated, and it relies on images, stories, and documents passed down from one generation to the next ("Surviving Images," 222). Even this, however, guarantees little when one takes into account the ineluctably selective and partial nature of memory, the imbrication of archival processes in structures of power, the necessarily incomplete state of the documentary record, and the capacity of photographs not only to be manipulated, but to generate widely divergent and conflicting interpretations. The other solution is what Hirsch, following Kaja Silverman, terms "heteropathic identification," a non-appropriative mode of identification that allows one to say, "it could have been me; it was me, also" and, at the same time, "but it was not me" ("Projected Memory," 9). This is the crux of Hirsch's claim that postmemorial identification is necessarily ethical. The problem, however, is that in Silverman, an "ethical relation to the other" is a precondition rather than a product of heteropathic identification (Silverman, 173). Hirsch's use of the heteropathic in fact assumes the prior existence of an ethical subject, thereby presupposing what it sets out to explain.

A final aspect of postmemory that seems to call for critical attention is that it is "distinguished from memory by generational distance and from history by a deep personal connection." As Hirsch's title *Family Frames* suggests, the place where generational distance and deep personal connection coincide is the nuclear family as the smallest unit of social organization. In her readings of photographs and other visual artifacts, she mobilizes what she terms the familial gaze. This is defined as a set of looking relations that "situate human subjects in the ideology, the mythology, of the family as institution and project a screen of familial myths between camera and subject" (*Family Frames*, 11). Hirsch's psychoanalytic approach to the visual construction of family relationships is by no means apolitical. She draws on Silverman's Lacanian-inspired discussion of the opposition between the look, the gaze, and the screen. If the screen is a "large, diverse, but ultimately finite range of representational coordinates which determines what and how members of our culture see — how they process visual detail, and what meaning they give it," the gaze imposes a normative "mortifying and memorial" way of seeing on the individual subject, while the look is "on the side of flux, memory, and subjectivity" (Silverman, 221, 222). The look thus possesses the capacity, in Hirsch's view, to resist the normative power of the screen and gaze, allowing the viewer of family images to unmask the unacknowledged relationships of "domination and subjection, of mutuality and interconnectedness" (*Family Frames*, 9) that structure the act of looking within the family.

But the emphasis on the family as the privileged context of postmemory restricts the ideological scope of Hirsch's work. Postmemory distinctly lacks explanatory force in situations where family matters are complicated by external socio-political factors and relations of power. Symptomatic of this is Hirsch's reading of Lorie Novak's installation "Past Lives," a composite projection that combines a photograph of the Jewish children from the French orphanage in Izieu who were eventually discovered and deported, a photograph of a mother holding a smiling baby (Novak herself in her mother's arms), and the face of Ethel Rosenberg, who, along with her husband Julius, was convicted of espionage and executed in New York in 1953. Hirsch sees "Past Lives" as staging "the moment of knowledge for the Jewish child growing up in the late 1950s whose needs, desires, and cares fade out in relation to the stories that surround her, the traumatic memories that preceded her birth but nevertheless define her life's narrative" ("Projected Memory," 8). By equating the "stories that surround her" with memories of the Holocaust, Hirsch reduces Rosenberg to the status of "a mother who couldn't protect her children" ("Projected Memory," 6), and a "distancing device" that somehow disrupts the process of identification with Holocaust victims ("Projected Memory," 17). What is missing from this account of Rosenberg's role within the image is the history of the Cold War and the equation of communism and Jewishness, which, far from disappearing with the defeat of Nazi Germany, led a dubious afterlife in McCarthy-era America.[13] That "Past Lives" might also constitute a critique of American anticommunism and anti-Semitism is something that Hirsch's scheme refuses to countenance.

Postmemory is thus a radically overdetermined concept. Even in Hirsch's own work it travels with striking facility and emerges, variously, as a subject-position, a structure of transgenerational transmission, an ethics of identification and remembering, a theory of familial ideology, a therapeutic aesthetic strategy, and a mode of cultural memory. This conceptual mutability threatens to diminish rather than enhance postmemory's explanatory and critical power.

Monika Maron's *Pawels Briefe*

Pawels Briefe points up some of these problems with postmemory. The external conditions for a postmemorial narrative are certainly there: the deportation and death of the narrator's grandmother, the murder of her grandfather, the threats and vulnerability to persecution of their offspring during the Third Reich, and the belated attempt by one who was born later to narrativize this potentially traumatic past. This establishes Maron as a postmemorial subject who is responsible for recuperating her mother's and her grandparents' histories.[14] Because she is a postmemorial subject, memory, conceived of as an internal psychological mechanism, cannot be her only source. As she herself points out, remembering ("Erinnern") does not adequately describe her narrative project, since there is within her no submerged knowledge that could be brought to light (*PB*, 8). She is reliant, then, on other external mnemotechnical supplements in addition to Pawel's letters: photographic and archival documents, and the stories told by her mother and her aunt about the Iglarz family's existence before and during the Second World War. The thematic concern with material traces goes hand in hand with the formal strategy of reproducing photographic images within the text, linking *Pawels Briefe* with other paradigmatically "postmemorial" texts that Hirsch discusses. An analysis of photography and narrative in Maron's construction of her grandfather Pawel, however, yields rather different conclusions from those adumbrated by Hirsch's theory.

On the third page of the text, Maron elects Pawel as the only ancestor she is prepared to acknowledge as such (*PB*, 9), and expands on this at a later point: "Wir, mein Großvater und ich, weil ich nach ihm und nur nach ihm kam, waren eben ein bißchen anders, ein bißchen unpraktisch, dafür verträumt und zu spontanen Einfällen neigend, nervös, ein bißchen verrückt" (*PB*, 63; We, my grandfather and I, because I am descended from him and him alone, were a bit different, we were a bit unpractical, but we were dreamers, prone to spontaneous whims, highly-strung, and a bit crazy). This represents a double process of identification and differentiation, identification with Pawel going hand in hand with an assertion of his (and therefore also the narrator's) individuality and difference from other people.

This process can be seen at work in the arrangement of the photographs in *Pawels Briefe*. With three exceptions, the photographs are first presented complete and with a caption, and are then followed by an uncaptioned close-up detail.[15] As Eigler points out, the reframing of individual details draws attention to the arbitrariness of framing, making the viewer aware that framing determines how the photograph is read, and exposing the illusion of photographic transparency. She also claims, however, that the photographs resist integration into the verbal narrative "because the biographical frame that is usually transmitted through 'communicative memory' and that makes family photos meaningful, is largely missing."[16] This, however, foreshortens the discussion. For if, as Eigler concedes, the meaning of photographs is determined by framing — that is, by context — then clearly their function within the narrative economy of *Pawels Briefe* is in need of critical investigation.[17]

In Hirsch's *Family Frames*, photography functions as a privileged vehicle of postmemory for two reasons. The first is that it is an indexical medium, a trace of the real etched by light onto the photosensitive plate. As such, the photograph possesses an enhanced relationship to both life and death:

> it is precisely the indexical nature of the photo, its status as relic, or trace, or fetish — its "direct" connection with the material presence of the photographed person — that at once intensifies its status as harbinger of death and, at the same time and concomitantly, its capacity to signify life. [. . .] Life is the presence of the object before the camera and the "carnal medium" of light which produces the image; death is the "having-been-there" of the object — the radical break, the finality introduced by the past tense. [. . .] Photography's relation to loss and death is not to mediate the process of individual and collective memory, but to bring back the past in the form of a ghostly revenant, emphasizing, at the same time, its immutable and irreversible pastness. (*Family Frames*, 19–20)

For Hirsch, indexicality is what gives Holocaust photographs their particular power. They bring out photography's unique capacity to hover between life and death, capturing "that which no longer exists" and suggesting "both the desire and the necessity and, at the same time, the difficulty, the impossibility of mourning" (*Family Frames*, 20). Elsewhere, Hirsch states that the repeated circulation of a narrow range of Holocaust images produces the trauma of the first generation for those born later: "it is not an anaesthetic, but a traumatic fixation." Only a recontextualization of such photographs, she adds, might enable a "postmemorial working through" that will, however, remain forever incomplete, the final integration forever postponed ("Surviving Images," 238). Hirsch sees photography as therapeutic, but only partially so, helping the second generation to work through a past that cannot be fully worked through, and being thus also symptomatic of ongoing trauma. This is effectively a psychoanalytically-inflected version of Roland Barthes's account of photography in *Camera Lucida*. In this text, Barthes posits the indexical as the essence of photography, but then rejects indexicality in favor of temporality as the *noeme* of the photograph. "In photography," he writes, "I cannot deny that *the thing has been there*."[18]

The second reason for photography's privileged status is that it facilitates a psychoanalytic investigation into structures of looking and the collusion of photographer, subject, and viewer in the production of familial ideology. This is what we might call the critical aspect of Hirsch's agenda.

At one level, the photographs in *Pawels Briefe* certainly fulfill these functions. The narrative of deportation and of a violent yet disturbingly anonymous death is juxtaposed with photographs of the living Pawel and Josefa in a way that foregrounds precisely the "having been there" of the past, but also its fundamental irretrievability. Certain images also allow an exploration of the "familial gaze." The indexical and the familial converge in a studio portrait of the Iglarz family that was taken as part of an abortive application for emigration to the United States. In her reading of this photograph, Maron is aware that it is a constructed image of togetherness that was choreographed by the photographer. But she is nevertheless susceptible to its power: "sie [wirken] auf mich einander so verbunden, einer so gesichert durch den anderen, daß mich das schon erwähnte irrationale Heimweh überkommt" (*PB*, 47; to me, they seem so close to one another, each offering the other such support and security, that I'm overcome with that irrational sense of homesickness I've mentioned before). She goes on to say, though, that it may well be that all she reads into or out of this picture is what she has already learned about the family from Hella's stories. A disinterested observer, she fears, would see nothing more in this image than a standard family photograph of the era (*PB*, 47). This is the familial gaze and its demystification in operation at the same time: Maron succumbs to the emotional and ideological pull of the image, while acknowledging that it is a function of compositional conventions and of the viewing relations imposed upon her as a member of the family group. Furthermore, the image represents a family that remains intact only within the layers of photographic emulsion. It was soon to be rent asunder in several ways: Josefa died of cancer, Pawel perished soon after in the Holocaust, their eldest child Bruno died as a result of gall-bladder surgery in 1937 (*PB*, 17), Hella split definitively with her brother Paul after an altercation between him and Karl Maron (*PB*, 187), and Marta, the elder sister with whom Hella continued to share a close relationship, died in 1973. So the photograph betokens death and irretrievable loss even as it promotes the desire for familial identification.

Indexicality, temporality, and psychoanalysis are not the only ways of reading photographs, however. By exploring other approaches to the functioning of photographic discourse in *Pawels Briefe*, the meaning of the family photograph can be shown to exceed the terms of Maron's commentary. Its relationship to other photographs is primarily contrastive, for it is the only image that depicts an entire family. There is no such portrait of Monika, Hella, and Karl Maron. Indeed, male relatives are conspicuous by their absence. There is a photograph of Hella, Marta, Monika, Paul, and his wife Erika, which was taken after Josefa's funeral, but the composition of this image centers on the triangular arrangement of Hella, Marta, and Monika. Paul and Erika are literally and figuratively peripheral, an effect that is strengthened by Paul's refusal to return the camera's gaze (*PB*, 138). This image reinforces Paul's marginal status within the narrative. More complex in its functioning is the remarkable studio portrait of Pawels' father, Juda Leib Sendrowitsch (*PB*, 26). A plurality of meanings coalesces around this image. First, it signals the unreliability of archival sources, since Sendrowitsch's hand placed on an open book, to which the viewer's attention is drawn by the subsequent close-up (*PB*, 29), suggests scholarship or at the very least literacy, whereas according to Pawel's birth certificate, Sendrowitsch could neither read nor write (*PB*, 27). It is later suggested that he might have been able to write Hebrew, even if he could not write Russian or Polish (*PB*, 110), but his degree of literacy remains indeterminate. This is one of many instances in which the incompleteness and inadequacy of the archive — including the photographic archive — is thematized. Second, it is an image of a rejected father: Pawel converted to Baptism at the age of twenty, and was thenceforth regarded as dead by the family he had left. Maron's inclusion of the image in her text reconstructs *post hoc* the succession of generations that Pawel's conversion had broken. But this patrilinear genealogy stops as soon as it starts: with Pawel. There are no photographs of Monika's biological father Walter, or of her stepfather Karl Maron.

This is a telling omission. It is a commonplace in writings on domestic photography that the father, as the one who wields the camera and depresses the shutter, is often the "structuring absence" of family snaps.[19] And yet the insistence with which male figures are excluded from visual representation suggests that this exclusion is not merely a contingent consequence of the circumstances under which family photographs are taken. At one point in the text, Monika comments that she had two mothers (Hella and Marta), but no father (*PB*, 58), and this assertion of a microcosmic matriarchy (which existed despite the fact that the flat was also shared by Karl Maron from 1951) is reinforced by the photographs of Monika, which show her almost exclusively in the company of women. By thus erasing Karl and Walter, Maron creates a genealogical gap in the visual record into which she can insert Pawel as the only father she is willing to acknowledge. This is tantamount to a belated symbolic accomplishment of what Pawel acknowledges to be impossible, namely the choosing of one's parentage (*PB*, 98).

Significantly, the choice of Pawel as an *ersatz* father is itself a photographic choice: "weil die Fotografie meiner Großmutter, die schmal gerahmt in meinem Zimmer hing, sie allzu deutlich als die Mutter meiner Mutter auswies, fiel meine Wahl als einzigen Ahnen, von dem abzustammen ich bereit war, auf meinen Großvater" (*PB*, 9; because the photograph of my grandmother that hung in a narrow frame in my bedroom showed her all too clearly to be my mother's mother, my choice fell upon my grandfather as the only ancestor from whom I was willing to be descended).[20] This attests to the capacity of photography to highlight family resemblance and thereby affirm lineage. And it is indeed striking that Josefa and Hella have the same full cheeks and sturdy build, confirming Maron's claim that Hella, a pretty and robust girl, was Josefa's child (*PB*, 57). The abundance of photographs of Pawel, on the other hand, show him to have been slender in face and body, with a squarish jaw and hollow cheeks.[21] This has a twofold effect. Within the text, he is visually differentiated from both his wife and his daughter: the difference and individuality ("Anderssein") that Monika attributes to him is thus affirmed, at the level of imagery, as a bodily difference. Furthermore, for those acquainted with photographs of Monika Maron as an adult, it is difficult to overlook the facial resemblance between Pawel and Monika, which is considerably more marked than her resemblance to either Josefa or Hella.[22] Rather than *referring indexically*, then, photographs are forced to *signify physiognomically*, the face becomes legible as a sign that discloses the inner qualities of the person and constructs a facial typology that places Monika and Pawel in one category, Josefa and Hella in another.[23]

The way in which the body is made to signify in *Pawels Briefe* can be seen, further, in the photographs of Hella, especially those depicting her as an adult, where she is always shown in the company of others. This applies even to the enlarged details: in one enlargement she is part of a funeral gathering, in another she is participating in a demonstration, in a third, she is attending the *Parteihochschule* (SED leadership training school). Hers is a body that is easily integrated into the collective and resists individuation — unlike Pawel, who is photographically isolated from his family (*PB*, 35) and the cycling club (*PB*, 63). Of these, the image of the *Parteihochschule* is particularly telling (*PB*, 177). Its enlargement is unusually long and thin, whereas all the other photographs and their enlargements are in more or less standard portrait or landscape format. Such conspicuous cropping invites critical attention because it endows the image with unusual formal properties. While on first glance it might appear that Hella has been singled out from the group, she remains flanked by comrades. Moreover, the image is now organized down a central vertical axis, which aligns Hella's head with another member of the group and an enormous Soviet flag with hammer and sickle on prominent display. Hella and the two young men in the back row gaze openly and smilingly at the camera, while the emaciated, sunken-cheeked, bespectacled man standing immediately behind her has adopted a sinister facial expression halfway between a grin and a sneer. The Soviet flag that appears to protrude from his head combines with his uniform to link him metonymically with East Germany's ruling party, the SED, the Sozialistische Einheitspartei Deutschlands. Hella, with her dark hair and dark jacket, partly merges with him, but remains partly distinct. The overall effect is to contrast the ostensible naiveté of Hella and the other comrades with what appears to be a cynical, if not malign, representative of a repressive regime, while also implying her partial identity with that regime. The undecidability between naiveté and knowing collusion characterizes the portrayal of Hella throughout.

The photographic discourse in *Pawels Briefe* thus performs several important functions. It establishes a visual gap in the genealogical record into which Pawel can be inserted, thereby providing a visual counterpart to Maron's declaration that he is her only legitimate ancestor. The strategy enables the act of identification with the grandfather, which is further assisted by the physiognomic opposition between Josefa and Hella on the one hand, and Pawel and Maron herself on the other. These photographic oppositions combine with the verbal narrative to constitute Pawel as an individualist in contrast to the communist conformism of Hella. As this analysis suggests, then, the photographic discourse of *Pawels Briefe* exceeds by far the terms of postmemory. Maron's agenda is not purely the mourning of an irretrievable loss; it is also a sustained critique of Hella as an embodiment of GDR communism and the configurations of memory that it supported.

The critique of the GDR is explicit. Maron attacks the vulgar-Marxist lexicon, ridiculing the idea of "Klasseninstinkt" (class instinct) as a political concept (*PB*, 127), and showing that the notion of the "Klassenfeind" (class enemy) could be used to justify hypocrisy, naiveté, and bad faith (*PB*, 161). She sets up an equation between Nazism and GDR socialism (*PB*, 80), and finds it inexplicable that Hella and her sister Marta should have espoused a political system in which opponents were imprisoned, Christians harassed, books banned, the entire population walled in, and a vast surveillance network set up to spy on the GDR's own citizens (*PB*, 154). Hella's blind loyalty to the SED and her unshakeable communist convictions are subjected to further criticism, culminating in the following verdict: "Ich glaube, Hella sieht in ihrer Treue eine Tugend; ich empfinde sie als Unbelehrbarkeit und, angesichts der Willkür und des Unglücks, das Kommunisten über einen halben Kontinent gebracht haben, als Herzlosigkeit" (*PB*, 179; I think Hella sees her loyalty as a virtue. But I see it as incorrigibility and, in view of the arbitrary rule and the unhappiness that communists visited upon half a continent, as heartlessness).

This critique carries over into the narrator's repeated devaluation of Hella as a witness to history and as an agent of memory. In the former case, Maron points out that Hella's diaries are purely personal, and omit all references to the Berlin workers' uprising of 1953, the Soviet suppression of the Hungarian uprising in 1956, or the construction of the Berlin Wall in 1961. 1968 is labeled "verflucht" (accursed), but only because of Karl Maron's post-retirement depression (*PB*, 191–92). In the latter case, Maron frequently thematizes the unreliability of her mother's memory, while making extensive use of the rhetoric of retraction: doubts are cast on Hella as a remembering subject, but then the narrator seeks to relativize or counteract these doubts. There are numerous examples of this pattern throughout the text, and the following can serve as an illustration. The context is Hella's forgetting of a letter written to Pawel by Josefa the day before she died, and forwarded to the family by Pawel with the instruction that Hella should translate it and keep a typescript.

Vor diesem Vergessen stehe ich ratlos, so ratlos wie Hella selbst. Das Jahr 1945 sei für sie wie eine Wiedergeburt, sagte Hella. Eine Wiedergeburt ohne Eltern, ein Neuanfang ohne die Vergangenheit? Mußten nicht nur die Täter sondern auch die Opfer ihre Trauer verdrängen, um weiterzuleben? Jeder hatte seine Toten, Söhne, Väter, Männer, Freunde. Regierten die einfachen Sätze: das Leben muß weitergehen; das macht die Toten nicht wieder lebendig? Und später, als das Leben längst weitergegangen wat, als die Zeitungen "Neues Leben," "Neuer Weg," "Neue Zeit" und "Neues Deutschland" hießen, als die Gegenwart der Zukunft weichen mußte und die Vergangenheit endgültig überwunden wurde, wurde da auch die eigene Vergangenheit unwichtig? Oder waren die Jahrzehnte davor so aufs Überleben gerichtet, daß zum Innehalten und Zurückblicken keine Zeit war? Wir haben immer so nach vorne gelebt, sagt Hella. (*PB*, 113–14)

[I am baffled when confronted with this forgetfulness, as baffled as Hella herself. Hella has said that 1945 was for her a kind of rebirth. A rebirth without parents, a new beginning without the past? Did victims as well as perpetrators have to repress their grief in order to carry on living? Everyone had suffered losses: sons, fathers, husbands, boyfriends. Was everything governed by the simple principles "life must go on," and "that won't bring them back"? And later, after life had gone on for quite some time, when the papers were called "The New Life," "The New Path," "The New Era" and "New Germany," when the present had to make way for the future and the past had been definitively overcome, was one's own individual past also of no importance? Or had the preceding decades been so thoroughly oriented towards survival that there had been no time to pause and look back? We always just lived for the future, says Hella.]

Hella's personal act of forgetting is here mapped onto the memory politics of the GDR, in which a thorough reckoning with the Nazi past was precluded by the official rhetoric of antifascism and orientation towards a future socialist utopia.[24] Only afterwards is a more indulgent account of Hella's forgetting offered, but this is not sufficiently powerful or developed to constitute a genuine relativization of the earlier critique.[25]

As we have seen above, Maron's rejection of her mother goes hand in hand with identification with Pawel. In good postmemorial fashion, this identification is only partial, for Pawel's death represents the moment at which identification and imaginative reconstruction fail (*PB*, 184). Identification is also threatened by Pawel's membership in the KPD (German Communist Party). How, Maron asks at one point, is she supposed to imagine her gentle, even-tempered, and pious grandfather as a member of a tightly-organized party that labeled Social Democrats "Social Fascists" and brawled with the Nazis (*PB*, 59)? She circumvents this question by constructing a grandfather who is not subject to majority resolutions and the discipline of the Party (*PB*, 63). She claims that anyone who can write as Pawel did from Belchatow as his death approached "zeigt niemals dem Kinde, daß es Haß, Neid und Rache gibt" (*PB*, 181; never let the child see that hatred, envy and revenge exist), would have been immune to the

Party's claim to infallibility and would not have remained indifferent to the victims of the East German dictatorship. Had he lived, she continues, Pawel would never have left the West Berlin district of Neukölln and would never have become an acolyte of the GDR. In particular, her image of Pawel is incommensurable with the image of Karl Maron in his general's uniform, or with the two armed guards sent to protect the family in the wake of the workers' uprisings of 17 June 1953 (*PB*, 182).

The refusal to see Pawel as subject to the same Party strictures as his communist offspring, and the desire to see him as a skeptic, represents an act of "imaginative investment and creation" that is structurally identical to the processes that Hirsch sees as characteristic of postmemory. It is also, however, an avowedly unregulated fantasy, based on no more than a fairly arbitrary conviction on the narrator's part (*PB*, 182). The way in which she constructs the past and projects the future of Pawel's life is determined not purely by familial identifications but by explicitly political considerations. The clash of interpretations of GDR history that governs Maron's relationship with her mother is far removed from Hirsch's notion of an ideologically-determined familial gaze or an ethically-conditioned identification with the victim. Both the photographic and narrative discourses of *Pawels Briefe* are organized in such as way as to consolidate Maron's ideological position while devaluing that of her mother.

The question remains, then, why such a large quantity of textual energy should be expended on the question of Maron's political identity. She had, after all, built her literary career on dissidence, and had left the GDR in 1988, shortly before the Berlin Wall came down. In this sense, she was, as she puts it herself, one of history's victors (*PB*, 130): the collapse of communism confirmed the superiority of capitalist democracy. Yet *Pawels Briefe* has other work to do, since in 1995, it was revealed by a journalist working for the German weekly news magazine *Der Spiegel* that Maron had had dealings with the Stasi, the GDR's Ministry of State Security. She was on the books of the "Hauptverwaltung Aufklärung," the department responsible for foreign intelligence, and as such was able to undertake several visits to West Berlin, which would otherwise not have been possible (*PB*, 197–98). She also wrote two reports for the intelligence services, both of them reprinted in her collection *quer über die gleise* (across the tracks), that are not only apparently harmless but overtly critical of the GDR's economic, social, and political failings.[26] In defending her Stasi activity, Maron adduces motives that, as Andrew Plowman points out, are utterly typical of those seeking to justify their collaboration with the GDR regime: her Stasi work was merely an extension of a more acceptable commitment to the GDR, and in any case, she refused to collaborate fully; her work for the Stasi was in fact an act of resistance.[27] But the value of resistance is profoundly compromised when it is predicated on the enjoyment of privileges and active participation in the system of secrecy, surveillance, and report-writing on which the Stasi's power depended. Not *what* she wrote but the fact *that* she wrote is what constitutes the moment of collaboration, and it is therefore not surprising that her pre-*Wende* biography should have been called into question as a result of the *Spiegel* report. The final irony of the text is that the one person to whom she turns for confirmation that her Stasi activity had harmed nobody is Hella (*PB*, 200) — the very person who, as the text repeatedly demonstrates, has a remarkable capacity to remember only that which is pleasant or anodyne.

Though the Stasi episode is addressed only at the end of *Pawels Briefe*, it is possible to read the entire narrative as being governed by Maron's desire to relegitimize her political identity following this moment of biographical crisis. The text as a whole gives the lie to her claim that she had to have ceased battling with her parents in order to concern herself with her grandparents' story in a way that transcended her own need to legitimate herself (*PB*, 13); *Pawels Briefe* remains obsessed with such self-legitimation, and this can only take place via identification with the victim and a simultaneous denigration of the GDR, metonymically represented by Hella. What emerges in *Pawels Briefe*, therefore, is a particular kind of post-GDR postmemory in which Maron's imaginative reconstruction of her grandparents' lives and deaths is mapped onto, or even overlaid by, a struggle for the memory of the GDR, and by Maron's desire to reaffirm her victim status and her political identity.[28] The "imaginative investment and creation," and the partial identification with the victim-position, both of which are central to Hirsch's account of postmemory, result in something different from therapy, symptom, or familial critique. What we see in *Pawels Briefe* is the manipulability of the image being enlisted in the service of a narrative whose unacknowledged purpose is self-exculpation.

This reading of *Pawels Briefe* exposes the gap between postmemory as a structure of transmission and postmemory as an ethics of remembering. It is not that these two things are incompatible, it is that that they belong to two completely different orders of psycho-discursive activity. I would not, however, wish to suggest that postmemory be abandoned altogether. Indeed, when understood as a structure of transgenerational transmission, it can function as a necessary complement to other influential theories of memory, such as Jan Assmann's. Assmann's account of collective memory mobilizes a distinction between "communicative" and "cultural" memory. Communicative memory refers primarily to generational memory, the tendency for the "living memory," embodied by those who experienced or witnessed specific events, to wane as the bearers of such memory age and die. He identifies the forty-year mark as the crucial moment, when those who have experienced a certain event as adults retire from professional life and enter old age, which brings with it an intensified desire to fix and record. Communicative memory thus becomes transformed into what Assmann calls "cultural memory," enshrined not in the intersubjective space of oral communication, but in the book, the monument, the ritual, or the archive.[29] If the organic succession of generations on which these processes depends is ruptured, it follows that we need a concept of memory that is reducible neither to communicative nor to cultural memory. And it is here that postmemory can play an important role, for it addresses the possibility of reading the remnants of communicative *and* cultural memory in order to repair (if only partially) that very rupture.

Postmemory continues to provide a useful starting point for the identification, description, and analysis of a major cultural trend of the past two decades, namely the second and third generations' engagement with their parents' pasts. At the same time, however, using postmemory to read a text like *Pawels Briefe*, which introduces emotional investments that go beyond the familial gaze and involve identifications that are not unequivocally ethical, reveals the limitations of Hirsch's account. These very limitations can be productive for our reading not only of *Pawels Briefe* but of numerous other German texts that thematize a kind of perpetrator postmemory,[30] because they enable us to say what is specific about German contributions to this ostensibly global (or at least European/American) cultural current. Such cultural products can also alert us, however, to Hirsch's more dubious claim that postmemory entails an *"ethical relation to the oppressed or persecuted other."* Such a claim runs the risk of fetishizing identification with the victim without regard to wider political configurations, and making postmemory available to those who wish to promote, for example, an apologetic perpetrator discourse or an uncritical victim discourse in Germany. The relationship between the ethics of identification and the structure of memory needs to be theorized in a far more differentiated fashion, rather than the two terms being accommodated — or even conflated — under the banner of postmemory.

Ultimately, *Pawels Briefe* tells us something about the transferability or lack thereof of memory paradigms. The work of Marianne Hirsch, Jan Assmann, Aleida Assmann, Dominick LaCapra, Andreas Huyssen, Marita Sturken, Richard Terdiman, and others continues to migrate across disciplines and national contexts. But amid this global flow of theory, we need the concrete engagement with specific texts to keep us alert to cultural specificity at a time when such specificity is often elided by the traveling concepts of the humanities.

Notes

[1] Monika Maron, *Pawels Briefe* (Frankfurt am Main: Fischer, 1999), 51. Subsequent references to this work are cited in the text using the abbreviation *PB* and page number.

[2] Friedericke Eigler, "Nostalgisches und kritisches Erinnern am Beispiel von Martin Walsers *Ein springender Brunnen* und Monika Marons *Pawels Briefe*," in *Monika*

Maron in Perspective: "Dialogische" Einblicke in zeitgeschichtliche, intertextuelle und rezeptionsbezogene Aspekte ihres Werkes, ed. by Elke Gilson (Amsterdam: Rodopi, 2002), 157–80; here: 168.

[3] Edward W. Said, "Traveling Theory," in *The World, the Text and the Critic* (London: Vintage, 1991), 226–47; here: 239.

[4] Eigler has twice noted the applicability of postmemory to *Pawels Briefe.* In "Nostalgisches und kritisches Erinnern," she sees Maron as achieving Hirsch's balancing act of putting oneself in another's place without displacing them (169). I shall argue below, however, that the narrator's identification with Pawel is not as positive as Eigler contends. In a later article, she argues that *Pawels Briefe* foregrounds "the absence of memory traces that mark an irretrievable loss," but goes beyond postmemory by using literary and poetic language to "facilitate an affective response to this lost past" ("Engendering Cultural Memory in Selected Post-*Wende* Literary Texts of the 1990s," *German Quarterly* 74/4 (2001): 392–406; here: 395). I do not see that such an "affective response" in any way goes beyond Hirsch's account of postmemorial narrative. *Pawels Briefe* does exceed the terms of postmemory, but in ways Eigler does not consider.

[5] Marianne Hirsch, "Surviving Images: Holocaust Photographs and the Work of Postmemory," in *Visual Culture and the Holocaust,* ed. Barbie Zelizer (London: Athlone, 2001), 215–46; here: 221. See also the definitions provided by Hirsch in "Projected Memory: Holocaust Photographs in Personal and Public Fantasy," in *Acts of Memory: Cultural Recall in the Present,* ed. Mieke Bal, Jonathan Crewe, and Leo Spitzer (Hanover and London: UP of New England, 1999), 3–23; here: 8. Both are taken almost verbatim from Hirsch's earlier book *Family Frames: Photography, Narrative and Postmemory* (Cambridge, MA: Harvard UP, 1997), 22. The significant change is the substitution of "displaced" for "evacuated" in the later essays. This is an important distinction, and it goes at least some way towards correcting the impression created by *Family Frames* that the second generation is nothing but a receptacle for the first generation's memories.

[6] In "Projected Memory" Hirsch writes: "As I conceive of it, postmemory is not an identity position, but a space of remembrance, more broadly available through cultural and public, and not merely individual and personal, acts of remembrance" (8–9). This, however, is incompatible with the claims Hirsch makes for postmemory in *Family Frames* and "Surviving Images," where it is set up unequivocally as a subject position. It transmutes into a "space of remembrance" only when Hirsch begins to develop the notion of a "postmemorial aesthetic."

[7] See e.g. *Family Frames,* 272, 276; "Projected Memory," 9–10.

[8] Kaja Silverman, *The Threshold of the Visible World* (London: Routledge, 1996), 173.

[9] Marita Grimwood, "Postmemorial Positions: Reading and Writing after the Holocaust in Anne Michaels's *Fugitive Pieces,*" *Canadian Jewish Studies* 11 (2003): 111–30; here: 114–15.

[10] Hirsch, "Surviving Images," 221; cf. "Projected Memory," 8–9 and *Family Frames,* 254–55.

[11] Hirsch, "Surviving Images," 221; cf. "Projected Memory," 9. Curiously, Hirsch maintains that the descendants of perpetrators, victims, witnesses and survivors

"have different experiences of postmemory, even though they share the familial ties that facilitate intergenerational identification" ("Surviving Images," 220). Quite how identification with the perpetrator might represent an "*ethical* relation to the oppressed or persecuted other," however, remains unclear.

[12] Karin Mylius, daughter of a former member of an SS Special Unit, was elected to the board of the Jewish Community in Halle without ever converting to Judaism. During her twenty-five-year tenure in this office, she buried her father in rabbinical robes, and sent her son to a rabbinical school in Budapest. Binjamin Wilkomirski, who published a memoir of his childhood in the concentration camps, was soon afterwards revealed to be the Swiss gentile Bruno Grosjean. Nevertheless, he continued to insist on his Jewishness, adopting the outward trappings of orthodoxy and cultivating a melancholy, emotionally fragile public persona. At stake in these cases is decidedly unethical identification with "the oppressed or persecuted other" for economic gain, enhanced self-image, cultural prestige, and power.

[13] See Peter Novick, *The Holocaust in American Life* (New York: Houghton Mifflin, 1999), 88–98.

[14] Hirsch's notion of "generations" implies an essentialized distinction between "first" and "second" generations. Maron is situated somewhere in between: born in 1941, she lived through the last four years of Nazi rule, and therefore falls within the first generation. But since she was still a very young child when the war ended, she has few conscious memories of the time, and most of them are banal. This is thematized throughout the text (*PB*, 70, 117, 145, 151, 165, 174). On the difficulties of defining "second generation" and the terms on which it depends (such as "survivor" and "refugee"), see Grimwood, "Postmemorial Positions," 115.

[15] I use the term "complete" only relationally: the visual rhetoric of the text leads one to assume that the first occurrence of each image is uncropped, even though this may not be the case.

[16] Fredericke Eigler, *Engendering Cultural Memory*, 396.

[17] No critic has yet provided anything more than a cursory discussion of the photographs in *Pawels Briefe*. In addition to secondary works cited elsewhere in this chapter, see Elke Gilson, " 'Nur wenige kurze Augenblicke, die sicher sind': Zur konstruktivistisch inspirierten Darstellung des Erinnerns und Vergessens in Monika Marons Familiengeschichte *Pawels Briefe*," *Colloquia Germanica* 33/3 (2000): 275–88.

[18] Roland Barthes, *Camera Lucida*, trans. by Richard Howard (London: Flamingo, 1984), 76.

[19] See e.g. Julia Hirsch, *Family Photographs: Content, Meaning, and Effect* (New York and Oxford: Oxford UP, 1981), 94–95.

[20] The photograph reproduced in *Pawels Briefe*, 54, bears a striking resemblance to that described in Maron's first novel *Flugasche* (Frankfurt am Main: Fischer, 1981), 7. For a comparison of the treatment of Pawel and Josefa's story in the two texts, see Sylvia Klötzer, " 'Wir haben so lange nach vorne gelebt': Erinnerung und Identität. *Flugasche* und *Pawels Briefe*," in *Monika Maron in Perspective: "Dialogische" Einblicke in zeitgeschichtliche, intertextuelle und rezeptionsbezogene Aspekte ihres Werkes*, ed. Elke Gilson (Amsterdam: Rodopi, 2002), 35–56.

[21] As Julia Hirsch points out, full-face, frontal composition allows genetic similarity to emerge clearly (*Family Photographs*, 95). Pawel is invariably photographed in this way.

[22] See, for example, the images disseminated as part of the Fischer Verlag's publicity material, or the portraits gracing the dustjackets of several of Maron's books.

[23] Much has been written about the role of photography in various physiognomic and classificatory discourses and the effect of these on the construction of the bourgeois, criminal, insane, racial, or pathological body. For comprehensive accounts, see Suren Lalvani, *Photography, Vision, and the Production of Modern Bodies* (Albany: SUNY Press, 1996) and Peter Hamilton and Roger Hargreaves, *The Beautiful and the Damned: The Creation of Identity in Nineteenth-Century Photography* (Aldershot and Burlington: Lund Humphries, 2001). See also Susanne Regener, *Fotografische Erfassung: Zur Geschichte medialer Konstruktionen des Kriminellen* (Munich: Fink, 1999).

[24] See Jeffrey Herf, *Divided Memory: The Nazi Past in the Two Germanys* (Cambridge MA: Harvard UP, 1997).

[25] What I have called the rhetoric of retraction can be seen in numerous other instances where Maron addresses Hella's status as an agent of memory. See *PB*, 10–12, 15–18, 50, 70–71, 77–79, 109. This rhetoric functions in conjunction with the thoroughgoing critique of the GDR to constitute Hella's memory as ineluctably flawed. To claim that *Pawels Briefe* implies a relativist notion of memory and upholds the value of tolerance is a simplification. For although the narrator is cognizant of the unreliability of any memory — including her own — she nevertheless constructs a hierarchy that privileges her version of affairs over Hella's. See Eigler, "Nostalgisches und kritisches Erinnern," Lothar Bluhm, "'Irgendwann, denken wir, muß ich das genau wissen': Der Erinnerungsdiskurs bei Monika Maron," in *Mentalitätswandel in der deutschen Literatur zur Einheit (1990–2000)*, ed. Volker Wehdeking (Berlin: Erich Schmidt, 2000), 141–51, and Katharina Boll, *Erinnerung und Reflexion: Retrospektive Lebenskonstruktionen im Prosawerk Monika Marons* (Würzburg: Königshausen und Neumann, 2002), 97.

[26] Monika Maron, *quer über die gleise: Essays, Artikel, Zwischenrufe* (Frankfurt am Main: Fischer, 2000), 24–33.

[27] Andrew Plowman, "Escaping the Autobiographical Trap? Monika Maron, the Stasi and *Pawels Briefe*," in *German Writers and the Politics of Culture: Dealing with the Stasi*, ed. Paul Cooke and Andrew Plowman (Basingstoke: Palgrave, 2003), 227–42. Here: 231.

[28] A similar conclusion is reached — albeit from a very different starting point — by Plowman, "Escaping the Autobiographical Trap?," 233. In her essay "Rollenwechsel" (*quer über die gleise*, 95–116), Maron takes issue with a series of criticisms of *Pawels Briefe*. In particular, she strenuously denies ever having felt herself to be a victim (100). Later, however, she argues that the desire for a clear distinction between victims and perpetrators does not allow a better understanding of history, nor does it facilitate justice, but merely bolsters the self-righteousness of those who demand the clear distinction in the first place. "Unsere Verhältnisse und wir sind gemischt" (111), she adds (our situation and we ourselves are mixed). This contradicts the earlier part of the essay, since here Maron clearly does claim partial victim status

for herself. More dubious, however, is her apparent blindness to the implications of her argument. Dismantling the victim-perpetrator binary can lead to historical distortions and impede justice in ways that are ultimately far more problematic than those caused by an insistence on the distinction. It is difficult not to read "Rollenwechsel" as a disingenuous exercise in self-justification that lacks the subtlety, self-questioning, and formal interest of *Pawels Briefe*.

[29] Jan Assmann, *Das kulturelle Gedächtnis: Schrift, Erinnerung, und politische Identität in frühen Hochkulturen* (Munich: Beck, 1992), 50–52.

[30] Marcel Beyer's *Spione*, Kurt Drawert's *Spiegelland*, and Ulla Hahn's *Unscharfe Bilder* are cases in point.

Ethnicity/Hybridity

8: Imagined Identities: Children and Grandchildren of Holocaust Survivors in Literature

Dagmar C. G. Lorenz

THE REPRESENTATION OF JEWISH IDENTITY after the Shoah in German and Austrian texts is a complex and often problematic issue, showing up the highly contentious nature of German-Jewish memory contests. On the one hand post-Shoah Jewish identity continues to be negotiated within firmly established traditions; on the other hand any such negotiation involves an engagement with the Austrian and German cultural contexts. The destruction of the Jewish communities and cultural networks in Europe caused an unprecedented breakdown in continuity and a divide across which the search for an authentic Jewish tradition seems impossible. Jewish intellectuals and poets left behind a rich textual legacy in a variety of European languages. Innumerable literary and autobiographical works by authors such as Arthur Schnitzler, Else Lasker-Schüler, Gertrud Kolmar, Jakob Wassermann, and Joseph Roth convey an impression of Jewish life before the Shoah. These works explore the identity struggles of Jews between assimilation and self-assertion, between those who sought citizenship within Christian societies and those who wished to preserve their difference, opting instead to coexist alongside the dominant population, albeit within an ambiguously defined cultural context.

Throughout the following article the works of one of the most prominent post-Shoah writers, Ilse Aichinger, will be examined and revisited to assess different phases in the re-emergence of a literary Jewish culture after 1945. Aichinger's career began with the publication of her novel *Die größere Hoffnung* (1948, *The Greater Hope*, published in English as *Herod's Children*, 1963), a text whose radical position of alienation from the dominant culture has often been overlooked, and continues in the twenty-first century.[1] Like many Austrians of Jewish descent, the author had been raised Catholic. In response to her experience of discrimination and the threat of deportation during the Nazi era she focused in her works on the experiences and perceptions of the Jewish minority. During her career she interacted personally and through her texts with different generations of authors in search of a Jewish identity after the genocide. They included members of the exile and survivor generations such as Nelly Sachs, Paul Celan and others, whose works were anthologized but largely ignored, the intermediate generation — Jurek Becker, Cordelia Edvardson, Jakov Lind —, the post-Shoah generation — Ruth Beckermann, Nadja Seelich, Esther Dischereit, Robert Menasse, and Robert Schindel — and, finally, the third and fourth generations: Doron Rabinovici and Vladimir Vertlib.[2] Aichinger was a pioneer in helping to shape a new Jewish literary discourse in the German language, but her later later works reveal that she, in turn, learned from and responded to younger authors. A key figure and an active participant in contemporary German and Austrian Jewish literary culture, Aichinger and her writings provide the paradigm for the literary processes examined in this article.

Even before the emergence of National Socialism the use of Jewish languages — Yiddish, Hebrew, Ladino — was decreasing in areas where German was spoken, especially in middle-class circles. The German language, more precisely Hochdeutsch, had in fact become the "hidden" language of the Jews. However, anti-Semites did not tire of listening for and identifying the mark of difference in the German of assimilated Jews.[3] During the nineteenth century certain cultural practices and political views had increasingly taken the place of traditional religious observance. Considered revolutionary by mainstream conservatives, these movements — Zionism, cosmopolitanism, pacifism, and Marxism — came to be identified as Jewish. Indeed, all of these models were attractive to Jews looking for an alternative to traditional Judaism and an escape from oppression and persecution. In the interwar period an entire spectrum of Jewish identities and communities existed in the big cities of Germany, Austria, and Central and Eastern Europe. In *Die Mazzesinsel* (The Matzoh Island, 1984), a photo documentary of Vienna's Second District during the interwar period, Ruth Beckermann evokes a vivid picture of the diversity of the Jewish community there:

> Hier lebten nicht nur die Religionen, sondern auch die Klassen eng beisammen [. . .]. Eine Vielzahl jüdischer Vereine, Clubs und Organisationen, die sich den verschiedensten weltanschaulichen Lagern verpflichtet fühlten — von ganz weit links über sämtliche zionistische Schattierungen bis hin zu den Ultrafrommen —, waren nicht nur den Leopoldstädter Juden, sondern auch den 120.000 anderswo in Wien lebenden gesellschaftliche Heimat. Das war Weltrekord, denn in keiner anderen Stadt gab es damals ein ähnlich dichtes Netz jüdischer Vereine.[4]

> [Not only the different religions but also the different classes lived closely together in this neighborhood [. . .]. A multitude of Jewish associations, clubs, and organizations indebted to the most diverse ideological orientations — including the extreme Left, all forms of Zionism and the ultra religious — were home to the Jews of Leopoldstadt as well as to the 120,000 Jews living elsewhere in Vienna. That was a world record. In no other city was there a similarly dense network of Jewish associations.]

During the Holocaust these cultural networks were destroyed. Beyond their personal losses, Shoah survivors faced not only a Europe without Jewish life but they also had to deal with their traumatic memories survivors.

Eine ganze Kultur wurde vernichtet [. . .]. Bis in unsere Erinnerung hinein wurde sie vernichtet, von der Bilderflut der Nazis überschwemmt. Mit Tausenden Photos und Filmen haben sie ihre Macht in unsere Gehirne eingebrannt.[5]

[An entire culture was destroyed [. . .]. Even in our memory it was destroyed, inundated by the flood of Nazi images. With their thousands of photographs and films they branded our brains with their power.]

The works of post-Shoah authors writing in German reveal a variety of approaches to the problem of identity. They range from attempts at reconstructing a lost or destroyed identity to the construction of new Jewish identities that reflect the changed historical situation and the absence of a community context. In the following I will examine Jewish identity construction as demonstrated by authors from different generations. There are a number of themes raised and strategies implemented by the respective authors. Jurek Becker and Lea Fleischmann, for example, posit the Holocaust as the fundamental divide between Jewish and non-Jewish identity. Others, such as Ilse Aichinger, Anna Mitgutsch, Robert Menasse, and Vladimir Vertlib construct oppositional Jewish narratives in the face of an antagonistically configured German or Austrian mainstream. The experience of alterity in Germany or Austria is a dominant theme, while the search for alternative spheres of existence, both within these countries and beyond them — the mapping of an alternative Jewish geography — also preoccupies many of these writers. Finally, another tendency is the introduction of literary and cultural characteristics to mark the text as Jewish. None of these strategies are exclusive to individual works, but are instead ubiquitous in the body of post-Shoah Jewish writing.

Jurek Becker, a child survivor of the ghettos of Lodz and Ravensbrück, uses Jewish elements and themes on multiple levels. Sander Gilman raises the question of Becker's mother tongue. He finds it hard to decide whether the author's native language was Polish, which he had spoken as a child, or whether it was perhaps Yiddish, used by Becker's parents in the ghetto, or if it was the "Lagersprache," the *lingua franca* of the concentration camps.[6] For historical reasons Becker's literary language was German. For numerous prominent pre-Shoah authors, writing in German was a deliberate decision. Elias Canetti and Claire Goll could conceivably have published in a different language. For Becker, who grew up in the GDR, writing in German was a matter of course.

Becker was the first East German author who wrote about the Nazi persecutions from a Jewish point of view. He portrayed the Holocaust as a specifically Jewish experience in *Jakob der Lügner* (Jacob the Liar, 1969), a novel set in two different locations and time frames, in the GDR and in a ghetto about to be liquidated.[7] The narrator, who is the sole survivor, resides in the GDR. His life continues to be overshadowed by the past as the dominant collective memory in the GDR marginalizes that of the Shoah survivors. In keeping with the doctrine that the Nazi regime was the culmination of the class struggle pitting the proletariat against capitalists and the lower middle class, the East German "Workers and Farmers' State" (Arbeiter- und Bauernstaat) considered itself the heir to socialist antifascism and as such not responsible for the crimes of National Socialism. The murder of the Jews was considered collateral damage in the fight for a classless society. While their status as victims of fascism was recognized, Judaism and the legacy of German Jewish culture were repudiated as reactionary and bourgeois. In the GDR a revitalization of Jewish life was discouraged because of the association of Jewishness with capitalism.

Becker, similar to the protagonist of his second and most autobiographical novel *Der Boxer* (The Boxer, 1976), was reunited with his father by JOINT, the American Jewish Joint Distribution Organization. In the novel, the boy Mark, aged seven, is small and weak for his age. Father and son do not recognize one another.[8] Their alienation from each other anticipates their differing reactions to the problem of Jewish identity after 1945. While Mark's father is keen to remove all traces of this — for him — traumatic identity from their lives, his son embraces his Jewish identity and goes to Israel where he is killed in the Six Day War. Arno, Mark's father (who is not identical with the character of Arno in *Bronsteins Kinder*) wonders why his son chose to define himself in this way; after all, he had tried to protect his son from the dangers of Jewish identity by denying him a Jewish education. The text thus thematizes Jewish identity as negotiated differently by different generations. In Mark's case, it raises an important question concerning Jewish self-definition after 1945: the orientation towards a clearly demarcated sense of one's Jewishness as a reaction to anti-Semitism. In his 1976 address "Der ehrbare Antisemitismus" (Respectable Anti-Semitism), for example, the Austrian-born Holocaust survivor, philosopher, and critic Jean Améry drew attention to a fast-spreading, specifically Leftist anti-Semitism, which came in the guise of anti-Zionism and was inspired by the attitude toward Jews and Judaism in the GDR and the Soviet Union.[9]

In his third novel, *Bronsteins Kinder* (Bronstein's Children, 1986), Becker explores the residues of Jewishness in children of Shoah survivors who grew up in a non-Jewish environment. Elle, the older sister of the protagonist Hans, survived in hiding with Gentiles. She remembers more of the past than her brother, hence her fits of aggression against adult Germans. Unable to cope with her trauma, she has to live in a mental institution in the GDR. Hans, on the other hand, grew up identifying with the East German worker's and farmer's state. He seems oblivious to the fact that his circle of friends consists almost exclusively of Jewish survivors and their children, including his first girlfriend. Finally his father's past catches up with him; Arno Bronstein and some of his fellow survivors kidnap a former concentration camp guard from Neuengamme. This capture seems as arbitrary as Nazi actions; none of the men had ever been in this particular camp. Observing his father and the other men interrogating and humiliating their prisoner, Hans is outraged by the violence committed. He is also taken aback by the fact that the men speak Yiddish, and that, after some initial difficulty, he too understands the language perfectly well.[10]

Becker's *Jakob der Lügner* is replete with Jewish elements including Jewish names (Chana, Frankfurter, Fajngold, Herschel Schtamm), foods (Tscholent, Chale), institutions such as the Jewish sports club "Hakoah," references to Jewish institutions, offices, and customs — "Synagoge," the house of worship, "Rabbiner," the teacher knowledgable in Jewish law and scripture, "Schamess," the synagogue attendant, "Schläfenlocken," peyos, "Schabess," Shabbat.[11] Finally, Jakob Heim's occupation prior to his deportation calls to mind the Eastern European shtetl culture and Jewish food: He had been a vendor of "latkes" — potato pancakes. By naming Jewish phenomena, Becker calls to mind pre-Shoah Jewish culture and its diverse expressions, but he also sets these terms as linguistic markers emphasizing the untranslatability of things Jewish into a non-Jewish language. Set in East Germany, the Jewish elements in *Der Boxer* and *Bronsteins Kinder*, the second and third volumes of Becker's Jewish trilogy, are overlaid with allusions to National Socialism, anti-Fascism, and GDR history.[12] In these two novels the survivor/fathers, both of whom call themselves "Arno" to avoid their actual name, Aron, steer their sons away from the Jewish past. However, even in the absence of a Jewish education or a discussion of the past, Mark in *Der Boxer* constructs for himself a Jewish identity in response to anti-Semitism, and Hans in *Bronsteins Kinder* appears forever changed after his confrontation with the legacy of the Holocaust in his home environment.

Throughout *Bronsteins Kinder* there are hints that Hans is not as well integrated into socialist society as he thinks. For example, while taking a shower Hans has a dispute with another student and resorts to physical violence. His teacher tries to explain this incident by pointing out that Hans is Jewish. He presumes that Hans reacted defensively because he was circumcised. Ironically, this is not the case, as Hans's father did not believe in marking his only son as Jewish.[13] The well-intended cultural overinterpretation on the part of the non-Jewish teacher reveals Hans's outsider status. Another example is the production of a Holocaust film in which Hans's girlfriend is asked to participate because she is Jewish, and, finally, Arno's regression into the *universe concentrationnaire* as a result of yielding to his desire for revenge and ultimately justice. Thus, he and his friends kidnap the former concentration camp guard from Neuengamme and imprison him in Arno Bronstein's weekend cottage, where they beat and torture him. For Arno the situation becomes so stressful that he begins to neglect himself, takes up smoking again, and eventually dies of a heart attack while the perpetrator, released by Hans, is able to walk away and presumably begin a new life in the West. The situation Becker evokes is one of traumatic memory repressed and reemergent. Arno relives the horrors of the concentration camp while replaying events reminiscent of it. In order to free himself of the past he assumes the position of power: he is the torturer, he is the henchman. However, as LaCapra reveals in the context of Holocaust testimonies, the traumatic event

> may actually be relived in the present, at times in a compulsively repetitive manner. It may not be subject to controlled, conscious recall. But it returns in nightmares, flashbacks, anxiety attacks, and other forms of intrusively repetitive behavior characteristic of an all-compelling frame.[14]

In *Bronsteins Kinder*, reliving the past by recreating concentration-camp-like conditions ends up costing the former victim, but not the perpetrator, his life. At the same time, at the pivotal moment when Hans realizes what is going on he is pulled into his father's experience, linguistically and emotionally. In other words, Becker suggests that Jewish identity is an ongoing process of negotiating checks and balances between external pressures imposed by family and society, and internal, subjective needs. He also introduces the element of personal choice in the identity process. Mark in *Der Boxer* chooses to become a Jew, while Hans in *Bronsteins Kinder* is hesitant and undecided. The example of Hans's girlfriend Martha Lepschitz, like Hans the child of survivors, shows that a secular Jewish identity can also evolve through confrontation under specific social, emotional, and intellectual conditions. For all these types of identity formation the final touchstone is the Holocaust and the communality it created.[15] Already in his first novel, *Jakob der Lügner*, Becker shows how a community of quite dissimilar characters forms in the ghetto. This community arises from the experience of suffering and an unrealistic hope that revolves around a simple man, who presumably owns a radio and unites persons of different status, age, and ideology. In the postwar society depicted in *Bronsteins Kinder* the common experiences of persecution, survival, and marginalization as Jews provide close ties between Holocaust survivors and their children. Hans, for example, considers Martha his only logical choice as a girlfriend even though she is older and more mature than he is. The surivors Bronstein, Kwart, and Rotstein are united by their common trauma that drives their transgressions as it would a conspiracy. The Lepschitzs, even after the breakup of Hans and Martha's relationship, invite Arno Bronstein's orphaned son to live with them until he graduates and can take care of himself.

Lea Fleischmann's autobiographical account of growing up in and eventually leaving West Germany, *Dies ist nicht mein Land* (This Is Not My

Country, 1980) is equally motivated by Holocaust memory.[16] In the post-war period an "unprecendented forgetting of the historic events" charac-terized West Germany, followed by an epidemic of remembrance in the 1970s, Manuela Günter writes.[17] Jews still or again living in Germany were not an issue in a country trying to reestablish its national unity.[18] Hence the avoidance of the term "Jude," and the government's focus on Israel as the recipient of restitution. In the Federal Republic Shoah memory was the memory of a marginalized minority. Fleischmann, the daughter of Polish survivors born in the Bavarian Displaced Persons' (DP) Camp Föhren-walde, and a *Berufsschullehrerin*, a vocational school teacher, left West Ger-many in 1978 to live in Israel. In *Dies ist nicht mein Land* she recounts how she resisted being shaped by German people, institutions, and the "Disziplin-Begriff," the belief in discipline that, as Henryk Broder writes, is common in Germany."[19] Her opposition to what she perceives as a lin-gering Nazi mentality and Nazi practices in the Federal Republic culmin-ates in her decision to go to Israel: "Fünf Jahre lebte meine Mutter unter den Deutschen, und fünf Jahre lebte ich mit ihnen. Es ist genug," she con-cludes (250; My mother lived among the Germans for five years, and I lived with them for five years. That is enough).

Fleischmann begins her narrative with a chapter entitled "Die Tür wird luftdicht abgeschlossen. Schma Israel" (The Door Closes Airtight. Sh'ma Israel). It is an account of an imagined alternative Jewish biography that begins in a Polish shtetl and ends in the gas chamber. Fleischmann envisages traumatic events that she escaped by having been born after the Shoah. She describes what might have happened to her and her parents had they been captured by the Nazis.[20] Her intimate and emotional narrative attempts to bridge the gap between herself and the previous generation. Writing from the point of view of a near-victim, Fleischmann characterizes herself as an exception to the Ashkenazy fate and as an oddity in post-Shoah Germany. Her legitimate home is the shtetl, where she would have grown up among pious men and women practicing "jahrhundertealte Bräuche" (century-old customs) that the Nazis disrupted and that van-ished within a generation.[21] She imagines how it might have felt being "geborgen" (safe), a feeling she never had among Germans. She evokes the Yiddish language and pleasures of which she believes she was deprived, such as joyful celebrations and closeness to nature. Her dream ends with the shocking arrival of the Germans, "ganz andere Goim als die Polen [. . .]. Alle Deutschen sehen gleich aus. Schwarze Stiefel, Uniform und eine Mütze" (non-Jews altogether different from the Poles [. . .]. All Germans look the same. Black boots, a uniform, and a cap) and with the deportation of the entire village to Auschwitz. The final vision is that of a gas chamber disguised as a shower room.[22]

Fleischmann constructs Jews and Germans as opposites, motivated by different goals and perceptions. Her fictional mother's tenderness during the journey to the death camp, the forbearance and wisdom her fictional father musters, despite being abused by the Nazis, reveal idealized character traits and behavior patterns that are constructed as fundamentally different from those of the Germans. The Jews portrayed in the opening section of the book also differ from the characters of Fleischmann's actual parents in the following chapters. Fleischmann idealizes the imaginary parents of the Holocaust segment and portrays her actual parents as complex people, who are difficult to get along with. Despite her conflicted relationship with the actual parents Fleischmann maintains the binary opposition between Germans and Jews throughout the text, as well as the divide between the pre-Shoah and post-Shoah era, making the Shoah the touchstone of Jewish and German identity. These dualities also reveal an interdependence between the two opposing aspects of Fleischmann's identity: the Jewish and, despite her protestations, the German. *Dies ist nicht mein Land* confirms Dan Diner's thesis of a negative German-Jewish symbiosis produced by the Shoah.[23] Fleischmann's career as an Israeli author of German literature epitomizes the post-Shoah paradox even further. The author resides in Jerusalem but publishes in German with German publishing houses, and she lectures to German audiences. There are other Germanophone authors who are identified or identify themselves as Jewish and who position themselves in opposition to an antagonistically constructed German culture, for example Henryk Broder and Ruth Beckermann.[24] The base of their criticism comes from the history of their families and their Jewish identity, which separates them from the dominant culture and motivates them to write deliberately Jewish texts.

The authors who played a key role in late twentieth-century Jewish literary circles included writers of the Shoah generation who, like Ilse Aichinger, had transformed themselves in response to the changing historical situation. In contrast to the younger writers, Aichinger had experienced the violent end of Jewish assimilation under the Nazi regime and the shock of suddenly being made a social outcast. Already in the last years of the Nazi regime she had begun to construct a literary Jewish identity informed by her disillusionment with Austrian society, her exclusion, and the persecution suffered by her maternal family.

Under the Nazis Aichinger had been classified as a "half-Aryan" minor, a status that had enabled her to protect her mother from deportation. Her novel about persecuted children in Vienna, *Die größere Hoffnung*, is an early example of post-Shoah textual revisionism as a strategy of marking a text as Jewish. The author was the daughter of a non-Jewish father and a mother of Jewish descent, and she introduces this dilemma in her novel.[25] In the novel she emphasized the solidarity of her autobiographical protagonist Ellen with children facing deportation. Like the author, Ellen is positioned between Jews and non-Jews. Without being forced to do so, Ellen decides to wear the Yellow Star, which she re-interprets as a repeatedly her uncertainty about how a Jew can define herself after the destruction of the Jewish culture and its traditional communities by the Nazis. In a sarcastic reference to the Nuremberg Laws she suggests that for many non-Jews Nazi concepts still had validity in the 1980s.[40] Hannah's question "Who is a Jew?" also points to the loss of Jewish diversity after the Shoah discussed by Sem Dresden, who deplores the reduction of Jewish identity to the generic category of victim.[41]

The revision of mainstream narratives is an important strategy for Doron Rabinovici, who was born in Tel Aviv in 1961. He was a child when he moved with his Polish-born parents to Vienna. His dissertation in History, completed at the University of Vienna in 2001 and published as a book, is a controversial contribution to the debates on the Austrian past. Rabinovici re-examines the role of the *Judenräte* (the Jewish Councils) who have been commonly vilified as traitors and collaborators.[42] Rabinovici underscores the powerlessness of Jewish institutions and agents. He identifies the Nazi establishment as the sole source of power, which demanded that specific functions be carried out by Jews during the deportations and in the ghettos. Thus he exonerates Jews who were browbeaten or lured into cooperating with the perpetrators; he assigns exclusive responsibility for the genocide to the perpetrators, rather than implicating and assigning blame to subalterns and victims.

Die jüdische Gemeindeleitung Wiens unterlag denselben Zwängen wie alle Juden, sie verfügte über keine eigene Macht, sondern war zur bloßen Instanz geschwunden, zu einer Instanz der Ohnmacht. Auch im nachhinein tut sich keine Handlungsalternative zum damaligen Dilemma auf. Mit jüdischen Traditionen, mit der Identifikation des Opfers mit dem Täter oder mit etwaigen Wiener Eigenheiten hängt dies alles nicht im geringsten zusammen. Keine Opfergruppe hätte unter ähnlichen Bedingungen anders reagieren können; keine könnte heute anders handeln.[43]

[The leadership of the Vienna Jewish community was subject to the same oppression as all Jews. It did not have any power of its own. It had been reduced to a mere administrator, an administrator of powerlessness. Not even in hindsight does a possible alternative to their dilemma emerge. The events in question did not have the least bit to do with Jewish tradition, the victims' identification with the perpetrators, or possible Viennese idiosyncrasies. Under similar conditions no victim group could have reacted differently; none could act differently today.]

The Jewishness of Rabinovici's literary texts and his polemics rests on the construction of an oppositional point of view that undermines the discourse on the Shoah in Austrian mainstream writing, Jewish identity and history, and popular perceptions about Jewish and Austrian identity.

A large-scale revision of historical narratives about Jewish culture across the centuries is the focal point in Robert Menasse's novel *Die*

symbol of pride. Throughout the novel, Aichinger attributes a degree of integrity to the persecuted children that is unattainable to their persecutors, including Ellen's Nazi father. In an encounter between father and daughter Aichinger reveals that the Nazis' aggression and apparent strength are based on fear and insecurity.

The rift between the pre- and post-Shoah generations, Jews and non-Jews, recurs in Aichinger's later poem entitled "Mein Vater" (My Father). Here, winter images and the contrast of mobility and stagnation express the distance between the former victimizer and his once persecuted daughter.[26] In many of her later poems and prose works Aichinger takes a position apart from Austria's Catholic mainstream.[27] Most explicitly Aichinger's recent collections of short prose provide autobiographical details and express critical distance from her Austrian contemporaries.

> Diejenigen, die zusahen, wie meine Großmutter und die jüngeren Geschwister meiner Mutter auf offenen Viehwagen über die Schwedenbrücke in Folter und Tod gefahren wurden, sahen jedenfalls mit einem gewissen Vergnügen zu. Es war das letzte Mal, daß ich meine Großmutter sah. Als ich nach ihr rief, wichen sie links und rechts zurück. Aber das war drei Jahre früher gewesen. "Der Jude" war jetzt keine Gefahr mehr, jetzt war "der Russe" der Inbegriff der Bedrohung.[28]

> [Those who watched as my grandmother and my mother's younger siblings were driven on an open cattle car across the Swedish Bridge toward torture and death looked on, to be sure, with a certain glee. It was the last time that I saw my grandmother. When I called out for her they stepped back left and right. But that had been three years earlier. "The Jew" was no longer a danger at that point. Now "the Russian" had come to epitomize the threat.]

Another important element in the construction or reconstruction of Jewish identity in Aichinger's writing is the shaping of an alternative Jewish topography or geography. The emphasis on certain sites and their meaning differ from those in Gentile writing. A map of Vienna highlighting the places mentioned most frequently by Jewish writers would certainly differ from one drawn from a mainstream narrative. Associating specific locations with Jewish history and the Shoah, Aichinger creates a Jewish memory discourse. Sites reminiscent of Vienna Jewish history are introduced in the prose vignettes *Plätze und Straßen* (Places and Streets, 1954). They include "Judengasse," Jewish Alley, "Seegasse," the site of an ancient Jewish cemetery, "Verbindungsbahn," the railway line close to the location where Jews were rounded up and loaded on deportation trains, "Im Werd," the site of Vienna's second ghetto in the Leopoldstadt (Second District), which was destroyed in a pogrom in 1420 and that, in the nineteenth century, became a center for Jewish immigration.[29]

In their rigor, Aichinger's texts call to mind the autobiography of Cordelia Edvardson, daughter of the prominent writer Elisabeth Langgässer.[30] Like Aichinger, Edvardson was Catholic, but her father had been Jewish, and she was deported to Auschwitz. During her ordeal Edvardson became acquainted with other Jews and the Yiddish language. In her autobiography *Gebranntes Kind sucht das Feuer* (Burnt Child Seeks the Fire, 1986) she examines her problematic relationship with her mother, notably her sense that her mother had betrayed her, first, when she let her child face the Jewish transport alone, and second, when she asked her about her experiences and used the information in the context of her novel *Märkische Argonautenfahrt* (The Argonauts' Journey in Mark Brandenburg, 1950) in a way Edvardson did not approve of.[31] Thus the novel reflects upon the intergenerational conflict between Edvardson and her mother: for similar reasons as Aichinger, Edvardson had constructed for herself a Jewish identity and emotionally distanced herself from her mother. She even converted to Judaism separating herself from her in terms of religion as well.

Textual revisionism, the recasting and reinterpreting of German and Austrian mainstream narratives of different time periods and genres features in many Jewish novels.[32] Such mainstream material includes Christian legends and stories, fairy tales, non-Jewish folklore, and well-known literary works. By reading such texts against the grain, Jewish authors reveal ways in which they can be read in a Jewish context. Ilse Aichinger, for example, in the chapter "Das große Spiel" (The Great Play) in her novel *Die größere Hoffnung* reinterprets the story of Mary and Joseph to fit the situation of Jewish children persecuted by the Nazis — in the twentieth century the Jewish children, indeed, are persecuted as the Christians once were.[33] Not only Aichinger, but also later authors such as the Holocaust survivor Eva Deutsch, represented Jesus as a Jewish man and a paradigm of Jewish suffering. The Holocaust survivor Eva Deutsch, a native speaker of Polish and Yiddish, had entrusted the Austrian author Brigitte Schwaiger with the writing of her memoir *Die Galizianerin* (The Woman from Galicia, 1974). Schwaiger based the book *Die Galizianerin* on interviews she had conducted with Deutsch and on written accounts Deutsch had provided.[34] Eva Deutsch describes Jesus as "ein Jude durch und durch" (a Jew through and through).[35] Using Jewish markers æ vocabulary, references to holidays, food items, dress codes, specific historical references — Deutsch participates in one of the major practices of post-Shoah Jewish writing. She rewrites Christian or secular non-Jewish narratives from her point of view. Jewish narratives written in German, are overlaid with a network of references to Jewish debates and historic events, but their authors also employ patterns and structures of the German and Austrian tradition. This is the case with the works of Ilse Aichinger, Robert Schindel, Vladimir Vertlib, and notably Robert Menasse, whose expansive narrative networks are modeled after Heimito von Doderer's great novels. Vertlib is inspired by

the classical Russian authors, Pushkin, Gogol, Turgenev, Dostoevsky, stoy, and Chekhov, and the twentieth-century elite, Gorky, Bulg Mayakovsky, Pasternak, Nabokov, and Solzhenitsyn. However, no these authors uses any of these models uncritically.

Austria's repression of the Nazi past became a public issue for th time when Kurt Waldheim ran for President in 1986. In the course election campaign it was revealed that Waldheim, who served as Secr General of the United Nations (1972–1981), had been a member of Nazi German units during the Second World War. This notwithsta he won the Austrian Presidency after much public debate. As a resul Waldheim affair Austria began to examine critically the dominant hi narrative of the Second Republic according to which Austria had b first victim of National Socialism. Austrian Jewish intellectuals bo the Shoah took an active part in the controversy. They protested r against the denial of Austrian guilt in the mainstream media but al cized the Jewish community for placating the former perpetrators i midst they had lived for more than four decades. Ruth Beckerman in 1989: "Die Kinder der Überlebenden wollen nicht mehr schwei Antisemiten diskutieren oder um Mitleid werben" (The childre survivors no longer want to be silent, have discussions with anti or plead for compassion).[36]

The political activism and the polemical contributions pub Austrian Jewish intellectuals during and after the Waldheim camp hand in hand with the emergence of a new Jewish intellectual cul tria. Doron Rabinovici, a younger writer and political activist raises the issue of Jewish identity and unmasks the widespread denial in Austria, emphasizing that denying the Holocaust is offense. Thus he concludes that the fight against Holocaust den political issue but a matter for the courts.[37] In addition, Rabir fronts post-Shoah anti-Semitism: in his short story "Der richtig (The Right Nose for Things) he describes anti-Semitism as insidiou even those persons who try to be politically correct. The Jewish pr non-Jewish friend opposes Waldheim, who had made the ment that joining the Nazi military was his duty.[38] Nonetheless, ers orthodox Jews fair game for jokes and ridicule. Rabinovici's ends the friendship by punching his former buddy in the face the sentiments conveyed through Jurek Becker's protagonists seems to consider physical retribution the only possible react Semitic invectives.[39]

Already prior to the Waldheim affair the feature film *Kiese* bles, 1981) by the Czech-Austrian filmmaker Nadja Seelich h question of what it means to be a Jew in post-1945 Aust Seelich's protagonist, dismisses the notion of race, national gion, but is haunted by the question of Jewish identity. S

Vertreibung aus der Hölle (The Expulsion from Hell, 2001). Assuming a biographical link with Sephardic Jewry because of his Spanish-origin name Menasse, the author draws attention to Sephardic culture and its representatives that include the scholar Samuel Manasseh ben Israel (1064–1657) and the philosopher Barukh Spinoza (1632–77). Menasse uses two historical frames of reference, the Sephardic past, and the post-Shoah present to explore suffering caused by intolerance directed at the Jewish collective from the outside as well as from within Jewish communities against nonconformists. By telling the story of the expulsion from the Spanish peninsula Menasse's twenty-first century, protagonist Viktor Abravanel, a descendant of Shoah survivors, establishes a connection with seventeenth-century Sephardic Amsterdam and the Spanish Jewish tradition that has been virtually ignored in Central and Eastern European literature. Parallels emerge between the ordeal of the survivors of the Inquisition and those of the Shoah, in light of which, the novel implies, inner-Jewish disputes are absurd. Yet, the religious and social intolerance Menasse reveals seems insurmountable. The persecution by the Inquisition is the first horrendous instance of intolerance. It pits Christians against Jews.[44] Examining the minority status of Sephardic Jews in Amsterdam Menasse exposes inner-Jewish sectarianism. Finally, he shows the tenuous situation of the exiles from Spain within the established Sephardic community. Inequity suffered by intellectuals within the doubly marginalized exile group and the larger Sephardic community eventually led to Spinoza's excommunication (herem) in 1656. Past and present suffering connects the Vienna of Menasse's protagonist with Spinoza's Amsterdam. Immersing himself in history Abravanel frees himself from the emotional burden of his mundane existence. The knowledge of the atrocities of centuries past gives him the strength to confront former Nazis with their past. Menasse establishes through multiple levels of otherness and marginalization a position of radical individualism for his protagonist.

Other prominent German-Jewish authors have written about the Sephardic experience and culture. Yet, in contrast to Menasse, who views Sephardic life as an integral part of Central European history, they have associated it with the border regions of Europe and Northern Africa. Elias Canetti's travelogue *Die Stimmen von Marrakesch* (The Voices of Marrakesh, 1967) culminates in a visit to Marrakesh's Jewish quarter, its ancient Jewish cemetery and, finally, a Jewish home. Esther Dischereit in *Merryn* (1992) and Barbara Honigmann in *Sohara's Reise* (Sohara's Journey, 1996) thematize the contrasting experiences of North African Sephardic and Ashkenazic Jews. Canetti and Dischereit envision a coming together and a possible understanding between the two traditions in the present.[45] Menasse, by contrast, stresses their common history of suffering, of persecution, torture, expulsion, and exile. The survivor's trauma he addresses in the case of the Spanish Jews who escaped to the Netherlands, a society less than hospitable society to them, call to mind the fate of European Jews under Nazism. The fascination of Jewish intellectuals such as Spinoza with the progressive, increasingly secular Christian philosophy, and their ultimate failure to reconcile Jewish and Gentile values is reconstructed in such a way as to call to mind the history of Ashkenazic emancipation and assimilation up until the collapse of the German-Jewish symbiosis in the twentieth century. From his post-Shoah perspective Menasse sheds a critical light on the optimism of Spinoza and later thinkers such as Moses Mendelssohn, who tried to establish a basis of mutual respect for the coexistence between Jews and Gentiles. The repeated failure of such attempts, the novel suggests, could have been taken as an omen that the efforts to bring about a German-Jewish symbiosis in the twentieth century would also end in a catastrophe because of the ingrained anti-Judaism and anti-Semitism in Christian and secular society. In Aichinger, Becker, and Fleischmann, Jewishness represents an alternative position to German or Austrian culture within this context. Menasse adopts a point of view marginal even to the dominant Jewish position. He breaks up the monolithic juxtaposition of Germans and Jews by introducing Sephardic, Spanish, and Dutch characters and settings in contradistinction to Ashkenazim, Germans, and Poles.

Jewish writing articulates experiences deviating from mainstream German narratives that construct their own outsiders, for example Böll and Grass in *Billiard um Halbzehn* (Billiards at Half Past Nine, 1959) and *Die Blechtrommel* (The Tin Drum, 1959). In Jewish texts the outsider status implies decisions and issues that are not necessarily individual and personal. As Deleuze and Guattari argue in the case of Kafka, Jewish marginality involves and reflects upon the entire group and is thus always political.[46] This observation applies to Jewish intellectuals in Germany and Austria as well. They are aware that statements they make are all too often interpreted as representative of a collective Jewish viewpoint. Conversely, some of the authors in question at times articulate what they believe to be a Jewish perspective or point of view, explaining, as it were, Jewish reactions to non-Jews. This is true for West-German born Lea Fleischmann, for the Viennese filmmaker Ruth Beckermann, and also for Barbara Honigmann, who grew up in the GDR. By criticizing the conventions, practices, and mentality of their respective Germanophone countries, these authors set themselves apart as Jewish Others. Their criticism goes hand in hand with the search for an alternative Jewish sphere within or outside Germany or Austria. Fleischmann in *Dies ist nicht mein Land*, Beckermann in *Unzugehörig*, and Honigmann in *Roman von einem Kinde* (Novel about a Child, 1986) carve out outsider positions that call for a decision both personal and political.[47] For Fleischmann and Honigmann the physical relocation to a viable Jewish community, Jerusalem or Strasbourg respectively, brings about an at least temporary solution. Beckermann, in her films *Wien*

Retour (A Return Ticket to Vienna, 1983), *Die papierene Brücke* (The Paper Bridge, 1987), *Nach Jerusalem* (To Jerusalem, 1990), and *Ein flüchtiger Zug nach dem Orient* (A Fleeting Passage to the Orient, 1999), which take her from Vienna to Romania, Israel, and Egypt, embarks on a global quest for a viable space appropriate to a contemporary secular Jewish woman. Yet, her filmic narratives, *Jenseits des Krieges* (Beyond War, 1997) and especially *Home mad(e)* (2001), produced in the shadow of the victories of Austria's Freedom Party, take her back to Vienna and the Viennese.[48] Beckermann's implied decision is acceptance of the *galuth*, the freely accepted dispersion of the Jews in contrast to the diaspora, which implies being exiled or driven out, and the determination to maintain her position as an Austrian intellectual.

The expansion of the Jewish sphere in analogy to the patterns of exile of the 1930s and 1940s is reflected in the works of many authors. Menasse takes his readers to South America, Spain, and the Netherlands in *Selige Zeiten, Brüchige Welt* (Blissful Times, Brittle World, 1991) and *Die Vertreibung aus der Hölle*, Rabinovici to Eastern Europe and the Middle East in his *Suche nach M.* (Search for M., 1999), Anna Mitgutsch to Israel in *Abschied von Jerusalem* (Farewell to Jerusalem, 1995), and the United States in *In fremden Städten* (In Strange Cities, 1992). Jeanette Lander includes France, the United States, and Poland in her narrative universe in *Die Töchter* (The Daughters, 1976), as she does Sri Lanka in *Das Jahrhundert der Herren* (The Century of the Lords, 1993). Elias Canetti and Esther Dischereit do likewise in the case of Morocco.[49]

The works of Aichinger, Dischereit, Beckermann, Mitgutsch, and Rabinovici have a metropolitan Germanophone center as their focal point: Vienna or Berlin. These cities constitute the point of departure for these authors' narratives. Historically, this center is associated with the Shoah, and the travel undertaken by the lead character progresses into a world perceived as a global crime scene. Similar to Rabinovici's *Suche nach M.*, the earlier novels of Robert Menasse show that the victims of Nazi crimes and the perpetrators and their children can be found everywhere on the globe. In his earlier novels *Selige Zeiten, brüchige Welt* and *Sinnliche Gewissheit* (Sensual Certainty, 1996), which are set in Brazil and in Austria, Menasse examines the effects of the ubiquitous Nazi connections in terms of morality and international crime. While Rabinovici focuses on Austria, Israel, and the Middle East, Menasse looks toward the Spanish and Portugese speaking world. In view of an assumed global criminal mentality that emerged and spread in the Holocaust era Rabinovici in *Suche nach M.* trivializes everyday crimes such as shoplifting, manslaughter, and even serial murder.

For Rabinovici and Menasse, Vienna represents the geographical and intellectual center from which their plot and subplots evolve. For Dischereit and Lander, Berlin constitutes a similar center.[50] In the prose works of Vladimir Vertlib, born in Leningrad in 1966, such a center is absent. Vertlib immigrated to Austria in 1981 after an odyssey that took him to Israel, Austria, the Netherlands, Germany, back to Israel again, and the United States. He has lived in Vienna and Salzburg. His works differ from those that establish an affinity for a particular place as do the Viennese works of Ruth Beckermann and Robert Schindel. Common reference points and close interaction produced a group of Viennese intellectuals, who reference and cite one another. Schindel, for example, discusses the production of Beckermann's film *Die papierene Brücke*, while she refers to Nadja Seelich's film *Kieselsteine*, which included Schindel as one of the collaborators, in her essay *Unzugehörig* (Not Belonging, 1989).[51] Vertlib stands apart from these "Viennese" authors. For him, it is not the quest for identity or security that defines his sense of space, but rather the experience of continual deportation and migration.

Vertlib's first major narrative "Abschiebung" (Deportation, 1995) is an account of his and his parents' struggle with the US-American immigration service.[52] He reveals the existence of an international underclass of migrants after the collapse of the Eastern Bloc. His perceptions are shaped by chance, coincidence, and uncertainty, and his narratives preclude choice and identity, as they occur in Beckermann's films. In Vertlib's works persons of different ethnicities interact randomly in makeshift migrant abodes. They are pushed around by other agencies and, like the narrator's mother, are exploited and demeaned. Yet even for Vertlib, Jewish identity is linked with memory, as in the novel *Das besondere Gedächtnis der Rosa Masur* (The Special Memory of Rosa Masur, 2001), which harkens back to the pre-Shoah era in a Russian shtetl.[53]

Regarding his recent decision to move to Salzburg, Vertlib downplays Jewish considerations, stating that he had private reasons for relocating, and as a result positive aspects of his move were foremost on his mind.[54] Vertlib moved to Salzburg knowing that it was a provincial town unlike Vienna, a town that did not even offer the rich Jewish history of a place like Czernowitz or Brünn. Indeed, for him Salzburg played virtually no role in Jewish history. He defied the warnings of Viennese friends, revealing that his worst experiences with anti-Semitism occurred during his underprivileged youth in Vienna. He writes that he remembered that in Vienna he was exposed to anti-Semitic and racist insults wherever he went, on the streets, in the subway, and in the apartment house where he and his parents lived. He even wonders if this constant exposure desensitized him to the ubiquitous everyday fascism in his Austrian surroundings.[55] Unlike Fleischmann, Honigmann, Schindel, and Beckermann, who position themselves in history-laden places that add to their sense of Jewishness (for example Beckermann's film *Homemad(e)* celebrates her Jewish street in Vienna), Vertlib stresses the element of coincidence in his global migration.

Jewish markers are present in all of the works under discussion. In *Bronsteins Kinder*, for example, Becker plays with the notion of circumcision. Schindel in *Gebürtig* (Born-Where, 1992) uses Yiddish elements that exceed the range of the Yiddishisms commonly used in the anti-Semitic Austrian *Kronen-Zeitung*. "Sch'ma Jisruel, kalt is ma in die Fiß Sch'ma, die Fiß so kalt, oh is ma in die Fiß Israel. Sch'ma Jisruel, in die Fiß is ma soi koit in die Fiß adonai."[56] (Sh'ma Israel, cold is me footsie, Sh'ma, footsies so cold, oy me ma footsies Israel. Sh'ma Israel, in the footsies is me so coldy, adonai.[57]) In this passage Schindel brings together the sublime, the physical, and the ridiculous, parodying the prayer for the dead, the "Sh'ma," at a moment when his narrator is so cold that he thinks of impending death. Ironically this scene takes place during the shooting of the Theresienstadt sequences of Herman Wouk's monumental film series *War and Remembrance* (1988) in Yugoslavia — filming in Theresienstadt was forbidden. Schindel participated as an extra in Wouk's film, and during this time Beckermann interviewed him for her film *Die papierene Brücke*.[58] Playing a Nazi victim in a film about the Holocaust in the dead of winter, Schindel gets cold, but he ridicules his pains because they cannot be compared to the suffering of the Holocaust victims. Like Becker in *Bronsteins Kinder* and Beckermann in *Die papierene Brücke* he calls into question the authenticity and moral validity of Holocaust films and the representation of the Holocaust in general.

Through his use of language he identifies his point of view as Jewish. The parody of the "Sch'ma" occurs in the last paragraph of his novel in a parodistic "Jüdeln" or "Mauscheln," an imitation of the idiom ascribed to Jews by anti-Semites since Gustav Freytag: "Da denk ich mir, wann endlich warm warden die Füße, und Kopf bleibt wunderbar kühl, kann passieren, daß kommt nicht der Messias, sondern ein schönes Gefühl."[59] (There, I think when my feet finally warm up and the head remains wonderfully cool, it can happen, that there comes not the Messiah but a beautiful feeling.) The word order of the German text mimics the standard word order in Yiddish, defining the speaker as a Jew. For a contemporary audience sensitive to stereotypes the effect might be funny but is more likely somewhat embarrassing. As a Jewish author, Schindel can rightfully claim Jewish language usage and expressions as his own. However, for non-Jewish Austrians and Germans it would be politically improper to laugh at jokes relying on the use of the Jewish German idiom (mauscheln), which the Nazis had deployed to perpetuate racial stereotypes as for example in Veit Harlan's propaganda film *Jud Süß* (1940) commissioned by Josef Goebbels' ministry of propaganda.[60] Names that are identified as Jewish often appear as markers for Jewish characters, as is to be expected. However, some authors also use names to create confusion — the choice of a name is, after all, random, and can be used to mislead. Often Jewish names occur in the title in order to evoke certain reader expectations: Becker's *Bronsteins Kinder*,

Rafael Seligmann's *Rubinsteins Versteigerung* (Auctioning Off Rubinstein, 1989), Esther Dischereit's *Joëmis Tisch* (Joëmis Table, 1988), and Didi Danquart and Thomas Strittmatter's film *Viehjud Levi* (Cattle Jew Levi, 2001).[61] Titles alluding to Jewish history or specific sites likewise create reader expectations, e.g. Edgar Hilsenrath's *Der Nazi und der Friseur*, Maxim Biller's *Harlem Holocaust*, and Anna Mitgutsch's *Abschied von Jerusalem*.

A common element is the subversion of anti-Semitic stereotypes.[62] In *Kieselsteine* Nadja Seelich inverts the process of stereotyping by placing German and Austrian characters under scrutiny by a Jewish woman, who sees them through the eyes of the child of Holocaust survivors. Seelich's Hannah becomes increasingly aware of the fascist structures in her environment. Hannah observes the gratuitous brutalization of a homeless woman, the openly displayed homophobia of a man bragging about his Nazi affiliations, and the fear other Jews have of identifying themselves in public. Hannah is exposed to jokes about Jews, the Holocaust, and her "race," and finally becomes the victim of a date rape. Irene Dische, an American-born author whose works enjoyed a wider reception in German translation than in the English original uses a similar strategy to uncover the Nazi legacy within contemporary German society in her novella "Eine Jüdin für Charles Allen" (A Jewess for Charles Allen, 1994).[63] Here it is a Jewish impersonator, Esther, who creates a stereotypically Jewish persona. The son of Jewish exiles, Charles, who was raised as a Catholic in the United States, takes her for a genuine Jewess until he learns of her parents' Nazi past. Maxim Biller's *Harlem Holocaust*, too, sets forth Jewish stereotypes and cultural clichés just to undermine them, suggesting in the end that the stereotypes are part of the "große deutsche Krankheit" (the big German disease).[64] Such cleverly executed satirical texts draw on a great deal of research into Jewish history, National Socialism, and anti-Semitism.

Finally, the construction of an alternative geography foregrounding sites of memory significant for Jewish history features in many Austrian narratives. Vienna's Second District, the Leopoldstadt, is featured in the fiction of Ilse Aichinger and Robert Schindel, and in Ruth Beckermann's documentary books and films, including *Die Mazzesinsel* and *Wien Retour*. During the interwar period the Leopoldstadt was the preferred neighborhood of Jewish immigrants. In the Second Republic it became the primary site of Vienna's Jewish memory. In Schindel's novel *Gebürtig* the Second District is featured as the location of the protagonist's apartment, a gathering spot for his Jewish and non-Jewish friends. It suggests the renewal of Jewish life and a changed relationship between Jews, Austrians, and Germans. Austrian authors often differentiate between Vienna, the former Habsburg capital, which played an important role in Jewish history, and provincial Austria, viewed as hostile territory. "Ich fühle mich irgenwie verloren, sobald ich die Grenzen Wiens überschreite und die österreichische

Provinz betrete" (I feel somewhat lost as soon as I cross the boundaries of Vienna and enter the Austrian province) says Rabinovici's Russian-born character Lew Feininger.[65] Vertlib's autobiographical narrator reports that his father tried to prevent him from leaving Vienna, "die einzige Stadt, wo man unter Umständen noch leben kann" (the only city where one can possibly live these days). His mother equates the move to Salzburg with "sein Leben wegschmeißen für nichts und wieder nichts" (throwing away one's life for nothing at all).[66] One of his acquaintances predicts that he will "an den Menschen [in Salzburg] zu leiden haben" (suffer under the people of Salzburg).[67] Vertlib, however, downplays these notions by reporting about the xenophobia he faced in Vienna.

The choice of Jewish sites is particularly obvious in literary texts and films that deliberately by-pass tourist spots to show Jewish Vienna from their point of view, as is the case in Seelich's *Kieselsteine* and Beckermann's *Wien Retour*. Seelich's film is set exclusively in Vienna. Its most significant settings here include the synagogue in the Seittenstettengasse and coffeehouses historically linked to Jewish history, such as the Café Museum, Elias Canetti's former mainstay. More touristy places such as Café Landtmann or the famous Dehmel pastry shop are ignored. Since the Nazi era, authors such as Friedrich Torberg, Aichinger, and Lind have configured Vienna as a site of Jewish suffering and Nazi crime. Esther Dischereit in her afterword to the new edition of Gertrud Kolmar's *Die jüdische Mutter* (A Jewish Mother, 1978) describes how the lingering effect of the past shapes her sense of Berlin's topography:

> Ich könnte nicht in ihrem [Kolmar's] Haus einziehen. Es ist besser in Häuser einzuziehen, von denen ich nichts weiß. Das Lehrerzimmer der Liebfrauenschule ist in der Bibliothek eines ehemaligen jüdischen Privathauses eingerichtet. Oder irre ich mich, es war vielleicht doch das Wohnzimmer. Da konnte ich meine Tochter auch nicht hingeben. Besser, ich weiß nichts von den Schulen und den Häusern, damit noch welche in Frage kommen.[68]

> [I could not move into her [Kolmar's] house. It is better to move into houses about which I know nothing. The teacher's meeting room in the School of our Lady is located in the library of a former Jewish residence. Or am I mistaken? Perhaps it was the living room. I would not be able to send my daughter there either. Best of all, I don't know anything about the schools and the houses so that some of them remain an option.]

Likewise, the perception of international geography in these works differs from that in mainstream texts. Beckermann, Schindel, Hilsenrath, and Lander, similar to Claude Lanzmann in *Shoah*, represent Eastern Europe as the cemetery of Ashkenazic culture, a site of mourning.[69] In one of Rabinovici's stories the response of a certain Professor Rubinstein encapsulates the opposing Jewish dreams. "Ich liebe Israel . . . New York is more fun."[70]

The strategies for establishing distance from the mainstream and dominant cultural memory, such as invoking the Holocaust experience, articulating oppositional Jewish experiences, searching for an alternative sphere, and the use of Jewish textual markers and geography, do not produce a homogeneous Germanophone Jewish literature. The strategies are not uniformly applied, and the heterogeneity of the authors is reflected in a diverse body of literature. The literary models to which authors take recourse in shaping their Jewish experience also vary widely. They include paradigms of classical German literature, Romanticism, realism, existentialism, Austrian fin-de-siécle and interwar literature, the Yiddish narrative, even the novels of Heimito von Doderer and Thomas Mann. Even though many authors use some of the same topoi and strategies, it would be as incorrect to speak of a school or movement of German Jewish writing as it would be to describe contemporary non-Jewish German literature in terms of homogeneity. In the case of Jewish authors, because of the history of deportation, exile, and post-Shoah emigration, certain international perspectives come into play, but the emphasis varies from author to author.

Jewish postwar writing constructs new identity positions and establishes specifically Jewish networks of association and dissociation; it thus assumes a supra-national character that seems particularly appropriate in the context of the global developments of the late twentieth and early twenty-first centuries. However, rather than subscribing to the optimism of traditional cosmopolitanism, a profound distrust pervades many of the works under discussion, as the authors reject and disengage from traditional identity clichés. This is true also for authors who have rediscovered for themselves a traditional Jewish lifestyle such as Honigmann and Fleischmann. The fact that they are and present themselves as public figures, writers, and intellectuals who address German audiences places them into a position that differs markedly from traditional Jewish gender roles. Often they embrace positions of retreat, as is the case with Rabinovici in *Suche nach M.* In Rabinovici's and Schindel's work it is the intimacy of the lovers bordering on isolation, in Honigmann's, Behrens's, and Dische's texts that of mother and child, and in Fleischmann's and Honigmann's the yearning for traditional religious life that suggest alienation from the secular global culture of the late twentieth century. The most extreme positions of retreat occur in Aichinger and Mitgutsch, who like Aichinger had had a Catholic upbringing. Both authors portray radically disconnected individuals. A similar isolation is also evoked in Menasse's painstaking inquiry into the past and the failure of his protagonists to integrate themselves into Jewish or Christian society in *Vertreibung aus der Hölle*.

The perspective of the nomadic post-Shoah Jewish protagonists tends to be self-protective and individualistic. The emphasis on the individual corresponds with the precise manner in which the transmission of knowledge from one generation to the next is envisioned, namely as a process between two individuals, as in the interchange between interviewer and interviewee in Beckermann, teacher and student in Menasse, lover and beloved in Schindel, father and son in Becker, mother and daughter in Behrens, and husband and wife in Fleischmann).[71] Indeed, most German Jewish writing casts Jewish identity as a position of an isolation impossible to overcome except on a personal level, an isolation so great that it undermines any vision of a larger community.

Notes

[1] References are to the edition: Ilse Aichinger, *Die größere Hoffnung* (Frankfurt: Fischer, 1974). Since the turn of the millennium Aichinger has been extremely productive. She contributed to Wolfgang Benz, Claudia Curio, Andrea Hammel, eds., *Die Kindertransporte 1938/39: Rettung und Integration* (Frankfurt am Main: Fischer 2003); furthermore she published: *Der Wolf und die sieben jungen Geislein* (Vienna; Edition Korrespondenzen, 2004), and *Unglaubwürdige Reisen* (Frankfurt am Main: Fischer, 2005).

[2] Major anthologies containing works by little-known Holocaust-era poets include Heinz Seydel, ed., *Welch Wort in die Kälte gerufen* (Berlin: Verlag der Nation, 1968) and Manfred Schlösser and Hans-Rolf Ropertz, eds., *An den Wind geschrieben* (Darmstadt: Agora, 1960).

[3] See Sander Gilman, *Jewish Self-Hatred: Anti-Semitism and the Hidden Language of the Jews* (Baltimore: Johns Hopkins UP, 1986). Ruth Klüger writes about her multiple identities in pre-Shoah Austria in *weiter leben*: "Zunächst jedoch sind wir in der ersten Schulklasse alle zusammen Österreicher gewesen und haben das Dollfußlied gesungen [. . .] Zu Hause war man sozialdemokratisch [. . .]" (37). And she continues: "Ich war für ein Heimatgefühl sehr empfänglich gewesen: Donauweibchen und Basiliskenhaus, Stock im Eisen und Spinnerin am Kreuz [. . .]" (39). "Und nun, als mein ungefestigter Glaube an Österreich ins Schwanken geriet, wurde ich jüdisch in Abwehr" (40). (Göttingen: Wallstein, 1992).

[4] Ruth Beckermann, *Die Mazzesinsel* (Vienna: Löcker, 1984), 12.

[5] Beckermann, *Die Mazzesinsel*, 9.

[6] Sander Gilman, *Jurek Becker: Die Biographie* (Berlin: Ullstein, 2002).

[7] Jurek Becker, *Jakob der Lügner* (Frankfurt am Main: Suhrkamp, 1988). [Original publication 1969].

[8] Jurek Becker, *Der Boxer* (Frankfurt am Main: Suhrkamp, 1976). Gilman, *Becker*, 36–37.

[9] Jean Amery, "Der ehrbare Antisemitismus," in *Weiterleben* (Stuttgart: Klett-Cotta, 1982), 151–84.

[10] Becker, *Bronsteins Kinder* (Frankfurt am Main: Suhrkamp, 1986), 221–23.

[11] Becker, *Bronsteins Kinder*, 28–29, 68, 70, 119.

[12] Becker's three novels are, strictly speaking, not sequels even though there is a historical continuity. They feature distinct characters and plots. *Jakob der Lügner* is

190 ♦ Dagmar C. G. Lorenz

set in Poland during the Shoah, *Der Boxer* in post-1945 East Berlin, and *Bronsteins Kinder* in the GDR in 1973, the year of Walter Ulbricht's death.

[13] Becker, *Bronsteins Kinder*, 47–48.

[14] Dominick LaCapra, *Writing History, Writing Trauma* (Baltimore: Johns Hopkins UP, 2001), 89.

[15] Sem Dresden, *Persecution, Extermination, Literature* (Toronto: U of Toronto P, 1995), 24–26.

[16] Lea Fleischmann, *Dies ist nicht mein Land: Eine Jüdin verläßt die Bundesrepublik* (Hoffmann & Campe, 1980).

[17] Manuela Günter, "Überleben schreiben," in *Überleben schreiben: Zur Autobiographik der Shoah*, ed. Manuela Günter (Würzburg: Königshausen & Neumann, 2002), 9–20; here: 9.

[18] Stephan Braese, "Überlieferungen," *Beiheft zur Zeitschrift für deutsche Philologie. Deutsch-jüdische Literatur: Die Generation nach der Shoah*, ed. Sander L. Gilman and Hartmut Steinecke (Berlin: Erich Schmidt Verlag, 2002), 9–16; here: 6–8.

[19] Henryk Broder, "Zur Demokratie angetreten — ein Volk macht Dienst nach Vorschrift," in Fleischmann, *Dies ist nicht mein Land*, 251–72; here: 271.

[20] Fleischmann, *Dies ist nicht mein Land*, 8–21.

[21] Fleischmann, *Dies ist nicht mein Land*, 8.

[22] Fleischmann, *Dies ist nicht mein Land*, 12.

[23] Dan Diner, "Negative Symbiose: Deutsche und Juden nach Auschwitz," *Babylon: Beiträge zur jüdischen Gegenwart* 1/9 (1988): 9–20.

[24] Cf. Henryk Broder, *A Jew in the New Germany*, ed. Sander L. Gilman and Lilian M. Friedberg (Urbana: U of Illinois P, 2004); Ruth Beckermann, *Unzugehörig: Österreicher und Juden nach 1945* (Vienna: Löcker, 1989).

[25] Ruth Klüger, in her "Die Ödnis des entlarvten Landes. Antisemitismus im Werk jüdisch-österreichischer Autoren," in *Katastrophen: Über deutsche Literatur* (Göttingen: Wallstein, 1994), 59–82, comments: "Das ist kein Land, das eine ethnische Minorität abschiebt, sondern ein Österreich, das seine eigenen Kinder aussetzt oder verschlingt" (81).

[26] Ilse Aichinger, "Mein Vater," *Verschenkter Rat* (Frankfurt am Main: Fischer, 1978), 19.

[27] For example the poem "Winter, gemalt," in *Verschenkter Rat*, 39. The speaker envisions herself on lofty heights, looking down upon "die Österreicher" walking below in the snowy landscape. "Und in den weißen Röcken/ im Schnee die Österreicher. / Laß uns aufschauen . . ." [And in their white coats/ in the snow the Austrians. / Let us look upwards . . .].

[28] Ilse Aichinger, "Wien 1945: Kriegsende," in *Film und Verhängnis: Blitzlichter auf ein Leben* (Frankfurt am Main: Fischer, 2001), 56–61; here: 59–60.

[29] Aichinger, "Plätze und Straßen," *Jahresring* 3 (1959): 19–24; here: 19, 20.

[30] Cordelia Edvardson, *Gebranntes Kind sucht das Feuer* (Munich: Hanser, 1986).

[31] Elizabeth Langgässer, *Märkische Argonautenfahrt* (Hamburg: Claassen, 1950).

[32] Egon Schwarz, "Austria, Quite a Normal Nation," *New German Critique* 93/3 (2004): 175–91 writes: "Ilse Aichinger, Robert Schindel, Doron Rabinovici, Robert Menasse, Hilde Spiel and other authors are engaged in a continuous discussion, sometimes ironic and critical, sometimes insightful and moving, of the true history of Austria" (187).

[33] Aichinger, *Die größere Hoffnung*, 86–108.

[34] See: Dagmar C. G. Lorenz, "Hoffentlich werde ich taugen: Zu Situation und Kontext von Brigitte Schwaiger/Eva Deutsch *Die Galizianerin*." *Yearbook of Women in German* 6 (1991): 1–25.

[35] Eva Deutsch and Brigitte Schwaiger, *Die Galizianerin* (Reinbeck: Rowohlt, 1982), 81.

[36] Beckermann, *Unzugehörig*, 10–11.

[37] Doron Rabinovici, *Credo und Credit* (Frankfurt am Main: Suhrkamp, 2001). See especially: "Warum die Milch vom Fleisch getrennt werden mußte. Oder 'Die gerettete Zunge' und das drohende Messer," 7–21. Also see: "Ein Aberglaube der Zukunft. Oder Gedanken zur Leugnung der Vergangenheit," 122–29.

[38] Schwarz in "Austria, Quite a Normal Nation," terms the Waldheim election an instance in history that proved the "robust survival" of Austrian anti-Semitism (180).

[39] Doron Rabinovici, "Der richtige Riecher," in *Papirnik* (Frankfurt am Main: Suhrkamp, 1994), 7–18.

[40] *Kieselsteine*, script Nadja Seelich, dir. Lukas Stepanik. Filmverleih Hans Peter Hofmann, Vienna, 1982.

[41] Dresden, *Persecution, Extermination, Literature*, 72.

[42] Doron Rabinovici, *Instanzen der Ohnmacht: Wien 1938–1945: Der Weg zum Judenrat* (Frankfurt am Main: Jüdischer Verlag, 2000).

[43] Doron Rabinovici, *Instanzen der Ohnmacht*, 426.

[44] Robert Menasse, *Die Vertreibung aus der Hölle* (Frankfurt am Main: Suhrkamp, 1993).

[45] Elias Canetti, *Die Stimmen von Marrakesch* (Munich: Hanser, 1967); Esther Dischereit, *Merryn* (Frankfurt am Main: Suhrkamp, 1992); Barbara Honigmann, *Sohara's Reise* (Berlin: Rowohlt, 1996).

[46] Gilles Deleuze and Felix Guattari, *Kafka: Toward a Minor Literature* (Minneapolis: U of Minnesota P, 1986), 17: "The second characteristic of minor literatures is that everything in them is political. In major literatures, in contrast, the individual concern [. . .] joins with other no less individual concerns. [. . .] Minor literature is completely different: its cramped space forces each individual intrigue to connect immediately to politics."

[47] Barbara Honigmann, *Roman von einem Kinde* (Darmstadt: Luchterhand, 1986).

[48] Ruth Beckermann and Josef Aichholzer dir. *Wien Retour* (Vienna, 1983); Ruth Beckermann dir., *Die papierene Brücke* (Vienna, 1987); *Nach Jerusalem* (Vienna, 1990); *Ein flüchtiger Zug nach dem Orient* (Vienna, 1999); *Jenseits des Krieges* (Vienna, 1997); *Homemad(e)* (Vienna, 2001).

[49] Robert Menasse, *Selige Zeiten, Brüchige Welt* (Frankfurt am Main: Suhrkamp, 1994); Anna Mitgutsch, *Abschied von Jerusalem* (Berlin: Rowohlt, 1995); *In fremden Städten* (Munich: dtv, 1994); Jeanette Lander, *Die Töchter* (Frankfurt am Main: Insel, 1976); *Jahrhundert der Herren* (Berlin: Aufbau, 1993).

[50] Doron Rabinovici, *Suche nach M* (Frankfurt am Main: Suhrkamp, 1997); Robert Menasse, *Sinnliche Gewissheit* (Frankfurt am Main: Suhrkamp, 1996).

[51] Schindel, *Gebürtig*, 353; *Born-Where*, 285.

[52] Vladimir Vertlib, *Abschiebung* (Salzburg: Otto Möller, 1995).

[53] Vladimir Vertlib, *Das besondere Gedächtnis der Rosa Masur* (Munich: dtv, 2001).

[54] Vladimir Vertlib, " 'Jude, wie interessant' — 'A Jew, how interesting!' " in *Juden in Salzburg*, ed. Helga Embacher (Salzburg: Anton Pustet, 2002), 104–11; here: 105.

[55] Vertlib, "Jude, wie interessant," 105.

[56] Robert Schindel, *Gebürtig* (Frankfurt: Suhrkamp, 1994), 353. English translation: Robert Schindel, *Born-Where*. Trans. Michael Roloff (Riverside: Ariadne Press, 1995).

[57] Schindel, *Born-Where*. Trans. Michael, 285.

[58] Herman Wouk, dir. *War and Remembrance*. ABC Circle Films, 1988.

[59] Schindel, *Gebürtig*, 353; trans. Roloff, *Gebürtig*, 294.

[60] Veit Harlan, dir. *Jud Süß* (Berlin: UFA, 1940).

[61] Featured in the "Jewish Film Archive Online": http://www.jewishfilm.com/jz14.html

[62] For example the provocative novella by Jakov Lind, *Eine Seele aus Holz* (Darmstadt: Luchterhand, 1962).

[63] Irene Dische, "Eine Jüdin für Charles Allen," in *Fromme Lügen*, aus dem Englischen übersetzt von Otto Bayer und Monika Elwenspoek (Reinbeck: Rowohlt, 1994), 7–74; "Fromme Lügen," 140–283.

[64] Maxim Biller, *Harlem Holocaust* (Cologne: Kiepenheuer & Witsch, 1990), 61.

[65] Doron Rabinovici, *Ohnehin* (Frankfurt am Main: Suhrkamp, 2004), 94.

[66] Vladimir Vertlib, *Zwischenstationen* (Vienna: Deutike, 1999), 283.

[67] Vertlib, *Zwischenstationen*, 285.

[68] Esther Dischereit, "Nachwort," in Gertrud Kolmar, *Die jüdische* Mutter (Frankfurt am Main: Suhrkamp, 2003), 195–215; here: 196.

[69] The United States, traditionally a site of hope in terms of material advancement and personal freedom in contradistinction to Israel, the site of spiritual hope, is problematized in contemporary texts, for example Beckermann's *Nach Jerusalem*, Lander's *Die Töchter*, and Mitgutsch's *Abschied von Jerusalem*.

[70] Doron Rabinovici, "Der richtige Riecher," in *Papirnik* (Frankfurt am Main: Suhrkamp, 1994), 60–73; here: 63.

[71] Lea Fleischmann, *Ich bin Israelin: Erfahrungen in einem orientalischen Land* (Hamburg: Hoffman & Campe, 1982).

9: Of Stories and Histories: Golem Figures in Post-1989 German and Austrian Culture

Cathy S. Gelbin

A FIGURE FROM JEWISH TRADITION seized upon by Christian writers during the early nineteenth century and only later adopted by Jewish authors, the Golem has since embodied the ambivalent in- and outside perspectives on Jews in the German-speaking lands.[1] Its recent revival in German and Austrian culture reflects the shifting political and cultural constellations in post-1989 Europe, and exemplifies the Golem's heightened popularity during periods of radical change. The following exploration of the Golem in contemporary literature and film will show how this abject figure has come to embody the competing and overlapping discourses around the Nazi and GDR past, and serves to configure Jewish and German identities in the New Europe.

The term "Golem" first appears in the Hebrew Scriptures. In Psalm 139:16 it connotes a shapeless mass, perhaps an embryo, while a derivative of the root in Isaiah 49:21 indicates female infertility.[2] Medieval Jewish mystics adopted the term to describe an artificial man created from clay and brought to life by a cabbalistic ritual of words. By the nineteenth century, Jewish folk-tale traditions featuring an ever-growing Golem animated by an amulet had entered German literature.[3] A century later, the Golem had metamorphosed into a figure of haunted memory. Following the large number of renditions of the Golem and related figures of the uncanny during the early twentieth century, including Paul Wegener's 1920 film *Der Golem, wie er in die Welt kam* (The Golem: How He Came Into the World), Jewish writers adopted the Golem's association with haunted memory during the first two decades after the Shoah in order to commemorate the destroyed prewar Jewish life and the Shoah itself.[4] Current versions of the Golem reveal the rich tradition of this trope that both Jewish and non-Jewish writers helped to shape. The cabbalistic tradition had infused the making of a Golem with ethical questions regarding the relationship between humans and divine creation, while Jewish folktales portrayed Rabbi Löw's Golem as a figure of protection in a hostile Christian environment. While some recent works draw on these cabbalistic connotations of the android and its later associations with horror to position second- and third-generation Jews within the context of European unity, others employ this figure as a universal signifier of endangered human survival in the twentieth century, often with anti-Semitic implications.

Constructing Postwar Jewish Life

Benjamin Stein's novel *Das Alphabet des Juda Liva* (The Alphabet of Juda Liva, 1995) traces the disenchantment of second-generation East German Jews with their parents' communist ideals since the 1980s.[5] Stein rewrites the historical figures of the false seventeenth-century Messiah Shabbatai Zevi and his prophet Nathan of Gaza into the hilarious tale of young Alexander Rottenstein and the mysterious Jacoby, alias Nathan ben Gazi. The narrator's presentation of this story in the shape of seemingly scattered incidents mirrors the mosaic of Rottenstein's family history and forces the reader to repair the disjointed narrative, translating the cabbalistic imperative of *tikkun* (repair) into the acts of storytelling and reading. Mocking the Jewish belief that wishes made on the eve of Hoshanah Rabbah come true should lightning strike during that night, the young non-Jew Rottenstein wishes for the seemingly absurd: that the Golem will walk across the Charles Bridge of Prague and that he himself will become an Orthodox Jew. Lightning promptly does strike, though Rottenstein initially fails to recognize that his wish has been granted. During the following years, which also see the fall of the Berlin Wall, Rottenstein learns about the hidden Jewish origins of his paternal family and of its total assimilation, a process he finally repudiates.

The protagonist's surreal awakening as the Messiah with magnificent side locks in Prague, propelled by the threshold figure of the Golem, invokes and inverts the animal symbolism of Kafka's "Die Verwandlung" (The Metamorphosis, 1915).[6] Where, as Ritchie Robertson argues, Kafka's "hybrid" beetle represents the individual disintegration of the assimilating Western Jew,[7] Stein's adolescent Golem signifies the protagonist's disavowal of assimilation, which the novel compares to the Shoah. Thus Rottenstein's assimilating great-great-grandfather envisions his death in a garden of ash, an image that repeats itself three communist generations onward in Rottenstein's own death in the fire, which effects his transformation into the Hasidic Messiah. The novel's gist, however, is anti-assimilationist rather than anti-communist, as the consumerism fun-seeking western youths bring to post-socialist Prague does not represent a capitalist solution to the protagonist's dilemma; instead, it merely appears as the last manifestation of the "real" world that Rottenstein must overcome to bring on the messianic repair of the world.

The Golem signifies the political transitions occurring between Rottenstein's two encounters with the Rabbi Löw's creation, but also his schism into "der jüdischste Goi, den die Welt je gesehen hat" (249; the most Jewish Goy the world has ever seen). Yet Rottenstein's ruptured Jewish genealogy and his subsequent rejection by traditional Jewish law play an important part in the novel's mystical scheme of redemption. Indeed, cabbalism placed great emphasis on the flawed origins of the Messiah, claiming that the Messiah would either be reincarnated from the sinner Adam through David to his current manifestation, or even appear as a new soul not circulated through previous Jewish generations.[8] However, while challenging the prevailing insistence on ethnic and religious homogeneity in traditional Jewish communities, Stein's construction of a "hybrid" Messiah falls back on the negative inscription of ethnic, cultural, and religious boundary crossings.[9] In line with the frequent association of racial hybridity with sexual transgression, the Golem betrays Rottenstein's sexual misdemeanors. Although Scholem rejects this connotation,[10] the term Golem has been translated as "embryo," perhaps owing to its original meaning of "shapeless mass." By embodying both Alex's sinful wasting of his seed twelve years previously and the aborted child he unknowingly fathered as an adult, the Golem stands for the novel's construction of unrestrained masculinity as a sign of flawed human nature. In the realm of the real, the text's men abuse and forsake the women who love them, a chain of betrayals leading to the violent destruction of Rottenstein and his male predecessors. Stein's gendered representation of the worlds below and above conveys the traditional Jewish elevation of the masculine to the higher symbolic, which the feminine merely mediates or represents in its negative aspects. Female figures operating on the realm of the symbolic are destructive or catalyze the transformation of Rottenstein's unethical male nature, without themselves entering the realm of the divine. The Golem ultimately represents the overcoming of the female principle of exile that alienates the sons of Israel from their male God, with the fires of the Shoah — symbolized in the Angel of Death's garden of ash — problematically configured as the divine punishment for the vice of assimilation.

In contrast, Esther Dischereit's volume of poetry *als mir mein golem öffnete* (when my golem opened onto me, 1996) emphasizes the disruption of Jewish cultural traditions through the Shoah as the irreversible predicament of postwar Jewish life.[11] Following Gershom Scholem's observation that the Golem represents an image of the Jewish people, Dischereit employs this figure to construct the shared Jewish experience of annihilation during the Shoah.[12] At the same time, her construction of the particularities of female Jewish identity, which Itta Shedletzky has explored,[13] follows the long tradition of android figures symbolizing the interplay between gender and Jewish subjectivities. Dischereit employs the heterogeneous figure of the Golem to negotiate multiple alterities within a Jewish collective that takes its central signifiers from the European-Jewish experience.

The first poem's ambiguous casting of the Golem as the target and source of destruction suggests an annihilation from within, paralleling the rise of the genocide from the German culture in which Central European Jews had partaken. The lyrical addressee represents the German betrayal of the prewar Jewish dream of the "German-Jewish symbiosis" and, in her disappearance from the second line of the poem, the impossibility of dialogue across the divides of the genocide. Dischereit cites the older notion of the Golem as an image of haunted memory, but also evokes the Jewish icons of poetry after the Shoah that continue to shape the German imagination of Jewish culture. The Golem in Nelly Sachs's poem "Golem Tod" (Golem Death, 1949) similarly represents both the Jews' adversary and the indestructibility and sanctity of the Jewish people,[14] while Paul Celan's Rabbi Löw poem "Einem, der vor der Tür stand" (To One Who Stood Before the Door, 1963) imbued the Golem with the duality of slaughterer and messiah.[15]

In the second poem of Dischereit's volume, the Golem returns in the form of the lyrical narrator, however, it is now *a* golem rather than *the* Golem (6). The lower-case spelling of "golem" signifies the diminishment of Jewish communities through the Shoah and the postwar perception of Jews as an anonymous mass of victims, a guilt returning to haunt Germans after the genocide. At the same, the collation of Arabic, German, and Yiddish words in expressions such as "Chabibi / mein waibele" (my beloved / my little wife, 13) resists the forging of coherent linguistic and cultural identities from the Jewish experience. This linguistic strategy points to the alienated and jumbled nature of Jewish identity and culture after the Shoah, parodying the attempted appropriation of Jewish traditions and culture by postwar Jews and non-Jewish Germans. In this phrase and others, Dischereit ridicules the farcical German fascination with Klezmer music in the 1990s, while also parodying young Jews' construction of a supposedly authentic Jewish identity by resorting to the annihilated Eastern-European Jewish culture. "Chabibi" casts young Jews' flirtation with Jewish tradition as a dance with a *dibbuk*, like the Golem an undead figure associated with the magical traditions of a mythologized Jewish past.

Through the missing *mezuzah* (an amulet attached to the right door post) and the flawed genealogy indicated in her inaccurate transliteration of the Yiddish word for family, "mespoche" (13) instead of *mischpoche*, Dischereit insists on the inherently partial and distorting nature of such appropriations. As her poetry suggests, fragmentation marks both the postwar Jewish experience at large and female Jewish subjectivity in particular. Young Jews' attempts to reclaim fragments of Jewish tradition merely testify to the death of the culture that sustained the physical presence of Jews. While this construction overtly fixates Jews in a victim position, other writings by Dischereit pose self-conscious fragmentation as a form of political agency to resist new cultural and political hegemonies, such as the policies of exclusion, displacement, and physical violence perpetrated by Israeli Jews on the Palestinians.

The Golem returns as the twin symbol of the deadly past and the fraught continuity of postwar Jewish life in Andreas Kleinert's recent TV sequel of the popular German detective series *Schimanski*, entitled *Das Geheimnis des Golem* (The Secret of the Golem, 2003).[16] Set in Duisburg and Antwerp, the film unravels the mysterious murder of the Hasidic Jew Rosenfeldt from Antwerp, who was killed for the sake of a Hebrew notebook. Rosenfeldt had received the booklet containing the encrypted numbers of deceased Nazi victims' Swiss bank accounts from his former fellow camp inmate Goldmann, who had collected monthly payments from one of them. When Goldmann died a few decades after the war, Rosenfeldt began to impersonate his friend in order to prevent the expiration of the Swiss account, henceforth living a double life as Rosenfeldt in Antwerp and Goldmann in Duisburg and donating all of Goldmann's money to Jewish charity causes. Rosenfeldt was murdered for the sake of the secret notebook before he could destroy his second identity, which he had secretly named "Golem."

Citing the folktale of the ever-growing Golem that kills its creator, the film ambiguously straddles anti-Semitic perceptions of the Jewish presence in postwar Europe and their counter-images. Hasidic Jews' black garments, the dark and blue lighting of their synagogue in Antwerp and the eerie non-diegetic music featured in the film's opening sequences powerfully play on the anti-Semitic image of the uncanny Jew who is relegated to a dark and irrational past. For example, the portrayal of the Jewish market in Antwerp as the site of tough bartering, theft, and crime invokes such highly charged images. Both anti-Jewish and anti-Arab stereotypes seem additionally confirmed when König, the German state security officer on the case, declares that Rosenfeldt and his alleged Jewish pursuer had worked for the Israeli secret service and were killed by Islamic extremists because of their weapons deals. Gradually, however, the film dismantles these images as Rosenfeldt turns out to be a charitable victim rather than a Mossad arms dealer and König emerges as Rosenfeldt's killer, a German trying to appropriate the last belongings of Jews killed during the Shoah. In a similar vein, the initial image of the uncanny and mysterious Jew is revealed as part of the visual repertoire of anti-Semitism when the Hasidic Rabbi Ginzberg, in divulging the secret of Rosenfeldt's Golem to Schimanski, asserts that the formula of Judaism's survival lies in its embrace of both tradition and modernity. Set in modern surroundings and shot in sober lighting, the Jewish Orthodox prayer service in Duisburg emphasizes the contemporary setting of traditional Jewish life. In this context, Rosenfeldt's grasp for the Golem no longer appears motivated by an innate Jewish tendency towards mysticism but rather by the acute need for protection. The monitoring of synagogue visitors by a security camera and guard, accompanied by police protection outside, connotes the beleaguered reality of postwar Jewish communities in Germany and starkly contrasts with König's construction of the Jews as foreign conspirators damaging the vital security interests of the Federal Republic of Germany.

While state servant König, Rosenberg's killer, represents the ideological uses of anti-Semitism to distract from his own crimes, the figure of the liberal detective Schimanski serves to illustrate the omnipresent legacy of anti-Semitism in everyday life; thus a Jewish dealer at the Antwerp market mentions his gassed grandmother and lack of family inheritance when Schimanski attempts to sell his own grandmother's silver. Furthermore, although Schimanski debunks König's conspiracy theories as anti-Semitic garbage, he himself occasionally associates Jews with the stereotypical notions of the lying Jews and their "mauscheln."[17] In contrasting Schimanski's repeated telling of jokes about Jews with the silent dismay of his various Jewish counterparts, the film exposes the profound inappropriateness of such jokes when related by non-Jews and portrays a genuine dialogue between Jews and non-Jewish Germans after the Shoah as impossible. Yet the film itself circulates potent anti-Semitic images when it shows the stereotypically "Jewish" profile of a Jewish woman listening to one such joke about Jewish noses. The Yiddish accents of practically all Jewish characters in the film and their frequent accompaniment by a Klezmer soundtrack additionally convey a stereotypically coded Jewish milieu.

Goldmann's illegitimate daughter Kaminski epitomizes the film's efforts to disrupt clichéd representations of Jews and its simultaneous perpetuation of such discourses. More than any other Jewish character in the film, Kaminski — born to the man whose legacy returns as the "Golem" — embodies the construction of Judaism as a meeting point of tradition and modernity. Her double appearance as a secular woman in Duisburg and in Hasidic outfit in Antwerp reiterates the early twentieth-century perception of Eastern European Jewry as the atavistic Other of German Jews and sets up the Jewish woman as an object of the non-Jewish male gaze. Dark, shorthaired, and athletically slim, the beautiful Jewess Kaminski both represents the supposed special sexual allure of the Jewess and exemplifies shifting modern gender roles.[18] Her masculine qualities are shown most clearly when she knocks down the male attacker of Schimanski's lover, the latter a long-haired non-Jewish blonde, with an iron pole symbolizing the Jewish woman's phallic aspects. The secret notebook in Schimanski's pocket shields his genitalia from a devastating shot, imbuing Jewish spirituality and learning with special masculine qualities, yet the film portrays everyday Jewish life as a site of emasculation by contrasting strong Jewish women with submissive Jewish men. Traditional power constellations regarding gender and Jews are suspended altogether when Kaminski responds to Schimanski's question whether circumcision indeed heightens sexual satisfaction by describing the temporarily defunct penis after this ritual, obviously referring to adult conversion. This plotline follows the melodramatic love-between-foes pattern with its momentary destabilization of masculinity in the domestic realm of love.

The film conveys Schimanski's evolving enthrallment with Kaminski, who falsely claims to be a Belgian police detective, in terms of a sado-masochistic relationship symbolizing what Dan Diner has termed the "negative symbiosis" of Jews and Germans after the Shoah.[19] As the plot moves from the protagonists' sexually suggestive attempts to arrest and overpower each other to Jewish folkdancing, Schimanski's infatuation with Kaminski offers exotic titillation to mainstream German audiences and suggests the remasculation of the German subject in the new republic. Kaminski's tragic attributes as the daughter of a Holocaust survivor only heighten her sexual appeal. This postwar variation of the trope of the beautiful Jewess with its romantic associations of victimization and passivity ultimately reinstates the male non-Jewish subject in a position of power over the feminized Jewish object. The film's interethnic romance functions precisely in order to equate the plight of second-generation Jews and second-generation Germans in a bid to redeem postwar Germans from the crimes of their parents' generation. The relativizing of German and Jewish positionalities[20] emerges most clearly in the showdown among König, Schimanski, and Kaminski between cattle cars on an abandoned railroad track, a site laden with Holocaust symbolism where Schimanski is to hand over Goldmann's notebook in order to release his non-Jewish lover from her abduction by König. As Schimanski recovers from his sexually debilitating bullet wound, Kaminski, speaking off-screen, declares him a righteous man according to the Jewish tradition of the thirty-six just men required in every generation to ensure the world's continued existence. Kaminski's disappearance from the scene ensures the restoration of Schimanski's relationship with his old-time lover, suggesting that Jews' role in the new German Republic is to forgive but to remain conveniently invisible in order to facilitate the smooth running of the German-German relationship.

Not insignificantly, Schimanski is played by Götz George, the son of the famous stage and film actor Heinrich George. The father features prominently in Veit Harlan's Nazi film *Jud Süß* (Jew Süß, 1940), the rendition of the Rabbi Löw story that marked the end of the prewar German-Jewish encounter. Heinrich George was interned as a Nazi collaborator at the Soviet special camp at Sachsenhausen and died there in 1946; his political rehabilitation by the Soviets occurred in 1998. The backdrop of the lives and complementary film projects of two male generations of the George family add piquant meaning to Kleinert's gendered portrayal of the empowerment of Germans within the post-Wall German-Jewish encounter and their subsequent emancipation from the Nazi past.

Universal Atrocity in a Globalized World

While the previously discussed texts concern themselves, in one way or another, with the conditions of postwar Jewish existence, a number of recent Golem texts construct non-Jewish Germans and Austrians after the Iron Curtain as the victims of a boundless internationalism frequently controlled by the US and, by implication, by the Jews. Drawing on the early twentieth-century anti-Semitic discourse linking Jews to a destructive and internationalist modernity, these texts map the Golem's dual associations of messianism and the Shoah onto their bleak vision of a globalized world ruled by technology. In *Kafka der Golem und Fußball und Prag* (Kafka the Golem and Soccer and Prague, 1998), the Viennese-based writer Ernst Petz presents a host of anti-Semitic stereotypes, including his oversexed or castrated male Jewish figures[21] Kafka, the Golem, and Rabbi Löw.[22] Petz's asexual yet pining Golem symbolizes the history of atrocities. In one sweep, the novel mentions the Hussite wars and SS-head Heydrich's crimes against the Czechs along with "murderous" feminism (21) and the arrival of cheap "Original Chikago-Pizza" (21), the latter connoting the lack of authenticity ascribed to American culture, followed by ecological disaster, religious fundamentalism, and nuclear war. These dangers to human civilization and physical survival result from the fanatical and superstitious nature of Rabbi Löw, the Jewish maker of the monster (23).

The Austrian dramatist Hilde Langthaler takes a similarly universalizing approach in her play *Golem Now* (2000), yet from a feminist viewpoint.[23] Langthaler uses the Golem as a metaphor for the alienated woman in the male-dominated age of technology. Increasingly isolated among the multiplying computers in their apartment, the play's protagonists Hanna and Helmut represent a modern-day version of Adam and Eve after the fall from grace. Hanna's futile attempts to rebel against Helmut's total surrender to his machines occur against the backdrop of news reports about the global destruction of national economies, environmental disaster, and the threat of another holocaust, this time a nuclear one (25). Langthaler first locates the origins of these destructive uses of technology in the medieval Christian separation of the materialistic aspects of life from spiritual ones, a division that the cabbalists had resisted in insisting that God alone was truth (16). Later, however, the play contrasts the soulless and externally animated Golem (27) with ancient Asian philosophies about a non-materialistic, autonomous soul and Native American concerns with nature, thus constructing Jews as the materialistic antidote to spirituality before its split from nature. Lurking behind this construct is the notion of the Judeo-Christian origin of Western civilization, which traditionally has configured Jews and Judaism as its negative antecedent. Hannah's Jewish name and Helmut's preoccupation with the modern Golem of technology signal that Langthaler's drama is indebted to the 1980s German feminist construction of women as the victims of Jewish-generated patriarchy, which, as Susannah Heschel has observed, rewrote the historical constellations of Germans and Jews, perpetrators and victims.[24] Post-1989 German texts employing the Golem as a symbol of technology equally tended to universalize atrocity, configuring Jews as the creators of a murderous modernity. In addition, these texts map the themes of the Golem and its corrupt master, of victims and perpetrators, onto the constellation of East and West Germans in a globalized world.

Ulla Berkéwicz's lyrical drama *Der Golem in Bayreuth* (The Golem in Bayreuth, 1999) interweaves the present-day narrative of the disruption of the annual Bayreuth festival of Wagner music by the rioting "Haßkappen" (caps of hatred) with that of the sixteenth-century Golem of Rabbi Löw.[25] By paralleling its characters in both realms of the narrative, that is, the Hitlerian Bayreuth pharmacist with Rabbi Löw, and the *Haßkappen* and their leader Hoffmann with Löw's cabbalists and the Golem, the play imbues Judaism with the seed of fascism alongside a number of other anti-Semitic stereotypes, such as that of Judaism as a religion of hatred and superstition. Most prominently, the term *Haßkappen* variously evokes the *kippah* (Jewish skullcap) and the pointed infidel's hat forced upon medieval German Jews, but also the headdress of the Ku Klux Klan and the disguise of extreme leftist protesters at West German demonstrations. In turn, the cabbalists gesticulate madly, screech in falsetto voice, and mock the divine creation with their making of the Golem. The Golem's hoarse and clipped voice, together with his Hebrew proclamation that numbers epitomize divine mercy (35), reiterates the stereotypical notion of the Jews' flawed discourse and cold rationality. The Jews and their Golem appear as harbingers of the totalitarian control that the pharmacist and city council, the latter representing the German state, are trying to unleash.

In contrast, the *Haßkappen* emerge as a symptom of rising fascism in postunification Germany rather than its agents. The disaffected youth descended from the desolate cities and countryside after Jericho's trumpets brought down the walls of the promised land (20), a biblical twist on the messianic promises of socialist East Germany and the fall of its Wall. Through the Golem, Berkéwicz constructs the rise of right-wing extremism among postunification East German youth as a vain revolt against the bourgeois totalitarianism reigning from the Western city of Bayreuth. In fact, the festival guests call for the Storm Troopers to remove the rioting *Haßkappen* as un-German: "Entartung, [. . .] Nürnberg, Wannsee / Vergasen, Vergessen" (14; degeneracy, [. . .] Nürnberg, Wannsee / gas, oblivion). This reiterates the stages of Nazi Germany's racialized classification of its Others, their extermination, and Germans' denial of responsibility for these crimes after 1945. Right-wing German youth hence appear as the victims of the pervasive fascism among the mainstream Germans in Wagner's Bayreuth, a town itself ripe with Nazi associations. These are highlighted in the pharmacist's vocation and his euphemistic announcement of a messianic and murderous white roar about to engulf Hoffmann, inferring the Nazis' chemical means of mass annihilation (19). The pharmacist's grasp for total control of his victim also anticipates the play's vision of a bleak future in which humans in the biological sense cease to exist and where self-determination is, in the pharmacist's words, exterminated (17).

Here Berkéwicz's conflation of all modern atrocities and ideologies of hatred turns from the racist, antileftist, homophobic, and sexist slogans of the *Haßkappen* to an "Endlösung" (final solution) linking Nagasaki and Hiroshima with the computer technology and cyborg creations now affecting humanity at large (16). Indeed, Berkéwicz herself falls back on these tainted discourses of gender and sexuality in constructing the hermaphroditic machine Kleene, "hybrid, but normal frigid" [*sic*] (22; hybrid but frigid in the normal way) as the horror vision of the future.[26] Kleene's ambiguous gender and sexual orientation, as well as its fragmented language, correspond to the emasculated features of its cabbalist originators, who now speak English with a Yiddish accent and invoke the stereotype of the Jews' corrupt bodies and discourse. Indeed, the cabbalists' control of the entire set and the cast's gradual slippage into fragmented English as the play's clock races forwards convey the pervasive notion of a destructive American world order led by Jews. In a nod both to Wegener's 1920 film and the modern-day stereotype of Jewish dominance in Hollywood, the cabbalists project the nuclear destruction of the entire set onto an imaginary screen: the building collapses and its contents are consumed by the heat of the explosion. Berkéwicz's conflation of the perceived evils of cybernetics with nuclear destruction reverses the positive understanding of computer technology as a modern Golem, a helper in the sense of Jewish tradition, that Norbert Wiener, the Jewish creator of cybernetics, put forth. Instead, the Golem serves to translate the fin-de-siècle stereotype of destructive Jewish modernity into the unequal post-1989 power constellations between East and West Germans, and to pinpoint the supposed emasculation of Germans in an American-Jewish controlled age of technological progress and globalization.

In a similar vein, Jörg Kastner's thriller *Wenn der Golem erwacht* (When the Golem Awakens, 2000) configures the Golem as a signifier of the Nazi and GDR legacies and global technology in unified Germany.[27] The novel relates the quest of its first-person narrator, a cyborg without memory, to ascertain the history of his creation, from the Nazi's attempts to create a superhuman soldier to the GDR's abandoned Operation Golem — meant to defeat the capitalist class enemy — and the realization of this project by a ruthless international corporation after the Wall.

While the cyborg's childhood as a human in Berlin-Wannsee, where the Nazis planned the Final Solution of European Jewry, implicates present-day Germans in the Nazi crimes, his enforced transformation into a machine based in the Uckermark, a locality rife with associations with the Ravens-brück concentration camp, conveys the sense that contemporary Germans are the victims of an uncanny legacy. In fact, the thriller elides any representation of the Nazis' actual Jewish victims. Instead, the Golem, awakening in a blood-spattered mass of anonymous dead (91), serves to transfer the iconography of Jewish suffering onto second-generation Germans. This strategy is evident in the portrayal of the cyborg's lover Max, whose house in the formerly Jewish *Scheunenviertel* neighborhood symbolizes the cultural and political continuities of Weimar, Nazi, and post-1989 Germany. Her family once owned the building, a converted theater charged with memories of Berlin's "Golden Twenties." After running afoul of the Nazis due to the plays he chose to stage, Max's great-grandfather was murdered at Sachsenhausen and the family was forced to sell the house. Yet the family, recognized as Nazi victims, regained the estate under socialist rule until the wartime owners returned after unification, now claiming the house as victims of the GDR. Max's characterization as one of the last "Widerständler [. . .] umgeben von den Legionen der Wendegewinner" (64; resisters [. . .] surrounded by the legions of post-Wall winners) parallels the main protagonist's associations of Jewish victimization and resistance through the Golem figure.

Asserting that the similarities of Stasi und Gestapo exceeded the three letters their names had in common (189), the android marks Kastner's relativizing of the Nazi past within the larger German and international contexts after 1945 and 1989. The Golem signifies the GDR's adoption of a Jewish iconography of victimization and defense in order to mask, according to the text, the socialist objective of military aggression. With this aim of aggression, paired with its universalizing ideology, Kastner constructs the socialist state as having surpassed the discredited Nazi racism and having paved the way for the culmination of both legacies in today's international corporatism. By representing the supposed dangers of internationalism through the Jewish signifier of the Golem, Kastner implicitly reiterates the anti-Semitic cliché of rootless Jewish modernity and its destruction of national harmony.

Conclusion

Renditions of the Golem since the 1990s signify the competing discourses around twentieth-century Jewish, German, and Austrian histories and positionalities. A Jewish figure of destruction and messianic rebirth, the Golem now embodies the resistance, continuity, and revival of Jewish culture in Europe after the genocide and Cold War ideological divides. However, the Golem's associations with persecution and defense and its casting as a Frankensteinian symbol of destructive posthumanity[28] have led other

authors to rewrite the historical constellations of Nazi victims and perpetrators and construct a discourse of German and Austrian victimization in
the present. As German Chancellor Gerhard Schröder stated in a recent
Spiegel interview, his invitation to the D-Day commemoration ceremony in
June 2004 marked the overcoming not only of the Second World War, but
also of the postwar order in the "New Europe." This historical relativism
has come full circle during the sixth decade after the war, such as in the
2004 debate in the German Parliament around the renaming of 8 May,
which the old Federal Republic had termed *Tag der Kapitulation* (Capitulation Day), into the GDR's *Tag der Befreiung* (Liberation Day), and
Chancellor Schröder's scandalous opening of the Flick art collection, an
institution established from the German profits of slave labor in the Nazi
concentration camps. Furthermore, the series of German commemoration
events in 2005, such as the debate around the "Bombenholocaust" (holocaust of bombs)[29] at Dresden and the commemoration of the former concentration camp at Sachsenhausen as "Ort doppelter Geschichte" (site of a
dual history),[30] emphasized the dual associations of many German sites
with Nazi atrocities and the alleged or real postwar victimization of Germans. Recent Golem texts reflect this trend. The literary Golem trope,
shaped in the last two hundred years of cultural interaction between Jews
and non-Jews in the German-speaking lands, represents a potent site for
these memory contests and their transformation of the social and historical
meanings of being Jewish, Austrian, and German beyond the racial, ethnic-
religious, cultural, and political delineations of the twentieth century.

Notes

[1] Parts of this article originally appeared in "The Monster Returns: Golem Figures
in the Writings of Benjamin Stein, Esther Dischereit and Doron Rabinovici," in
Jewish Writing in Austria and Germany Today, ed. Hilary Herzog, Todd Herzog,
and Benjamin Lapp (New York: Berghahn, forthcoming). I thank Berghahn Publishers for the kind permission to reprint these excerpts.

[2] Wilhelm Gesenius, *Hebräisches und aramäisches Handwörterbuch über das Alte
Testament* (Berlin: Springer-Verlag, 1962), 142.

[3] The amulet contained the Hebrew word *emet* (truth), which contains within it
the word *met* (death).

[4] Dagmar C. G. Lorenz explores the saliency of the Golem for constructions of the
destroyed European Jewry in her article "Transcending the Boundaries of Space
and Culture: The Figures of the Maharal and the Golem after the Shoah —
Friedrich Torberg's *Golems Wiederkehr*, Leo Perutz's *Nachts unter der steinernen
Brücke*, Frank Zwillinger's *Maharal*, and Nelly Sachs's *Eli: Ein Mysterienspiel vom
Leiden Israels*," in *Transforming the Center, Eroding the Margins: Essays on Ethnic
and Cultural Boundaries in German-Speaking Countries*, ed. Dagmar C. G.

Lorenz and Renate S. Posthofen (Columbia, SC: Camden House, 1998), 285–302.

[5] Benjamin Stein, *Das Alphabet des Juda Liva* (Munich: dtv, 1998). Subsequent references to this work are cited in the text.

[6] Franz Kafka, "Die Verwandlung," in *Sämtliche Erzählungen* (Frankfurt am Main: Fischer, 1995), 56–99.

[7] Ritchie Robertson, *Kafka: Judaism, Politics, and Literature* (Oxford: Oxford UP, 1985), 189–90.

[8] Gershom Scholem, *Von der mystischen Gestalt der Gottheit: Studien zu Grundbegriffen der Kabbala* (Frankfurt am Main: Suhrkamp, 1977), 201 and 211.

[9] Cathy S. Gelbin, *An Indelible Seal: Race, Hybridity and Identity in Elisabeth Langgässer's Writings* (Essen: Blaue Eule, 2001), 13–47.

[10] Gershom Scholem, *Zur Kabbala und ihrer Symbolik* (Frankfurt am Main: Suhrkamp, 1973), 212.

[11] Esther Dischereit, *als mir mein golem öffnete. Gedichte* (Passau: Karl Sturz, 1996). Henceforth cited with page number.

[12] Gershom Scholem, *Zur Kabbala und ihrer Symbolik* (Frankfurt am Main: Suhrkamp, 1973), 259.

[13] Itta Shedletzky, "Eine deutsch-jüdische Stimme sucht Gehör — Zu Esther Dischereits Romanen, Hörspielen und Gedichten," in *In der Sprache der Täter: Neue Lektüren deutschsprachiger Nachkriegs- und Gegenwartsliteratur*, ed. Stephan Braese (Opladen: Westdeutscher Verlag, 1998), 199–225.

[14] Nelly Sachs, "Golem Tod," in *Das Leiden Israels. Eli. In den Wohnungen des Todes. Sternverdunkelung* (Frankfurt am Main: Edition Suhrkamp, 1996), 118.

[15] Paul Celan, "Einem, der vor der Tür stand," in *Gedichte in zwei Bänden* (Frankfurt am Main, 1978), 142–43. See also the explorations of Celan's poetry by Peter Horst Neumann, *Zur Lyrik Paul Celans: Eine Einführung* (Göttingen: Vandenhoek & Ruprecht, 1990) and Jacques Derrida, "Shibboleth: For Paul Celan," in *Word Traces: Readings of Paul Celan*, ed. Aris Fioretos (Baltimore: Johns Hopkins UP, 1994), 3–72.

[16] Andreas Kleinert, *Schimanski: Das Geheimnis des Golem* (Germany, 2003).

[17] For an exploration of the anti-Semitic concept of *mauscheln* as an indicator of Jewish corruption, see Sander L. Gilman, *Jewish Self-Hatred: Anti-Semitism and the Hidden Language of the Jews* (Baltimore: Johns Hopkins UP, 1986).

[18] Sander L. Gilman, "Salome, Syphilis, Sara Bernhardt and the Modern Jewess," in *German Quarterly* 66 (1993): 195–211.

[19] Diner develops this term from the prewar notion of a "German-Jewish symbiosis" to describe the ways in which self-definitions of postwar Germans and Jews have become inextricably linked to each other in relation to Auschwitz. See Dan Diner, "Negative Symbiose — Deutsche und Juden nach Auschwitz," in *Jüdisches Leben in Deutschland seit 1945*, ed. Micha Brumlik et al. (Frankfurt am Main: Athenäum, 1988): 243–57.

[20] Leslie Adelson describes positionality as the discursive fixation of individuals in contrast to the notion of position as a self-determined choice. As Adelson argues,

this concept allows for a critical pursuit of constructions of difference, such as "configurations of race, nationality, class, ethnicity, and other signifying social practices through which power is manifested." See Leslie Adelson, *Making Bodies, Making History: Feminism and German Identity* (Lincoln: U of Nebraska P, 1993), xiv.

[21] Sander L. Gilman has described this ambivalent stereotype as one of the central images of the anti-Semitic imagination. See Sander L. Gilman, *Difference and Pathology: Stereotypes of Sexuality, Race, and Madness* (Ithaca, NY: Cornell UP, 1985).

[22] Ernst Petz, *Kafka der Golem und Fußball und Prag. 1 phantastischer Roman* (Vienna: Aarachne, 1998). Henceforth cited in the text.

[23] Hilde Langthaler, *Golem Now* (Vienna: Triton, 2000). Henceforth cited in the text.

[24] During the 1980s, German-speaking feminist discourses constructed women as a universal category of victims of patriarchy beyond responsibility for anti-Semitism, racism, and genocide. The simultaneous assertion that ancient Judaism had destroyed pre-existing matriarchal cultures and ushered in the subjugation of women to patriarchal rule culminating in Nazism enabled non-Jewish German women to stylize themselves as victims of an alleged Jewish patriarchy. For examples, see Irene Stoehr, "Machtergriffen? Deutsche Frauenbewegung 1933," in *Courage* 2/1983, 24–32; Gerda Weiler, *Ich verwerfe im Lande die Kriege: Auf den Spuren des Matriarchats im Alten Testament* (Munich: Verlag Frauenoffensive, 1984), and Helke Sander, "Telefongespräch mit einem Freund," in *Die Geschichten der drei Damen K.* (Munich: dtv, 1991), 104–14. A discussion of this trend can be found in Susannah Heschel, "Konfigurationen des Patriarchats, des Judentums und des Nazismus im deutschen feministischen Denken, in *Der feministische "Sündenfall"? Antisemitische Vorurteile in der Frauenbewegung*, ed. Charlotte Kohn-Ley and Ilse Korotin (Vienna: Picus), 160–208; as well as Cathy S. Gelbin, "Die jüdische Thematik im (multi)kulturellen Diskurs der Bundesrepublik," in *AufBrüche: Kulturelle Produktionen von Migrantinnen, Schwarzen und jüdischen Frauen in Deutschland*, ed. Cathy S. Gelbin et al. (Königstein/Ts.: Ulrike Helmer Verlag, 1999), 87–111.

[25] Ulla Berkéwicz, *Der Golem in Bayreuth* (Frankfurt am Main: Edition Suhrkamp, 1999). Henceforth cited in the text.

[26] In contrast, feminist theoreticians such as Donna Haraway have held up the cyborg as an inherently transgressive figure able to disrupt traditional discourses of Otherness, including gender, sexuality, and race. See Donna Haraway, "Manifesto for Cyborgs: Science, Technology, and Socialist Feminism in the 1980s," in *Coming to Terms*, ed. Elizabeth Weed (New York: Routledge, 1985), 173–204, 279–88.

[27] Jörg Kastner, *Wenn der Golem erwacht* (Bern: Scherz Verlag, 2000). Henceforth cited as in text.

[28] I owe this term to Elaine Graham's recent exploration of cyborgs and other transgressive figures in popular culture. See Elaine Graham, *Representations of the Post/human: Monsters, Aliens and Others in Popular Culture* (Manchester: Manchester UP, 2002).

[29] Jürgen Gansel, elected representative of the German rightwing party NPD, used this relativizing term in the regional parliament of Sachsen in January 2005 for the Allied bombings of Dresden. Although this incident caused an uproar in the Sächsische Landtag and the German press and led the government to consider a crackdown on the NPD's status as a political party, a significant portion of the German population had no such reaction. According to a survey by Infratest Dimap Institute, nineteen percent of West Germans and fifteen percent of East Germans did not find the term objectionable. As regards age patterns, twenty-seven percent of Germans under age thirty and fifteen per cent of those under sixty did not consider the usage of this term in this context objectionable. The hightest rate of consent was found among the constituency of the leftist PDS, where thirty-one percent agreed, closely followed by twenty-eight percent of CDU supporters. See *Welt am Sonntag* 5/30 (January 2005): 4; Stefan Wirner, "Dresden geht in sich," *Jungle World* 6 (9 February 2005): 5.

[30] Thus stated by Brandenburg's Minister of Culture Johanna Wanka (CDU) in August 2005 at the opening of a special exhibition marking the sixtieth anniversary of the creation of a Soviet internment camp at Sachsenhausen. See the webpage of the Ministry of Science, Research and Culture of the Federal State of Brandenburg, http://www.brandenburg.de/sixcms/detail.php?id=238933&_siteid=60.

10: Multi-Ethnicity and Cultural Identity: Afro-German Women Writers' Struggle for Identity in Postunification Germany

Jennifer E. Michaels

GERMAN UNIFICATION BROUGHT for Afro-Germans,[1] as well as for African and other non-white immigrants and asylum seekers, an increased feeling of vulnerability and not belonging. As Marilyn Sephocle observes: "Before German unification African Germans had to grapple with identity/image issues. Today their focus is on something even more pressing: fear of being attacked."[2] In the following, I will focus in particular on texts by May Ayim, Helga Emde, and Ika Hügel-Marshall, who played an important role in founding the Afro-German group. Theirs are strong voices against the increase in racist violence in the immediate postunification years. In their postunification texts, these and other Afro-German women writers contest the euphoric memories of unification. Their texts shed light on their efforts to build a community, define their biracial identities, and understand their heritage: theirs is a "struggle for cultural space in the New Germany."[3] By fighting against racism and reclaiming their erased history in Germany they contest notions of a monoethnic German society, what Helga Emde calls "the myth of Germanic ethnic-nationalism."[4]

Like most Germans with biracial African or African American and German heritage, Ayim, Emde, and Hügel-Marshall grew up isolated from other black people in a predominantly white society that marginalized them. Only in the mid-1980s did Afro-Germans begin to define themselves as a cultural group. In 1984, the American black activist poet Audre Lorde taught a course on black American women poets at the Free University in Berlin where she got to know black German women. From 1984 until her death in 1992, Lorde visited Germany often, and she enjoyed close friendships in particular with Ayim, Emde, and Hügel-Marshall. Her influence was important because she encouraged black German women to write about their experiences and to create a community, and she remained their mentor and friend. A result of her encouragement was the publication in 1986 of *Farbe bekennen: Afro-deutsche Frauen auf den Spuren ihrer Geschichte* (translated as *Showing Our Colors: Afro-German Women Speak*

Out, 1992)[5] edited by Ayim and the Afro-German Katharina Oguntoye, who grew up in the GDR, and the white feminist Dagmar Schultz. This volume is a collection of life stories, essays, and poems that document the experiences of Afro-Germans. In several of their texts, Afro-German women acknowledge Lorde's impact on them. In "I Too Am German," for example, Emde writes that Lorde "was a touchstone for most Black German women in their struggle and political development. She became a friend whom I respected and loved" (38).

Afro-German women who were close to Lorde have been among the strongest voices in the Afro-German movement and have written many of its literary, autobiographical, and theoretical texts. Ayim, Emde, and Hügel-Marshall played a leading role in founding the Afro-German community, and in speeches and essays they have all been active in speaking out against racism. Until her suicide in 1996 Ayim, who was born in 1960, was the group's most prominent poet. Her father came from Ghana and her mother was German. Shortly after her birth, she was placed in an orphanage and was adopted by a white German family in 1962. She decided to change her name from Opitz, that of her foster family and the name that appears on her early publications, to Ayim, her father's name. She worked as an educational specialist and speech therapist in Berlin. In addition to numerous essays she wrote two collections of poetry, *blues in schwarz weiss* (blues in black and white, 1995) and *nachtgesang* (nightsong), published posthumously in 1997. Emde, one of the contributors to *Farbe bekennen*, was born in 1946, the daughter of a German mother and an African American soldier. She grew up in her mother's family, trained as a nurse, a profession in which she worked for several years before deciding to study for a teaching certificate, and she helped develop antiracist curricula for public schools. Hügel-Marshall was born in 1947. Her mother was German and her father was an African American soldier. When she was seven, she was placed in an orphanage. She later studied social pedagogics and since 1990 she has been in charge of publicity for the Orlanda Frauenverlag, which published *Farbe bekennen*, Ayim's poetry, and also Hügel-Marshall's autobiographical work *Daheim unterwegs* (1998). She lectures on racism at both the Technical University and the Free University in Berlin.

Experiences of Unification

Afro-German women writers offer a sober perspective on German unification. Instead of the togetherness experienced at least initially by white Germans, it gave them an increased sense of exclusion. In her essay "Rassismus und Verdrängung im vereinten Deutschland" (Racism and Oppression in Unified Germany, 1994), Ayim writes that unification has not yet brought anything positive for minorities. Instead, they have experienced growing racism.[6] In her poem "grenzenlos und unverschämt" (borderless and brazen), her subtitle "ein gedicht gegen die deutsche sch-einheit" (a poem against the German "u-not-y") suggests the hollowness of a unification that did not embrace all.[7] She writes in her poem "blues in schwarz weiss" that reunified Germany celebrates itself in 1990 without immigrants, refugees, or Jewish and black people: it celebrates in white (*blues*, 82). Like Afro-Germans, students in the GDR from Namibia, South Africa, Nicaragua, and Cuba sensed that they would be excluded from postunification society. One of these students, Sithebe Nombuso, who was also known as Yoliswa Ngidi, was a refugee from South Africa. She suspected that unification would be a setback and that the new German government would not make room for them.[8]

A key text for understanding Afro-Germans' reactions to unification is Ayim's essay "Das Jahr 1990: Heimat und Einheit aus afro-deutscher Perspektive" (The Year 1990: Homeland and Unity from an Afro-German Perspective, 1993). Ayim recollects talk in the media about German-German brothers and sisters, about being united and reunited, and about solidarity with one another (*Grenzenlos*, 88). In the celebrations of unification, however, black Germans and immigrants were absent. For those with dark skins, even owning a German passport did not give them an invitation to participate in the East/West celebrations. They realized that the new German "we" in "diesem unserem Lande" (this our country), as Chancellor Helmut Kohl liked to put it, did not include everyone (*Grenzenlos*, 90). Particularly disturbing to Ayim was the outpouring of nationalism. She was dismayed by the sudden availability of German flags, patriotic T-Shirts, and other black-red-gold articles, by the high demand for such items, and by the resurgence of nationalist rhetoric. Words such as "folk," "home," and "fatherland," which were tainted because of their use by the Nazis, suddenly became respectable again, and Germany's past was forgotten. To her it seemed as if the white Christian-German collective guilt complex had dissipated overnight, thereby wrenching the present away from the past. Because the celebrations were so white, she wonders for whom and for how many there would be room in the new homeland. She asks who embraced whom in German-German reunification, who was embraced, who was brought in, and who was excluded (*Grenzenlos*, 89). Afro-Germans and other minority groups sensed that German reunification would bring with it an increasing closing off from the outside, an outside that would include them (*Grenzenlos*, 90).

Ayim speaks out in this essay against the erasing of cultural memory in the GDR. In her view, West Germany was dictating how the GDR would be remembered, and she sees this process as yet another example of those in power shaping the past according to their ideological views. This is for her a sensitive issue since she notices a similar pattern in the erasure of the history of Africans in Germany. Two years after unification, the former

GDR was no longer recognizable, and the takeover by the West was progressing rapidly. Virtually everything in the East, such as textbooks, laws, and institutional structures, had either been adapted to those of the West or had been abolished. Neon signs demonstrated that capitalism had taken root in even the smallest villages, and unemployment, especially among women, was increasing. Streets that had been named after those who resisted Hitler now were named for flowers or had names with colonial and racist overtones. The East Berlin U-Bahn station "Thälmannstrasse" was changed, for example, to "Moorstrasse," an indication to Ayim that racist language and thinking was tolerated in the highest echelons of the new government. Such insensitivity was also evident in the West, where street names and monuments that continued to glorify the colonists and humiliate the colonized were retained. Ayim wonders what we will remember and what we have already forgotten (*Grenzenlos*, 96). In her view, unification could have been a moment of critical self-examination and a stimulus for change in both parts of Germany (*Grenzenlos*, 95), and she regrets this lost opportunity.

Particularly worrying for Afro-Germans and other blacks was the worsening climate of racism and racially motivated attacks in both former East and former West Germany in the immediate postunification years. In *Stoppt die Gewalt! Stimmen gegen den Ausländerhaß* (Stop the Violence! Voices Against the Hatred of Foreigners, 1992), the editors Michael Jürgs and Freimut Duve chronicle the many incidents of violent racism in Germany just in the two-month period from the attack in Hoyerswerda on 17 September 1991 to 12 November of that year. The strong protests in this volume come from journalists and from a wide array of prominent people, such as the writers Peter Härtling, Christoph Hein, and Lew Kopelew, as well as from ordinary citizens. As the editors observe, Hoyerswerda has become a synonym for non-German residents' fear of German national feeling.[9]

Afro-Germans, African residents, and black visitors all felt this fear. Nombuso relates that many foreigners left Dresden because they were afraid of the increasing racist violence. She mentions a colleague from South Africa who was beaten up by neo-Nazis on three occasions, twice in Weimar and once in East Berlin (*EV*, 230). Afraid for his life, he left Germany. In her view, the situation in the whole of Germany was becoming more and more alarming (*EV*, 231). When the Ghanaian writer Amma Darko was on a reading tour in East Germany in 1999 she was accosted by a group of young men who called her "nigger" and threw a bottle at her. Audre Lorde notes that for the first time in six years of coming to Germany she felt afraid as she read her poetry there.[10] In her poem "East Berlin December 1989," Lorde depicts the fear that blacks felt: "Already my blood shrieks/ through East Berlin streets/ misplaced hatreds/ volcanic tallies rung upon cement/ Afro-German woman stomped to death/ by skinheads in Alexanderplatz."[11]

Ayim, Emde, and Hügel-Marshall respond to this climate of fear in their texts. Ayim observes in "Rassismus und Verdrängung im vereinten Deutschland" (Racism and Persecution in Unified Germany) that especially in the five new federal states racist violence was a reality of daily life (*Grenzenlos*, 138). In "Das Jahr 1990" she remembers that for the first time she felt threatened in Berlin, where she now experienced not only hostile looks and insults but also open racism. A friend who was holding her Afro-German daughter on her lap in the S-Bahn, was told: "Solche wie euch brauchen wir jetzt nicht mehr, wir sind hier schon selber mehr als genug" (We don't need people like you any more. There are already more than enough of us, *Grenzenlos*, 91). Ayim points to the increase since 1990 of racially motivated attacks on black people and criticizes the media for paying scant attention to the violence and white German citizens and politicians for looking on and not protesting. In "Die Wut der Schwarzen Frauen sollte auch die Empörung der weißen Frauen sein" (The Rage of Black Women Should Also Be The Outrage of White Women, 1993), Ayim notes that several of her black friends have left Germany, some after experiencing violence themselves and others because they were afraid. She adds that in the not too distant future she might have to do the same (*Grenzenlos*, 108).

Not only in her essays but also in her poetry Ayim speaks out strongly against such racial violence. In "soul sister," she defines racism as the pale face of an illness that secretly and openly devours us (*blues*, 57) and in the poem "die farbe der macht" (the color of power), she writes that racism is the pale face of violence that shows itself increasingly openly again in Germany.[12] Ayim notes in her poem "im exil und hiv positiv" (in exile and HIV positive), written in memory of Yoliswa Ngidi (Sithebe Nombuso), that Yoliswa was not only threatened with racist murder in her native South Africa but also in Germany, her last place of refuge (*blues*, 95). Ayim's poem "tagesthemen" (topics of the day) satirizes those Germans who sit comfortably at home watching television and eating chocolates, unconcerned about an arson attack on a Turkish travel agency they hear about on the news (*nachtgesang*, 37). In "die unterkunft" (shelter), she speaks out against hate crimes, specifically against the arson attack on a refugee home. She evokes the loneliness of the refugees in a strange land and the barrenness of their refugee home with its lack of flowers, pictures, or carpets, and its harsh neon light that burns night and day. Her reference to those killed in the attack: "die menschen sind tot/ nur noch asche und rauch/ verkohlte/ knochen und haut" (the people are dead/ only ashes and smoke/ charred/ bones and skin, *nachtgesang*, 74) is a chilling reminder of the Holocaust and reinforces the fatalistic sense of the circularity of German history.[13] In "deutschland im herbst" (Germany in Autumn), Ayim draws even closer parallels between atrocities of the National Socialist past and the racially motivated murder in November 1990 of Antonio Amadeo, an Angolan man. Her poem, which begins with references to Kristallnacht, lists those targeted by the Nazis:

> kristallnacht:
> im november 1938
> zerklirrten zuerst
> fensterscheiben
> dann
> wieder und wieder
> menschenknochen
> von juden und schwarzen und
> kranken und schwachen von
> sinti und roma und
> polen von lesben und
> schwulen von und von
> und von und von
> und und.
>
> [kristallnacht:
> in November 1938
> first shattered
> were windowpanes
> then
> again and again
> human bones
> of jews and blacks
> of the weak and the sick
> of sinti and roma and
> poles of lesbians and
> gays of and of
> and of and of
> and and.][14]

The last lines suggest that the list of those persecuted goes on and on. The neo-Nazis' murder of Amadeo fits into what she sees as a continuing pattern of racial violence in Germany and an unconfronted past. She stresses that the police did not hurry to help, and the media did not protest loudly. Then as now people either participated and approved or looked on passively. She concludes: "so ist es:/ deutschland im herbst/ mir graut vor dem winter" (that's how it is:/ autumn in germany/ i dread the winter, *blues*, 68–70).[14]

Like Ayim, Emde speaks out against racial violence. In her autobiographical essay "I Too Am German," she writes that seven years after unification, *Ausländerfeindlichkeit* (hostility to foreigners), which she defines as a German combination of xenophobia and racism, has "reached a semi-fascist racist dimension" (37). Although she acknowledges that the nineteenth-century "scientific" racism expounded by Houston Stewart Chamberlain and Joseph Arthur Comte de Gobineau is not restricted to Germany, she argues that such racist myths found fertile ground in "the tense situation after German 'unification'" (38). She recalls a newspaper article about a group of white East Germans in Wittemberge who on 2 May 1991 went on a rampage of "Nigger bashing" that ended in the murder of one young man. For her, 1991 was "the year of riots, violence and killing" (41). Afraid of being killed because she was black, she moved to the United States in 1991 and did not return to Germany until the end of October 1997. In her view, the riots and killings "made it clear that the German justice system could not protect Blacks and other visible ethnic groups" (41).

In her autobiography *Daheim unterwegs: Ein deutsches Leben* (On the Move at Home: A German Life, 1998),[15] Hügel-Marshall also discusses the increasing racial violence in Germany since the fall of the Wall. Her title, *Daheim unterwegs*, a line from Ayim's poem "entfernte verbindungen" (distant connections), underscores her search for identity and a cultural home, and her subtitle emphasizes not only that her story gives voice to the experiences of other Afro-Germans but also that, however much white Germans may protest, hers is indeed a German life. In the talk she gave at the University of Massachusetts at Amherst in October 1992, which she includes in her autobiography, she depicts the climate of fear among blacks and other ethnic groups. After dark, many did not dare go outside; mothers were scared to bring their children to kindergarten for fear of racist attacks; black people were assaulted on the street; Jewish cemeteries and memorials were vandalized; and refugee homes were attacked. This was when the Angolan man, Antonio Amadeo, was killed. As a result, some Afro-Germans left Germany, despite the fact that they saw it as their home, because they could no longer endure the situation (103).

Afro-German women writers also speak out in their postunification texts about the increased stress on Germanness and the hostility to foreigners and those seeking asylum. Ayim was disturbed by the restrictions on asylum and by white Germans' lack of solidarity with asylum seekers. In "Das Jahr 1990" she observes that scarcely any white Germans participated in demonstrations against the tightening of immigration and asylum laws, which especially affected people from poor, non-European countries (*Grenzenlos*, 93–94). That specific groups were targeted demonstrated to her the racially motivated origins of the restrictions.[16] She suspects that even for asylum seekers who are permitted to stay, the Federal Republic will not be, for the foreseeable future, a place that they can call home. This is also true for immigrants, black Germans, and Jews who have either always lived in Germany or have done so for a long time (*Grenzenlos*, 100). In her essay "Rassismus und Verdrängung im vereinten Deutschland"

Ayim acknowledges, however, that laws restricting immigration, residence, and job possibilities are not only characteristic of Germany but have become typical of the European Union as a whole (*Grenzenlos*, 138), an indication to her of widespread European hostility to those considered different.

Nombuso experienced this restrictive climate herself. She gives a grim picture of her struggle with immigration authorities after unification. Like other foreign students in the GDR, she had GDR identity papers. After unification, she had to turn in these documents, which were no longer valid, but was unable to obtain new ones. Immigration officials demanded, for example, that she procure a passport and other documents from South Africa but, since she was a refugee from the South African government, this was not possible. She was afraid that she would be deported to South Africa, where she would be arrested, and she struggled unsuccessfully with the authorities until her death from AIDS in 1993 (*EV*, 228–29).

Afro-Germans sensed apathy in postunification Germany regarding problems they faced. In "Das Jahr 1990," Ayim notes that there was little interest after unification in a North-South dialogue and that even in the women's movement, German-German issues were discussed and celebrated, as if Germany were exclusively white (*Grenzenlos*, 93). She was disturbed by the silence in regard to and denial of racism, apparent even among "progressive" leftists and in the women's movement (*Grenzenlos*, 97). In her opinion, Germans only remember immigrants, black Germans, and Jews when they need them to participate in congresses on tolerance, racism, immigration, or multiculturalism, such as before the elections in 1990. In her poem "gegen leberwurstgrau — für eine bunte republik: talk-talk-show für den bla-bla kampf" (against liverwurst gray — for a colorful republic: talk talk show for the blah blah struggle), Ayim satirizes the hypocrisy of such endeavors. Afro-Germans and other minorities sit with white activists, politicians, prominent people, and the socially committed and debate such issues as protest actions. They draw up demands, which are neatly listed. The lists are filed and sent on to the right places. Then the show is over and everyone goes home. The socially committed feel relieved, whereas minorities feel as if they have been duped (*blues*, 62–65). Their problems will be forgotten again until the next election.

The Importance of Community

For Afro-Germans, an important part of finding cultural space was creating a community. Beginning in the mid-1980s, Afro-Germans worked to create the community they had previously lacked, and this effort increased after unification. In "Weiße Taktik, weiße Herrschaft" (White Tactics,

White Supremacy) Sheila Mysorekar points out that their history as blacks in Germany is one of isolation and struggling alone. They lack a community and generations of older black Germans who could be role models and could pass on their experiences as blacks in Germany to them (*EV*, 110). As Emde observes: "We had no Black schools, churches, communities, or other institutions to teach us about heritage; what it means to be Black!" (37). In "Weißer Streß und Schwarze Nerven: Streßfaktor Rassismus" (White Stress and Black Nerves: Stress Factor Racism, 1995), Ayim emphasizes the absence of continuity between generations of Afro-Germans. Afro-Germans, she writes, lack both a sense of their historical roots and black role models, so crucial for forming an identity (*Grenzenlos*, 113). Growing up isolated from other blacks made her feel that she was an alien body in West German society (*Grenzenlos*, 126). In her view, while a visible and strong community does not protect from discrimination, it does protect against isolation (*Grenzenlos*, 127). Both Ayim and Oguntoye stress the significant role groups such as the *Initiative Schwarze Deutsche* (Initiative of Black Germans), established in 1986, and the black German women's group ADEFRA[17] play in fostering self-esteem and cultural identity among their members and fighting for the rights of blacks in German society (*Colors*, xvi).

In the atmosphere of fear after unification, these groups became increasingly important. In "I Too Am German," Emde recalls that when she met with black Germans for the first time it was overwhelming and breathtaking to see "black people of all shades, sizes and ages" (40), all of them speaking German. She recalls too the hostility of some whites, such as evidenced by the postcard sent to the television station, the Saarländischer Rundfunk, on which was written: "Germans are white. Niggers can't be Germans" (40). Hügel-Marshall, who like other Afro-Germans grew up in a completely white environment, stresses in *Daheim unterwegs* that her involvement in the Black German movement made her feel she was no longer alone. The community gave her strength and helped her gradually find her way to herself (91–92). Ayim points out in "Die Wut der Schwarzen Frauen" (The Rage of Black Women) how important it is to have a space in which Afro-Germans can exchange views among themselves (*Grenzenlos*, 107). In "Die afro-deutsche Minderheit" (The Afro-German Minority, 1995), she writes that such groups promote the interests of black people, fight along with progressive whites against racism and anti-Semitism, and solidify connections with politically active immigrant and black groups (*Grenzenlos*, 156). Afro-Germans reached out to other "hyphenated" groups and forged coalitions with other people of color, not only in Germany but in other countries as well. The essay collection *Entfernte Verbindungen* (Distant Connections, 1993), for example, was put out by such a coalition and sought to contribute to redefining German identity.[18]

Reclaiming an Afro-German History

An important part of Afro-German women's struggle for cultural space in the new Germany is not only contesting memories but creating them. Reclaiming their erased history in Germany is important because of the role history plays in shaping culture and identity. Oguntoye and Ayim write: "In disentangling the threads of our histories within Africa and Germany and connecting them to our subjective experiences, we are becoming more sure of our identity and are able to assert it more aggressively to the outside world" (*Colors*, xxii). By demonstrating that there has been a black presence in Germany for centuries, they also contest the myth of Germany as a monoethnic country. In "Rassismus und Verdrängung im vereinten Deutschland," Ayim notes that, despite its many immigrants, Germany still does not see itself as a land of immigration, and white Germans perceive those who are German and black as exotic combinations. Since they do not conform to the Aryan ideal, a mode of thinking she still finds prevalent in Germany, they are not typically German and thus do not belong (*Grenzenlos*, 137).

In "Wir wollen aus der Isolation heraus" (We Want to Get Out of Our Isolation, 1987) John Amoateng-Kantara quotes the Jamaican-born Marcus Garvey, who likens a people that does not know its history to a tree without roots (*Grenzenlos*, 47). Afro-German women writers, especially Ayim, have worked to provide the roots for the tree. As Hügel-Marshall stresses in *Daheim unterwegs*, creating a black history in Germany is necessary for all who come after them (103).

Recovering the historical record of Africans in Germany is crucial, since Afro-Germans grew up knowing nothing about their history or culture. As Ayim observes in "Weißer Stress und Schwarze Nerven," only when she began her own research did she realize that the history of blacks in Germany did not begin after the Second World War (*Grenzenlos*, 113). In "Rassismus und Verdrängung im vereinten Deutschland" Ayim points out that at school Afro-Germans learned nothing about the long presence of Africans in Germany and were unaware that black Germans were persecuted in the National Socialist period. They did, however, learn about African natives, among them cannibals and cruel barbarians, who through the "great deeds" of European explorers were exposed to civilization (*Grenzenlos*, 136–37). In her opinion, on the topics of colonial history, National Socialism, and racism they were misinformed and made ignorant at school (*Grenzenlos*, 137).

Already before unification, Afro-German women made the first important step in recovering their history and heritage with the publication in 1986 of *Farbe bekennen*. Ayim's research into the history and presence of Africans in Germany from the Middle Ages to the present provides the framework for the individual life histories and the poems in the volume.

Present-day racism in Germany, she argues, stems from Germany's colonial history and colonial consciousness. Thus, an understanding of the past sheds light on the way that Afro-Germans are treated in the present. She addresses in particular Africans' mistreatment under nineteenth-century German colonialism, a part of German history that for many years was largely ignored. She highlights the hostility in Germany to the so-called "Rhineland Bastards," children born to German mothers and black French occupying troops after the First World War, and the hateful propaganda campaign against these soldiers, during which German nationalists warned of racial and cultural pollution. When the Nazis came to power, some of these biracial children were sterilized and others were sent to concentration camps. Ayim also observes that German society marginalized and stigmatized the approximately 3000 "occupation babies," children of African-American and German couples, who were born after the Second World War. By reclaiming their history, Afro-Germans began to understand that their past "was closely linked with Germany's colonial and National Socialist history" (*Colors*, xxii). As Ayim and Oguntoye observe: "Our unknown background and our invisibility as Afro-Germans are consequences of the suppression of German history" (*Colors*, xxii).

In *Daheim unterwegs*, Hügel-Marshall underscores the urgency of making their own history visible (93). Ayim and others have continued to explore the history of blacks in Germany in their postunification texts.[19] In "Die afro-deutsche Minderheit," Ayim writes that in Germany in the 1990s black Germans were still generally seen as foreigners, and their residence in Germany was considered temporary (*Grenzenlos*, 139). To combat such thinking, Ayim traces a black presence in Germany back to the times of Caesar, who had Africans among his soldiers. As in *Farbe bekennen*, Ayim links the history of blacks with the history of racism. During the crusades she notes that Christian Ethiopians were considered allies and thus Christian blacks were a frequent motif in legends of the saints in medieval art and literature. However, positive images of black people became less frequent as Islam penetrated the African continent and during the course of colonialism. The word Moor, applied to blacks until the eighteenth century, already implies religiously formed prejudices and the rejection of black people as heathens. In church vocabulary of the Middle Ages, for example, "Aegyptius" became a synonym for the devil (*Grenzenlos*, 140).

Such religious prejudice, Ayim argues, formed the basis of racial thinking in the colonial period. In the biologically based racial theories of the nineteenth century, as propagated for example by Gobineau, white European males were classified at the top of the racial hierarchy and black men, followed by black women, were at the very bottom (*Grenzenlos*, 142). Black Africans were depicted as cannibals or as exotic objects or, patronizingly, as naive children of nature. She states that some were even stuffed and displayed in natural history museums. Others were brought to Germany to be exhibited in various venues, including zoos (*Grenzenlos*, 144). Although the German colonial period was short, such racial thinking, Ayim argues, continued uninterrupted into the present. In Ayim's opinion, Germany's failure to confront its colonial past and its insufficient confrontation with its recent history of racism and anti-Semitism are responsible for today's discrimination and prejudice (*Grenzenlos*, 150).

By reclaiming their history, Afro-Germans demonstrate their long connection to Germany and challenge Germany's ethnic nationalism, what Ayim terms "the myth of the German people as an ethnic monolith" (*Colors*, 136). In "Die Wut der Schwarzen Frauen," Ayim recollects that since her childhood she was told that she had no right to be in Germany (*Grenzenlos*, 108). In her poem "afro-deutsch I" (afro-german I), Ayim both challenges German perceptions of who is German and addresses the difficulty white Germans have accepting people of biracial heritage as German. The white speaker in the poem tells the Afro-German woman that she is lucky she grew up in Germany and not in the bush, and that if she studies hard she will be able to go back to help her people in Africa (*blues*, 18–19).

Afro-Germans also write in order to make Germans aware of the racist thinking embedded in language. In her poetry, Ayim, who as both a poet and a speech therapist was particularly sensitive to language, struggles with the German language. She writes in "Ein Brief aus Münster" (A Letter from Münster, 1984) that she uses the German language, with its racist elements that are often directed at her, mostly unreflectedly (*Grenzenlos*, 11). In several poems, she uses puns to unmask the racist elements in the language, and she creates new words when the old ones do not suffice. Ayim also examines insensitivity to racist language within the German women's movement. In "freiheit der kunst" (freedom of art), for example, a white German woman, who claims not to be racist, declares that, even though the words "Neger" (Negro) and "Mulatte" (Mulatto) are offensive to the anonymous Afro-German woman with whom she is talking, she intends to keep on using them because she finds them "melodisch und klassisch" (melodic and classic, *blues*, 76). Ayim stresses the frequency of racist notions in everyday language. In "Weißer Stress und Schwarze Nerven" she points out that black connotes something negative, evil, or even illegal, whereas white represents everything that is good and pure (*Grenzenlos*, 111–13). Other examples that Afro-Germans frequently cite include the Sarotti-Moor, the emblem of the Sarotti chocolate factory, which in "I Too Am German" Emde refers to as "a product of colonialism" (35), and "Negro Kiss," the name for the popular chocolates (*Colors*, 102).[20] Emde calls such terms "sweet tasting insults" (*Colors*, 102). As a child she loved such sweets but was ashamed to ask for them in a store (*Colors*, 102). In "Eistorte à la Hildegard" (Hildegard's Ice Cream Cake, 1989) Ayim notes that such terms as "Eisneger" (Ice Negro) or "Eismohr"

(Ice Moor) for ice cream with chocolate sauce made racism palatable. Although she loved the chocolate sauce, these names spoiled her appetite (*Grenzenlos*, 49). In "Ethnozentrismus und Geschlechterrollenstereotype in der Logopädie" (Ethnocentrism and Gender Role Stereotypes in Speech Therapy, 1989) Ayim points out that racist thinking permeates even her own field of speech therapy. One such example is "Hottentotism," a supposedly objective term for a speech impediment but also a derogatory name for the southwest African Herero tribe. Another is the term "Mongolism" for those with Down's syndrome. She sees a pattern of using names of peoples whose heritage is outside Europe to describe sickness or deviation from the norm (*Grenzenlos*, 69).

In their texts, Afro-German women also speak out against blatant racial stereotypes. Of particular concern to them are children's books where blacks were often depicted as uncivilized, wild, or stupid, as, for example, in such children's rhymes as "Zehn kleine Negerlein" (Ten Little Negroes). Such demeaning images of blacks were devastating to Afro-German children growing up isolated with no sense of their history, and these images also shaped white German children's perceptions of blacks as inferior (*Grenzenlos*, 151). Ayim also found such stereotypes in speech therapy, where one therapeutic strategy was the game "The Negroes play drums in the bush" (*Grenzenlos*, 70). Hans J. Massaquoi refers to insensitive racial epithets in the title of his autobiography, which was translated into German as "*Neger, Neger, Schornsteinfeger!*" *Meine Kindheit in Deutschland* (1999).[21] The original English title *Destined to Witness: Growing Up Black in Nazi Germany* does not capture the unthinking racism inherent in this German children's rhyme (Negro, Negro, Chimney Sweep). Such insensitive use of language and stereotypes, Afro-Germans stress, reflects the wider insensitivity to minorities in society as a whole.

The Search for Identity

Afro-German women struggle in their texts to define and affirm their biracial identities. They were supported in this by Lorde, whose thinking about difference has resonated strongly with them. As they were growing up, they experienced difference as negative. They internalized the racist stereotypes of the society that surrounded them and tried to be as white as possible, and rejected, and sometimes hated, being black. Lorde, however, insisted on recognizing and affirming people's differences. Difference is, she insists, "a creative force for change."[22]

Afro-German women began to write about their lives, and several chose autobiographical forms to explore their identity and gain their voices. Their voyage of self-discovery "becomes the source of rebirth and reconciliation, the mode of healing the narrating self."[23] Afro-German women's texts make visible not only their own individual lives but also the experiences of Afro-Germans as a group. Their personal narratives thus help to create a shared history on which future generations of Afro-Germans can build. In their texts, they struggle to overcome their negative self-image and to form identities that braid together their different cultural heritages.[24] Tina Campt uses the term "textured identities" to describe the identities that Afro-German women create for themselves, since texture "connotes multiplicity and plurality without fragmentation."[25]

In her autobiography, Hügel-Marshall traces her journey from a lonely outsider, exposed to racism and prejudice in a children's home, through her difficulties finding a job because she is black, to her growing political awareness and sense of community once she became involved in the Afro-German movement. She depicts her life in the orphanage where, instead of being praised for her accomplishments, she was criticized. When she did well at school, people assumed she had copied from another student, and she learned that, whatever they accomplish, black people are worth nothing (30). When she was ten, a priest exorcised her "devils" and made her repeat: "Weiche von mir, Satan" (leave me, Satan) and "Reinige meine schwarze Seele" (purify my black soul). For years afterwards, she had nightmares and was afraid both of herself and the dark: she imagined small black devils everywhere (38). This upbringing systematically destroyed her love of learning and alienated her from her own self: she began to hate her skin color and to wish she were white (39). She learned that she was black, ugly, immoral, dirty, and stupid (86). Black people were alien to her and she was afraid of them. Through her involvement in the black German community, Hügel-Marshall came, however, to love herself and her skin color (EV, 29). She concludes her autobiography with a strong affirmation of her biracial identity: when she looks in the mirror, she writes, she is happy because she does not want to be different from what she is (140).

Emde struggled for many years to accept her biracial identity. She notes in "I Too Am German" that National Socialist racist thought was still evident in Germany after the war: "The ideology of a white Aryan superior nation with blue eyes and blond hair was still there and part of my daily life" (33). Being raised in a white world led to a radical alienation from herself. She saw blackness as "frightening, strange, foreign, and animalistic," and when as a child she saw black soldiers she ran from them "in fear and terror" (Colors, 102). When she was growing up she perceived white people as beautiful, noble, and perfect, and blacks as inferior and "unworthy of existence" (Colors, 102–3), and she rejected being black and wanted to be as white as possible. In "I Too Am German," she recalls that when she was young her mother was offered five marks and free coffee and cake to let Emde participate as the "Sarotti-Moor" in the Mardi Gras parade, an indication to her that Afro-Germans "were exotic objects on display for the amusement and entertainment of the larger white society"

(35). She tells of a friend who desperately tried to overcome her blackness by scratching, cutting, and brushing her skin until it bled. Emde recollects that she felt "fragmented, confused, and disoriented, without an identity of my own" (*Colors*, 103). In "I Too Am German," she stresses that "the psychological impact of growing up Black in Germany was devastating" (36). Only gradually could she come to terms with being black and accept her white and black heritages without feeling any breaks between them (*Colors*, 110).

Ayim tells of similar painful experiences. For many years she thought of herself as ugly because she was black (*Colors*, 146) and she asked her foster mother to wash her white and even secretly ate soap in an attempt to become white (*Grenzenlos*, 116).[26] In various ways, she believes, "the idea is transmitted that white skin color is the better skin color and that European (i.e., white) consciousness is progressive thinking" (*Colors*, 35). In second grade she was assigned the role of the devil in a school play. It was clear to everyone that she could not play an angel: who had ever seen a black angel (*Grenzenlos*, 109)? In the children's books she read, blacks were depicted as inferior beings or as monsters (*Grenzenlos*, 116), and she found it easier to identify with white princesses (*Grenzenlos*, 136). She expresses society's negative attitude to skin color in her poem "winterreim in berlin" (winter rhyme in Berlin) in which she writes: "du bist so weiss wie schnee/ und ich so braun wie scheisse/ das denkst du dir" (you are as white as snow/ and I am as brown as shit/ you think, *nachtgesang*, 68).

Like Hügel-Marshall and Emde, Ayim comes to overcome her rejection of self and affirm her bicultural identity. She declares, for example, that she finds broad noses "super" and that she does not want to be put "into a black or white compartment" (*Colors*, 157). Although many of her poems present a bleak view of exclusion and repetitive patterns of racism and discrimination, many also contain a vision of new possible identities and a new and inclusive world. The poem "die zeit danach" (the time thereafter), for example, written in memory of Martin Luther King, expresses her dream that one day people will not come into the world crying but "lachend/ in regenbogenfarben" (laughing/ in the colors of the rainbow, *blues*, 53), and in "entfernte verbindungen," she underscores her belief that bridges can be built between cultures (*blues*, 29). In the essay "Racism Here and Now," she gives one section the heading "The 'In-between World' as Opportunity" (*Colors*, 141) to suggest the opportunities offered by what Karein Goertz terms "the creative space between cultures as a site from which dichotomous notions of ethnic identity are dismantled."[27]

In her autobiography Hügel-Marshall observes that Afro-Germans have been struggling since they existed for a place in their own society, for the place to which they are entitled (103). Lorde writes: "Afro-German women have existed in a terrible isolation from each other for so long, and have not had the words sometimes even to identify themselves."[28] As Anne V. Adams points out, Afro-German refers to "a population *native* to Germany, raised and enculturated as Germans" and she observes that "the ironic paradox of being viewed and therefore treated as foreigners but having, in most cases, no personal Black reference — conscious or unconscious, individual or collective — within their lives as Germans, creates a limbo-life with no analog among Black populations in ex-colonial Europe or in North America" (*Colors*, 236). Through their writing and their involvement in the Afro-German community, Ayim, Emde, Hügel-Marshall, and others break out of this "limbo-life," and come to affirm their biracial identities. Their texts contest notions of cultural identity and national belonging in postunification Germany. Ayim writes: "I share a background with these people here even if they don't accept me. 'Yes, I'm German,' I say, perhaps out of spite, to shake up their black-and-white thinking" (*Colors*, 150). By shaking up such black-and-white thinking, Ayim, Emde, and Hügel-Marshall argue for a redefinition of German identity and a more inclusive and tolerant multicultural society in which, in the words of Awa Thiam, Afro-Germans can "wear their black colour with dignity and pride."[29]

Notes

[1] Although not all Germans with African or African American heritage prefer to be called Afro-German, I will use the term here because the writers I discuss were close to the American black activist poet Audre Lorde, who helped them coin it to connect them to their diverse heritages.

[2] Marilyn Sephocle, "Black Germans and Their Compatriots," in *The African-German Experience*, ed. Carol Aisha Blackshire-Belay (London: Praeger, 1996), 13–27; here: 15.

[3] Dedication to *The African-German Experience*, ed. Blackshire-Belay.

[4] Helga Emde, "I Too am German — An Afro-German Perspective," in *Who is German? Historical and Modern Perspectives on Africans in Germany*, ed. Leroy T. Hopkins (Washington: American Institute for Contemporary German Studies, 1999), 33–42; here: 37. Future references are given in the text.

[5] Katharina Oguntoye, May Opitz, Dagmar Schultz, eds. *Farbe bekennen: Afrodeutsche Frauen auf den Spuren ihrer Geschichte* (Berlin: Orlanda Frauenverlag, 1986).

[6] May Ayim, "Rassismus und Verdrängung im vereinten Deutschland," in May Ayim, *Grenzenlos und unverschämt* (Berlin: Orlanda Frauenverlag, 1997), 133–38; here: 137–38. Future references to materials in this collection will be given in the text as *Grenzenlos*.

[7] May Ayim, *blues in schwarz weiss: gedichte* (Berlin: Orlanda Frauenverlag, 1995), 61. Future references to this collection are given in the text as *blues*. An English version of this poem, translated by Ayim, is contained in May Ayim, *Blues in Black and White: A Collection of Essays, Poetry, and Conversations*, trans. Anne V. Adams (Trenton, NJ: Africa World Press, 2003), 48–49.

[8] Sithebe Nombuso, "Ost- oder Westdeutschland, für mich ist das kein großer Unterschied," in *Entfernte Verbindungen: Rassismus, Antisemitismus, Klassenunterdrückung*, eds. Ika Hügel, Chris Lange, May Ayim, Ilona Bubeck, Gülsen Aktas, Dagmar Schultz (Berlin: Orlanda Frauenverlag, 1993), 224–32; here: 228. Future references to essays in this collection are given in the text as *EV*.

[9] Michael Jürgs and Freimut Duve, eds. *Stoppt die Gewalt: Stimmen gegen den Ausländerhaß*, Luchterhand Flugschrift 4 (Hamburg/Zürich: Luchterhand, 1992), 7.

[10] Audre Lorde, "Foreword to the English Language Edition," in *Showing Our Colors: Afro-German Women Speak Out*, eds. May Opitz, Katharina Oguntoye, and Dagmar Schultz, trans. Anne V. Adams (Amherst: U of Massachusetts P, 1992), vii–xiv; here: xiii. Future references are given in the text as *Colors*. This is the translation of *Farbe bekennen* and contains a new foreword by Lorde and a new preface by Ayim, Oguntoye, and Schultz.

[11] Audre Lorde, "East Berlin," from *The Marvelous Arithmetics of Distance* (1993), in *The Collected Poems of Audre Lorde* (New York, London: Norton, 1997), 465.

[12] May Ayim, *nachtgesang: gedichte* (Berlin: Orlanda Frauenverlag, 1997), 72. Future references to this collection are given in the text as *nachtgesang*.

[13] Translation taken from *Blues in Black and White*, 112–13.

[14] Translations taken from *Blues in Black and White*, 109–11.

[15] Ika Hügel-Marshall, *Daheim unterwegs: Ein deutsches Leben* (Berlin: Orlanda Frauenverlag, 1998). Future references are given in the text. The book was translated as *Invisible Woman: Growing Up Black in Germany* (New York: Continuum, 2001). She received the Audre Lorde Award in 1996 to enable her to complete the work.

[16] In contrast to the Kohl government, the Red-Green government was more sympathetic to asylum seekers. As the recent "visa scandal" demonstrates, however, Joschka Fischer's relaxed policy of granting visas to Eastern Europeans was harshly criticized for being too permissive and allowing people involved in organized crime and prostitution to gain visas. As this debate suggests, the granting of asylum and visas is still a divisive issue in Germany.

[17] In Amharic, the official language of Ethiopia, the name "Adefra" means "The Woman Who Shows Courage," http://www.woman.de/katalog/politik/adefra. html, February 20, 2002.

[18] See note 8.

[19] Other Afro-German writers have built on Ayim's work, see for example, Katharina Oguntoye, *Eine Afro-Deutsche Geschichte: Zur Lebenssituation von Afrikanern und Afro-Deutschen von 1884 bis 1950* (Berlin: Hoho Verlag, 1997).

[20] The German name is "Negerkuss." Emde and other Afro-Germans tend to use the more pejorative "Nigger" rather than "Negro" when they translate.

[21] Hans J. Massaquoi, "*Neger, Neger, Schornsteinfeger!" Meine Kindheit in Deutschland* (Bern, Munich, Vienna: Scherz, 1999). It was published first in English as *Destined to Witness: Growing Up Black in Nazi Germany* (New York: William Morrow, 1999).

[22] Audre Lorde, "Turning The Beat Around," in *A Burst of Light, Essays by Audre Lorde* (Ithaca, NY: Firebrand Books, 1988), 39–48; here: 45–46.

[23] Françoise Lionnet, "*Métissage*, Emancipation, and Textuality," in *Life/Lines: Theorizing Women's Autobiography*, ed. Bella Brodzki and Celeste Schenck (Ithaca and London: Cornell UP, 1988), 260–78; here: 263. Both here and in *Autobiographical Voices*, Lionnet draws on the Martinican writer Edouard Glissant's notion of *métissage* as the braiding together of cultural forms. While she does not apply this notion to Afro-German writers, it sheds light on the strategies Afro-German women writers use.

[24] Françoise Lionnet, *Autobiographical Voices: Race, Gender, Self-Portraiture* (Ithaca and London: Cornell UP, 1989). Lionnet sees *métissage* as "the fertile ground of our heterogeneous and heteronomous identities as postcolonial subjects," 8.

[25] Tina M. Campt, "Afro-German Cultural Identity and the Politics of Positionality: Contests and Contexts in the Formation of a German Ethnic Identity," *New German Critique* 58 (Winter 1993): 109–26; here: 117.

[26] See also Maria Binder's video *Hoffnung im Herz*, put out with subtitles as *Hope in My Heart: The May Ayim Story* (New York: Third World Newsreel, 1997).

[27] Karein Goertz, "Borderless and Brazen: Ethnicity Redefined by Afro-German and Turkish German Poets," *The Comparatist* 21 (1997): 68–91; here: 68.

[28] Ilona Pache and Regina-Maria Dackweiler, "An Interview with Audre Lorde (1987)," in *Conversations with Audre Lorde*, ed. Joan Wylie Hall (Jackson: U of Mississippi P, 2004), 164–70; here: 170.

[29] Awa Thiam, *Speak Out, Black Sisters: Feminism and Oppression in Black Africa*, trans. Dorothy S. Blair (London: Pluto Press, 1986), 107–8, quoted in *Colors*, eds. Opitz, Oguntoye, and Schultz, 36.

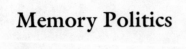
Memory Politics

11: The Anxiety of German Influence: Affiliation, Rejection, and Jewish Identity in W. G. Sebald's Work

Mary Cosgrove

The Desire for Influence

IN A STIMULATING ARTICLE on travel in W. G. Sebald's writing, John Zilcosky puts forward the argument that Sebald overturns a Romantic and postmodern travel strategy, which consists of getting lost only to recover oneself finally with greater clarity and a more assured sense of identity.[1] Such a travel paradigm is based on upholding a clear dichotomy between home and away. Zilcosky argues that Sebald's deconstruction of this traditional opposition differentiates him from contemporaries such as Roland Barthes, who transform the margin into a new home, making it into familiar territory. Resisting any "disingenuous attempt to turn the margin into a new centre," Sebald's travel texts instead present all locations in terms of the in-between zone of the familiar-strange, the uncanny. According to Zilcosky, being hopelessly lost is therefore not the central image of these texts. On the contrary, it is the ". . . *in*ability to lose one's way that haunts Sebald's travel narratives" (*Z,* 104). With this in mind, Zilcosky goes on to provide an interesting psychoanalytically-based reading of *Schwindel. Gefühle* (Vertigo, 1990) and *Die Ausgewanderten* (The Emigrants, 1992), arguing that in these texts the glimpse of the familiar-strange is always accompanied by a sense of dismay and fear (*Z,* 107).[2] This is because familiarity is an impediment to the invention of a creative self. The consequences of the persistence of the familiar and the already-known are devastating for the burgeoning writer, as in the case of *Schwindel. Gefühle,* where the narrator lurches from one European cultural metropolis to the next and is haunted in all by figures from the canon of great writers (*SG,* 41–42). Much as he tries, he cannot escape the well-trodden path of established literary tradition, and so cannot invent himself as an original writer. In this context, *Heimat* or the territory of the known is anything but a comfort zone. It is instead a space of impotence and lack, as time and again the would-be writer is overwhelmed by the ghosts of literature past.

Zilcosky's insight provides a precise point of contrast for what I will be advancing in the following. While there is no quibble with his general claim that Sebald's travel narratives are more fundamentally about orient-ation than disorientation, one could nevertheless argue that being pre-vented from writerly self-development by an army of literary ghosts in fact constitutes a kind of homelessness. If we accept that the narrator of *Schwindel. Gefühle* does indeed want to find his own particular creative lit-erary identity, then it would seem that as he physically retraces and re-imagines the paths taken in the past by Kafka, Stendhal, or Grillparzer, he must remain eternally lost to himself as a literary creator. Following this line of argument, being lost, in direct contrast to Zilcosky's reading of *Schwindel. Gefühle*, is the only existential possibility. The notion of aspiring to being lost, of aspiring to "lose" those oppressive literary ancestors, how-ever, is viable only if we accept Zilcosky's underlying presumption that the narrator in fact *wants* to be lost, *wills* the banishment from his imagination of his literary forefathers, but finds that he cannot muster up the necessary self-assertion. For if a kind of literary tabula rasa is in fact what the narrator wants, why then does he undertake a trip to Riva, retracing not only Kafka's trip to the same location in 1913, but also weaving into this jour-ney, and indeed into the wider narrative of his own odyssey, the motif of the barque from Kafka's "Der Jäger Gracchus" (The Hunter Gracchus, *SG*, 178–83)?[3] If the narrator wants to lose all thoughts of past literary greatness, why is he so dedicated to reconstructing the events contempora-neous to Kafka's stay in Verona from the same year, digging deep in the archives of the local library (*SG*, 133)? Why does he, in fact, actively con-tribute to the sense of a great writers' clique by constructing a link between Stendahl and Kafka through the Gracchus figure and through comments made by an aging general who was also a guest at the spa in Riva at the same time as Kafka (*SG*, 171–72)? When we consider the precise attention paid to accounts of Kafka's languishing person on beds in Italian hotel rooms in 1913 and then observe how carefully the narrator assumes iden-tical poses on hotel beds of the same Italian region in the 1980s, it becomes clear that the narrator of *Schwindel. Gefühle* does not suffer from a melancholic form of the anxiety of influence, as Zilcosky's interpretation seems to suggest (*SG*, 72, 161). Rather, he prefers to orient himself within his select group of European writers, his reconstructive trips, his reflective journeys, and even his body language betraying the desire to affirm this legacy, not to deny and escape it. As such, it becomes questionable whether the narrator ever reaches the margins of a literary tradition — how marginal is Kafka, for example? It would seem rather that the old intel-lectual *Heimat* of Sebald's preferred writers was never deserted in the first place, even if he chooses to represent this situation through the mildly distorting, but fundamentally affirmative psychoanalytic trope of the uncanny.[4]

Many scholars have pointed out, like Zilcosky, the various influences, old and new, that inform Sebald's work: travel writing, the reproduction of and sustained commentary on photography and other visual media in his prose works, the German-European inward-looking tradition of the novel, the Western tradition of melancholy, to name but a few.[5] Studies that explore the intertextual nature of his work highlight the impressive range of literary and cultural references alluded to throughout.[6] Currently, Sebald is regarded as the instigator of increasingly frenzied memory work on the controversial issue of German suffering during the Second World War;[7] his essay on *Luftkrieg und Literatur* (Air Raids and Literature, 1999) put this theme firmly on the contemporary German memory map.[8] The general reception of Günter Grass's novella *Im Krebsgang* (Crabwalk, 2002) seems to confirm the timeliness of Sebald's invective against the German inability to mourn.[9] His interest in individual and collective memory processes has also made his work the subject of analyses that stress the connections between it and current trends in Holocaust historiography, American and French thought in the ethics of memory, witnessing theory, and trauma theory.[10] There is a general consensus that Sebald understood history predominantly as the history of victimization, a perspective that has repercussions for the ethical content of his work.[11] In other words, Sebald's attention is almost exclusively focused on the victims of history and their ongoing trauma. The reader is thereby presented with the image of a depressingly terminal world, whose cancerous destructiveness constantly reappears in the ruins and corruption of all cultural and natural forms. Ethically speaking, this view of history seems to veto any chance of mankind getting over historical trauma, implying that it is impossible to distance oneself from the victim other's experience. This has uncomfortable ethical implications, to which I return in my discussion of Sebald's narrative style.

In the English-speaking world little has been said, however, about the more local German literary context within and against which Sebald wrote with a vengeance. American Sebald scholarship, which often relies on his works in translation, tends to examine the prose work in isolation from his essayistic work, emphasizing the themes outlined above.[12] With the exception of *Luftkrieg und Literatur* his essayistic work has not been analyzed to the same extent as his prose work.[13] I would argue, however, that close reading of his many essays, particularly on German and Austrian writers of the post-1945 period, reveals much about where Sebald perceived himself to be placed within postwar German language literature, what he endorsed and what he rejected about this field. These essays frequently stray in tone and in subject matter from an objective academic register. For example, a writer's private life and personal decisions are often examined as closely as the literary work the writer produced.[14] Furthermore, certain favorite tropes are repeated regularly, perhaps the most well-known refrain being the inability of German 1950s writers to mourn the trauma of the Holocaust and of the war.[15]

My analysis focuses on the special place Sebald accorded to German- and Austro-Jewish writers of the postwar era, and further, how this outlook impacts on his literary work. In his essays concerning this period, Sebald's attention often returns to the literary discourse of the 1960s, the point when postwar German literature, both non-Jewish and German-Jewish, first began to consider the National Socialist past and the trauma of the Holocaust from the perspective of the victims.[16] In other words, it was the point in time when the theme that was to preoccupy him in some of his own works some thirty years later first surfaced. When discussing the non-Jewish German writers of this epoch, however, Sebald frequently complains that there is a lack of authenticity about their writing. What he means, in fact, is that non-Jewish German literature about the experiences of persecuted and exiled Jews under National Socialism continually hits the wrong note in its attempt to portray sympathetically the plight of the Jews. According to Sebald, this is because personal accounts of trauma are eclipsed by a politically correct trend that, in the context of the Auschwitz trials of the 1960s, made it morally necessary to write about the Holocaust and Jewish suffering. For example, the efforts of Alfred Andersch and Günter Grass in this sensitive area are deemed to be opportunistic and self-serving (*CS*, 118–19; *LL*, 139). Viewed alongside the essays on Grass and Andersch, works such as *Austerlitz* (2001), *Die Ausgewanderten*, and even *Schwindel. Gefühle* suddenly emerge as a critical response to — perhaps even correction of — these earlier works, a point I return to in the final section.[17]

I argue that this critique of non-Jewish German writers has a double genealogical function in Sebald's complex negotiation of his own identity as a contemporary German writer. While the often disapproving tone of these essays dissociates him from his German predecessors, at the same time this tendency is part of a larger drive for affiliation within a post-Holocaust German-Jewish or Austro-Jewish literature that Sebald perceives as ethically superior to that produced by non-Jewish German writers of the same time. At the same moment that Sebald attempted to write himself out of one literary enclave, he wrote himself into his preferred alternative by seeking to model his work, in terms of the politics and ethics of memory, on a number of Jewish writers he most admired from this time. To pinpoint my opening argument: Sebald's choice of literary influence within the German post-1945 context is the German-Jewish literature of the survivor generation; his anxiety of influence centers around the same generation of non-Jewish German writers who have tried, and in his view failed, to find an adequate literary language through which to engage with and represent Jewish suffering.

My use of the term "anxiety of influence" derives from, but also modifies and adapts somewhat, Harold Bloom's theoretical study on the psyche of great writers.[18] Bloom observes how great writers, in their desire to be recognized as original creators of the literary new, often deny the role their erudite forefathers might have played in their creative development. The anxiety of influence we encounter in Sebald's case is not an anxiety about the desire for absolute literary originality. It is much more specifically about the rejection of any association with writers whom he perceives to be embarrassingly and opportunistically either exploiting or eliding the Jew in their literary work. If we turn this critical perspective back onto Sebald himself, however, the question arises to what extent he struggled with his identity as a non-Jewish German writer who, like Andersch for example, wrote about the Jewish experience of persecution. For whether he embraced it or not, this is one of the more immediate and specifically German literary contexts to which Sebald belongs. I argue, however, that he acknowledged this fact only indirectly through his essayistic condemnation of this very literary context and, as I show later, through regular slips in his prose work.

This conflicted local dimension to Sebald's work has thus far gone unnoticed. In fact, with the exception of Stuart Taberner's and Maya Barzilai's excellent analyses, most scholars have thus far avoided addressing what might be problematic about Sebald's discourse on Jews.[19] In discussions of the Jewish character of Sebald's writing, the tendency has been to emphasize how he can be seen to have been working in positive established traditions. Thus, Katharina Hall shows how it is possible to understand Sebald as writing within the old Jewish tradition of Yizkor or memory books, but does not problematize confusions of German and Jewish identity that arise, for example in the case of Ambrose Adelwarth from *Die Ausgewanderten*, a theme I return to in the third section of this essay.[20] Similarly, Ralf Jeutter highlights the centrality of the Jewish experience for Sebald's German narrators, without, however, considering the problems of identity and identification raised by the ambivalent merging of German and Jewish identity after the Holocaust.[21] Against the generalizing trend of these analyses, I wish to focus on the more immediate context of what specific post-1945 Jewish writers meant to Sebald.

Elsewhere, I have drawn parallels between Sebald and the German-Jewish writer of the survivor generation, Wolfgang Hildesheimer.[22] In the present essay, I focus on the legacy of the Austro-Jewish writer Jean Améry in Sebald's work, the subject of no less than three of his critical essays.[23] I will show how Sebald's ethics of memory overlaps with Améry's concept of *Ressentiment* (resentment), which I describe in detail in the next section.[24] Indeed, I will argue that the figure of Austerlitz is in part inspired by Jean Améry. I also argue that the basic narrative situation of *Austerlitz* — a series of dialogues between German and Jew — along with characterization strategies in *Die Ausgewanderten* present a problematic understanding of

Ressentiment. In my view, Sebald's depictions of the connection between Germans and Jews is fundamentally nostalgic; these portrayals express a melancholy resuscitation of the nineteenth-century ideal of German-Jewish symbiosis in a self-consciously sentimentalizing way that rather too eagerly sidelines the alienation of German-Jewish relations in the post-Holocaust context. Ironically, this tendency serves only to reinforce the sense of prevailing awkwardness between Germans and Jews; when read in conjunction with Sebald's essays, this nostalgia becomes a thin veneer for his struggle with his identity as a German writer. As Stuart Taberner has recently pointed out, the leap from sentimentality of this type to philo-Semitism is not far: the question I consider is whether Sebald crossed this fine line.[25]

Again, most critics have not examined this tendentious aspect of Sebald's work because much is made of the ethical drive behind his narrative aesthetic of emphatically not speaking for the Jewish victim other, of allowing the other to bear witness to his or her experiences and to give voice finally to the silenced trauma of the past.[26] The novel *Austerlitz* is particularly interesting in this regard. It tells the story of Jacques Austerlitz, a Czech-Jewish refugee who arrived in England as a child during the Second World War and who has repressed all memory of his previous life in Prague, his Jewish identity, and his parents. The novel is based on a series of dialogues between Austerlitz and the German narrator, also living in England, and documents Austerlitz's gradual recovery of his traumatic past. These conversations are the outcome of an initial chance meeting between the two men in the 1960s and carry on, not without interruption, up to the late 1990s.

In contrast to the prevailing secondary literature on *Austerlitz*, my analysis of the novel is more concerned with the perspective of the German narrator/listener in the framework of the dialogue. I ask how ethically driven narrative aesthetics and the larger narrative framework of idealized communication between German and Jew after 1945 interrelate in the case of *Austerlitz*; whether, in fact, they interrelate at all. Sebald's wish is never to usurp the voice of the other, never to claim the Jewish experience as his own through pathos-ridden overidentification;[27] his narrative technique is the expression of this desire. Yet is his narrative formula of pointing up the distinct identity of speakers not overburdened by vast ethical expectation? Close inspection of the narrator figure in *Austerlitz* shows how the desired ethical effect of carefully choreographed narration is often reversed by the narrator's near adulation of Austerlitz, suggesting that the relationship between German and Jew in Sebald's work is more problematic than his ethical narrative style admits.

My reading of *Die Ausgewanderten* follows a similar pattern of inquiry: the book is composed of four thematically interconnected stories of exile, three of which deal with the exile of Jewish figures and one that deals with German emigration. The character of Ambrose Adelwarth in *Die Ausgewanderten* is of particular note; he stands out as the only German emigrant in a sequence of stories about Jewish exile and persecution. For this reason, my analysis of *Die Ausgewanderten* focuses on his tale and the symbolic construction of his character. Interestingly, he converges with Améry in some critical points that, on a symbolic level, partly transform this enigmatic German character into a Jewish figure. In the case of *Austerlitz*, the focus on Améry also allows the novel to be regarded more closely within the context of a continuing debate on how to represent Jewish suffering, for it can be argued that *Austerlitz* is in part a correction of Andersch's *Efraim*, whose central character, Georg Efraim — a German-Jewish journalist living in London who is sent by his editor to Germany to find out what became of a Jewish girl he knew during the war — was based on Jean Améry.[28] Finally, I suggest that Sebald's desire for affiliation within a tradition of German-Jewish writing is also expressed in his frequent appropriation of a specifically Jewish perspective on the condition of exile, most notably in *Schwindel. Gefühle* and *Die Ausgewanderten*.

Ressentiment

Born in Vienna 1912 into an assimilated Jewish family, Hans Mayer went into exile after the Nazi annexation of Austria in 1938. He subsequently changed his name to Jean Améry, not just a choice of nom de plume, as Sebald and other commentators point out, but more crucially an expression of complete alienation from his Austrian *Heimat*, and from the person he once was before the period of exile, resistance, incarceration, and torture began.[29] Améry never again resided in Austria, remaining in exile in Belgium until he committed suicide in Salzburg in 1978. In the early 1950s he began working as a correspondent for Swiss newspapers, an activity that was to last until his death, but in early 1964 he started work on a number of essays that dealt with moral and intellectual questions raised by his experiences of Auschwitz. This collection of essays was published with great success in 1966 under the title of *Jenseits von Schuld und Sühne: Bewältigungsversuche eines Überwältigten* (At the Mind's Limits: Contemplations by a Survivor on Auschwitz and Its Realities); a fifth edition with a second introduction appeared in 1977. *Ressentiments* (resentments) is one of the essays in this collection, alongside other famous essays on the intellectual in Auschwitz, enforced Jewish identity, and the experience of torture.[30]

Of interest for an understanding of Sebald's reception of Améry is the preface to the 1977 edition, which is in large part directed at the generation of *Nachgeborene* (those born at the end of or after the Second World War), Sebald's generation. Améry points to Germany's failure to take responsibility for the Nazi past, evident in the widening gulf he observes between victim and perpetrator collectives and in new forms of anti-Semitism that threaten the democratic foundation of West Germany (*JSS*, 10–12). This builds on his statement in the preface to the first edition — also included in the second edition — that the book is aimed at the German audience, not at his fellow survivors (*JSS*, 17). For a thinker like Sebald, who during the 1960s looked to Jewish schools of thought for moral impetus, these insights will have had a clear resonance;[31] he too went into a kind of self-elected exile in the late 1960s, moving first to Switzerland and from there to England. His many descriptions of Germany in the latter twentieth century are for the main part negative; in *Schwindel. Gefühle*, Vienna is also the site of the narrator's disintegration into dazed homelessness, a metamorphosis he can escape only by fleeing the city (*SG*, 43–44). However, it is through the mnemonic moral category of *Ressentiment* that we can most clearly observe Améry's influence on Sebald.

Ressentiment is the moral outrage of the victim survivor who has undergone a double betrayal: first, by being persecuted and victimized, second, by realizing that after the defeat of Germany this disgraced nation was soon integrated back into world politics, as if the Nazi crimes could now be consigned to a place in the past forever. Améry argues that the experience of the victims is forgotten through this process of normalization (*JSS*, 108). His *Ressentiment*, which he grittily tends and nourishes, is the individual response to this greater social amnesia (*JSS*, 109). It focuses on the subjective constitution of the victim and demands that the individuals who suffered should not be forgotten by their persecutors (*JSS*, 104). *Ressentiment* is a paradoxical condition in that it pits itself against the logical, socio-biological processes of time and history, which have short and selective memories. Instead, *Ressentiment* demands the reversal of historical time and the undoing of the crimes committed in the past (*JSS*, 115). Thus, it is an absurd temporal concept, but its very absurdity is the condition of its moral superiority; as Améry points out, the moral person demands the reversal of time (*JSS*, 116). In order for society's relationship to the past to become fully ethical, therefore, the perpetrator collective must also develop the absurd temporal sensibility of *Ressentiment*, the intense desire to undo what happened (*JSS*, 113–14).

As Irene Heidelberger-Leonard points out, this demand issued to Germans and Austrians makes of *Ressentiment* a communicative form with the therapeutic aim of healing the ongoing wounds of the victims, not, however, by looking forward to the future, but by revisiting the past.[32] A further critic notes that, despite its therapeutic core, *Ressentiment* does not represent an altruistic drive for reconciliation between victim and perpetrator; rather it stems from the victim's need to be released from the unbearable isolation that started with deportation and torture and that continues as an existential reality in the survivor's present.[33] *Ressentiment* is thus the demand for a difficult dialogue between perpetrators and victims, for the actualization of unresolved conflict between these two groups with the aim of finding justice for the victims. The only way to do this, according to Améry, is to make the perpetrators feel the terrible loneliness felt by the victims, as sufferers during torture and incarceration, and as survivors in a world that has abandoned the memory of their ordeal (*JSS*, 114).

In his essays on Améry, Sebald pays homage to his insistence on history as the experience of violence and terror, the value of *Ressentiment* as a morally superior way of counteracting the indifference of passing time, and the solidarity with the victims of history voiced therein (*CS*, 158–60; *UH*, 142). For Sebald, Améry's discourse of *Ressentiment* counteracts the danger of forgetting the pain of victims that is inherent in acts of representation after the Holocaust. He sees Améry as one of the few German-language writers of the 1960s who addressed the legacy of the Holocaust with any kind of authenticity. Améry's scrupulous sense of reserve is expressed in the sober linguistic register employed in his essays, and his desire to reverse the irreversible — historical time — is part of his attempt to find a language that does not fall into the reductionism and amnesia of representation (*CS*, 157). A further ethical feature of Améry's discourse is his precise focus on the internal life of the individual victim, an approach that also counteracts generalizing and misleading abstract talk of victims so apparent in most literary works of the time. Sebald clearly saw himself as the descendant of a literary process initiated in the 1960s by writers such as Améry: a process of finding, through the act of writing, justice for the victims of recent German history (*CS*, 150).

The centrality of *Ressentiment* for Sebald's poetics of memory has been remarked upon; Anne Fuchs points out how the focus on subjective experience in Améry's essays has influenced the biographical or microhistorical representation of history offered in Sebald's prose work.[34] However, the dangers of this identification with the victim experience have been noted in recent scholarly works on history and trauma.[35] Identification can lead to an over-emotional, ethically suspect usurpation of the victim's experience by — in this case — a member of the perpetrator collective. A further consequence of identification is the reduction of history to the experience of trauma, with the Holocaust serving as the authentic standard of trauma against which all other historical experience is defined.[36] Fuchs argues that while at some points in Sebald's narrative prose an excess of emotional identification can be detected, by and large his narrative self-reflexivity counteracts this trend and restores ethical balance to his memory discourse and representation of victims.[37]

In *Austerlitz* and *Die Ausgewanderten*, the dialogues between Sebald's narrator-interviewers and the interviewees — who are either Jewish Holocaust survivors or who were at one time close to the deceased victims — employ as a main tool of self-reflexivity the regular reminders of different and distinctive voices by pointing up the identity of who is speaking at any given moment. Thus, as interviewees delve deeper into their memories and begin to report conversations from the past, or indeed at one further remove, report on conversations that they had been told about in the past, Sebald's narrators attempt to prevent the loss of distinct speaker identity by reasserting mid mise-en-abîme the specificity of the layered conversational frameworks. Austerlitz's conversations with Věra, a family friend in Prague and his childhood nanny before the destruction of his family, use this narrative technique in a pronounced fashion; the closer he gets to discovery of his mother's deportation and the tragedy of Prague's Jews, the more the narrative voice insists on erecting these pointers of distinct identity:

> Ich erinnere mich, *so sagte Věra, sagte Austerlitz,* an einen solchen Hausierer, einen gewissen Saly Bleyberg, der in der Leopoldstadt, unweit von Praterstern einen Garagenbetrieb aufgebaut hatte in der schweren Zwischenkriegszeit und der uns, als Agáta ihn auf einen Kaffee hereinbat, die schauderhaftesten Geschichten von der Niedertracht der Wiener erzählte. (*Aus,* 249 my italics)

> [I remember, *said Věra, Austerlitz added,* one such hawker, a man called Saly Bleyberg, who had built up his own garage business in the Leopold-stadt district of Vienna not far from the Praterstern during the difficult inter-war years, and who when Agáta invited him in for a cup of coffee told us the most appalling tales of the despicable conduct of the Viennese.] (241, my italics)

The narrator has been careful to signal via his layering technique that the integrity of Austerlitz's telling of the discovery and reconstruction of his past has not been compromised or contaminated by the narrator's intervention. He is a listening and recording vessel here and merely channels Austerlitz's account of Věra's memories. Such a view of Sebald's narrative technique concludes that the narrator keeps his distance from the interviewee by reminding us constantly of who speaks and thereby refrains from usurping the unique experience of the other. Some critics have argued, however, that voice ultimately becomes confused in Sebald's prose: Bernhard Malkmus points out that in *Austerlitz* narrative voice and the voice of Austerlitz are intertwined and at times indistinguishable while Katharina Hall makes the same observation with reference to *Die Ausgewanderten.*[38]

Both these interpretations of Sebald's narrative ethics are correct, if contradictory. As such, they testify to the ambivalence of his relationship to the Jewish others he constructs in his texts, an ambivalence that sees him oscillate between tendentious identification and critical distance, or, as Dominick LaCapra terms it, "empathetic unsettlement."[39] In the mode of empathetic unsettlement we should be able to uphold a resolute barrier of difference between the self and the other so that the alterity of the other's suffering is maintained. Crucially, empathetic unsettlement should also help to prevent this suffering from becoming a debilitating cultural norm of identity through its uncritical appropriation by individuals who did not experience this suffering first hand. The critical perspective outlined in empathetic unsettlement has been endorsed by scholars of the Holocaust who are agreed upon the dangers of transference when writing about the Holocaust and the desirability of heightened self-reflexivity.[40] Thus, there is consensus that ethical writing about the Holocaust is possible only if the writing individual can subject him or herself to a rigorous program of critical self-observation at all times, a constant splitting of the self into ever more policed parts, and an ongoing battle against the pull of affect.

Despite his stylistic efforts to avoid transference, however, Sebald's use of *Ressentiment* in his literary work reveals his capitulation to the sway of affect and to the vicariousness of identification. Recalling briefly Améry's demand that the perpetrators should feel to the point of unbearable remorse the isolation of the victim, it is clear that *Ressentiment* is a raw call to identification as the only possible way of exacting justice for the victims. Sebald's narratives fundamentally obey the moral command of *Ressentiment*, something that is evident in his narrators' relationship to their Jewish counterparts. However, the spirit of resistance and the sense of outrage that are so central to Améry's concept of *Ressentiment* are lacking in Sebald's prose, as solidarity with the victims continually lapses into wistful sentimentality. The "resentful" desire to turn back time mutates into the desire for a world unspoiled by the caesura of the Holocaust, a longing that is expressed in the many idealized images of German-Jewish symbiosis in *Austerlitz* and *Die Ausgewanderten*.

Negative Symbiosis

A rather heavy-handed representation of "Germanness" and "Jewishness" emerges in *Austerlitz* and *Die Ausgewanderten*. While on the surface, the relationships between the German narrators and their Jewish counterparts appears to be positive — it is undeniably sympathetic — nevertheless, I would argue that the basis of this interaction can be described in terms of Dan Diner's concept of negative symbiosis.[41] Diner argues that after 1945, Germans and Jews can relate to each other only negatively because at the heart of any interaction is the burden of the Holocaust. Sebald's representation of this relationship confirms the governing principle of negative symbiosis, as I will show in my discussion of Austerlitz, Paul Bereyter — the Jewish subject of the second story in *Die Ausgewanderten* — and the German narrators of their stories.

Paul Bereyter's sudden suicide in 1984 propels the narrator, who as a child had been his pupil, to investigate and reconstruct his former teacher's life. Interestingly, it emerges that Bereyter's personal and professional life had been disastrously interrupted by the period of National Socialist rule. The narrator devotes much of his homage to Bereyter's exceptional and unconventional qualities as a teacher (*A*, 56). This is a pattern of interaction that extends from *Die Ausgewanderten* to *Austerlitz*: the teacher-pupil relationship serves as a prototype for the relationship between the German narrator and his Jewish interviewee. Thus, in *Austerlitz* we learn that the narrator views Austerlitz as the first real teacher he has encountered since his time at school (*Aus*, 51–52). Jewish figures are portrayed as people from whom something of value can be learned; the respective narrators' persistence in helping to re-establish these Jewish life stories suggests that they are hopeful of learning some truth that will be of value to them too. Indeed, in *Austerlitz* the narrator seems from a very early point in the narrative to be highly dependent on his contact with Austerlitz. The day after their initial encounter in the Antwerp train station, the bombastic style of which gives rise to Austerlitz's veritable lecture on the meaning of architectural forms, the narrator positions himself in a café near the glove market with the intention of engineering a further encounter with Austerlitz (*Aus*, 32). Although this does not happen, by some stroke of fate they accidentally meet a few days later in Lüttich (*Aus*, 44). From this point on in the year 1967, they maintain contact until the end of 1975 when the narrator, resident in England for the previous nine years, decides to return to Germany. Although at this stage in the narrative, reader, narrator, and even Austerlitz himself do not know of his Prague Jewish origins, it is significant that, despite the narrator's efforts, the contact between the two ends after the narrator returns to Germany, an indicator of the difficulty of German-Jewish relations anywhere other than in mutual exile (*Aus*, 53–54). This development also suggests that the responsibility for improved relations between Germans and Jews after the Holocaust falls squarely onto the shoulders of the German. Thus, symbolically Sebald is already marking out a fairly one-sided pattern of interaction between the two men, who sense a connection but do not know yet what that connection is. Viewing the chemistry of their interaction as an indicator of their shared, submerged historical legacy, it should come as no surprise that the narrator's return to the host country of National Socialism means the end of his relationship with Austerlitz. The relationship can only be resumed two decades later, long after the narrator returns to England from Germany. What Wilfried Wilms has argued in relation to *Luftkrieg und Literatur* is equally true here: Sebald's representation of Germans and Jews shows up his blind spot: the bad conscience of his generation and the bad conscience of the FRG.[42]

German and Jew, despite the considerable odds, are destined to meet again many years later in a miraculous, deeply gratifying, and productive way. This momentous event reinforces the sense that Sebald was trying, rather awkwardly, to reverse a negative symbiosis, an impression that continues in the satisfying nostalgia of a happyish end: in the closing pages of the novel we see the narrator sentimentally retracing his steps in Antwerp in 1967, returning to the place where he first met Austerlitz. We furthermore learn that he now possesses the keys to Austerlitz's house in London (*Aus*, 414). This information suggests the success of the relationship: the narrator has been enlightened through his extended encounter with the enigma of Austerlitz and the latter has been restored to his true identity. Both have thus undergone a healing process of sorts — with the help of the other. Austerlitz's discovery of his true Jewish identity opens the door to his own past, but it also opens the door of alternative identity to the keenly listening German. This is expressed in spatial terms: by the end of the novel the narrator has unlimited access not only to Austerlitz's house, but also to the adjoining Jewish cemetery, which has only recently come to Austerlitz's attention (*Aus*, 414–15). It is unclear what Sebald wanted to communicate with this image, but I would argue that it can be read as an incidence of ethically questionable, vicarious identification: the alternative identity open to the German at the end of a two-way therapy is an appropriately sepulchral Jewish identity, further evidence of unease with German identity after the Holocaust. Thus, the same strategy of rejection and affiliation that was observed earlier in Sebald's essays continues into the literary work, particularly in the representation of Germans and Jews.

The theme of enlightenment is represented in an almost comically evident way through the sequence of events that lead up to the second chance encounter of the narrator with Austerlitz in 1996. Like Paul Bereyter of *Die Ausgewanderten*, the narrator has trouble with his failing eyesight and must undergo a procedure in London. Afterwards, plagued by nausea and unsettled by exploding points of light in his eyes, he goes into the Salon Bar of the Great Eastern Hotel in Liverpool Street where he observes the disorienting movement of people around him. Finally, his troubled eyes settle upon a point of indisputable clarity, the almost unchanged person of Austerlitz (*Aus*, 60–62). It is as if they have never been separated; their last conversation of the mid 1970s simply picks up seamlessly where it left off in a way that strongly suggests an undeniable connection, a bipolar magnetism, and an ideal symbiosis:

> So habe Austerlitz, ohne auch nur ein Wort zu verlieren über unser nach solch langer Zeit rein zufällig erfolgtes Zusammentreffen, das Gespräch mehr oder weniger dort wieder aufgenommen, wo es einst abgebrochen war. (*Aus*, 64)

> [Accordingly, and without wasting any words on the coincidence of our meeting again after all this time, Austerlitz took up the conversation that evening in the bar of the Great Eastern Hotel more or less where it had broken off.] (56–57)

Notably it is Austerlitz who takes the conversational lead, a pattern of interaction that is repeated in their encounters over the next period. For the narrator always comes when summoned by Austerlitz, whether the call is issued from London or Paris he is unconditionally on standby for this enigmatic acquaintance (*Aus*, 173, 362). It is as if the narrator owes Austerlitz, has something to make up to him, the unspoken premise of negative symbiosis that pervades all their encounters. Moreover, the narrator's sense of self-validation is considerably threatened when he does not hear from Austerlitz. In his anxious self-reprimands we can hear sotto voce the self-conscious stigmatization that surrounds the fact of belonging to the post-1945 German collective, and the fear that the negative legacy of this identity has somehow clumsily expressed itself in conversation with Austerlitz:

> Mehr und mehr hatte ich im Laufe der Wochen gezweifelt, je wieder von ihm zu hören, fürchtete verschiedentlich, eine unbedachte Äußerung ihm gegenüber getan zu haben oder ihm sonst irgendwie unangenehm gewesen zu sein. (*Aus*, 173)

> [As the weeks went by I had felt less and less sure whether I would ever hear from him again, fearing at various times that I might have made a thoughtless remark, or offended him in some way.] (165)

We never find out if in fact this was the case; the narrator simply lives with this doubt continually, as the next excerpt shows. He has just read of the gruesome suicide of a grieving widower and, for no clear reason, relates this tale to Austerlitz.

> Als ich Austerlitz, der mich gegen elf abgeholt hatte, diese Geschichte erzählte, während wir durch Whitechapel und Shoreditch zum Fluß hinabgingen, sagte er lange Zeit nichts, vielleicht weil er, wie ich mir nachher zum Vorwurf machte, mein Herausstreichen der absurden Aspekte dieses Falles als eine Geschmacklosigkeit empfand. (*Aus*, 147)

> [Austerlitz had come to fetch me around eleven, and when I told him this story as we walked down to the river through Whitechapel and Shoreditch he said nothing for quite a long time, perhaps, I told myself reproachfully afterwards, because he felt it was tasteless of me to dwell on the absurd aspects of the case.] (139)

Significantly, this incident occurs before either the narrator or Austerlitz is fully aware of all details concerning the latter's traumatic past, the deportation and murder of his mother, the disappearance to Paris of his father. Yet the narrator's self-reproach suggests that he has instinctive, if unconscious, antennae for sensing Austerlitz's tragic past and Germany's role in it, an explanation, perhaps, for his unreflective choice of a lamentable story to tell Austerlitz and for the self-thwarting that follows. Negative undercurrents notwithstanding, the secret connection between German and Jew that emerges here is a further instance of a privileged and special relationship after the Holocaust. Like any good pupil, the narrator also feels utterly compelled to record everything Austerlitz tells him, as if there resides in all of Austerlitz's commentary on cultural forms and their melancholy meaning a fundamental truth (*Aus*, 146). This truth finally begins to emerge in the course of their second set of discussions: the truth of Austerlitz's identity. Of note in this regard is the narrator's desire, expressed earlier, for release from the difficult task of reading and writing to which he feels driven, the desire for numbness and oblivion (*Aus*, 146). The second chance encounter in the Great Eastern Hotel corrects this desire to obliterate thought and analysis, and again the Jewish figure as bearer of truth, moral guide, and pedagogue emerges in full significance.

To return to an issue raised earlier: while it might be exaggerated to suggest that Sebald's portrayal of the Jewish other is in essence philo-Semitic, nevertheless Jewish characters in his work are positively overdetermined through the doe-like narrative gaze of unconditional contrition. They are therefore compromised figures that do not in the first instance signify the Jewish experience of victimization, but instead become ciphers of a problematic German identity. The above quotations communicate as much: the narrator is overdetermined by a self-deprecating awareness of his helpless devotion. However, I would argue that the self-awareness of "German self-hatred" provides a chink in the narrative armor; this chink prevents sentimentalization from turning in on itself and coagulating into philo-Semitism.

The same level of personal dependency is not apparent in the Bereyter story of *Die Ausgewanderten*. Another problem of representation crops up here, however, and is repeated in the story concerning Ambrose Adelwarth: the creation of uncomfortable and, again, potentially vicarious hybrids of German and Jewish identity, a further symptom of a sentimentalizing perspective on German-Jewish relations. Bereyter's myopia corresponds to the eye problems of the *Austerlitz* narrator; this motif causes the two characters to converge on a symbolic level across both works. Yet one is a German Jew who suffered greatly under the National Socialist regime, so much so that he is driven to suicide late in life, while the other is a German who, as a member of the immediate postwar generation, bears no direct responsibility for the crimes committed during National Socialism, but who is nevertheless burdened with this legacy. The symbolic confusion of German and Jewish identity, which in this case are biographically and historically distinct, could be regarded as a further wishful expression of the desire for a renewed German-Jewish symbiosis; along with the behavior of the devoted *Austerlitz* narrator, it testifies to a fundamental narrative position that wishes to retrieve a golden past of German-Jewish relations, but, in transposing this vision onto a post 1945 narrative world, ends up in unreflective identification with an idealized Jewish prototype.

The convergence of German and Jewish identity comes across clearly in the tale of the German emigrant, Ambrose Adelwarth, the narrator's great-uncle who immigrated to America at the turn of the century and who worked for many years for the Solomons, a wealthy New York Jewish family. Like the narrator is to Austerlitz, Adelwarth is the devoted servant to the son of this family, Cosmo. Thus the same basic interaction prevails here as it does in *Austerlitz*: the attentive and obedient German who ardently strives to meet the needs of his Jewish counterpart (*A*, 133). However, Adelwarth and Cosmo are also lovers (*A*, 128). Again, viewing the representation of relationships between Germans and Jews across the two works, their discreet sexual relationship makes explicit the romantic undercurrent in the outwardly platonic interaction between Austerlitz and his conversational partner. The narrator's fretting and oversensitivity where Austerlitz is concerned comes close to the attentive and highly-strung behavior of the smitten, as does his impressive mobility whenever he is summoned by his friend. At the same time, the relationship between Cosmo and Adelwarth also provides us with a sexualized image of German-Jewish symbiosis, complete with its tragic dimension. Cosmo, who suffers from mental illness, dies at a young age; despite this, Adelwarth remains in the service of the family until his retirement, shortly after which he voluntarily commits himself to the mental home Sanatorium Samaria, in Ithaca in upstate New York (*A*, 150). The narrator, who has traced his great-uncle's steps to the now dilapidated sanatorium, reconstructs through conversations with the elderly Dr. Abramsky, once director of the institution, his uncle's gruesome death. Adelwarth requested to undergo electric shock therapy, at that time a new and unknown treatment. Abramsky remembers with horror Adelwarth's docility, his desire to put himself through terrible pain, a procedure that even now Abramsky remembers as pure torture:

> Bemerkenswert war auch, mit welcher Bereitwilligkeit Ambrose sich der Schockbehandlung unterzog, die zu Beginn der fünfziger Jahre, wie mir rückblickend erst aufgegangen ist, wahrhaftig an eine Folterprozedur oder ein Martyrium heranreichte. Mußten die anderen Patienten nicht selten mit Gewalt in die Apparatekammer gebracht werden [. . .], so saß Ambrose zum anberaumten Zeitpunkt jedesmal schon auf dem Hocker vor der Türe und wartete, den Kopf an die Wand gelehnt, die Augen geschlossen, auf das, was ihm bevorstand. (*A*, 163)

> [It was also remarkable how readily Ambrose submitted to shock treatment, which in the early Fifties, as I understood only later, really came close to torture or martyrdom. Other patients often had to be frogmarched to the treatment room, said Dr Abramsky, but Ambrose would always be sitting on the stool outside the door at the appointed hour, leaning his head against the wall, eyes closed, waiting for what was in store for him. (*E*, 111)]

Adelwarth dies as a result of this treatment; we are never told the exact reason for his decision to commit himself and to opt for this kind of therapy.

Although Abramsky states that Adelwarth presented the worst case of melancholy he had ever seen, we are not given a precise cause (*A*, 162). All we know is that he desires the complete annihilation of his powers of memory (*A*, 167). It is on this point that the characterization of Adelwarth becomes difficult. For Sebald's description of Jean Améry's terrible suffering as a victim of National Socialist persecution conforms rather uncomfortably with Adelwarth's memory complex. Of Améry Sebald remarks:

> Es ist, als sei ihm ein jegliches Bruchstück seiner Erinnerung ein neuralgischer Punkt [. . .]. Die Problematik, daß die Erinnerung — [. . .] — kaum mehr auszuhalten ist, bestimmt weitgehend den seelischen Zustand der Opfer der Verfolgung. (*CS*, 153)

> [It is as if every fragment of memory touched a sore point, as if he were compelled to ward off everything immediately and translate it into reflective form to make it at all measurable by any standard. (*NHD*, 153)]

Adelwarth's desire to isolate and delete the problematic neuralgic sore point of memory can be compared to Améry's suffering as it is described here. However, Adelwarth is a German whose biography is untouched by the Holocaust. This does not prevent his character being based on Améry; even the language Sebald uses to describe the clinical act of memory destruction in the novel — *vernichten* (to annihilate, 170) and *Annihilationsmethode* (method of annihilation, 168) — evoke uncomfortable associations with the Holocaust. And while Sebald notes above that Améry, unlike Adelwarth, tried to overcome the pain of memory through intellectualization, arguably he too succumbed to its power when he ended his life in Salzburg. Thus, in a further display of problematic identification processes in Sebald's work, yet another German character symbolically metamorphoses into the Jewish victim other. The question arises whether we can truly speak of empathetic unsettlement here.

Adelwarth's willing martyrdom also links him to the self-effacement of the narrator in *Austerlitz*, whose raison d'être, as we have seen, is his relationship with Austerlitz. Is the Adelwarth-Cosmo story a less subtle symbol of the German need to atone, also suggested by the narrator's behavior in *Austerlitz*? In Adelwarth's past there is the specter of a dead Jewish lover; one possible interpretation is that his self-annihilation many years after Cosmo's death is an allegory of the ethical demands of *Ressentiment*. As we have seen, Améry demands that the perpetrator collective turn back the clock and experience the intense suffering of the victims — the excruciating pain, spiritual and physical, that they endured. It is suggested that Cosmo died as a result of his mental illness; Adelwarth re-enacts Cosmo's demise many years later in the Sanatorium Samaria. If we accept this allegorical reading of the relationship between Adelwarth and Cosmo, then it becomes clear that Sebald's portrayal of German-Jewish relations before the Holocaust is told in a way that simply cannot get around this historical caesura. Thus, even the portrayal of an idealized symbiosis of relations between Germans and Jews is tainted by the negative symbiosis of their relations after the Holocaust. This does not stop the narrator figure of *Die Ausgewanderten* from trying to resuscitate the imagined ideal of German-Jewish harmony before the Holocaust; his efforts to reconstruct Cosmo's gambling heyday in Deauville at the turn of the century express this desire (*Aus*, 180).

The figure of Austerlitz embodies less problematic references to Jean Améry. The book begins and ends with descriptions of the fortress of Breendonk near Antwerp, where Améry was imprisoned and tortured by the Nazis in 1943 (*JSS*, 46–73). Austerlitz's description of his visit to Breendonk includes a specific reference to Améry and is furthermore characterized by his effort at all times to identify with the individual pain suffered by the tortured, which for him is still palpable in this building, now a museum (*Aus*, 42). Austerlitz's understanding of the nature of human suffering in history derives to a great extent from Améry's essay on *Ressentiment*; he tells the narrator of how he is constantly attuned to the submerged and marginalized suffering of individuals, whose pain goes unnoticed by the rest of the world (*Aus*, 23). The narrator in turn provides the recognizing instance needed by Austerlitz in the gradual excavation of his own suffering (*Aus*, 68) and as illustrated above, he also addresses his own need for validation through his relationship with Austerlitz. Austerlitz's criticism of the widespread indifference to history's victims, expressed in the march of official historical time, also recalls Améry's similar invective against the socio-biological processes of forgetting (*Aus*, 149–52; *JSS*, 116). The power of suppressed memory overcomes him in 1992 and he suffers a breakdown, which propels him to further investigate his past (*Aus*, 331). Thus, the subjective time of the victim rears its head in the form of repressed trauma and forces him to ignore the march of official time; the narrator becomes involved in this quest, long before it takes on such a sense of urgency. Outwardly it seems as if the ethical mode of *Ressentiment* has been successfully transformed into a narrative situation; German and Jew reconstruct together the submerged suffering of the past, the traumatized underside of historical time that is ignored by official history. However, as argued above, Sebald's sentimentalization of the relationship between German and Jew weakens the moral standard of *Ressentiment* and compromises his own ethically driven narrative aesthetics.

Further evidence of the drive to identification with Jewish experience comes across in Sebald's frequent appropriation of specific Jewish markers in the representation of exile.[43] Exile is the existential condition of all Sebaldian narrators; however, in *Schwindel. Gefühle*, a narrative that otherwise has little to do with Jewish themes, the mention of Jerusalem gives the narrator's sense of exile a distinctly Jewish flavor (*SG*, 72). The crisis of identity this narrator experiences in Vienna is assuaged only when, on one of his nightmarish promenades through the city, he mysteriously ends up in the synagogue (*SG*, 44). The focus on his worn-out shoes evokes the pathos of homelessness and exile and associates him with the figure of the wandering Jew. Only after having returned to the "home" of the synagogue does a sense of calm descend on him and he finds himself able to decide to travel to Venice. Once there, he ends up in the ghetto and again seems to don markers of Jewish identity; after one hour of wandering fruitlessly in the Venetian ghetto, he starts to feel persecuted and is glad when he finally gets out (*SG*, 61). The army of tourists that upon his arrival he encounters sleeping in the open air in front of Santa Lucia train station is also described in a pathos-ridden way that evokes connotations of Jewish homelessness, evidence of a romanticizing projection that ignores the fact of relative wealth that goes with the possibility of tourism in the first place (*SG*, 95). In *Die Ausgewanderten*, Adelwarth's exiled existence moves between the twin poles of a negatively connoted Hellenic culture, implied by his tragic end in "Ithaca," and a positive odyssey of Jewish spiritualism, implied by his happy journey to Jerusalem with Cosmo (*A*, 202).[44] In *Austerlitz*, the Welsh village of Bala is a terrible exile for the child Austerlitz, yet he identifies much more with a pictorial representation of Jewish exile in his Welsh children's bible than with his own lived experience (*Aus*, 88). The latter case reveals itself in the fullness of time as a signifier of Austerlitz's submerged, yet innate, sense of Jewishness. Thus, if we regard the development of character from the *Schwindel. Gefühle* narrator to Adelwarth and then to Austerlitz, these characters seem to merge increasingly with an ideal Jewish identity that culminates in the figure of Austerlitz. In all the novels, being Jewish is seen to be a highly desirable identity aspiration, with Austerlitz as a model of ethical behavior in general and as a kind of provider of spiritual sustenance to the morally impoverished German of the present.

In conclusion, I return to my opening argument concerning Sebald's desire for affiliation within a specific tradition of 1960s German-Jewish writing and his rejection of non-Jewish-German writers from the same period. Despite following Améry's lead in his conceptualization of certain characters and in his development of an ethics of memory, the above analysis suggests that a central strand of Sebald's work is troubled German identity and that his often confused and overdetermined depictions of Jewish identity reflect the difficulties of the German subject in trying to represent the Jewish other. Sebald accused Alfred Andersch of creating a wholly unconvincing Jewish character in the figure of Georg Efraim, the eponymous hero of his 1967 novel; Andersch's opportunistic and politically correct voice could be all too loudly heard as it chimed through the inadequate literary vessel of Efraim (*LL*, 141). Focusing on the negative reception of *Efraim* by some critics, Sebald also conveniently leaves out the fact that Améry and a number of other Jewish writers of the time were very pleased with the novel and recognized in its main character a convincing Jewish figure (*LL*, 143).[45] Despite these efforts to distance himself from his immediate German literary predecessors, however, I would argue that Austerlitz is similarly a thin screen for Sebald, who has split himself between two ideal notions of identity: the contrite and receptive German and the lucid Jewish other. What Sebald identifies in *Efraim* — an artificial representation of Jewish experience from a politically correct German standpoint — is what he tries to avoid, particularly in *Austerlitz*. I read this as further evidence of Sebald's anxiety of German influence: his rejection of recent German writers and his pronounced preference for Jewish literary role-models. And as I have shown, close inspection of the narrative situation and strategies of characterization in Sebald's novels shows up the artificiality of his own ethical-aesthetic strategy. *Austerlitz* is undoubtedly a far more sophisticated and considered work than *Efraim*; despite its studied self-reflexivity, however, it is testimony to the ongoing difficulties that German writers experience in their representation of the Jewish other.

Notes

[1] John Zilkosky, "Sebald's Uncanny Travels: the Impossibility of Getting Lost," in *W. G. Sebald: A Critical Companion*, ed. J. J. Long and Anne Whitehead (Edinburgh: Edinburgh UP, 2004), 102–20; here: 102. Henceforth cited in main text in brackets as Z followed by page number.

[2] All references are henceforth abbreviated as *SG* and cite the following edition: W. G. Sebald, *Schwindel. Gefühle* (Frankfurt am Main: Fischer, 1994). Likewise, *Die Ausgewanderten* is henceforth abbreviated as *A* and cites the following edition: W. G. Sebald, *Die Ausgewanderten. Vier lange Erzählungen* (Frankfurt am Main: Fischer, 1994). The English translation appeared under the title *The Emigrants*, translated from the German by Michael Hulse (London: Harvill, 1996). Quotations in English are taken from Hulse's translation and cited as *E*.

[3] See Martin Klebes, "Infinite Journey: From Kafka to Sebald," in *W. G. Sebald: A Critical Companion*, 123–39.

[4] Here I refer to Ernest Gellner's pugnacious but convincing critique of the Freudian unconscious, which asserts that the unconscious is not as radically alien to the conscious mind as psychoanalysis claims. Ernest Gellner, *The Psychoanalytic Movement or the Coming of Unreason* (London: Paladin/Grafton, 1985).

[5] On travel in Sebald, see, in addition to Zilcosky (note 1), Ruth Klüger, "Wanderer zwischen falschen Leben," in *Text + Kritik* 158 (2003), *W. G. Sebald*, ed. Heinz Ludwig Arnold, 95–102; Massimo Leone, "Textual Wanderings: A Vertiginous Reading of W. G. Sebald," in *W. G. Sebald: A Critical Companion*, ed. Long and Whitehead, 89–101. On visual media in his work see Carolin Duttlinger, "Traumatic Photographs: Remembrance and the Technical Media in W. G.

Sebald's *Austerlitz*," in *W. G. Sebald: A Critical Companion*, ed. Long and White-head, 155–71; J. J. Long, "History, Narrative and Photography in W. G. Sebald's *Die Ausgewanderten*," *The Modern Language Review* 98 (2003): 117–37; Stefanie Harris, "The Return of the Dead: Memory and Photography in W. G. Sebald's *Die Ausgewanderten*," *German Quarterly* 74.4 (2001): 370–92. On melancholy see Peter Morgan, "The Sign of Saturn: Melancholy, Homelessness and Apocalypse in W. G. Sebald's Prose Narratives," *German Life and Letters* 58 (2005): 75–92; Sigrid Löffler, " 'Melancholie ist eine Form des Widerstands'; Über das Saturnische bei W. G. Sebald und seine Aufhebung in der Schrift," *Text + Kritik* 158 (2003), *W. G. Sebald*, 103–11; Mary Cosgrove, "Melancholy Competitions: W. G. Sebald reads Günter Grass and Wolfgang Hildesheimer," *German Life and Letters* 59/2 (2006), special issue: *Memory Contests*, ed. Anne Fuchs and Mary Cosgrove, 217–32. See also Martin Swales, "Theoretical Reflections on the Work of W. G. Sebald," in *W. G. Sebald: A Critical Companion*, ed. Long and White-head, 23–28.

⁶ See Susanne Schedel, "*Wer weiß, wie es vor Zeiten wirklich gewesen ist?*" *Textbeziehungen als Mittel der Geschichtsschreibung bei W. G. Sebald* (Würzburg: Königshausen & Neumann, 2004). See also Anne Fuchs, *Die Schmerzensspuren der Geschichte: Zur Poetik der Erinnerung in W. G. Sebalds Prosa* (Cologne, Weimar, Vienna: Böhlau 2004), 76–107.

⁷ See Andreas Huyssen, "On Rewritings and New Beginnings: W. G. Sebald and the Literature about the Luftkrieg," *Zeitschrift für Literatur und Linguistik* 31 (2001): 72–90. See also Anne Fuchs's essay on *Heimat* and ruins in Sebald's work in this volume.

⁸ W. G. Sebald, *Luftkrieg und Literatur: Mit einem Essay zu Alfred Andersch* (Munich, Vienna: Carl Hanser, 1999). This edition is henceforth cited as *LL*.

⁹ Günter Grass, *Im Krebsgang* (Göttingen: Steidel, 2002). On the media frenzy surrounding the novella, see Elizabeth Dye, " 'Weil die Geschichte nicht aufhört': Günter Grass's *Im Krebsgang*," *German Life and Letters* 57 (2004): 472–87.

¹⁰ See Anne Fuchs's discussion of Sebald's ethics of memory, *Die Schmerzensspuren der Geschichte*, 21–39. See also Greg Bond, "On the Misery of Nature and the Nature of Misery: W. G. Sebald's Landscapes," in *W. G. Sebald: A Critical Companion*, 31–44.

¹¹ See Fuchs, *Die Schmerzensspuren der Geschichte*, 165–205. See also Andreas Huyssen, "W. G. Sebald and the Literature about the Luftkrieg," 72–90.

¹² Four volumes of Sebald's essayistic work have been published, two on Austrian literature of the nineteenth and twentieth centuries. The first of these is *Unheimliche Heimat: Essays zur österreichischen Literatur* (Frankfurt am Main: Fischer, 1994). All references to this edition use the abbreviated form *UH*. The second is *Die Beschreibung des Unglücks: Zur österreichischen Literatur von Stifter bis Handke* (Salzburg, Vienna: Residenz, 1985). A third is *Logis in einem Landhaus: Über Gottfried Keller, Johann Peter Hebel, Robert Walser und andere* (Munich: Carl Hanser, 1998). A further posthumous collection appeared more recently: *Campo Santo*, ed. Sven Meyer (Munich, Vienna: Carl Hanser 2003), henceforth cited as *CS*. The English translation appeared under the title *Campo Santo*, translated from the German by Anthea Bell (London: Hamish Hamilton, 2005).

[13] Given the controversy that ensued after Sebald, in Zurich in 1997, held the lectures that became *Luftkrieg und Literatur*, this is hardly surprising. See Winfried Wilms's excellent essay on this topic, "Taboo and Repression in W. G. Sebald's *On the Natural History of Destruction*," in *W. G. Sebald: A Critical Companion*, ed. Long and Whitehead, 175–89. See also Andreas Huyssen, "W. G. Sebald and the Literature about the Luftkrieg," 72–90; Christian Schulte, " 'Die Naturgeschichte der Zerstörung': W. G. Sebalds Thesen zu 'Luftkrieg und Literatur,' " in *Text + Kritik* 158 (2003), *W. G. Sebald*, 82–94; see also Anne Fuchs's contribution on this theme in the present volume.

[14] This very personal approach is most evident in Sebald's attack on Alfred Andersch, "Der Schriftsteller Alfred Andersch," in *Luftkrieg und Literatur*, 113–47.

[15] See, for example, *Luftkrieg und Literatur*, 17; "Mit den Augen des Nachtvogels: Über Jean Améry," in *Campo Santo*, 149–70; here: 149–50; "Konstruktionen der Trauer: Günter Grass und Wolfgang Hildesheimer," in *Campo Santo*, 101–27; here: 101–3; "Zwischen Geschichte und Naturgeschichte: Über die literarische Beschreibung totaler Zerstörung," in *Campo Santo*, 69–100; here: 69–71.

[16] For a discussion of this development, see Dieter Lamping, *Von Kafka bis Celan: Jüdischer Diskurs in der deutschen Literatur des 20. Jahrhunderts* (Göttingen: Vandenhoek & Ruprecht, 1998), 151.

[17] All subsequent references are abbreviated as *Aus* and are taken from the following edition: *Austerlitz* (Frankfurt am Main: Fischer, 2003). Quotations in English are taken from Anthea Bell's translation, also titled *Austerlitz* (London: Hamish Hamilton, 2001).

[18] Harold Bloom, *The Anxiety of Influence: A Theory of Poetry* (New York, Oxford: Oxford UP, 1973).

[19] Stuart Taberner, "German Nostalgia? Remembering German-Jewish Life in W. G. Sebald's *Die Ausgewanderten* and *Austerlitz*," *The Germanic Review* 3 (2004), special issue: *W. G. Sebald*, 181–202; Maya Barzilai, "Facing the Past and the Female Spectre in W. G. Sebald's *The Emigrants*," in *W. G. Sebald: A Critical Companion*, ed. Long and Whitehead, 203–16.

[20] Katharina Hall, "Jewish Memory in Exile: The Relation of W. G. Sebald's *Die Ausgewanderten* to the Tradition of the Yizkor Books," in *Jews in German Literature since 1945: German-Jewish Literature?*, ed. Pól O'Dochartaigh (Amsterdam: Rodopi, 2000), 152–64; here: 160.

[21] Ralf Jeutter, " 'Am Rand der Finsternis': The Jewish Experience in the Context of W. G. Sebald's Prose," in *Jews in German Literature since 1945: German-Jewish Literature?*, ed. Pól O'Dochartaigh, 165–77; here: 171.

[22] Mary Cosgrove, "Melancholy Competitions," 217–32.

[23] W. G. Sebald, "Verlorenes Land: Jean Améry und Österreich," in *Unheimliche Heimat*, 131–44; "Mit den Augen des Nachtvogels: Über Jean Améry," in *Campo Santo*, 149–70; "Jean Améry und Primo Levi," in *Über Jean Améry*, ed. Irene Heidelberger-Leonard (Heidelberg: Carl Winter, 1990), 115–23. The second essay was translated by Anthea Bell as "Against the Irreversible: On Jean Améry," and appears in *On the Natural History of Destruction*, 147–71. Quotations in English are taken from Bell's translation and cited as *NHD*.

[24] Jean Améry, "Ressentiments," in *Jenseits von Schuld und Sühne: Bewältigungsversuche eines Überwältigten* (Stuttgart: Klett-Cotta, 1977), 102–29. This edition is henceforth cited as *JSS*. The first edition was published in 1966 by Szczesny Publishers.

[25] Stuart Taberner, "Philo-Semitism in Recent German Film: *Aimée und Jaguar*, *Rosenstraße* and *Das Wunder von Bern*," *German Life and Letters* 58:3 (2005): 357–72. See also Jack Zipes, "The Contemporary German Fascination for Things Jewish: Towards a Jewish Minority Culture," in *Reemerging Jewish Culture in Germany: Life and Literature since 1989*, ed. Sander Gilman and Karen Remmler (New York, London: New York UP, 1994), 15–46.

[26] See in particular Ernestine Schlant, *The Language of Silence: West German Literature and the Holocaust* (New York, London: Routledge, 1999), 71–78. Anne Fuchs notes the tendency to identification in Sebald's narrative aesthetics but argues that the self-reflexive nature of his style prevents this (*Die Schmerzensspuren der Geschichte*, 28–34). Stuart Taberner also emphasizes that Sebald's narrative technique prevents identification in *Austerlitz*, if not in *Die Ausgewanderten* ("Remembering German-Jewish Life in W. G. Sebald's *Die Ausgewanderten* and *Austerlitz*," 198).

[27] In the closing pages of *Die Ausgewanderten* the narrator discusses this narrative scrupulousness, mentioning the highly questionable nature of all attempts to tell stories, 344–45.

[28] Alfred Andersch, *Efraim* (Zurich: Diogenes, 1967); see also Andersch's assessment of Améry's life and work: "Anzeige einer Rückkehr des Geistes als Person," in *Merkur* 25 (1971): 689–700; here: 699. See also Dieter Lamping's discussion of the divided reception of the book in *Von Kafka bis Celan*, 145–51.

[29] W. G. Sebald, "Verlorenes Land: Jean Améry und Österreich," in *Unheimliche Heimat*, 131–44; Irene Heidelberger-Leonard, "Jean Amérys Selbstverständnis als Jude," in *Über Jean Améry*, ed. Heidelberger-Leonard, 17–27.

[30] Jean Améry, "An den Grenzen des Geistes," 18–45; "Die Tortur," 46–73; "Über Zwang und Unmöglichkeit, Jude zu sein," 130–56; all in *Jenseits von Schuld und Sühne*.

[31] W. G. Sebald, *Logis in einem Landhaus*, 12.

[32] Heidelberger-Leonard, "Jean Amérys Selbstverständnis als Jude," in *Über Jean Améry*, ed. Heidelberger-Leonard, 17–21; here: 20.

[33] Jean-Michel Chaumont, "Geschichtliche Verantwortung und menschliche Würde bei Jean Améry," in *Über Jean Améry*, ed. Heidelberger-Leonard, 29–47; here: 32.

[34] Fuchs, *Die Schmerzensspuren der Geschichte*, 28–31.

[35] Dominick LaCapra, *Writing History, Writing Trauma* (Baltimore, London: Johns Hopkins UP, 2001).

[36] Cathy Caruth's argument that traumatic experience serves as a model for the understanding of historical experience is representative for this intellectual streamlining of historical understanding. See Cathy Caruth, *Unclaimed Experience: Trauma, Narrative, and History* (Baltimore, London: Johns Hopkins UP, 1996),

chapter 1. Sigrid Weigel provides an excellent critique of the generalizing tendencies inherent in Caruth's work, "Télescopage im Unbewußten: Zum Verhältnis von Trauma, Geschichtsbegriff und Literatur," in *Trauma zwischen Psychoanalyse und kulturellen Deutungsmustern*, ed. Elisabeth Bronfen, Birgit Erdle, Sigrid Weigel (Cologne, Weimar, Vienna: Böhlau, 1999), 51–76.

[37] Fuchs, *Die Schmerzensspuren der Geschichte*, 37–38. J. J. Long follows a similar argument in his article "History, Narrative, and Photography in W. G. Sebald's *Die Ausgewanderten*," in *The Modern Language Review* 98 (2003): 117–37.

[38] Bernhard Malkmus, " 'All of them Signs and Characters from the Type-Case of Forgotten Things': Intermedia Configurations of History in W. G. Sebald," in *Memory Traces: 1989 and the Question of German Cultural Identity*, ed. Silke Arnold-de-Simine (Oxford, Bern, Berlin: Lang, 2005), 211–44; Katharina Hall, "Jewish Memory in Exile: The Relation of W. G. Sebald's *Die Ausgewanderten* to the Tradition of the Yizkor Books," in *Jews in German Literature since 1945: German-Jewish Literature?*, ed. Pól O'Dochartaigh, 152–64.

[39] LaCapra, *Writing History, Writing Trauma*, 41.

[40] The awareness of transference is a major concern in a collection of articles on the theme of Holocaust representation that was published in the aftermath of the historians' debate of the late 1980s. *Probing the Limits of Representation: Nazism and the Final Solution*, ed. Saul Friedländer (Cambridge, MA, London: Harvard UP, 1992).

[41] Dan Diner, "Negative Symbiose: Deutsche und Juden nach 1945," in *Ist der Nationalsozialismus Geschichte? Zu Historisierung und Historikerstreit*, ed. Dan Diner (Frankfurt am Main: Fischer, 1987), 185–97.

[42] Wilms, "Taboo and Repression in W. G. Sebald's *On the Natural History of Destruction*," in *W. G. Sebald: A Critical Companion*, ed. Long and Whitehead, 175–89; here: 188.

[43] For a discussion of these markers of Jewish exile and of the distinction between exile generally and Jewish exile, see *Placeless Topographies: Jewish Perspectives on the Literature of Exile*, ed. Bernhard Greiner (Tübingen: Niemeyer, 2003).

[44] On the theme of Jerusalem as a signifier of redemption in Sebald's work, see Jan Cueppens, "Seeing Things: Spectres and Angels in W. G. Sebald's Prose Fiction," in *W. G. Sebald: A Critical Companion*, ed. Long and Whitehead, 190–202; here: 198–99.

[45] See Dieter Lamping, *Von Kafka bis Celan*, 150.

12: Between "Restauration" and "Nierentisch": The 1950s in Ludwig Harig, F. C. Delius, and Thomas Hettche

Andrew Plowman

IN *WER MIT DEN WÖLFEN HEULT, wird Wolf* (Whoever Runs With the Pack Becomes a Wolf, 1996), his third autobiographical novel, Ludwig Harig repeatedly reflects upon the Zeitgeist defining the Federal Republic of Germany during the 1950s.[1] His recurring preoccupation is the contradictory outline retrospectively presented by the era. "Zu keiner anderen Zeit lagen die großen und die kleinen Dinge weiter auseinander als Anfang der fünfziger Jahre" (at no other time were the important and the small matters further apart than at the start of the fifties), he writes:

> Was ging's uns an, wenn in Korea die Kanonen wieder krachten, wenn zur gleichen Zeit Konrad Adenauer und François-Poncet [. . .] zusammensaßen auf dem Weg nach Paris, den Vertrag zum Gemeinsamen Markt für Kohle und Stahl zu unterzeichnen! [. . .] Wie wir Hermanns Plattenspieler unter der Dachschräge unserer Mansarde am zweckmäßigsten installieren könnten, war uns wichtiger.[2]

> [What did we care, if the guns blazed in Korea, if at the same time Adenauer and François-Poncet [. . .] were en route to Paris to sign the treaty of the Community for Steel and Coal! [. . .] More important to us was how properly to install Hermann's record player under the slanted attic roof.]

Setting a pragmatic *Lebensgefühl* against broader political developments, this passage illustrates a disjunction between the personal and the political, between life history and history that frames the diverse elements of the novel. On the personal side these include Harig's early career as a teacher and his beginnings as a writer in the experimental circle surrounding Max Bense; and on the political side, reflections on West German recovery in the wider context of economic and military integration into the West.

What is so intriguing about *Wer mit den Wölfen heult* is how Harig's contradictory recollections of the 1950s are reflected in its construction of memory. They are underpinned, first, by an autobiographical discourse of "self-invention,"[3] as Harig self-consciously constructs a new personal beginning after the childhood enthusiasm for National Socialism described in *Wehe dem, der aus der Reihe tanzt* (Woe to Him Who Steps Out of Line, 1990). Significantly, Harig expresses skepticism toward the synthetic thrust usually ascribed to autobiographical memory.[4] A toy kaleidoscope "das eine ganze Kindheit und Jugend mit Bildern des schönsten Scheines begleitet hatte" (*W*, 226; which had accompanied childhood and youth with images of the most beautiful appearance), provides the metaphor for an autobiographical memory, which seeks to combine heterogeneous recollections in a broader narrative arc without sacrificing their singularity. With every turn, the central mosaic changes form: "Was uns aber am meisten beeindruckte, war die stets neu entstehende Radialsymmetrie, die bei der geringsten Erschütterung wieder zerfiel, um einer anderen Platz zu machen" (*W*, 227; what impressed us most was the symmetry which formed ever new around the central axis, collapsing at the slightest touch to make way to a new pattern).

The kaleidoscope appears here as the object of and a figure for autobiographical memory. There is, however, a less obvious sense in which it offers a fitting image for the process of memory in the text. The symmetry of its central axis arguably also provides a filter for a conspectus of historical and contemporary discourses *about* the 1950s. A pervasive discourse which figures prominently in the text (for example in the first passage cited) is that of "Restauration." The term was coined late in the 1940s by leftist intellectuals to "understand the gap between their expectations and the reality of developments after the collapse in 1945."[5] It has since enjoyed wide (and vague) usage to describe critically various processes in the 1950s: the restoration of capitalism; rearmament and military integration into the West; the continuity of personnel and elites from the Third Reich; the prevailing outlook of a paternalistic, authoritarian state and chancellor; the ascendancy of a popular "Wir-sind-wieder-wer" (we are someone again) mentality that hid from the Nazi past in economic success; or simply a conservative social morality and a diffuse climate of conformity.[6] In social and political discourses the restoration thesis enjoyed widest currency in the 1950s themselves and again in the 1970s.[7] From Wolfgang Koeppen's *Das Treibhaus* (The Hothouse, 1953) to Rainer Werner Fassbinder's film *Die Ehe der Maria Braun* (The Marriage of Maria Braun, 1978), it informs a wide range of cultural production in and beyond these periods.

But Harig's autobiographical novel refracts other discourses about the 1950s too. Take the following passage, in which Harig seeks to capture a social and cultural profile for which his mentor Bense around 1955 coined the phrase "das neue deutsche Nivellement" (the new German leveling-out):

In Köln endet die deutsche Hausrats- und Eisenwarenmesse mit wachsenden Profiten. Die Hausbars werden mit Leder, die Damensessel mit

Seidensatin und die Einbauküchen mit Resopal bezogen. In Dingolfing
rollt das tausendste Goggomobil vom Band. (*W*, 241–42)

[In Cologne the German household and iron goods trade fair ends with
growing profits. Domestic bars are upholstered with leather, ladies' arm-
chairs with satin, and fitted kitchens finished in melamine. In Dingolfing
the 1,000th Goggomobil rolls off the production line.]

The term "Nivellement" invokes Helmut Schelsky's famous diagnosis of the
FRG in the 1950s as a society in which class differences were being eroded
through processes of upward and downward mobility and values reoriented
toward leisure and consumption.[8] Further, references to "Einbauküchen"
(fitted kitchens) finished in "Resopal" (melamine) or the "Goggomobil"
point to more recent popular and nostalgic discourses. The 1986 film *Rendezvous unter dem Nierentisch* (Rendezvous Beneath the Kidney-Shaped
Table), a collage of advertising and *Wochenschau* clips, exemplifies a wave of
documentaries and picture books endlessly recycling key signifiers of
the transformation of the Federal Republic in the 1950s into a modern
consumer society. Design and consumer icons have pride of place: cars like
the Borgward Isabella or the curious "Goggomobil," music systems like the
"Musiktruhe," fitted kitchens equipped with mixers and refrigerators, the
"Nierentisch," and stockings or petticoats made from synthetic fabrics.[9]
Besides that of restoration, Harig's autobiographical act reveals itself to be
shaped by a network of competing discourses about the decade.

This essay offers an examination of post-1990 literary representations
of the 1950s in the Federal Republic of Germany. Harig's *Wer mit den
Wölfen heult* brings to life the contradictory place the decade has occupied
within the popular and historical imagination in the Federal Republic. The
1950s — to the extent they can be regarded as a historical period[10]— were,
historians remind us, "both a dramatic endpoint and a new beginning":
the end of a period of "economic chaos, political extremism and wanton
mass destruction that had disfigured German history and experience since
1914," and the beginning of "the first successful implantation of liberal
democracy in German soil and [. . .] the country's full transformation
[. . .] to a welfare state."[11] And they continue to be broadly associated, as
Harig's text memorably illustrates, with the stasis of restoration on the one
hand, the dynamism of modernization on the other, and with the birth of
consumer culture. Since unification, fascination with the 1950s has
mounted as the origins of the enlarged Federal Republic have come under
the spotlight.[12]

This essay reads recent literary representations of the 1950s as part of
a broader revaluation of the decade's legacy beginning in the 1980s and
gaining momentum after 1990. The next section introduces a range of
post-1990 literary texts about the period, placing them in the context of
contemporary debates about the legacy of the "old" Federal Republic. If

the 1950s in the West are increasingly understood in popular and historical discourses as marking the beginning of a successful German story of liberalization and modernization, then these literary constructions of the early Federal Republic constitute a historical "imaginary" that offers a differentiated, critical account of this story. The subsequent sections of the essay pursue this theme in two texts in which a received image of West German restoration is reviewed from a more liberal post-1968 perspective: F. C. Delius's *Der Sonntag, an dem Ich Weltmeister wurde* (The Sunday I Became World Champion, 1994), and Thomas Hettche's *Der Fall Arbogast* (The Arbogast Case, 2001). Contemporary literary representations are not, of course, historical documents, but, as Harig's novel illustrates, acts of memory in which the past is reconstructed. Thus the texts also bring into focus the issue of cultural memory.

There are important differences here between the texts by Harig, Delius, and Hettche that are also the subject of this essay. Harig's autobiographical act, I have suggested, brings into play personal memories as well as competing discourses from and about the time recalled. His autobiographical memory exhibits *some* continuities with what theorists of cultural memory term communicative memory. Here, personal memories are not so much the product of private individual activity as formed intersubjectively and in the medium of language.[13] Not unlike in Harig's kaleidoscope, this construction of memory is marked by its richness, diversity, and even contradictoriness. By contrast, the manner in which his text refracts diverse discourses about the period he describes suggests the operation of a cultural memory. This is characterized by the shifting of the work of memory onto material discourses and systems of transmission, which are constantly revalued and contested according to the needs of the present.[14]

A striking contrast with the autobiographical focus of Harig, who was born in 1927 and experienced the early Federal Republic as a young adult, is the structure of memory in texts by authors whose biographies situate them differently toward the decade. Born in 1943, Delius experienced the central event in his text only as a boy; Hettche, born in 1964, not at all. The concepts of communicative and cultural memory are of course ideal types. In practice what is often at issue is their interplay within cultural artifacts and the way cultural forms locate themselves at the borders between them, for instance when one memory passes historically into another.[15] Autobiographical theory has distinct preoccupations of its own with respect to the act of memory.[16] A synthesis of autobiographical and cultural memory theory might understand autobiography as a genre that partakes of communicative and cultural memory and performs the transformation of the former into the latter. By contrast, the Delius and Hettche texts exhibit a progressive shift of the burden of memory towards the material transmission and storage of data identified as crucial to cultural memory. The act of memory proceeds as the recoding of texts to which identifiable meanings have already accrued. It is, in short, an engagement with a pre-existing cultural archive.

Reviewing the Republic?
The FRG in Contemporary Texts

Besides Harig, Delius, and Hettche, a number of writers have since 1990 offered striking representations of the early Federal Republic. Among figures already well established before 1990, Uwe Timm has examined the social climate that gave birth to the Federal Republic in the late 1940s in *Die Entdeckung der Currywurst* (The Discovery of the Curried Sausage, 1993), and Wilhelm Genazino the mood going into the 1960s in *Eine Frau, eine Wohnung, ein Roman* (A Woman, a Room, a Novel, 2003). Better known for poetry, Ulla Hahn has delivered a classic novel of development that illuminates the period from a gendered perspective in *Das verborgene Wort* (The Hidden Word, 2001). Memorable novels have also catapulted writers who were only just beginning to make their name before 1990 to the fore. The shadow of the past that hung over the period dominates Hans-Ulrich Treichel's *Der Verlorene* (The Lost One, 1993) and Claire Bayer's *Rauken* (Rauken, 2000), novels which respectively explore the memory of Germans as victims of war and as Nazi perpetrators. Jochen Missfeldt's *Gespiegelter Himmel* (Reflected Sky, 2001) is a multi-layered novel about *Luftwaffe* pilots caught between outdated military codes of honor and democratic values in the context of Cold-War integration into the West, Kurt Oesterle's *Der Fernsehgast* (The Television Guest, 2002) an account of the dawn of television in the rural *Heimat* in the late 1950s. The early Federal Republic has provided rich material also for younger authors who have made their mark exclusively in postunification literary markets. Exploring the ruptured biography of a protagonist who flees from creditors in the FRG to the German Democratic Republic, Michael Kumpfmüller's *Hampels Fluchten* (Hampel's Flights, 2000) takes in the merry-go-round of the "economic miracle" and postwar German division. Finally, Bianca Döring's *Hallo, Mr Zebra* (Hello, Mr. Zebra, 1999) offers a portrait of antagonistic family relations, and Gerhard Henschel's *Die Liebenden* (The Lovers, 2002) a detailed appraisal of the politics of everyday life in the 1950s at the heart of an epistolary novel spanning from the end of Third Reich to beyond the *Wende*.

These texts belong, first, in the context of a proliferation since the mid-1990s of writing about the pre-unification Federal Republic.[17] With the exception of a lively interest in novels about 1968 such as Timm's *ROT* (RED, 2001) or Erasmus Schöffer's *Ein Frühling irrer Hoffnung* (A Springtime of Vain Hope, 2001),[18] this trend has been scrutinized only fitfully as scholars privilege postunification writing about the GDR and its transformation. During the later 1990s, literary engagements with the pre-unification Federal Republic have, as Stuart Taberner argues, become less critical and more affirmative in tone.[19] As such the texts can also be placed in the context of a wider assessment in the 1990s of the legacy of the old Federal Republic, to which the 1950s are central.

Since unification, initial controversy over that legacy has generally given way to a more positive appraisal. In the early 1990s, critics from the right seeking to promote national identity and historical consciousness derided the old Federal Republic as provincial in outlook;[20] the left, meanwhile, in an irony often noted, discovered a retrospective attachment to the constitutional achievements and civil society of a state previously regarded with mistrust.[21] With the fading of the challenge of the right, the election of the Red-Green coalition and the preparations for the fiftieth anniversary in 1999, greater consensus emerged. The history of the Federal Republic, it is more widely agreed, marks a success story leading from inauspicious beginnings to the attainment by the 1980s of a significant measure of self-acceptance. This, it is argued, is a story valorized by unification, and at its heart stands the acceptance of liberal western values.[22]

Central to this view is the intensification of a revaluation of the 1950s begun, perhaps not coincidentally, during the period identified as one of self-acceptance for the Federal Republic. Since the 1980s, and with increasing momentum since 1990, the lingering image of the 1950s as a period of restoration has come to be contested by a picture of radical social and economic modernization.[23] It is, of course, the *topos* of modernization that underwrites the popular discourses about consumption and youth culture in the 1950s identified in the opening section. Arguably, the optimistic tone of these discourses simply presents a reverse image of the restoration thesis (as surely do the journalistic tributes to economic reconstruction and the birth of democracy appearing on the occasion of the fiftieth anniversary in 1999).[24] Significantly however, recent historical scholarship offers a more differentiated account. What is at issue here is rather the interaction and conflict between processes of social and economic modernization on the one hand and entrenched structures and attitudes on the other which look back across the Third Reich to previous epochs.[25] (The heavy and ornate throwback to the *Biedermeier* that was the "Gelsenkirchener Barock," we learn, captures the public taste of the era more accurately than the "Nierentisch" that has retrospectively become one of its principle icons.)[26] The 1950s, as Axel Schildt puts it, are best understood in terms of a tension between conservative moments and modernizing tendencies and of a discontinuous process of modernization within the framework of a conservative social formation.[27]

To what extent does this contemporary discourse about the ambivalences of the 1950s inform recent literary representations that are after all imaginative reconstructions rather than works of historiography? What is striking about Harig's *Wer mit den Wölfen heult* and other texts introduced above is precisely the acute sense of the contradictoriness of the decade. Indeed, if the generally more affirmative tone of recent writing about the old Federal Republic since the mid-1990s can be linked to a positive appraisal of its history, literary discourse is also ideally suited to an exploration of tensions and discontinuities at its heart. It functions as a historical imaginary in which shifting relationships between the private and the political, between the fabric of everyday life and the social processes underlying it are reconstructed from the perspective of the present. The following sections examine how the monolithic image of West German restoration gives way to a more dynamic reconstruction in Delius's *Der Sonntag, an dem ich Weltmeister wurde* and Hettche's *Der Fall Arbogast*. An interesting feature in the texts is the review of the era from a more liberal post-1968 perspective. While the 1950s have been marked out as the site of a fraught process of modernization, the student movement of 1968 is frequently associated in postunification discourses with a fundamental liberalization of social and cultural values in the Federal Republic.[28] Here the texts also bring into focus the issue of cultural memory and its mechanisms. In contrast to the autobiographical focus of memory in Harig's novel, they enact a more visible shift of the burden of memory toward the inscription of new meanings into texts forming part of a pre-existing cultural archive.

Reimagining "Restoration" I: F. C. Delius's *Der Sonntag, an dem ich Weltmeister wurde*

A prominent figure associated with the generation of 1968, F. C. Delius has written many works critical of the Federal Republic such as *Held der inneren Sicherheit* (Hero of Internal Security, 1981), *Mogadischu Fensterplatz* (A Window Seat in Mogadishu, 1987), and *Himmelfahrt eines Staatsfeindes* (Ascension of an Enemy of the State, 1992). Perhaps it is surprising, then, that his 1994 narrative *Der Sonntag, an dem ich Weltmeister wurde* appraises more positively an event more usually seen on the left as the embodiment of the spirit of West German restoration: the World Cup final of June 1954. In a famous victory, a West German team starting as underdogs defeated an unbeaten Hungarian side that went into the match as *de facto* world champions. The symbolic overtones of victory in a game that was, as Herbert Zimmermann's famous radio commentary noted, "das populärste Spiel der Welt" (the most popular game in the world) were controversial enough at the time.[29] Initially with official encouragement, popular sentiment seized upon the triumph as the expression of a national self-consciousness reborn after 1945. Yet faced with concern also from abroad at a resurgence of nationalist rhetoric, the government of the day soon found itself having to tread cautiously, with Bundespräsident Theodor Heuss at once downplaying any symbolic significance and chiding as "töricht" (foolish) critics who sought to deny Germans pride in their sporting success.[30] It is precisely the symbolic dimension of the event that has continued to fascinate, however. Zimmermann's exclamation "Deutschland ist Weltmeister!" (Germany is World Champion) at the close of the game becomes the expression of a sinister "Wir-sind-wieder-Wer" mentality in Fassbinder's *Die Ehe der Maria Braun* from 1978. In the film, it follows soon after Adenauer's announcement of rearmament on the radio and it accompanies the gas explosion, linking West German recovery motivically to the bomb blast and the calamity of German fascism at the opening of the film. More recently, Sonke Wortmann's 2003 film *Das Wunder von Bern* (The Miracle of Bern) presents the event anew as an untroubled moment of revival and integration in the bond it forges between a boy and his father, one of the former German soldiers returning home late from imprisonment in the Soviet Union.

In Delius's text the more positive appraisal of the event resides structurally in the escape it offers the first-person narrator, a pastor's son in a village in Hessen in 1954, from the physically and morally stifling routine ordinarily governing Sundays. The usual "Sonntagsgefahren" (Sunday dangers) and "Sonntagspflichten" (*S*, 80; Sunday duties) are underwritten by the religious injunction "*Du sollst den Feiertag heiligen!*" (*S*, 13; you must honor the day of rest). These dangers and duties include being woken by the forceful ringing of church bells (*S*, 8), a breakfast taken in moderation and in a spirit of "Stillsitzen und Bravsein" (*S*, 20; sitting still and behaving), the prohibition from playing football "vormittags wegen der Sonntagsruhe, nachmittags wegen der Sonntagskleidung" (*S*, 14; in the mornings because of Sunday peace and quiet, in the afternoon because of wearing one's Sunday best), the Sunday service and his father's monotonous "Predigtsätze, die ohnehin nur für Erwachsene gedacht waren" (*S*, 47; sentences of sermons in any case only meant for adults), and the Sunday roast, in which in almost grotesque fashion "*das Wort ward Fleisch*" (*S*, 69; the Word became flesh). Sundays mean, in short, reverence, rules, religious injunctions and for the narrator the debilitating "Schwermut und Lähmung" (*S*, 15; melancholy and paralysis), of a loss of fantasy and speech. The narrator's power of imagination is stifled: "Mein Kopf war belagert [. . .] von der Macht Gott, die in alle Gedanken hineinregierte" (*S*, 15; my head was taken over by the power of God, which extended its rule into my very thoughts). His ability to speak with his own voice is undermined: "Ich [. . .] stürzte ab mit meiner Sprache [. . .], fand keinen Halt und fiel" (*S*, 55; my speech crashed, I found nothing to hold onto and fell). There is, however, a bleak irony at work when the narrator concedes that the rituals of the Sunday are in fact "Erleichterungen des Sonntags" (consolations of

Sunday), when compared to the "gewöhnlichen Gefangenschaften der Woche" (*S*, 12; the normal tribulations of the week).

The text offers a vision of the stifling conformity of provincial restoration in the early Federal Republic that would scarcely be out of place in a text coming directly out of the student movement like Bernward Vesper's *Die Reise* (The Journey, published posthumously 1977). Indeed, Delius mobilizes a discourse of *Heimat* to set the small village in Hessen in relation to the state, fixing it as a microcosm of a Federal Republic shaped by prewar traditions and by war and its legacy. The stratification of social groups in the church service is a case in point: "die Adligen in ihrem Familiengestühl, [. . .] Flüchtlinge, die immer noch Flüchtlinge genannt wurden, Mechaniker und Angestellte, mürrische Bauern" (*S*, 44; the aristocracy in their family pews, refugees from the lost territories who were then still known as refugees, mechanics and employers, surly farmers). Also striking in this regard is the way the village is bound into the fabric of the Cold War. The nearby land, on which American forces exercise their tanks, overlooks "die düstere Ostzone Walter Ulbrichts" (*S*, 37; the dismal Eastern Zone of Walter Ulbricht).

Into this context the World Cup final opens an almost utopian perspective. Like most Germans the narrator follows the game by means of Zimmermann's commentary: "[seine] Stimme [. . .], die geschmeidig und erregt die Begeisterung von Silbe zu Silbe trug und sich schnell steigerte zu Wortmelodien" (*S*, 88; his voice, which transferred the excitement supply and agitatedly from one syllable to the next and soon heightened into verbal melodies). In contrast to his father's deadening sermon, the language of the commentary mobilizes the narrator's fantasy:[31] "Meine Phantasie flog voraus zu dem fernen Spiel, ich sah die stürmenden Ungarn auf mich zukommen" (*S*, 78; my fantasy flew ahead to the distant game, I saw the attacking Hungarians coming at me). It offers a gratifying identification with the West German team: pride at having reached the final (*S*, 64); and joy at the unexpected final score (*S*, 114). The game moreover appears as a pleasurable activity free of the usual Sunday injunctions — "ein Können ohne Gehorsam und Gebet, [. . .] das nicht von oben abgesegnet war, und [. . .] Glück [. . .] ohne Wenn und Aber und Scham" (*S*, 106; a skill that dispensed with obedience and prayer, that was not sanctioned from above, and a joy without qualification and shame). Some of the promise held by the commentary fleetingly but tangibly spills over into the narrator's routinized Sunday existence at the close, when he and friends celebrate in front of the church — inspired by the unusual power of the words they have heard and liberated from the routine of the typical Sunday (*S*, 119).

Solidarity, spontaneity, the liberation of speech and of fantasy from everyday injunctions: these are qualities typically associated with the initial stirring of the student movement in novels like Timm's *Heißer Sommer*

(Hot Summer, 1974) or *ROT*, Schöffer's *Ein Frühling irrer Hoffnung* or Delius's own *Amerikahaus* (1997). In short, the World Cup final of 1954 offers in the text an anticipatory glimpse of 1968, or rather an anticipation of 1968 is written back into the 1954 event. Thus the text provides a vivid example of what commentators have identified as the way in which postunification constructions of 1968 as a central moment of liberalization allowed an embattled left in the immediate wake of unification to identify itself with a previously mistrusted Federal Republic.[32] In *Der Sonntag* the implicit memory of 1968 functions as a prism through which a more positive vision of the Federal Republic is projected back into the restoration of the 1950s. Significantly, though, the text does not surrender a critical vision of West German restoration to a rose-tinted account of the German success story, but rather moves dialectically between them.

The text's dialectical perspective resides in the contrast between Sunday norms and the extraordinary commentary, but also in a structure of memory that is grounded in Herbert Zimmermann's commentary itself. Delius's narrative was widely received as autobiography, yet it eschews the self-conscious gestures of remembering that abound in Harig's text. Zimmermann's commentary is cited extensively by Delius, and here the act of memory shifts toward a recoding of another text. Moreover, if *Der Sonntag* gives a utopian twist to the commentary, it also preserves its inherent ambiguities. Zimmermann's descriptions of German players and their formation — "eisern" (iron, *S*, 92), "Windhund[e]" (agile hounds, *S*, 92), "Schlachtenkolonne" (battle formation, *S*, 114) — suggest a militaristic rhetoric that points back to National Socialist Germany. This is shored up with postwar anticommunism where the Hungarians are dubbed an "Angriffsmaschine" (assault machine, *S*, 108). The ambiguities in the commentary indeed appear as open contradiction when German supporters simultaneously sing the permitted third verse of the national anthem — "*Einigkeit, Recht und Freiheit*" — and the forbidden first verse — "*Deutschland, Deutschland über alles*" (*S*, 116). The text constructs the World Cup victory as a point of a retrospective identification with the Federal Republic from a post-1968 perspective, but acknowledges a reality in which the liberal values that came to define it had been far from accepted. Thus the utopian reading of Zimmermann's commentary in *Der Sonntag* illustrates a structure of memory that not only preserves its ambivalences but also the possibility of other interpretations, a central attribute associated with cultural memory according to Aleida Assmann.[33] An important feature of the commentary is that it is a well-known text that has already accrued diverse meanings, including that of restoration in Fassbinder's *Die Ehe der Maria Braun*. These surely remain part of the meaning of Delius's text. Admittedly the commentary is reviewed from a first-person perspective informed by the later experience of 1968. But the central act of memory hinges on the accretion of meaning to this text, the signifiers of which are already the carriers of a cultural memory.

Reimagining "Restoration" II: Thomas Hettche's *Der Fall Arbogast*

The review of the early Federal Republic from a post-1968 perspective and by means of contemporaneous texts also marks Hettche's *Der Fall Arbogast*, published in 2001. Hettche's novel lacks the utopian moment of identification with the Federal Republic of the 1950s that characterizes Delius's text. And it exhibits a structure of memory that proceeds yet more visibly in the assignation of new meanings to texts, a process foregrounded thematically and formally. Perhaps this is unsurprising given the biography of a writer who made his name after 1990 with the texts *Inkubation* (1992) and *Nox* (1995), which explored in different contexts the inscription of the human body with meaning.[34] Born in 1964, Hettche did not know the 1950s and so cannot have needed the retrospective identification with the Federal Republic in this period which is so central in Delius's text.

Der Fall Arbogast fictionalizes a notorious criminal case of the 1950s and 1960s. In Hettche's version, Hans Arbogast, a married sales representative for a U.S. billiard tables firm, is tried in 1955 for the murder in 1953 of Marie Gürth, a married woman from a refugee camp whom he had picked up for sexual intercourse, during which, by a roadside in the Black Forest, she died. Though the first autopsy indicated heart failure, Arbogast is convicted when a respected pathologist identifies strangulation marks on photographs and infers a sexual murder. The novel closes with the quashing of the verdict in 1969 after the crime writer Fritz Sarrazin's "German League for Human Rights" takes up the case. With no West German pathologist willing to break from closed professional ranks, the crucial evidence comes from Katja Lavans, a pathologist from the GDR. The marks on the photographs, she testifies, were probably *post mortem* bruising, a process accepted by forensic science already in 1896.[35]

The novel constructs an impressive panorama of the Federal Republic between the early 1950s and the late 1960s. For critics, what is advertised as a "Kriminalroman" in the subtitle proved to be more a novel of society in which the murder case indexes the change of social climate during the Adenauer years and the liberalization of the late 1960s.[36] Indeed, the appeal hearing of 1969 makes it possible to recognize the extent to which the guilty verdict of 1955 comprised a moral judgment about the depravity of a sexual act that involved biting and possibly sodomy. The change in attitudes is clear when Lavans laconically backs the original assumption that the death was caused by heart failure: "Diese Art des Todes [. . .]

kommt übrigens häufiger extramarital vor als in der Ehe" (*F*, 317; this kind
of death incidentally occurs more often outside than within marriage).

The changing climate is evident too in the emergence of a dynamic
public sphere. By the 1960s critical organs like *Der Spiegel* were quick to
expose flaws in the original verdict; soon even *Bunte* declared it untenable
(*F*, 251). And shortly after Arbogast's release a relaxing of moral attitudes
was reflected benignly under the miscellaneous rubric "Deutschland und
die Welt" in the *Frankfurter Allgemeine Zeitung*:

> Nach einem [. . .] Aufenthalt in München, während dem Arbogast nach
> Angaben des Leiters des MÜNCHNER RATIONALTHEATER, Rainer
> Uttmann, als Berater für das "Knast"-Programm des politischen Theaters
> fungierte, reiste der ehemalige Häftling mit der [. . .] Ehefrau des
> Kabarettisten Jürgen Froemer ab. Dieser soll erklärt haben, er gebe seinen
> Eigentumsanspruch auf seine Frau auf. Uttmann bezeichnete den Vor-
> gang als bestes Beispiel zur Resozialisierung eines Gefangenen (*F*, 351).

> [After a stay in Munich, during which, according to Rainer Uttman, the
> director of the Munich "Rational Theater," Arbogast acted as advisor for
> the political theater's "prison"-cabaret, the former prisoner made off with
> the wife of the cabaret performer Jürgen Froemer. The latter is said to
> have renounced all claims on his wife. Uttman described the incident as
> the best possible example for the resocialization of a prisoner.]

In this mix of sexual permissiveness, politics, and performance, the text
radiates at the close the afterglow of 1968, in which the original events
emerge in a new light.

Yet neither a liberalization of attitudes nor a critical press finally secure
the appeal hearing for Arbogast, but the intervention of a pathologist from
the GDR. (Lavans is allowed by her state to travel to the FRG for the
appeal hearing for reasons of prestige.) If the history of the Federal Republic appears as a process of liberalization, it is neither seamless nor heroic.
On the contrary, it is a struggle fraught with tensions and with a real
human cost. The case, for example, illuminates a central contradiction of
the modern consumer society the Federal Republic was becoming in the
1950s. As Arbogast and Gürth drive off together at the opening in his
Borgward Isabella (a staple of the picture books about the 1950s mentioned near the opening of the chapter), his illicit sexual desires find a striking counterpoint in the sensuous way he strokes the car's "kühle und glatte
Holz der Türblätter" (*F*, 7; cool and smooth wooden door panels). Here is
an ascendant consumer society that depends for its existence on the investment of commodities with libido, yet maintains a strictly regimented sexual
and moral code. And when the case comes to appeal, the backward-looking
nature of an entrenched legal superstructure emerges with new clarity. The
criminal law used to convict Arbogast in 1955, according to his lawyer at
the appeal hearing, still bears the imprint of "den schleppenden, eitlen Ton

der Kaiserszeit [. . .], die gehetzte Diktion der Zwischenkriegszeit, [. . .] und schließlich die erschreckend planvolle Nüchternheit der Nazis" (*F*, 170; the vain and dragging tone of Imperial Germany, the hurried diction of the interwar years, and finally the shockingly methodical sobriety of the Nazis). The significance of the case is thus that it forcefully brings into motion contradictions between modern and backward-looking elements in society. Or as Sarrazin puts it near the close: "ich denke schon, daß jenes Geschehen damals so etwas wie ein Unfall war. Zugleich aber auch ein Ausbruch, eine Art von Ladungsübertragung, [. . .] ein letzter Rest des Krieges, der sich plötzlich entlud" (*F*, 340; I do think that what happened back then was a kind of accident. But at the same time also an explosion, the release of a charge, a last reminder of the war that was suddenly released.)

Der Fall Arbogast offers a contradictory and dynamic representation of the early Federal Republic. But in contrast to the autobiographical focus in Harig's text, Hettche's novel proceeds in its reconstruction of the era entirely through an engagement with pre-existing texts. The novel after all self-consciously fictionalizes an actual case, a procedure which commentators note, involved both archival research and citation from press sources so as to designate the textual material as "überprüfbar" (verifiable).[37] (In the original case it was a Hans Hensel who was convicted of killing Magdalene Gierth; Hettche's substantive alteration substitutes a male pathologist from the GDR with a woman, enabling a final sexual encounter all too pointedly laden with an ambiguity befitting of a "Kriminalroman" when Arbogast grasps Lavans's neck.)

It is the fictionalizing process that reveals the case's full social significance in the context of references to the changing times, from news about Adenauer (*F*, 98) to beginning political unrest (*F*, 106). Yet the reconstruction of the past through archival research in which texts are uncovered and placed in new contexts to produce new meanings is a central motif throughout. Bringing the case to appeal, Arbogast's legal team reviews various materials from the first trial and its coverage in the press. The original murder trial and the appeal hearing in the more liberal 1960s provide, not unlike the dialectic of Delius's text, a twin perspective through which documents — photos, the pathologists' reports — reveal differing meanings. The appeal, though, marks not just the reinterpretation of original evidence but also a critique of the process of interpretation, or rather misinterpretation, in which the earlier meanings were constructed.

Indeed, the inscription of new meanings into diverse discourses is perhaps the central aesthetic principle in the text. Hans Deppe's *Schwarzwaldmädel* (Black Forest Girl, 1951), for example, an archetypal escapist 1950s *Heimatfilm*, appears in a sinister light when Arbogast, in prison, recalls that he had thought about the car the film's female protagonist wins as he drove Gürth in his own new Isabella past one of the filming locations to her death (*F*, 51). The references to the Isabella too, with its characteristic "Geruch aus Holz und Plastik" (*F*, 172; smell of wood and plastic), typify a structure of memory that embeds the popular icons of the 1950s in a more complex social dynamic. Or consider Hettche's engagement with the "Kriminalroman," a favored popular form of the 1950s self-consciously employed in the exploration of the social and cultural meaning of the period.[38] It is arguably here, in the subject matter of the crime novel, that the novel reveals its link, finally, to the theme dominating Hettche's previous work: the human body and the construction of meanings about it. *Der Fall Arbogast* also examines how the body and bodily practices are inscribed in criminological, sexual, and moral discourses, discourses about consumption, and in philosophical critiques. This is most clearly evident, for example, in the way the sexual, moral, and criminological meanings of the encounter between Arbogast and Gürth are reshuffled between 1953 and 1969. Also striking in this regard is the contradiction highlighted in the text, reminiscent of Herbert Marcuse's critique of 1950s capitalism in his *Eros and Civilization* (1956), between desire regimented into the service of the act of consumption and given reign in the illicit sexual act.[39] A further example of the way the text explores the construction of meanings about the human body is the sub-Foucauldian "discipline and punish" discourse of the prison chaplain, who urges Arbogast to confess and who tells him that in prison his body is, "im Verhältnis zum Staat, der ihn einsperrt, sozusagen exterritoriales Gelände" (*F*, 62; exterritorial, as it were, in relation to the state imprisoning it).[40] *Der Fall Arbogast* joins the texts by Harig and Delius in offering a differentiated reconstruction of the history of the Federal Republic in the 1950s neither simply as West German restoration nor uncritically in thrall to simplistic accounts of the postwar success story of the FRG. Yet Hettche suggests a structure of memory progressively stripped of its (individual) subjective component. Harig's autobiographical act offers some of the richness of the communicative memory posited by theorists of cultural memory. In Delius's text, the act of memory proceeds as the recoding of a previously transmitted text, if from the perspective of a first-person narrator and on the basis of a recollection of 1968. *Der Fall Arbogast* points finally to the blank materiality of the body and the discourses with which it is encoded as the underlying "transmission system" of cultural memory.[41]

Conclusions

A wealth of recent writing points to an ongoing interest in the 1950s in the Federal Republic of Germany. Not least the caesura of 1989/90 has served to ensure the enduring fascination exerted by the formative years of the Federal Republic as they continue to be cast into new historical light.

Against the background of a range of discourses, I have argued that the recent literary presentations of the decade contribute to a breaking open of the received idea of West German restoration to reveal a more dynamic and contradictory conception of the period. In Harig's *Wer mit den Wölfen heult*, restoration figures as one among a number of competing discourses that are filtered through an autobiographical perspective. Delius's *Der Sonntag, an dem Ich Weltmeister wurde* introduces a dialectical, even utopian moment into an apparently monolithic atmosphere of restoration from a more liberal post-1968 perspective. Hettche's *Der Fall Arbogast* reconstructs the era in terms of central contradictions between the consumer society the Federal Republic was becoming and an entrenched moral and legal superstructure. The differentiated picture of the era painted here is informed by other more recent discourses about modernization and the "success story" of the Federal Republic, though these too are thrown into critical relief. But what is perhaps most memorable about the texts in question are the issues they raise about the construction of cultural memory as the era starts to recede from living memory. In Harig's text, an autobiographical act of memory comprised elements of both communicative and cultural memory within the framework of a literary genre that might serve the transformation of the first into the second. By contrast, the shift towards a cultural memory appears yet more visibly in the works by Delius and Hettche, authors with a different biographical relationship to the period, in a shift of the burden of memory toward cultural texts previously encoded with meaning. In this process, literary discourse emerges not simply as the vehicle of cultural memory, but as a site in which its mechanisms are laid bare to become themselves the object of scrutiny. The 1950s will not fade from memory as long as writers continue to find such interesting ways to explore the process of remembering them.

Notes

[1] See Ludwig Harig, *Also Ordnung ist das ganze Leben* (Munich and Vienna: Hanser, 1986) and his *Wehe dem, der aus der Reihe tanzt* (Munich and Vienna: Hanser, 1990). See also the shorter pieces in *Und wenn sie nicht gestorben sind: Aus meinem Leben* (Munich and Vienna: Hanser, 2002).

[2] Ludwig Harig, *Wer mit den Wölfen heult, wird Wolf* (Munich and Vienna: Hanser, 1996), 190–91. Hereafter *W*.

[3] John Paul Eakin, *Fictions in Autobiography: Studies in the Art of Self-Invention* (Princeton, NJ: Princeton UP, 1985), 7–8.

[4] For instance Roy Pascal, *Design and Truth in Autobiography* (London: Routledge, 1960), 185.

[5] Axel Schildt and Arnold Sywottek, "'Reconstruction' and 'Modernization': West German Social History during the 1950s," in *West Germany under Reconstruction*, ed. Robert G. Moeller (Ann Arbor: U of Michigan P, 1997), 413–43; here: 414.

[6] Axel Schildt, *Moderne Zeiten: Freizeit, Massenmedien und "Zeitgeist" in der Bundesrepublik der 50er Jahre* (Hamburg: Christians, 1995), 19.

[7] Schildt, *Moderne Zeiten*, 19.

[8] Helmut Schelsky, "Gesellschaftlicher Wandel" (1956), in *Auf der Suche nach Wirklichkeit. Gesammelte Aufsätze* (Düsseldorf & Cologne: Diedrichs, 1965), 337–51; here: 340–41.

[9] Hajo Bücken and Dieter Rex, *Die wilden Fünfziger* (Reichelsheim: Edition XXL, 2001).

[10] On the question of periodization see Arnold Sywottek, "Wege in die 50er Jahre," in *Modernisierung im Wiederaufbau: Die westdeutsche Gesellschaft der 50er Jahre*, ed. Axel Schildt and Arnold Sywottek (Bonn: Dietz, 1993), 19–39.

[11] Paul Betts, "The *Nierentisch* Nemesis: Organic Design as West German Pop Culture," *German History* 19 (2001): 185–217; here: 185.

[12] Betts, "The *Nierentisch* Nemesis," 185.

[13] Aleida Assmann and Ute Frevert, *Geschichtsvergessenheit — Geschichtsversessenheit: Vom Umgang mit deutschen Vergangenheiten nach 1945* (Stuttgart: Deutsche Verlags-Anstalt, 1999), 36.

[14] Assmann and Frevert, *Geschichtsvergessenheit*, 49–50.

[15] Assmann and Frevert, *Geschichtsvergessenheit*, 50–51.

[16] A comprehensive account of issues in autobiographical theory is Laura Marcus, *Auto/biographical Discourses: Criticism, Theory, Practice* (Manchester: Manchester UP, 1994).

[17] Andrew Plowman, "'Westalgie?' Nostalgia for the 'Old' Federal Republic in Recent German Prose," *Seminar* 40 (2004): 1–14; and "'Was will ich als Westdeutscher erzählen?': The 'old' West and Globalisation in Recent German Prose," in *German Literature and The Age of Globalisation*, ed. Stuart Taberner (Birmingham: Birmingham UP, 2004), 47–66.

[18] See Ingo Cornils, "Long Memories: The German Student Movement in Recent Fiction," *German Life and Letters* 56 (2003): 89–101.

[19] Stuart Taberner, *German Literature of the 1990s and Beyond: Normalization and the Berlin Republic* (Rochester, NY: Camden House, 2005), 68–69, 78–79.

[20] Karl Heinz Bohrer, "Provinzialismus," *Merkur* 44 (1990): 1096–1102.

[21] Jan-Werner Müller, *Another Country: German Intellectuals, Unification and National Identity* (New Haven and London: Yale UP, 2000), 129–30.

[22] Axel Schildt, *Ankunft im Westen: Ein Essay zur Erfolgsgeschichte der Bundesrepublik* (Frankfurt am Main: S. Fischer, 1999), 17.

[23] Betts, "The *Nierentisch* Nemesis," 185 and Schildt, *Moderne Zeiten*, 19.

[24] For example Lothar Rühle, "Ein Patriarch vom Rhein. Der Kanzler Konrad Adenauer" and Gudrun Patricia Pott, "Die Flegeljahre der Republik. Der Aufstieg aus dem Nichts," *Der Spiegel*, 18 May 1999, 110–15 and 148–50.

[25] Schildt, *Moderne Zeiten*, 32.

[26] Schildt, *Ankunft im Westen*, 92.

[27] Schildt, *Moderne Zeiten*, 21.

[28] Gerd Koenen, *Das rote Jahrzehnt: Unsere kleine deutsche Kulturrevolution* (Cologne: Kiepenheuer und Witsch, 2001), 22.

[29] F. C. Delius, *Der Sonntag, an dem ich Weltmeister wurde* (Reinbek: Rowohlt, 1994), 115. Hereafter *S*.

[30] Michael Schaffrath, "'Wir sind wieder wer.' Die wachsende Bedeutung der Sportkultur," in *Die Kultur der 50er Jahre*, ed. Werner Faulstich (Munich: Wilhelm Fink, 2002), 145–57; here: 145–46.

[31] Simonetta Janna, "Sprachpuzzle und Selbstfindung. Delius' *Der Sonntag, an dem ich Weltmeister wurde*," in *F. C. Delius: Studien über sein literarisches Werk*, ed. Manfred Durzak (Tübingen: Stauffenberg, 1997), 163–80; here: 167.

[32] Müller, *Another Country*, 129–30.

[33] Assmann and Frevert, *Geschichtsvergessenheit*, 50.

[34] Timo Koslowski, "Thomas Hettche," in *Kritisches Lexikon Gegenwartsliteratur*, ed. Heinz Ludwig Arnold (Munich: Edition Text + Kritik, 2002), 4–8.

[35] Thomas Hettche, *Der Fall Arbogast* (Cologne: Dumont, 2001), 312. Hereafter *F*.

[36] Koslowski, "Thomas Hettche," 9.

[37] Koslowski, "Thomas Hettche," 9.

[38] Schildt, *Moderne Zeiten*, 129–30.

[39] Herbert Marcuse, *Eros and Civilization. A Philosophical Enquiry into Freud* (Boston: Beacon Press, 1956), 123.

[40] Michel Foucault, *Discipline and Punish: The Birth of the Prison*, trans. by Alan Sheridan (Harmondsworth: Allen Lane, 1977), 231–56.

[41] Paul Connerton, *How Societies Remember* (Cambridge: Cambridge UP, 1989), 1.

13: On Forgetting and Remembering: The New Right since German Unification

Roger Woods

The New Right and Postmemory

LOCATED AT THE INTERSECTION of culture and politics and to the right of mainstream conservatism, the New Right in Germany today provides an interesting case study in forgetting and remembering. What kind of collective political and cultural memory is the New Right trying to construct, and how much of a turning point was German unification for this construction? The New Right has seen generational change among its own ranks since it came into existence at the end of the sixties, and a key question of postmemory[1] — what happens to the memory of National Socialism with the passing of the generations that experienced it directly? — has a particular relevance for the New Right since some of the figures associated with its early years rejected National Socialism only after a period of direct support and involvement with it. The answers to these questions are complicated by the fact that the New Right is a political and a cultural movement, and the relationship between its political and cultural dimensions is far from harmonious. New Right culture was meant to function as a political resource, providing a set of values as the foundation for a New Right program. By the start of the seventies it had become apparent to advocates of a self-assertive German nationalism that the Right needed to give itself an intellectual dimension that would help it gain broad public support in the pre-political sphere before it could expect electoral success. But the New Right culture that emerged from this process of intellectualization has frequently been at odds with New Right politics. In contemporary Germany's memory contests New Right culture is not just doing battle with other cultures; it is doing battle with itself.

The following analysis will suggest how understanding the New Right as a cultural and political whole can shed light on its internal tensions over issues of remembering the past, and it will consider which models of culture provide an appropriate framework for analyzing these tensions. Three key aspects of New Right thought that are bound up with the question of memory will be examined: culture itself, the Nazi past, and the German nation.

What is the New Right?

The New Right has been a force in German political and cultural life for some thirty-five years, and in that time it has provided a loud and persistent voice, especially since German unification, in favor of a German identity that marks itself off from that of Western Europe. The loose network of politicians, writers, academics, and journalists that make up the New Right is constantly in the public eye, through the controversial activities of the political parties associated with it — virtually all parties of the radical or extreme right call themselves New Right — through its newspapers and journals, through its organizations, which run seminars, summer schools, and conferences, through its Internet presence, or through the hotly debated pronouncements of its most prominent representatives.[2] Botho Strauß's "Anschwellender Bocksgesang" (Swelling Tragic Chorus), a highly articulate attack on the foundations of German liberalism, was originally published in *Der Spiegel* in 1993 and provoked a public debate that continued for many months.[3] The New Right's best known advocates make the news by publishing detailed accounts of their political aims and cultural values. One example is the bestselling volume *Die selbstbewußte Nation* (The Confident Nation) which appeared in 1994 and may be regarded as the manifesto of the New Right.[4] Its voice is heard not least because it is one of the more articulate advocates of ideas to the right of the mainstream conservative parties. Whether the public debate is on German identity or the role of nationalism in postunification Germany, remembering National Socialism, or immigration and multiculturalism, the New Right is quick to speak out and sure of a sharp response from its left-wing and liberal opponents, and it is not least through this action and reaction that the New Right makes its presence felt in public debate in Germany.

Most commentators see a close link between the New Right and right-wing extremism: *Der Spiegel* described the movement as "Braune in Nadelstreifen" (brownshirts in pinstripes),[5] and academics and the Bundesamt für Verfassungsschutz (Federal Office for the Protection of the Constitution) regularly express their concerns about the New Right's attempts to gain cultural acceptance for an aggressive nationalism and about its attempt to undermine German democracy.[6] Yet its pronouncements generally serve to confirm its notoriety rather than to establish the cultural hegemony it aspires to. Its political significance is not as great as its significance as a symptom of cultural and political unease.

The secondary literature on the New Right defines it as an antidemocratic movement[7] dating back to the late sixties or early seventies and refers to it variously as the Young Right, Young Conservatism or neo-conservatism.[8] Political scientists home in on its rejection of universalism, pluralism, liberalism, parliamentarianism, equality, and multiculturalism, on its ranking of the collective above the individual, and its wish to see a strong state and a strong leader instead of political decision-making through negotiation and compromise. Jaschke defines the New Right by pointing to its rejection of the French Revolution and the associated principles of freedom, equality, and fraternity.[9] In their place the New Right seeks to establish a "Volksgemeinschaft" (community of the people), based on a supposed natural inequality of races and on the rule of an elite (Jaschke, 7). Gessenharter points out that the New Right rejects neo-Nazism and racism but is committed to the related concept of ethnopluralism (60–61). Underlying all these positions, he argues, is a resurgent nationalism: 1989 marked the end of Germany's postwar history for the New Right, which asserts that Germany should no longer allow itself to be led by the nose. It should overcome its long-established habit of putting other countries' interests ahead of its own, and it should become a culturally, economically, and politically dominant country (15–16). For Gessenharter the New Right represents a clearly delineated set of views and aims: rejection of individualism and liberalism in favor of the collective, and the promotion of a homogeneous society based on authoritarian structures (14).[10] These definitions and characterizations are notable for their clarity, and presenting the New Right as if there were clarity about what it stood for is a feature of much research on the movement. The debate among academics tends to be about which clear programmatic points to include in any definition and where the ideological line can be drawn between the New Right and other right-wing groups.

Yet these clear definitions do not fully reflect the multi-faceted, even contradictory nature of New Right sources: although the New Right has a set of recurrent themes, it is far from being united in its treatment of them. The political goals cited by observers to characterize the New Right do indeed feature in its thinking, but at one point or another they are all called into question by figures within the movement itself. Kurt Lenk suggests that the New Right displays an unbending obsession with a series of noble collective concepts that provide a kind of foundation for its worldview; furthermore he argues that the "Volk" (the people) and the "Reich" (the Empire) are invoked by the New Right as the fixed points and the substance of a new identity.[11] Yet this presentation of the New Right overlooks its capacity for self-doubt and the full complexity of New Right sources. This complexity is rooted in the culture of the New Right.

New Right Culture

New Right culture has two mutually exclusive functions: on the one hand culture is mobilized as the source of reassuring certainty and the foundation for political values in the midst of uncertainty and loss of direction. New Right culture that fulfills this function may be labeled feelgood culture. On the other hand New Right culture is the medium for reflecting on chaotic human experience that renders politics irrelevant. The cultural certainty and rootedness the New Right seeks to provide has to coexist with a current of cultural doubt and despair.

Stefan Ulbrich expresses the reassuring, feelgood version of culture when he describes it in the pages of *Junge Freiheit* (Young Freedom), the leading newspaper of the New Right, as one means by which the individual establishes roots and becomes at one with himself and with others. Culture, writes Ulbrich, is a complex network of behavior patterns that lends direction to people's lives. Cultural identity provides common goals and a sense of rootedness, of being at one with oneself and with shared traditions, of being part of a system of values and norms that is greater than the individual.[12]

This take on culture is widespread within the New Right, fulfilling what Karlheinz Weißmann refers to as the human need for permanence, community, and security.[13] The feelgood version of culture is present in the thinking of the Republikaner, the party that has been regarded at various points in the history of the New Right as its political wing. The 2002 party program proclaims Germany as one of the great cultural nations of the world, and this culture is thought to be Christian and Western. Western culture is the foundation of state and society, and this culture is in turn based on Christian principles that shape our views on the family, marriage, and the protection of the unborn child. They are the force behind the drive for freedom, democracy, and social justice.[14]

New Right feelgood culture is not a random collection of values but rather the sphere in which the individual has a fixed place. This version of culture is also a non-universalist concept, suggesting that it provides the contents of an exclusive national identity.[15] Ex-Bundestag member and New Right author Alfred Mechtersheimer takes these arguments one step further by seeing culture as the shared foundation for a political position in which the nation is based on a community of the will. This community lays claim to its right to be different from other communities, with its identity deriving from a shared culture, language, religion, or history. The sense of nation emerges from an awareness of shared values and aims, and it satisfies the basic human need to belong.[16] Mechtersheimer's points have a slightly different feel to them, with the wish for rootedness at their heart. His understanding of the link between culture and politics is different from Ulbrich's view of shared and unshakable cultural traditions and values. It is different also from the Republikaner view of culture as the driving force behind politics. For Mechtersheimer culture is one potential focal point for bringing a nation together. The community of the will indicates not an automatic and irrevocable belonging but rather a conscious commitment, a decision behind the concept of the nation. The need for absolute bonds and a sense of belonging comes first in Mechtersheimer's thinking, and the nation comes second as a means of satisfying the need.

The political consequences of cultural bonds are set out with great regularity in New Right publications. Karlheinz Weißmann quotes from an article written in 1927 by the conservative revolutionary Friedrich Hielscher. To the east of Germany, says Hielscher, lie the lands of culture. This culture has deep roots and a permanence lacking in the West. Germany also possesses a great culture and is therefore a brother to these lands, which sustain noble and powerful traditions.[17]

Yet the New Right also shows an awareness that the feelgood culture that was meant to provide the foundation for politics is no longer intact. What has been lost is a specifically German culture that was once not open to criticism but gave way to a Western pluralist culture after 1945.[18] The New Right wish for a feelgood culture to provide the basis for politics is not readily met.

This problem is relatively minor, however, when compared with the profound pessimism that pervades New Right culture — to the point of rendering politics irrelevant. Botho Strauß, whose "Anschwellender Bocksgesang" was the key essay in the volume *Die selbstbewußte Nation*, writes of human existence as a "beängstigendes Abenteuer der Selbstbegegnung" (an alarming adventure of encountering oneself) in his volume of philosophical reflections, *Beginnlosigkeit* (No Beginning, 1992), which appeared just one year before "Anschwellender Bocksgesang": the very delicate chemical balance at work in the body between chaos and ossification, form and formlessness allows us to create our image of the world, but the balance may be lost at any moment. In *Beginnlosigkeit* Strauß registers a crisis of consciousness that must shake us to the core. This effect reaches right into language, for many New Right authors one of the defining features of a *Volk*. Strauß does not reflect on language as the basis for a community. He is taken up instead with the language of public communication, which he describes as exhausted.[19]

If the original hope was that culture would provide a solid foundation for a political program, Botho Strauß throws a large spanner in the works. In his recent book of reflections, *Der Untenstehende auf Zehenspitzen* (Down Below on Tiptoes, 2004), he argues that in cultural terms the big bang was the exploding of myth. The fragments of myth hurtle past us and through us, traveling ever further away from their original wholeness and their religious core, and he identifies the irreversible process of expansion, slowing, and cooling at work in the universe with the process of spiritual decline.[20] This image is a novel formulation of the longstanding notion of a descent from culture into civilization that is at the heart of conservative cultural pessimism.[21] Strauß expresses this pessimism more directly and ties it to a rejection of political commitment in *Beginnlosigkeit*, where he declares that his attitude is characterized by "Kummer" (grief). He makes it clear that one cannot base politics on such a position: "Aus dem Kummer, aus dem aufrichtigsten Gefühl des Menschen, wird nie ein Manifest hervorgehen, kein Vorschlag für die Welt, sie in dieser oder jener Gestalt zu sehen, keine Lehre, keine Prophetie" (grief, humankind's most sincere emotion, will never give rise to a manifesto, a program for reshaping the world in this way or that, a doctrine or a prophecy).[22] In *Die Fehler des Kopisten* (The Copyist's Mistakes, 1997) Strauß paints a picture of society that is exhausted. One can only expect to see it bleed to death. And as for politics, Strauß cannot discern in political groups anything good or even the prospect of anything good.[23]

Other New Right figures take a similarly pessimistic line. Quoting Heidegger's famous image for existence, the writer Hartmut Lange declares:

> Wer aus nichtigem Grund in diese Welt geworfen ist und eben diese Nichtigkeit als Grund selbst zu übernehmen und wie eine Schuld abzuarbeiten hat, wie sollte der noch von Parteiprogrammen oder sonstigen politisch motivierten Hilfsversprechen zu beeindrucken sein? "Dasein heißt — Hineingehaltenheit in das Nichts" — vor diesem Satz besteht keine nationalistische Parole mehr, aber auch keine Sehnsucht nach einer verlorengegangenen völkischen Identität.[24]

> [How could anyone who is propelled out of the void into this world, having to accept the void itself as a foundation and work it off like some kind of guilt, be impressed by party programs or any other kind of politically motivated promises of help? "Existence means being held out into nothingness" — no nationalist slogan or yearning for some long-lost identity based on race can stand up to this declaration.]

This particular brand of New Right culture could hardly be more at odds with the feelgood culture, and it is a troublesome companion for New Right politics; its profound pessimism leaves no room for redemptive politics. In this respect the New Right illustrates what Zygmunt Bauman refers to as the functional and dysfunctional roles of culture. Culture as an exploring, questioning, even negating force can contribute to disorder rather than order.[25] Hermann Glaser refers to the "clair-obscur" nature of culture: creating meaning but also calling into question established sources of meaning. Culture is characterized by its lack of certainty and its tendency to find questions rather than answers.[26] Looking more closely at theorizing on the interaction of culture and politics gives a similar picture; sociological research on the relationship between culture and politics, more specifically between culture and national identity, seems to anticipate the New Right dilemma of wanting to project an intact national identity based on culture even as the movement sees through the cultural concepts it mobilizes. Stuart Hall points out that the anti-essentialist critique of ethnic, racial, and national conceptions of cultural identity has not supplanted inadequate concepts with "truer" ones. Rather it has put key concepts of identity "under erasure," indicating on the one hand that they are no longer serviceable, but on the other that they have not been superseded and there are no other, entirely different concepts to replace them. There is nothing to do but to continue to think with them.[27] Hall describes the concepts of identification and identity in the cultural sphere as "a construction, a process never completed." Identification is "conditional, lodged in contingency," and the "total merging" it suggests is a "fantasy of incorporation" (2–3). Cultural identity cannot be an "unchanging one-ness"; it is rather "fragmented and fractured," constantly in the process of change and transformation. Hall concludes that identities are about "questions of using the resources of history, language and culture in the process of becoming rather than being: not 'who we are' or 'where we came from' so much as what we might become" (4). Linked to this is also the idea of culture as a contested site or contested space rather than a fixed body of beliefs. One thinks of identity, argues Bauman, whenever one is not sure of where one belongs. Identity is a name given to the escape sought from uncertainty.[28]

These propositions about the nature of modern culture are cited here because they offer an apt description of the culture of the New Right. The search for absolute values through culture is without a doubt one of the deeper structures of New Right thinking. But New Right culture does not provide a simple and reassuring message. Hajo Funke regards the cultural-ization of politics, that is, the replacement of the traditional right-wing concept of race with the concept of culture, and presentation of culture as the basis of a German identity, as one of the key innovative features of the New Right. He argues that for the New Right culture is a source of collective meaning for the "Volk," which is born into this culture, through the myths of its origins, language, and history. Cultural identity is the basis for an ethnically homogeneous and hierarchically structured society.[29] This is in fact a description of what the New Right is trying, but largely failing, to achieve. Culturalization of politics turns out to be a very uncomfortable and costly process for the New Right, for it brings with it not only functionality but also dysfunctionality, as Baumann uses the terms. When New Right intellectuals turn their attention to cultural values, they do so in a highly critical way, concluding not only that stereotypical cultural images of German identity have little meaning but also that these images cannot be mobilized for political purposes. Moreover they demonstrate a cultural pessimism that politics can do little or nothing to alleviate. This suggests that the intellectuals who operate as more or less autonomous agents within the loose structure of the New Right and exercise their critical faculties may not be in the business of providing absolute values; they may be a disruptive presence rather than a homogenizing force. In terms of memory contests, New Right attempts at reviving the memory of an intact culture must compete with the New Right insight that when it thinks of the past it is thinking of what is irretrievable; this is what Botho Strauß means when he argues that the right-wing imagination does not deal in visions of the future but lives with an awareness of loss.[30]

Remembering the Nazi Past

A further tension in New Right thinking underlies the debate on remembering the Nazi past; the political drive to relativize the Nazi past competes with the cultural view that the Nazi legacy is Germany's property for all time.

The relativizing tendency is at work when Günter Rohrmoser stresses that the Germans did not know of Hitler's real aims,[31] when Karlheinz Weißmann argues that Germans were attracted to National Socialism by its idealism and religiosity and were not interested in the party program or anti-Semitism,[32] when the Allied plans to destroy Germany are given prominence,[33] and when the German people are portrayed as having been deceived by Hitler.[34] The New Right is also intent on rescuing something to remember with pride from the war years. The problem of remembering the war is presented through New Right eyes by Brigitte Seebacher-Brandt, who writes that whereas other countries honor their dead and find a unity through the act of remembrance, Germany does not allow itself this bond. "Mort pour la patrie" is the proud inscription on war memorials in every French village, she reflects, but for what German fatherland were Jews annihilated, resistance crushed, a war waged, and an army sacrificed?[35] Against this background the New Right creates its positive memories through a decontextualization of the war effort. German soldiers in the Second World War are portrayed as heroic and their heroism as an end in itself. Armin Mohler thus redefines the war "nicht im nationalsozialistischen Sinn als Befreiungskrieg eines eingekreisten Volkes" (not in the National Socialist sense of a war of liberation fought by an encircled people), but as struggle for its own sake.[36] In *Junge Freiheit* the virtues of the German soldiers are removed from their historical context and presented as laudable in their own right. Wolfgang Venohr thus describes the situation of the soldiers of the Wehrmacht, deep inside Russian territory and facing a military disaster on a Napoleonic scale.[37] He turns to the memoirs of a German flying officer to describe the conditions at the eastern front; in the vast snowy wastes the German soldiers were hopelessly equipped, but they held the line at every point, bringing the Soviet counterattack to a halt. Venohr praises the Germans who fought in these conditions as heroes whose achievements are unmatched in the military history of any nation (15).

For the New Right the memory of the soldiers who fought in the Second World War can be rescued if it is detached from Nazi war aims. Venohr has no doubts on this point: it is not the German soldiers' fault that they were involved in an unjust war. On the eastern front they were vastly outnumbered, and what they achieved was nothing less than miraculous (15).

Yet Venohr drifts from his original position in which the war is considered in its own right when he describes the Bolshevik offensive. German aggression seems ultimately to be justified in Venohr's eyes as he explains how the German soldiers rescued Germany from communism. If they had abandoned their positions the Bolshevik army would have been massed on Germany's eastern border by 1942, and on its western border by 1943. The whole of Germany would have had to put up with what the East Germans eventually had to bear on their own. There would have been no Federal Republic or European Community, nor would Germany have known freedom (15).

The New Right holds the Wehrmacht in high esteem as the German institution that offered the strongest resistance to the spirit of Nazism.[38] This is the reason for the New Right's hostile response to the exhibition "Vernichtungskrieg. Verbrechen der Wehrmacht 1941 bis 1944" (War of Annihilation: Crimes of the Wehrmacht 1941 to 1944). The exhibition, mounted by the Hamburg Institute for Social Research, dealt with crimes of the Wehrmacht during the Second World War. It toured thirty-three German and Austrian cities between 1995 and 1999, but it was then withdrawn after experts cast doubt on the accuracy of the descriptions of some of the photographic exhibits. A new exhibition on the subject was launched in November 2001 in Berlin. The New Right called the original exhibition one of those defamatory hate shows that is only possible in Germany,[39] and Erich Vad, a CSU specialist in foreign and security policy, asked what army ever remained blameless in war. The problem for Vad is that, despite the availability of a wealth of empirical historical evidence, an exhibition with a similar purpose would be unthinkable in Washington, Paris, London, or Moscow. In these capitals, he asserts, they honor those who lost their lives in war.[40]

In the wake of the exhibition some fifty articles for *Junge Freiheit* stress the Wehrmacht's opposition to Hitler and Hitler's mistrust of the Wehrmacht,[41] and in an interview with *Junge Freiheit* a colonel proposes a day of remembrance for the men who planned and carried out the bomb plot of 20 July 1944. These men, he argues, were the fathers of the tradition honored by the Bundeswehr.[42] Yet the substance of this tradition is called into question by the New Right itself. Stauffenberg, Goerdeler, and Tresckow are made to do service at one point as representatives of the other Germany,[43] but their political beliefs are dismissed elsewhere as outmoded. In the journal *Criticon* Harald Holz suggests a mental experiment of introducing a "Gedenktag der Nationalen Ehre" (Day of National Honor) to be celebrated each year on 20 July, but he adds immediately that he is not thinking of any particular socio-political models such as the corporative state put forward by the groups involved in the attempt on Hitler's life. Rather he is thinking of their commitment to rescuing Germany's honor, even at the cost of their own lives.[44] Holz is clearly uneasy about Stauffenberg's politics since the corporations of employers and employees that he favored had a model in fascist Italy. The limitations of this other Germany are formulated more forcefully by the New Right author Rainer Zitelmann, who supposes that the political views of men such as von Hassell, Goerdeler or Stauffenberg would today be regarded not just as right-wing but as extreme right-wing.[45] For the New Right the ideas of 20 July 1944 cannot provide the basis for any kind of alternative vision for Germany.

The New Right sees German unification as a turning point, marking the end of German postwar history and the start of a newly confident history. Yet this confidence is not so easily gained. Just as the political voice of the New Right is attempting to draw a line under the Nazi past, Botho Strauß is once more the prominent critical voice. In his "Anschwellender Bocksgesang" he raises National Socialist crimes to the existential level and thus puts them beyond any kind of "Vergangenheitsbewältigung" (overcoming the past): Nazi crimes are so enormous, writes Strauß, that they cannot be compensated for by moral shame or any other bourgeois sentiments. These crimes leave Germans under a massive burden, and guilt cannot be worked off through the passing of generations. Such is Germany's fate.[46] Strauß's interpretation flows from his cultural pessimism, and it is no mere passing thought. He returns to it in *Die Fehler des Kopisten*, where he writes that for five or six years the Germans had been intoxicated with the Nazi idea of community. Their punishment for this intoxication is to examine for a thousand years how it could have happened. Part of Germany's damned past is the eternal nature of its damnation.[47] Strauß's view is impossible to reconcile with the more conventional views expressed by politicians associated with the New Right: Franz Schönhuber, one-time leader of the Republikaner, argues that the guilt stemming from National Socialism can be worked off over time and that one can draw a line under the Nazi past by demonstrating that there was nothing unique about it.[48]

One further New Right strategy for dealing with the Nazi past is to argue for it to be forgotten for the sake of the present. Günter Rohrmoser develops the strategy in his consideration of why, as far as he is concerned, there was no debate in West Germany about fascism in the first twenty years after the war. His answer: because it would have been impossible to construct a democracy after 1945 with such a debate going on in the background. One could not put a large section of the population in the dock and expect to build a democracy with these people even as one was discriminating against them.[49] Taking this line of thought even further, Rohrmoser argues that the GDR declared any responsibility for National Socialism had been eliminated with the establishment of a socialist state. Rohrmoser seems to show a degree of admiration for this stance when he claims that the GDR would have collapsed much sooner if it had not ruled out any discussion about the Nazi past (37–38). The psychology of this attitude towards history, which wants nothing to do with Habermas's critical appropriation, is illuminated by Peter Meier-Bergfeld, correspondent for *Rheinische Merkur* in Austria and a contributor to *Die selbstbewußte Nation*. Meier-Bergfeld writes of the permanent Third Reich retrospective running in the cinemas of the Federal Republic. He argues that a preoccupation with the Nazi past makes Germany incapable of having a present or a future, and he quotes Nietzsche: "Es gibt einen Grad von Schlaflosigkeit, von Wiederkauen, von historischem Sinn, bei dem das Lebendige zu Schaden kommt und zuletzt zugrunde geht, sei es nun ein Mensch oder ein Volk oder eine Kultur" (there is a level of insomnia, of rumination, of historical awareness that is damaging to life and that ultimately causes life to perish, whether it is a person or a people or a culture).[50] Instead of presenting an intellectually coherent answer to the question of how to deal with the Nazi past, Meier-Bergfeld contents himself with a complaint about the debilitating effects of the act of remembering. Here again, the cultural dimension of the New Right sheds light on a mentality that is unable to bear uncertainty. If a simple faith in an unchallenged past is not to be had, then this past should not be discussed. Nietzschean vitalism provides the either-or construction, with reflection losing out to life.

Remembering the Nation

One might suppose that at least the nation and nationalism were beyond question in New Right thought. Certainly an assertive nationalism is a consistent feature of New Right political philosophy. Pierre Krebs of the Thule-Seminar argues that the revolution that swept away Marxism in the East is now surging ahead and demanding much more than German unification. It is seeking Germany's roots, its historical memory, and its essential character, and it is reaching out to those founding myths that made Germany special, unique, and different.[51]

There can be no doubt that nationalism is a key element in the psychology of the New Right. Karlheinz Weißmann argues that there is no discernible alternative to the nation, no other modern form of political community that satisfies the human need for clarity.[52] But strident New Right nationalism is like the feelgood culture. Beneath it runs a deeper current of doubt about the viability and relevance of nationalism. An examination of conflicting New Right attitudes reveals an acute awareness that nationalism is a compromised value. The tension over the issue of the nation is demonstrated in the very different diagnoses of Germany's problems offered by Pierre Krebs and Karlheinz Weißmann. For Krebs the obstacle to Germany reasserting itself on the world stage is the external one of Western allies imposing a re-education on Germany that forced it to break with its intellectual traditions. By contrast Karlheinz Weißmann traces Germany's lack of confidence to its military defeat, which was internalized to become a spiritual defeat. For this reason Weißmann quotes the poet Gottfried Benn's wartime diaries on his wishes for Germany:

> Wünsche für Deutschland: neue Begriffsbestimmung für Held und Ehre. Ausmerzung jeder Person, die innerhalb der nächsten hundert Jahre Preußentum oder das Reich sagt. Geschichte als Verwaltung mittleren Beamten des gehobenen Dienstes überlassen, aber als Richtung und Prinzip einer europäischen Exekutive öffentlich unterstellen. Die Kinder vom sechsten bis sechzehnten Jahr nach Wahl der Eltern in der Schweiz, in England, Frankreich, Amerika, Dänemark, auf Staatskosten erziehen.[53]

> [Wishes for Germany: new definition of hero and honor. Eradication of anyone saying the words Prussianism or Reich in the next one hundred years. History as an administrative matter to be left to middle-ranking civil servants, its direction and guiding principles to be publicly handed over to a European executive body. Children to be educated from the age of six to sixteen, according to the parents' preference and at the state's expense, in Switzerland, England, France, America, Denmark.]

Benn's words express a chronic loss of confidence, not a sense of being subjugated to Western re-education. If Armin Mohler imported the ideas of Alain de Benoist, the most prominent French New Right intellectual, in order to prompt the German New Right to work out a coherent set of positions for itself, the message de Benoist brings with him is a challenging one. Whereas de Benoist had been happy enough in the mid-eighties to see the nation and the fatherland as the ultimate realities, by the time he began thinking about globalization in the new millennium he had radically rethought the role of the nation. For de Benoist the fall of the Berlin Wall marked the start of the postmodern era, in which all political remains of Modernity are rendered obsolete. This obsolescence includes not only the competition between parties but also the nation state, an entity that is too big to respond to the everyday concerns of its citizens and too small to counter world-scale threats. In the face of globalization there is a temptation to emphasize one's own identity, notes de Benoist, yet if one says one is a Frenchman or a German one needs to explain what this means. Identity is not static but dynamic, and it cannot be limited to a more or less idealized past. Identity is no longer natural, and in the postmodern period there are no absolute foundations upon which it might rest. He dismisses the notion that one can escape globalization by clinging to ethnocentric notions of identity in a bunker mentality. It is also a mistake to attempt to stop history in its tracks. Right-wing movements have spent the previous century fighting battles that were lost from the start. There is no point in complaining about the present and mourning for the past.[54]

De Benoist's harsh judgment on so many items of faith, not just of traditional conservatism but also of the New Right, is anticipated within the

German New Right. The 1995 volume of essays, *Wir 89er* (We 89ers), authored by the younger generation of the New Right, has little time for a German identity based on the nation as a fixed point, supposedly providing absolute political bonds. Whereas Alfred Mechtersheimer, a representative of the older generation of the New Right, had argued that the nation fulfilled the basic human need to belong,[55] *Wir 89er* presents the nation as already permanently lost; with all attempts at creating an identity based on the nation doomed to failure, the German nation cannot be defined in terms of geographical borders or culture or language or genetic difference. The German nation is an empty space, a piece of history that has had its day.[56]

Conclusions

What do these tensions and contradictions tell us about the New Right and its future? They show that the New Right is not just engaged in an external memory contest with the Left and with liberalism; it is also caught up in an internal contest between its cultural and political voices. It is caught between remembering in the sense of reviving a culture or a nation, and remembering in the sense of acknowledging loss — a lost culture and a lost national identity. In the case of National Socialism it is caught between the wish to forget the past for the sake of the present and the impossibility of forgetting. These internal memory contests may not prevent the New Right from hitting the headlines and even being perceived as having a clear and confident message, but they do mean that in intellectual terms it is a self-limiting movement.

Notes

[1] Marianne Hirsch, *Family Frames: Photography, Narrative and Postmemory* (Cambridge, MA: Harvard UP, 1997), 22.

[2] See, for example, the websites of the New Right Thule-Seminar: http://www.thule-seminar.org, and two New Right journals, *Nation und Europa* and *Junge Freiheit*: http://www.nationeuropa.de, http://www.jungefreiheit.de. The latter has a searchable online archive of some 13,000 articles.

[3] Botho Strauß, "Anschwellender Bocksgesang," *Der Spiegel*, 8 February 1993.

[4] Heimo Schwilk and Ulrich Schacht, eds., *Die selbstbewußte Nation: "Anschwellender Bocksgesang" und andere Beiträge zu einer deutschen Debatte* (Berlin: Ullstein, 1994).

[5] Horst von Buttlar, "'Neue Rechte' in Deutschland: Braune in Nadelstreifen," *Der Spiegel*, 10 October 2003.

[6] See, for example, Wolfgang Gessenharter, *Kippt die Republik? Die Neue Rechte und ihre Unterstützung durch Politik und Medien* (Munich: Knaur, 1994); Bundesamt für Verfassungsschutz, *Rechtsextremismus in der Bundesrepublik Deutschland — Ein Lagebild* (Cologne: Bundesamt für Verfassungsschutz, 1996).

[7] Lars Rensmann points to the consensus among most researchers on the antidemocratic nature of the New Right. Because New Right thinkers and politicians generally commit themselves to the principles of a constitutional democracy, however, some researchers suggest that the movement does not qualify as anti-democratic but can be subsumed instead under the category of the radical right (Lars Rensmann, "Four Wings of the Intellectual New Right" [unpublished manuscript], 2003, 3).

[8] Gessenharter, *Kippt die Republik?*, 60–61. Benthin points to the line of research that suggests that neoconservatism and the New Right are two separate groups that merge or cooperate. See Rainer Benthin, *Die Neue Rechte in Deutschland und ihr Einfluß auf den politischen Diskurs der Gegenwart* (Frankfurt am Main: Lang, 1996), 28–29. The best known critic of neoconservatism, Jürgen Habermas, cites many sources that precede the emergence of the New Right and suggest neoconservatism is the precursor of the New Right. See *The New Conservatism* (Cambridge: Polity Press, 1989), especially the essay "Neoconservative Cultural Criticism in the United States and West Germany," 22–47.

[9] Hans-Gerd Jaschke, "Nationalismus und Ethnopluralismus. Zum Wiederaufleben von Ideen der 'Konservativen Revolution,'" *Aus Politik und Zeitgeschichte* B 3–4 (1993): 3–10; here: 3.

[10] Pfahl-Traughber rightly points out, however, that the characteristics Gessenharter detects in the New Right are features of virtually all extreme right-wing movements and therefore do not offer a specific enough characterization. See Armin Pfahl-Traughber, *"Konservative Revolution" und "Neue Rechte": Rechtextremistische Intellektuelle gegen den demokratischen Verfassungsstaat* (Opladen: Leske & Budrich, 1998), 157–58.

[11] Kurt Lenk, "Ideengeschichtliche Dispositionen rechtsextremen Denkens," *Aus Politik und Zeitgeschichte* B 9–10 (1998): 13–19; here: 13.

[12] Stefan Ulbrich, "Es entsteht eine neue Kultur," *Junge Freiheit*, 7 October 1992, 24.

[13] Karlheinz Weißmann, *Alles was recht(s) ist: Ideen, Köpfe und Perspektiven der politischen Rechten* (Graz, Stuttgart: Leopold Stocker, 2000), 170.

[14] *Parteiprogramm 2002 der Republikaner*, http://www.rep.de. Accessed 1 November 2004.

[15] Hajo Funke, *Paranoia und Politik: Rechtsextremismus in der Berliner Republik* (Berlin: Schiler Verlag, 2002), 246.

[16] Alfred Mechtersheimer, "Nation und Internationalismus: Über nationales Selbstbewußtsein als Bedingung des Friedens," in *Die selbstbewußte Nation*, ed. Schwilk and Schacht, 345–63; here: 357–60.

[17] Karlheinz Weißmann, *Alles was recht(s) ist*, 36. Weißmann is quoting from Hielscher's "Für die unterdrückten Völker!" which appeared in *Arminius* (16 March 1927).

[18] Weißmann sees this process at the heart of "re-education" in Germany. See Karlheinz Weißmann, *Rückruf in die Geschichte* (Frankfurt am Main, Berlin: Ullstein, 1992), 33.

[19] Botho Strauß, *Beginnlosigkeit: Reflexionen über Fleck und Linie* (Munich: dtv, 1997), 16. The first edition appeared in 1992.

[20] Botho Strauß, *Der Untenstehende auf Zehenspitzen* (Munich, Vienna: Carl Hanser, 2004), 43.

[21] See, for example, Oswald Spengler's *Der Untergang des Abendlandes* (Munich: Beck, 1922).

[22] Strauß, *Beginnlosigkeit*, 55.

[23] Botho Strauß, *Die Fehler des Kopisten* (Munich, Vienna: Hanser, 1997), 36.

[24] Hartmut Lange, "Existenz und Moderne: Über Selbsterkenntnis als Solidarität," in *Die selbstbewußte Nation*, ed. Schwilk and Schacht, 432–43; here: 440–41.

[25] Zygmunt Bauman, *Moderne und Ambivalenz: Das Ende der Eindeutigkeit* (Frankfurt am Main: Fischer, 1996), 22.

[26] Hermann Glaser, "Kultur und Identitäten," *Aus Politik und Zeitgeschichte*, B 50 (2001): 3–5; here: 5.

[27] Stuart Hall, "Who Needs 'Identity,'" in *Questions of Cultural Identity*, ed. Stuart Hall, Paul Du Gay (London: Sage, 1996), 1–17; here: 1.

[28] Zygmunt Bauman, "From Pilgrim to Tourist — Or a Short History of Identity," in *Questions of Cultural Identity*, ed. Stuart Hall, Paul Du Gay, 18–36; here: 19.

[29] Hajo Funke, *Paranoia und Politik*, 249–50.

[30] Strauß, "Anschwellender Bocksgesang," 25.

[31] Günter Rohrmoser, *Deutschlands Tragödie* (Munich: Olzog, 2002), 52.

[32] Karlheinz Weißmann, *Rückruf in die Geschichte*, 86.

[33] Weißmann, *Rückruf in die Geschichte*, 29–31.

[34] Rohrmoser, *Deutschlands Tragödie*, 52.

[35] Brigitte Seebacher-Brandt, "Norm und Normalität: Über die Liebe zum eigenen Land," in *Die selbstbewußte Nation*, ed. Schwilk and Schacht, 43–56; here: 50.

[36] Armin Mohler, *Liberalenbeschimpfung* (Essen: Heitz & Höffkes, 1990), 90–91.

[37] Wolfgang Venohr, "Vor 50 Jahren," *Junge Freiheit*, 1–2 (1992): 15.

[38] See, for example, Günter Rohrmoser, *Deutschlands Tragödie*, 39.

[39] Alexander Barti, "Die Schlammschlacht geht weiter," *Junge Freiheit*, 20 July 2001.

[40] Erich Vad, "Eine ganze Generation unter Generalverdacht," *Junge Freiheit*, 11 January 2002.

[41] See, for example, Stefan Scheil, "Argumentation mit der Brechstange," *Junge Freiheit*, 11 April 2003.

[42] "Immer von ihrem Gewissen geführt. Interview mit Oberst Kleyser," *Junge Freiheit*, 20 July 2001.

43 Ulrich Schacht, "Stigma und Sorge: Über deutsche Identität nach Auschwitz," in *Die selbstbewußte Nation*, ed. Schwilk and Schacht, 63, 67; Karlheinz Weißmann, *Alles was recht(s) ist*, 11.

44 Harald Holz, "Die Tragik der deutschen Geschichte," *Criticon* 135 (1993): 39.

45 Rainer Zitelmann, "Position und Begriff," in *Die selbstbewußte Nation*, ed. Schwilk and Schacht, 166. Peter Bochinski takes the same line in "War Stauffenberg ein Nazi?," *Nation und Europa* 47 (1997): no. 9, 50–52; here: 52.

46 Strauß, "Anschwellender Bocksgesang," 35.

47 Strauß, *Die Fehler des Kopisten*, 107, 114.

48 Franz Schönhuber, "Endzeit," *Nation und Europa* 1 (1997), 9–12; here: 9.

49 Günter Rohrmoser, *Deutschlands Tragödie*, 26.

50 Peter Meier-Bergfeld, "Deutschland und Österreich," in *Die selbstbewußte Nation*, ed. Schwilk and Schacht, 195–226; here: 215–16.

51 Pierre Krebs, "Eine Epoche in der Krise," *Elemente* (1990): 8–19; here: 8.

52 Karlheinz Weißmann, *Alles was recht(s) ist*, 247.

53 Quoted in Karlheinz Weißmann, *Rückruf in die Geschichte*, 26.

54 Alain de Benoist, "Netzwerke funktionieren wie Viren," *Junge Freiheit*, 13 September 2002.

55 Alfred Mechtersheimer, "Nation und Internationalismus: Über nationales Selbstbewußtsein als Bedingung des Friedens," in *Die selbstbewußte Nation*, ed. Schwilk and Schacht, 345–63; here: 357–58.

56 Michael Hageböck, "Endzeit," in *Wir 89er*, ed. Roland Bubik (Frankfurt am Main & Berlin: Ullstein, 1995), 145–62; here: 150–51.

14: A *Heimat* in Ruins and the Ruins as *Heimat:* W. G. Sebald's *Luftkrieg und Literatur*

Anne Fuchs

Published in 1999, the essay *Luftkrieg und Literatur* (Air Raids and Literature),[1] a revised version of Sebald's Zurich lectures on poetics from 1997, deserves particular attention in a present-day context as it thematizes the wartime destruction of the *Heimat* with a palpable vehemence. On a thematic level the essay deals superficially with a critical stock-check of postwar society and literature, against which Sebald levels the charge that they have up to the present day suppressed both the destruction of German cities during the Allied bombings of Germany and the disastrous long-term effects of this event on the collective psyche. The essay's characteristic tone is struck by Sebald at the very beginning when he formulates the following hyperbolically pointed notion that in several modifications will accompany almost refrain-like the broader strand of his argument:

> Die in der Geschichte bis dahin einzigartige Vernichtungsaktion ist in die Annalen der neu sich konstituierenden Nation nur in Form vager Verallgemeinerungen eingegangen, scheint kaum Schmerzensspuren hinterlassen zu haben im kollektiven Bewußtsein, ist aus der retrospektiven Selbsterfahrung der Betroffenen weitgehend ausgeschlossen geblieben, hat in den sich entwickelnden Diskussionen um die innere Verfassung unseres Landes nie eine nennenswerte Rolle gespielt, ist nie, wie Alexander Kluge später konstatierte, zu einer öffentlich lesbaren Chiffre geworden. (*LL*, 11–12)

> [The destruction, on a scale without historical precedent, entered the annals of the nation as it set out about rebuilding itself only in the form of vague generalizations. It seems to have left scarcely a trace of pain behind in the collective consciousness, it has been largely obliterated from the retrospective understanding of those affected, and it never played any appreciable part in the discussion of the internal constitution of our country. As Alexander Kluge later confirmed, it never became an experience capable of public decipherment. (*NHD*, 3–4)]

Sebald proceeds to examine this notion of repression in the second part of this essay with reference to the few postwar literary works that have actually engaged with the *Bombenkrieg* and its catastrophic consequences. Belonging to this category are above all Heinrich Böll's novel *Der Engel schwieg* (The Angel Was Silent, written in the early 1950s but published posthumously in 1992), Hermann Kasack's *Die Stadt hinter dem Strom* (The City Behind the River, 1947), Hans Erich Nossack's story *Der Untergang* (The Downfall, written in 1943 and published in 1948) and Peter de Mendelssohn's *Die Kathedrale* (The Cathedral, written in 1948 and published in 1983). As representatives of the second generation to deal with this topic, Sebald discusses writers such as Arno Schmidt, Hubert Fichte, and Alexander Kluge. He criticizes Arno Schmidt's "demonstrativen Avantgardismus" (demonstrative avantgardism), which obstructs the view of the reality described, and instead calls the reader's attention merely to what Sebald calls the author's "linguistische Laubsägearbeit" (linguistic woodwork). By contrast Sebald assesses Fichte's documentary tendency altogether more favorably. He writes:

> Im Dokumentarischen kommt die deutsche Nachkriegsliteratur eigentlich erst zu sich [. . .] und beginnt mit ihren ernsthaften Studien zu einem der tradierten Ästhetik inkommensurablen Material. (*LL*, 65)

> [It is with this documentary approach [. . .] that German post-war literature really comes into its own and begins the serious study of material incommensurable with traditional aesthetics. (*NHD*, 59)]

However, it is Alexander Kluge's text "Der Luftangriff auf Halberstadt am 8. April 1945" (The Air Raid on Halberstadt on 8 April 1945) that Sebald considers to be the only literary example to have made visible the reality of the destruction.[2] As a kind of postscript, the third part of the essay concerns itself at length with letters that Sebald received from witnesses of the *Bombenkrieg* following the press's discussion of the *Luftkrieg* essay. He asserts that as a result of the letters his hypothesis has been merely further validated. Everything he has read or heard has strengthened his opinion that the literary representations of the airraids were too inadequate to allow the generations born after the Second World War to imagine the scale and the consequences of the destruction (*LL*, 75). According to Sebald, the majority of private eyewitness accounts are also of no use to the required transgenerational communication of trauma. He states categorically that such autobiographical reports are inherently insufficient, notoriously unreliable, and, furthermore, characterized by linguistic stereotypes and a high degree of repetitiveness (*LL*, 86).

After its appearance, the *Luftkrieg* essay was the subject of discussion in most daily and weekly newspapers. Reinhard Baumgart argued in *Die Zeit* that with his essay and its evidence of the rarity of adequate literary representations of the *Bombenkrieg*, Sebald had succeeded in identifying an immense lapse in German collective memory.[3] Volker Hage's discussion of the essay in *Der Spiegel* largely concurred with Sebald's diagnosis as well, albeit with the addition of further authors to Sebald's list such as Borchert, Remarque, the forgotten Gert Ledig, Gerd Gaiser, Ralph Giordano, and Uwe Timm, all of whom have dealt with the *Bombenkrieg*. Hage also addresses the problem of German victim discourse within the context of Auschwitz. Since the majority of postwar German authors had understood Adorno's famous verdict, according to which writing poetry after Auschwitz is barbaric, as a ban of any literary representations of the unimaginable suffering in the camps, they could scarcely turn to their own suffering without falling under the suspicion of historical revisionism.[4] Also writing in *Der Spiegel*, Dieter Forte reacted less favorably to Sebald's essay, criticizing his downplaying of authentic eyewitness accounts.[5] However, the most virulent reaction was expressed by Willi Winkler in the *Süddeutsche Zeitung*, who polemicized against Sebald's "precipitous" and "schoolmasterly" assumptions, highlighting the role of non-literary forms of cultural memory and their manifestation in history workshops, cultural forums, and public libraries.[6]

Since the publication of the *Luftkrieg* essay more books have appeared that continue the discussion of the *Bombenkrieg* initiated by Sebald: Jörg Friedrich's controversial *Der Brand* (The Fire, 2002), which provides a historical account of the *Bombenkrieg* "from below," that is, from the perspective and experience of the German civilian population, and Volker Hage's *Zeugen der Zerstörung* (Witnesses of Destruction, 2003), which brings together numerous examples of the literary thematization of the *Bombenkrieg* from Brecht through Thomas Mann, Thomas Bernhard to Christa Wolf.[7] Sebald's essay has also been discussed within Sebald scholarship: for example, Andreas Huyssen reads the *Luftkrieg* essay as an exercise in intertextuality through which Sebald rewrites *Luftkrieg* texts by authors such as Kluge and Nossack. The point for Huyssen is, however, that Sebald is surprisingly blind to his dependency on these writers in his own text. His attack on earlier writers for their presumed failure to represent this catastrophic event is for Huyssen compensation

> for the fact that he, as a member of the first post-45 generation, born in the Allgäu in 1944 far away from the stream of bombers, has no access to the experience or memory of the air war except through these earlier texts which he is compelled to rewrite.[8]

Looked at from this psychological angle, the essay is evidence of transgenerational traumatization.

On the other hand, Wilfried Wilms has provided a nuanced psychological and historical critique of the *Luftkrieg* essay, above all of Sebald's treatment of the notion of trauma. In connection with the findings of trauma research, Wilms argues that Sebald's charge that the repression of the memory of the *Luftkrieg* is a collective moral failure of the German people, simplifies the notion of trauma. In contemporary discourse, trauma generally refers to events that, due to their overwhelming nature, cannot be integrated into a person's life story. Trauma is thus intrinsically non-representable and can only be accessed indirectly after a period of latency. In the light of this, it is quite obvious why Germans did not articulate their experiences of the bombings adequately after the war: the traumatic event was too close and too overwhelming to allow narration. Furthermore, Wilms takes issue with Sebald's political argument in view of the cultural and educational policies of the Allies, who were in no way interested in a widespread engagement with the *Bombenkrieg*. First, the issue of the bombings would have shifted the focus from Germany's responsibility for the war to an unwelcome debate about the legitimacy of the Allied bombings. Second, from an American point of view such a debate would have been detrimental to West Germany's integration into a western alliance, which became a policy issue in the emerging Cold War. Wilms concludes his analysis as follows: "Sebald's study itself bears the mark of a taboo typical of the 'bad conscience' of the Federal Republic of Germany. He himself is not a victim of the psychological taboo he observes on the side of his ancestors; rather, his interpretive wings are clipped from the start by the political taboo with which he himself grew up. The political taboo on criticizing the Allies for the attacks on civilians is the blind spot of his own observations."[9]

Against the background of this debate, the following article will deal with an aspect that has not been fully addressed: the obsessive tonality of Sebald's essay that shows through in the strikingly repetitive quality of his line of argument. Several times in the course of the essay, Sebald reiterates his basic notion of the fateful suppression of the *Luftkrieg*, providing visual support for this argument through a series of photographs of urban ruins. It is widely recognized that the complex relationship between text and image in Sebald's literary prose produces interesting tensions: because the relationship of the photographs to the narrative is often left unspecified, the reader is invited to reflect on the mediality of the process of remembrance. By contrast, in the *Luftkrieg* essay the photographs of ruined cities have a largely illustrative purpose, which runs counter to Sebald's poetics of indirection.[10]

The repetitive quality of the essay is demonstrated in a further respect: Sebald had already dealt with the subject in an essay published in 1982 in *Orbis litterarum*. Entitled "Zwischen Geschichte und Naturgeschichte. Versuch über die literarische Beschreibung totaler Zerstörung mit Anmerkungen zu Kasack, Nossack und Kluge" (Between History and the History of Nature: an Essay on Literary Representations of Total Destruction with Remarks on Kasack, Nossack and Kluge), the essay deals in a very condensed form with the question of how the three writers' representations of the *Bombenkrieg* and their respective literary means are to be appraised.[11]

Although Sebald transfers whole passages from the first essay to the *Luftkrieg* essay, the pitch of the latter is fundamentally different: while in the older essay Sebald confines himself to an analysis of selected examples, the *Luftkrieg* essay extends far beyond the deficits of postwar literature by providing a type of social pathography of the postwar era. Thus, Sebald claims with typical hyperbolic excess that the catalyst of the economic miracle was not only the Marshall plan but also the psychological effect of repression:

> Der Katalysator aber war eine rein immaterielle Dimension: der bis heute nicht zum Versiegen gekommene Strom psychischer Energie, dessen Quelle das von allen gehütete Geheimnis der in die Grundfesten unseres Staatswesens eingemauerten Leichen ist, ein Geheimnis, das die Deutschen in den Jahren des Kriegs fester aneinander band und heute noch bindet, als jede positive Zielsetzung, im Sinne etwa der Verwirklichung von Demokratie, es jemals vermochte. (*LL*, 20)

> [In addition to these more or less identifiable factors in the genesis of the economic miracle, there was also a purely immaterial catalyst: the stream of psychic energy that has not dried up to this day, and which has its source in the well-kept secret of the corpses built into the foundations of our state, a secret that bound all Germans together in the post-war years, and indeed still binds them, more closely than any positive goal such as the realization of democracy could. (*NHD*, 13)]

What is striking about such assertions is firstly their belated quality: Sebald argues that in spite of the student movement of the 1960s and the *Väterliteratur* (fathers' literature) in the late 1970s there has been no serious examination of the culture of repression that marked the 1950s. However mixed the success of the 1968 revolution may have been, it is hard to deny the generational break and paradigmatic change in literature and society ushered in by the 1968 generation.[12] In addition, it would be a mistake to interpret the intensity of recent public memory contests, such as the debate concerning the Wehrmacht exhibition, the Goldhagen and Walser-Bubis debates, or the controversy over the Holocaust memorial, only as evidence of a transgenerational trauma that continues to affect all Germans down to the third and fourth generation. In many ways the level of contemporary memory debates reflects a heightened historical consciousness on the part of the public, which on the whole deals quite self-critically with its own culture of repression.[13] Against the backdrop of the memory contests of the 1980s and 1990s, the historical reductionism of Sebald's argument is astonishing: at no point in the essay does he reflect on German reunification as the most dramatic historical turning point since 1945 or its consequences for cultural memory.

This is further compounded by the fact that Sebald in the *Luftkrieg* essay dispenses with precisely those stylistic characteristics that elsewhere lend his prose its signature. Sebald's style is the effect of a poetics of approximation and indirection that avoids the illusion that we have direct access to the past. In his prose works he is careful to mark the distance between his first-person narrator on the one hand and his protagonists on the other, many of which are Jewish survivors of the Holocaust, haunted by their traumatic pasts. Adopting the roles of empathic listener and historical researcher, the narrator figures of *Die Ausgewanderten* (The Emigrants, 1992) and *Austerlitz* (2001) pursue historical truth through those small imprints of history, the "Schmerzensspuren der Geschichte" (the painful traces of history), that, due to their apparent marginality, can hardly ever be found in history books.[14] Sebald's narrator-figure approaches history in the knowledge that the ultimate touchstone of his memory work is the otherness of the past. For Sebald the pursuit of historical truth must therefore constantly reflect back on the epistemological gap between what happened in the past and how we reconstruct it. However, the *Luftkrieg* essay abandons this poetics of approximation and indirection in favor of extremely graphic representations of destruction.

Against this background I propose to read the *Luftkrieg* essay as a symptomatic narrative that betrays Sebald's emotional ambivalence towards his German origins. In my view the essay is not so much an academic exercise as a disguised autobiographical reflection. This is already indicated in the preliminary remarks where Sebald explains that although he was born in 1944 and thus untouched by the experience of the war, the catastrophe had nonetheless left its mark on his mind (*LL*, 5). And he adds later in the preface:

> Trotz der angestrengten Bemühung um die sogenannte Bewältigung der Vergangenheit scheint es mir, als seien wir Deutsche heute ein auffallend geschichtsblindes und traditionsloses Volk. Ein passioniertes Interesse an unseren früheren Lebensformen und den Spezifika der eigenen Zivilisation, wie es etwa in der Kultur Großbritanniens überall spürbar ist, kennen wir nicht. Und wenn wir unseren Blick zurückwenden, insbesondere auf die Jahre 1930 bis 1950, so ist es immer ein Hinsehen und Wegschauen zugleich. (*LL*, 6)

> [In spite of strenuous efforts to come to terms with the past, as people like to put it, it seems to me that we Germans today are a nation strikingly blind to history and lacking in tradition. We do not feel any passionate interest in our earlier way of life and the specific features of our civilization, of the kind universally perceptible, for instance, in the culture of the British Isles. And when we turn to take a backward view, particularly of the years 1930 to 1950, we are always looking and looking away at the same time. (*NHD*, viii–ix)]

The nostalgic tenor of this passage is striking here, as it gives expression to Sebald's desire for an unbroken tradition and an intact cultural heritage without rupture. Sebald's comparison of the reputed German historical blindness with what he portrays as the exemplary British staging of history in terms of an uncontested "heritage," provides a first indication that his essay is an autobiographical lamentation on the loss of *Heimat* during the war. This in turn motivates Sebald's various denunciations of postwar German architecture and landscape, which he reads repeatedly as an expression of a collective amnesia: thus for example in *Schwindel. Gefühle.* (Vertigo, 1990) the homeward journey of the first-person narrator brings him through

> das mir von jeher unbegreifliche, bis in die letzten Winkel aufgeräumte und begradigte deutsche Land. Auf eine ungute Art befriedet und betäubt schien mir alles, und das Gefühl der Betäubung erfaßte bald auch mich.[15] (*S*, 287–88)

> [the German countryside, which has always been alien to me, straightened out and tidied up as it is to the last square inch and corner. Everything appeared to be appeased and numbed in some sinister way, and this sense of numbness soon came over me also.[16]]

Correspondingly the narrator of the Aurach story in *Die Ausgewanderten* explains as he visits Bad Kissingen "daß die rings mich umgebende Geistesverarmung und Erinnerungslosigkeit der Deutschen, das Geschick, mit dem man alles bereinigt hatte, mir Kopf und Nerven anzugreifen begann" (I felt increasingly that the mental impoverishment and lack of memory that marked the Germans, and the efficiency with which they had cleaned everything up, were beginning to affect my head and my nerves).[17] In an interview, Sebald himself expressed regret that all those marginal zones in Germany's postwar landscape that stand for the co-existence of different times have been eliminated:

> Als Besucher fällt mir auf, daß in Deutschland die Randzonen, die ja eine Ungleichzeitigkeit der Zeit garantieren würden, eliminiert worden sind. Es gibt keine Industriebrachen wie in England, nichts Darniederliegendes, keine Überreste von früher. Das Land hat kein Gefälle mehr. Das Ergebnis ist deprimierend. Alle deutschen Städte sind gleich, man kann sich nach nichts orientieren. Oldenburg, Braunschweig, Paderborn — alles gleich. Trostlos. Die Vergangenheit wird dauernd eliminiert.[18]

> [As a visitor it occurred to me that in Germany the peripheral zones, which would normally guarantee a non-synchronism of time, have been eliminated. There are no industrial wastelands as in England, nothing flat out, no remnants of former times. The land has no incline any more. The result is depressing. Every German city is the same — one can't get one's bearings at all. Oldenburg, Braunschweig, Paderborn — they're all the same. Dreary. The past is being continually eliminated.[19]]

Here one can object to Sebald, and not without a certain justification. His insistent repetition of the claim that all German cities are alike highlights the fact that he has no sensibility for contemporary architectural styles; his archaeological reading of architecture focuses on the nineteenth century and has no register for the present. In any case, it appears to me that in the current context the massive criticism of the dreariness of postwar German cities points to the nostalgic longing for an anchorage of subjectivity in meaningful traditions. However, since for Sebald National Socialism has delegitimized the notion of cultural heritage and devalued traditional forms of memory culture, this longing for tradition can no longer be fulfilled. Thus viewed, the awareness that National Socialism, the Holocaust, and the war destroyed the *Heimat* represents the basis on which Sebald's nostalgic longing for tradition is founded. This interdependence of *Heimat* critique and nostalgia is crucial for an understanding of Sebald's staging of sites of memory in the style of Pierre Nora: the family portraits incorporated into stories, the biographical narratives of the protagonists, the diaries and documents that the narrator quotes again and again, act as sacred islands of memory that suspend the negativity of the course of history in a fleeting gesture. This suspension of history's calamities can only occur because these sites of memory have no referents in reality. According to Nora they are themselves their own referent, pure signs that are withdrawn from the terror of history.[20]

The *Luftkrieg* essay reenacts the destruction of the *Heimat* with what is for Sebald an otherwise untypical graphic directness. Sebald describes the air raid on Hamburg of 28 July 1943 as an apocalyptic spectacle of nature that sweeps away any civilizing notion of historical progress:

> [Es] erhob sich ein Feuersturm von einer Intensität, wie sie kein Mensch für möglich gehalten hätte bis dahin. Mit solcher Gewalt riß das jetzt zweitausend Meter in den Himmel hinauflodernde Feuer den Sauerstoff an sich, daß die Luftströme Orkanstärke erreichten und dröhnten wie mächtige Orgeln, an denen alle Register gezogen wurden zugleich. Drei Stunden lang brannte es so. Auf seinem Höhepunkt hob der Sturm Giebel und Hausdächer ab, wirbelte Balken und ganze Plakatwände durch die Luft, drehte Bäume aus ihrem Grund und trieb Menschen als lebendige Fackeln vor sich her. Hinter einstürzenden Fassaden schossen haushoch die Flammen hervor, rollten gleich einer Flutwelle mit einer Geschwindigkeit von über 150 Stundenkilometern durch die Straßen, kreiselten als Feuerwalzen in seltsamen Rhythmen über die offenen Plätze. In einigen Kanälen brannte das Wasser. In den Straßenbahnwaggons schmolzen die Glasscheiben, der Zuckervorrat kochte in den Kellern der Bäckereien. Die aus ihren Unterständen Geflohenen sanken unter grotesken Verrenkungen in den aufgelösten, dicke Blasen werfenden Asphalt. (*LL*, 34)

> [A firestorm of an intensity that no one would ever before have thought possible arose. The fire, now rising 2,000 metres into the sky, snatched oxygen to itself so violently that the air currents reached hurricane force,

resonating like mighty organs with all their stops pulled out at once. The fire burned like this for three hours. At its height the storm lifted gables and roofs from buildings, flung rafters and entire advertising hoardings through the air, tore trees from the ground and drove human beings before it like living torches. Behind collapsing façades the flames shot up as high as houses, rolled like a tidal wave through the streets at a speed of 150 kilometres an hour, spun across open squares in strange rhythms like rolling cylinders of fire. The water in some of the canals was ablaze. The glass in the tramcars melted; stocks of sugar boiled in the bakery cellars. Those who had fled from the air-raid shelters sank, with grotesque contortions, in the thick bubbles thrown up by melting asphalt. (*NHD*, 27–28)]

One might read this drastic description as a critique of the power unleashed in the *Bombenkrieg*, which, according to the doctrine of the RAF Commander-in-Chief Arthur Harris, aimed to punish the civilian population.[21] Yet it appears to me that Sebald's language carries connotations of a sublime spectacle of nature that underhandedly exalts the brutality of the annihilation described. Similarly the photograph inserted a few pages before (*LL*, 29), which shows a night fighter surrounded by trails of light that shoot through the darkened sky, serves as an aestheticization of the *Bombenkrieg*. When the text at this point quotes an extract from a live BBC broadcast — "We are running straight into the most gigantic display of soundless fireworks" (*LL*, 29) — it underlines the aesthetic impact of this almost abstractly effective photograph. Thus viewed, the claim put forward by Sebald in his essay that there are only a few adequate literary representations of the *Bombenkrieg* disguises a fantasy of retribution: the German people, who committed themselves to National Socialism and total barbarity, deserve their apocalyptic downfall in debris and ashes.

A further indication of this reading against the grain is found in Sebald's revised interpretation of Kluge's text on the air raid on Halberstadt. In his earlier essay "Zwischen Geschichte und Naturgeschichte" Sebald argues that Kluge's linguistic montages stimulate a critical dialectics between the present and the past, which in turn triggers a learning process in the reader.[22] According to Sebald, Kluge's detailed reconstruction of the catastrophe contains die "unausgesprochene Hoffnung, daß ein richtiges Verständnis der von uns arrangierten Katastrophen die erste Voraussetzung wäre für die gesellschaftliche Organisation des Glücks" (the unspoken belief that the correct analysis of the catastrophes that have been caused by us would be the first condition for society's realization of happiness).[23] Kluge's montages are effective because they transform that which is merely documentary into something utopian. The *Luftkrieg* essay incorporates this deliberation on utopian hope (*LL*, 70), but then it casts fundamental doubt on its legitimacy. For Kluge the destruction through war is the direct result of the capitalist production process that with its accumulation of labor and material produced a destructive force beyond any moral legitimization. Although up to this point Sebald has followed Kluge's approach, he now comes to an entirely different conclusion:

> Die Geschichte der Industrie als das offene Buch des menschlichen Denkens und Fühlens — läßt die materialistische Erkenntnistheorie oder irgendeine Erkenntnistheorie überhaupt sich aufrechterhalten angesichts solcher Zerstörung, oder ist nicht diese vielmehr das unwiderlegbare Exempel dafür, daß die gewissermaßen unter unserer Hand sich entwickelnden Katastrophen in einer Art Experiment den Punkt vorwegnehmen, an dem wir aus unserer, wie wir so lange meinten, autonomen Geschichte zurücksinken in die Geschichte der Natur? (*LL*, 72)

> [The history of industry as the open book of human thought and feeling — can materialistic epistemology or any other such theory be maintained in the face of such destruction? Is the destruction not, rather, irrefutable proof that the catastrophes which develop, so to speak, in our hands and seem to break out suddenly are a kind of experiment, anticipating the point at which we will drop out of what we have thought for so long to be our autonomous history and back into the history of nature? (*NHD*, 67)]

Sebald's rhetorical question about the point when we sink back into the history of nature is characterized by the very allegorization of destruction that he accused Nossack of a few pages before. In so much as Sebald reads the *Luftkrieg* as an example of the transformation of anthropocentric history into natural history, he ultimately commits himself to a metaphysics of natural history, which, in my opinion, runs contrary to the basic principles of his poetics of memory. Andreas Huyssen arrives at a similar conclusion in his article on the *Luftkrieg* essay, in which he interprets Sebald's essay as a form of secondary, post-reunification traumatization. Huyssen comments on Sebald's bias towards a metaphysics of nature as follows: "Sebald's conceptual framework [. . .], especially in the idea of a 'Naturgeschichte der Zerstörung' which grounds his imagination, contains elements of a traditional metaphysics of nature absent from Kluge, but overbearingly present in Nossack's narrative."[24] Influenced by Kluge's documentary method and Benjamin's theories of history, Sebald's poetic of remembrance incorporates the messianic idea of historical alternatives. Only under the precondition that there might be the possibility of an alternative to the bad reality of history can Sebald's protagonists embark on their painful journey of remembrance. However, it would seem that in the *Luftkrieg* essay the principle of empathetic partisanship with the victims of history has been suspended in favor of a metaphysics of natural history that engulfs everybody.[25] At the end of his analysis of Kluge's text, Sebald lets Benjamin's angel of history appear once more (*LL*, 73–74); within the context of the implied metaphysics of natural history, the quotation appears, however, to be a fading reminiscence of a messianic hope already written off.[26]

However, the *Luftkrieg* essay does not end on this apocalyptic note. In the third part of the essay Sebald speaks of his childhood in the Allgäu. He explains that although, as someone born in 1944, he would hardly have any personal recollections of the war, he feels to this day that he is a child of the war "als fiele von dorther, von diesem von mir gar nicht erlebten Schrecknissen, ein Schatten auf mich, unter dem ich nie ganz herauskommen werde" (*LL*, 77–78; as if those horrors I did not experience had cast a shadow over me, and one from which I shall never entirely emerge, *NHD*, 71). He continues:

> In einem Festbuch über die Geschichte des Marktfleckens Sonthofen [. . .] heißt es: "Viel hat uns der Krieg genommen, doch uns blieb, unberührt und blühend wie eh und je, unsere herrliche Heimatlandschaft." Lese ich diesen Satz, so verschwimmen vor meinen Augen Bilder von Feldwegen, Flußauen und Bergwiesen, mit den Bildern der Zerstörung, und es sind die letzteren, perverserweise, und nicht die ganz irreal gewordenen früh-kindlichen Idyllen, die so etwas wie ein Heimatgefühl in mir heraufrufen, vielleicht, weil sie die mächtigere, übergeordnete Wirklichkeit meiner ersten Lebensjahre repräsentieren. (*LL*, 78)

> [A book on the history of the little market town of Sonthofen [. . .] contains a passage which runs: "The war took much from us, but our beautiful native landscape was left untouched, as flourishing as ever." Reading that sentence, I see pictures merging before my mind's eye — paths through the fields, river meadows and mountain pastures mingling with images of destruction — and oddly enough it is the latter, not the now entirely unreal idylls of my early childhood, that make me feel rather as if I were coming home, perhaps because they represent the more powerful and dominant reality of my first years of life. (*NHD*, 71)]

The kitschy appeal to "unsere herrliche Heimatlandschaft" in the local history of Sonthofen appears to Sebald as a mythologizing distortion of history that has no resonance in the commemorative subject. For Sebald it is not the idyllic images of the Allgäu countryside that imbue him with a feeling of *Heimat* but rather the images of destruction. The prevalence of such images of destruction demonstrates once again why after the war *Heimat* can no longer be understood in terms of an unalienated space of identity. Within the context of total war and total destruction, *Heimat* and the lack of *Heimat*, *Heimat* and exile, *Heimat* and the *Unheimliche* (the uncanny) are inextricably intertwined.

The physical manifestation of the disfigurement of the *Heimat* in war are the postwar ruins. Sebald reads their rapid removal and the ensuing reconstruction simultaneously as a sign of "fragloser Heroismus" (unquestioning heroism, *LL*, 13) and a symptom of the German people's

"Selbstanästhesierung" (self-anesthesia, *LL*, 19). For Sebald, the by-now legendary reconstruction of the country was tantamount to a "zweiten Liquidierung der eigenen Vorgeschichte" (second liquidation of the nation's own past, *LL*, 16), which produced precisely the new, faceless reality that cut the population off from any backward view in favor of a complete orientation to the future.

This is not a question of a renewed critique of the one-dimensionality of Sebald's theory of total repression but rather a question of his implied reading of the postwar ruin as a transitory place of memory, which concretizes Benjamin's image of historical heaps of rubble reaching to the sky.[27] In contrast to the romantic ruin that invites melancholy interpretation, the postwar ruins are, as shown by the photographs incorporated into the text, desolate ciphers of violence and self-destruction. Yet despite this desolateness, these ruins still convey the allegorization of history as natural history. Thus, Sebald recounts that after the firestorm in Hamburg nature's ability to regenerate did not appear to have been damaged: "ja, in Hamburg blühten im Herbst 1943, wenige Monate nach dem großen Brand, viele Bäume und Büsche, insbesondere Kastanien und Fliederstauden, ein zweites Mal" (in fact many trees and bushes, particularly chestnuts and lilacs, had a second flowering in Hamburg in the autumn of 1943, a few months after the great fire, *LL*, 46). The photograph inserted at this point, showing a sunlit path through a ruined city empty of people but overgrown with plants (*LL*, 47), underlines this transformation of history through nature. Sebald avails himself here of the established aesthetics of ruins, which, as the cultural philosopher Georg Simmel showed, consists in the displacement of the balance between human mastery of nature and nature's own mastery in favor of the latter. Simmel explains: "What has erected the building is human will, what gives it its current appearance is the mechanical power of nature — gnawing and pounding away, dragging it down."[28] Although the war ruin is a product of human force and not of any gradual decay, for Sebald it still demonstrates the victory of nature over history. With the figure of the war ruin Sebald pursues the allegorization of destruction and thus a metaphysical interpretation of history. The change from destructive history to natural history as embodied in the ruin evokes a utopian potential. The ruined buildings of the postwar era are hybrid places where the interior and exterior meet; they perforate the strict demarcation between inside and outside, the familiar and alien that had characterized the National Socialist discourse on *Heimat*. Although Sebald makes no mention of this, it is of course relevant in this context that in the aftermath of the war the ruins were indeed often occupied by displaced people, refugees, and strangers. Even from a socio-historical perspective life in the postwar ruins gave expression to an uprootedness that swept away the clear boundary between the familiar and the alien. As a product of war that now makes room for all that used to be excluded from the territory of the *Heimat,* the ruin thus unsettles the very foundation of National Socialist discourse: in the perforated space of the ruin the foreign takes root. The war-inflicted transformation of the *Heimat* into ruin and Sebald's striking interpretation of the ruin as *Heimat* appears in the following description of the ruins of Sonthofen. Sebald describes how he has kept in mind two particular buildings destroyed in the town. One is the image of the destroyed railway terminal, which was used for music lessons. The other is that of the Herz-Schloss:

> Die andere mir gegenwärtig gebliebene Ruine war das sogenannte Herz-schloß bei der protestantischen Kirche, eine Villa aus der Zeit der Jahrhundertwende, von der nichts mehr übrig war als der gußeiserne Gartenzaun und das Kellergeschoß. Das Grundstück, auf dem ein paar schöne Bäume die Katastrophe überstanden hatten, war in den fünfziger Jahren bereits völlig zugewachsen, und wir sind als Kinder oft nachmittagelang in dieser durch den Krieg mitten im Ort entstandenen Wildnis gewesen. Ich entsinne mich, daß es mir nie recht geheuer war, über die Treppe in die Kellerräume hinabzusteigen. Es roch dort faulig und feucht, und ich fürchtete immer, auf einen Tierkadaver zu stoßen oder auf eine Menschenleiche. (*LL*, 82)

> [The other ruin still present in my mind was the building known as the Herz-Schloss close to the Protestant church, a villa built at the turn of the century. Nothing was left of it now but its cast-iron garden railings and the cellars. By the 1950s the plot of land, where a few hundred trees had survived the catastrophe, was entirely overgrown, and as children we often spent whole afternoons in this wilderness created in the middle of town by the war. I remember that I never felt at ease going down the steps to the cellars. They smelled of damp and decay, and I always feared I might bump into the body of an animal or a human corpse. (*NHD*, 76)]

In this image of the romantically wild yet still eerie war ruin, the sentimental, nostalgic, and critical discourse on *Heimat* is brought together. For Sebald, National Socialism and the repression of the past in the postwar era have permanently ruined the *Heimat;* the reverse logic of this makes the postwar ruin with its transitory qualities the only adequate location for the memory of *Heimat.*[29] This overturning of the ruined *Heimat* into the ruins themselves as *Heimat* brings to the fore the uncanniness of *Heimat,* the latent underside of all *Heimat* discourse: the savaged Herz-Schloss is not a place where one can feel at home. For Sebald, as a space of wildness, the ruin of the destroyed villa anticipates that utopian point at which we possibly might leave behind our human history of destruction in favor of a reclaimed ethical relationship with the natural environment. Although Sebald is never entirely clear whether he advocates a postmodern version of Rousseau's state of nature, the *Luftkrieg* essays suggests that the idea of human autonomy and the attendant separation of human history from nature have had disastrous consequences for all forms of life.

Notes

[1] The German quotations are abbreviated as *LL* and taken from the following edition: W. G. Sebald, *Luftkrieg und Literatur: Mit einem Essay zu Alfred Andersch* (Frankfurt am Main: Fischer, 2001). The English translation appeared under the title *On the Natural History of Destruction: With Essays on Alfred Andersch, Jean Améry and Peter Weiss*, translated from the German by Anthea Bell (London: Hamish Hamilton, 2003). Quotations in English are taken from Bell's translation and abbreviated as *NHD*. The following chapter is a slightly adapted translation of a sub-chapter in my book *Die Schmerzensspuren der Geschichte: Zur Poetik der Erinnerung in W. G. Sebalds Prosa* (Cologne, Weimar, Vienna: Böhlau, 2004), 167–81.

[2] See Alexander Kluge, *Neue Geschichten. Hefte 1–18, Unheimlichkeit der Zeit* (Frankfurt am Main: Suhrkamp, 1977).

[3] Reinhard Baumgart, "Das Luftkriegstrauma der Literatur. W. G. Sebald entdeckt eine deutsche Gedächtnislücke," *Die Zeit*, 29 April 1999, 55.

[4] Volker Hage, "Feuer vom Himmel," *Der Spiegel*, 12 January 1998, 138–41; here: 141.

[5] Dieter Forte, "Menschen werden zu Herdentieren," *Der Spiegel*, 5 April 1999, 220–23.

[6] Willi Winkler, "Dumm debattiert sich's besser," *Süddeutsche Zeitung*, 30 March 2000, 23.

[7] See Jörg Friedrich, *Der Brand: Deutschland im Bombenkrieg 1940–1945* (Munich: Propyläen, 2002). Volker Hage, *Zeugen der Zerstörung: Die Literaten und der Luftkrieg* (Frankfurt am Main: Fischer, 2003).

[8] Andreas Huyssen, "On Rewritings and New Beginnings: W. G. Sebald and the Literature about the Luftkrieg," *Zeitschrift für Literaturwissenschaft und Linguistik* 31 (2001): 72–90; here: 84.

[9] Wilfried Wilms, "Taboo and Repression in W. G. Sebald's *On the Natural History of Destruction*," in *W. G. Sebald — A Critical Companion*, ed. J. J. Long and Anne Whitehead (Edinburgh: Edinburgh UP, 2004), 175–89; here: 188.

[10] See the photographs on *LL*,12, *LL*,13, *LL*, 35, *LL*, 72. An exception is the photograph of a bomber on *LL*, 29 which, because of the streaks of light against a black background, creates a certain aestheticization of the air raids.

[11] See W. G. Sebald, "Zwischen Geschichte und Naturgeschichte. Versuch über die literarische Beschreibung totaler Zerstörung mit Anmerkungen zu Kasack, Nossack und Kluge," *Orbis litterarum* 37 (1982): 345–66. Published again as "Zwischen Geschichte und Naturgeschichte. Versuch über die literarische Beschreibung totaler Zerstörung," in W. G. Sebald, *Campo Santo*, ed. Sven Meyer (Munich, Vienna: Hanser, 2003), 69–100.

[12] Elsewhere Sebald argues that it was the specific achievement of the 1960s to have brought the Holocaust to the literary fore. See W. G. Sebald, "Die Zerknirschung des Herzens. Über Erinnerung und Grausamkeit im Werk von Peter Weiss," *Orbis litterarum* 41 (1986): 265–78; "Konstruktionen der Trauer: Günter Grass und

Wolfgang Hildesheimer," *Der Deutschunterricht* 35 (1983): 32–46. Both appeared again in W. G. Sebald, *Campo Santo*, 128–48 and 101–27.

[13] See Bill Niven's nuanced study, *Facing the Nazi Past: United Germany and the Legacy of the Third Reich* (London, New York: Routledge, 2002).

[14] W. G. Sebald, *Austerlitz* (Munich, Vienna: Hanser 2001), 20. For a more detailed analysis of Sebald's poetics see Anne Fuchs, *Die Schmerzensspuren der Geschichte*.

[15] W. G. Sebald, *Schwindel. Gefühle* (Frankfurt am Main: Eichborn, 1990), 287–88.

[16] W. G. Sebald, *Vertigo*, translated from the German by Michael Hulse (London: The Harvill Press, 1999), 253.

[17] W. G. Sebald, *Die Ausgewanderten: Vier lange Erzählungen* (Frankfurt am Main: Eichborn 1992), 338. The English translation is taken from W. G. Sebald, *The Emigrants*, translated from the German by Michael Hulse (London: The Harvill Press, 1996), 225.

[18] Sigrid Löffler, " 'Wildes Denken.' Gespräch mit W. G. Sebald," in *W. G. Sebald*, ed. Franz Loquai (Eggingen: Edition Isele, 1997), 135–37; here: 136.

[19] Sigrid Löffler, "Wildes Denken," 136. All translations are mine unless otherwise stated.

[20] Pierre Nora, *Zwischen Gedächtnis und Geschichte*. Translated from the French by Wolfgang Kaiser (Frankfurt am Main: Fischer, 1998), 40.

[21] Sebald alludes to this connection at an earlier stage when he quotes Harris' words, "that those who have loosed these horrors upon mankind will now in their homes and persons feel the shattering strokes of retribution" (*LL*, 26).

[22] W. G. Sebald, "Zwischen Geschichte und Naturgeschichte," 98.

[23] W. G. Sebald, "Zwischen Geschichte und Naturgeschichte," 95.

[24] Andreas Huyssen, "On Writings and New Beginnings," 84.

[25] For this reason I cannot associate myself with Christian Schulte's following interpretation: "Unter 'Naturgeschichte der Katastrophe' versteht Sebald vor allem diese kreatürliche Dimension, das, was von Zivilisation, Kultur und Subjektivität übrig bleibt, wenn deren hypertrophische technische Hervorbringungen zu Mitteln der Zerstörung umgeschmiedet und zum Einsatz gebracht werden." Christian Schulte, "Die Naturgeschichte der Zerstörung. W. G. Sebalds Thesen zu *Luftkrieg und Literatur*," *Text + Kritik* 158 (2003), *W. G. Sebald*, 82–94; here: 92. In contrast it appears to me that Sebald's formulation that catastrophes develop "by our own hand" hints at the transformation of history into a metaphysics of natural history. This particular moment lies beyond the human ability to intervene — it is no longer about the self-destructive engagement with technological achievements.

[26] In his essay "Ruins and Poetics in the Works of W. G. Sebald," Simon Ward has, in contrast to Huyssen, argued that Sebald evades a metaphysics of history in that he invariably represents the fragments of a destroyed past. Ward concludes his deliberations as follows: "The ruination in the process of representation leads to an ambiguous aesthetic of ruination and construction. This aesthetic leaves the reader wandering through a highly constructed artifice, maybe even an edifice, that is also

a ruin, but which bears the traces of reality." Simon Ward, "Ruins and Poetics in the Works of W. G. Sebald," in *W. G. Sebald*, ed. J. J. Long and Anne Whitehead, 58–71; here: 70. Although I agree with Ward's thoughts on the self-reflexivity of the ruin in Sebald's works, it appears to me that this scarcely represents a counter-argument to the clear bias towards a metaphysics of natural history found here and elsewhere. The staged allegorization of the ruin that, as Benjamin has shown in his famous treatise, characterizes the baroque ruin forms the foundation for a meta-physical leap through time. See Walter Benjamin, *Über den Ursprung des deutschen Trauerspiels* (Frankfurt am Main: Suhrkamp, 1972).

[27] See Walter Benjamin, "Über den Begriff der Geschichte," in Walter Benjamin, *Illuminationen: Ausgewählte Schriften*, selected by Siegfried Unseld (Frankfurt am Main: Fischer, 1977), 251–61; here: 255.

[28] Georg Simmel, "Die Ruine," in Georg Simmel, *Philosophische Kultur: Über das Abenteuer, die Geschlechter und die Krise der Moderne* (Berlin: Klaus Wagenbach, 1998), 118–24; here: 120.

[29] See also Volker Hage's interview with Sebald, in which the latter explains: "Ich hatte immer den Eindruck und habe den Eindruck in zunehmendem Maße, daß ich aus dieser Zeit stamme. Wenn man von Zeitheimat sprechen könnte, dann sind es für mich die Jahre 1944 und 1950, die mich am meisten interessieren." (I have always had, and will continue to have to an increasing degree, the impression that I come from this time. When one speaks of a temporal *Heimat* (Zeitheimat), then for me it is the years 1944 and 1950 that interest me most.) In addition Sebald recounts that after his visit to a bombed-out Munich in 1949 he thought for a long time that the mountains of rubble were a "naturgeschichtliche Begebenheit größerer Städte" (a natural historical occurrence in big cities). And he explains: "Ich hatte immer die Vorstellung, Städte seien Orte, in denen es große Schuttberge gibt." (I always had the impression that cities are places in which there are huge mountains of rubble.) Volker Hage im Gespräch mit W. G. Sebald, *Akzente. Zeitschrift für Literatur* 1 (2003), 35–50; here: 35–36.

Works Cited

Adelson, Leslie. *Making Bodies, Making History: Feminism and German Identity*. Lincoln: U of Nebraska P, 1993.

Agamben, Giorgio. *Homo Sacer: Sovereign Power and Bare Life*. Trans. Daniel Heller-Rozen. Stanford: Stanford UP, 1998.

Aichinger, Ilse. *Die größere Hoffnung*. Frankfurt am Main: Fischer, 1974.

———. "Mein Vater." In *Verschenkter Rat*. Frankfurt am Main: Fischer, 1978.

———. "Plätze und Straßen." *Jahresring* 3 (1959): 19–24.

———. *Unglaubwürdige Reisen*. Frankfurt am Main: Fischer, 2005.

———. "Wien 1945: Kriegsende." In *Film und Verhängnis: Blitzlichter auf ein Leben*. Frankfurt: Fischer, 2001. 56–61.

———. *Der Wolf und die sieben jungen Geislein*. Vienna: Edition Korrespondenzen, 2004.

Amann, Jessica. "The Fantastic in the Post-Wende German Novel." Ph.D. dissertation, University of Nottingham, 2003.

Améry, Jean. "An den Grenzen des Geistes." In *Jenseits von Schuld und Sühne: Bewältigungsversuche eines Überwältigten*. Stuttgart: Klett-Cotta, 1977. 18–45.

———. "Der ehrbare Antisemitismus." In *Weiterleben*. Stuttgart: Klett-Cotta, 1982. 151–84.

Andersch, Alfred. "Anzeige einer Rückkehr des Geistes als Person." *Merkur* 25 (1971): 689–700.

———. *Efraim*. Zurich: Diogenes, 1967.

Anderson, Benedict. *Imagined Communities: Reflections on the Origin and Spread of Nationalism*. London: Verso, 1983.

Anonymous. "Landser auf dem Donnerbalken." *Der Spiegel*, 27 March 2000.

Arani, Miriam Y. "'Und an den Fotos entzündete sich die Kritik'. Die 'Wehrmachtausstellung,' deren Kritik und die Neukonzeption. Ein Beitrag aus fotohistorisch-quellenkritischer Sicht." *Fotogeschichte* 85/86 (2002): 97–124.

Arnold-de Simine, Silke, ed. *Memory Traces: 1989 and the Question of German Cultural Identity*. Oxford, Bern, Berlin: Lang, 2005.

Assmann, Aleida, and Ute Frevert. *Geschichtsvergessenheit — Geschichtsversessenheit: Vom Umgang mit deutschen Vergangenheiten nach 1945*. Stuttgart: Deutsche Verlags-Anstalt, 1999.

Assmann, Aleida. "On the (In)compatibility of Guilt and Suffering in German Memory." In *Memory Contests*, ed. by Anne Fuchs & Mary Cosgrove, *German Life & Letters* 59/2 (2006): 187–200.

———. "Persönliche Erinnerung und kollektives Gedächtnis in Deutschland nach 1945." In Hans Erler, ed., *Erinnerung und Verstehen: Der Völkermord an den Juden im politischen Gedächtnis der Deutschen.* Frankfurt am Main: Campus, 2003. 126–38.

Assmann, Jan. *Das kulturelle Gedächtnis: Schrift, Erinnerung und politische Identität in frühen Hochkulturen.* Munich: Beck, 1992.

Augstein, Rudolf, et al., eds. *"Historikerstreit," Die Dokumentation der Kontroverse um die Einzigartigkeit der nationalsozialistischen Judenvernichtung.* Munich, Zurich: Piper, 1987.

Ayim, May. *Blues in Black and White: A Collection of Essays, Poetry, and Conversations,* trans. Anne V. Adams. Trenton, NJ: Africa World Press, 2003.

———. *Blues in schwarz weiss: Gedichte.* Berlin: Orlanda Frauenverlag, 1995.

———. *Grenzenlos und unverschämt.* Berlin: Orlanda Frauenverlag, 1997.

———. *Nachtgesang: Gedichte.* Berlin: Orlanda Frauenverlag, 1997.

Bal, Mieke, Jonathan Crewe, and Leo Spitzer, eds. *Acts of Memory: Cultural Recall in the Present.* Hanover, London: UP of New England, 1999.

Barthes, Roland. *Camera Lucida.* Trans. Richard Howard. London: Flamingo, 1984.

Barti, Alexander. "Die Schlammschlacht geht weiter." *Junge Freiheit,* 20 July 2001.

Bartov, Omer. " 'Fields of Glory': War, Genocide, and the Glorification of Violence." In *Catastrophe and Meaning: The Holocaust and the Twentieth Century,* ed. Moishe Postone and Eric Santner. Chicago: U of Chicago P, 2003. 117–35.

Barzilai, Maya. "Facing the Past and the Female Spectre in W. G. Sebald's *The Emigrants.*" In *W. G. Sebald: A Critical Companion,* ed. J. J. Long and Anne Whitehead. Edinburgh: Edinburgh UP, 2004. 203–16.

Bauman, Zygmunt. "From Pilgrim to Tourist — or a Short History of Identity." In *Questions of Cultural Identity,* ed. Stuart Hall and Paul Du Gay. London: Sage, 1996. 18–36.

———. *Moderne und Ambivalenz: Das Ende der Eindeutigkeit.* Frankfurt am Main: Fischer, 1996.

Baumgart, Reinhard. "Das Luftkriegstrauma der Literatur: W. G. Sebald entdeckt eine deutsche Gedächtnislücke." *Die Zeit,* 29 April 1999, 55.

Becker, Jurek. *Der Boxer.* Frankfurt am Main: Suhrkamp, 1976.

———. *Bronsteins Kinder.* Frankfurt am Main: Suhrkamp, 1986.

———. *Jakob der Lügner.* Frankfurt am Main: Suhrkamp, 1988.

Beckermann, Ruth. *Ein flüchtiger Zug nach dem Orient*. Vienna: Aichholzer Filmproduktionen, 1999.

———. *Homemad(e)*. Vienna: Ruth Beckermann Filmproduktion, 2001.

———. *Jenseits des Krieges*. Vienna: Aichholzer Filmproduktionen, 1997.

———. *Die Mazzesinsel*. Vienna: Löcker, 1984.

———. *Nach Jerusalem*. Vienna: Aichholzer Filmproduktionen, 1990.

———. *Die papierene Brücke*. Vienna: Aichholzer Filmproduktionen, 1987.

———. *Unzugehörig: Österreicher und Juden nach 1945*. Vienna: Löcker, 1989.

Beckermann, Ruth, and Josef Aichholzer. *Wien Retour*. Vienna: Aichholzer Filmproduktionen, 1983.

Beer, Ann. "Watt, Knott and Beckett's Bilingualism." *Journal of Beckett Studies* 10 (1985): 37–75.

Benjamin, Walter. *Charles Baudelaire: Ein Lyriker im Zeitalter des Hochkapitalismus*, ed. Rolf Tiedemann. Frankfurt am Main: Suhrkamp, 1969.

———. *Das Kunstwerk im Zeitalter seiner technischen Reproduzierbarkeit*. Frankfurt am Main: Suhrkamp, 1963.

———. "Das Passagen-Werk: Aufzeichnungen und Materialien." In *Gesammelte Schriften*, vol. 1, ed. Rolf Tiedemann. Frankfurt am Main: Suhrkamp, 1982. 79–81.

———. "Über den Begriff der Geschichte." In Walter Benjamin. *Illuminationen: Ausgewählte Schriften*, ed. Siegfried Unseld. Frankfurt am Main: Fischer, 1977. 251–61.

———. *Über den Ursprung des deutschen Trauerspiels*. Frankfurt am Main: Suhrkamp, 1972.

Benthin, Rainer. *Die Neue Rechte in Deutschland und ihr Einfluß auf den politischen Diskurs der Gegenwart*. Frankfurt am Main: Lang, 1996.

Benz, Wolfgang, Claudia Curio, and Andrea Hammel, eds. *Die Kindertransporte 1938/39: Rettung und Integration*. Frankfurt am Main: Fischer 2003.

Berkéwicz, Ulla. *Der Golem in Bayreuth*. Frankfurt am Main: Edition Suhrkamp, 1999.

Bernig, Jörg. *Eingekesselt: Die Schlacht von Stalingrad im deutschsprachigen Romanen nach 1945*. New York, Bern, Berlin: Peter Lang, 1997.

Betts, Paul. "The Nierentisch Nemesis: Organic Design as West German Pop Culture." *German History* 19 (2001): 185–217.

Biller, Maxim. *Harlem Holocaust*. Cologne: Kiepenheuer & Witsch, 1990.

Binder, Maria. *Hoffnung im Herz, Hope in My Heart: The May Ayim Story*. (Video). New York: Third World Newsreel, 1997.

Bloom, Harold. *The Anxiety of Influence: A Theory of Poetry*. New York, Oxford: Oxford UP, 1973.

Bluhm, Lothar. "Irgendwann, denken wir, muss ich das genau wissen: Der Erinnerungsdiskurs bei Monika Maron." In *Mentalitätswandel in der deutschen Literatur zur Einheit (1990–2000)*, ed. Volker Wehdeking. Berlin: Erich Schmidt, 2000. 141–51.

Boa, Elizabeth, and Rachel Palfreyman. *Heimat — A German Dream: Regional Loyalties and National Identity in German Culture 1890–1990.* Oxford: Oxford UP, 2000.

Bochinski, Peter. "War Stauffenberg ein Nazi?" *Nation und Europa* 47 (1997): 50–52.

Bodenheimer, Alfred. "Kenntlichkeit und Schuld. Zur literarischen Jugendautobiographie G.-A. Goldschmidts." In *In der Sprache der Täter: Neue Lektüren deutschsprachiger Nachkriegs- und Gegenwartsliteratur*, ed. Stephan Braese. Opladen: Westdeutscher Verlag, 1998. 149–66.

Boehnecke, Heiner. "Clair obscur: W. G. Sebalds Bilder." *Text + Kritik* 158 (2003): *W. G. Sebald*, 43–62.

Bohrer, Karl Heinz. "Provinzialismus." *Merkur* 44 (1990): 96–102.

Boll, Bernd. "Vom Album ins Archiv. Zur Überlieferung privater Fotografien aus dem Zweiten Weltkrieg." In *Mit der Kamera bewaffnet: Krieg und Fotografie,* ed. Anton Holzer. Marburg: Jonas, 2003. 167–78.

Boll, Katharina. *Erinnerung und Reflexion: Retrospektive Lebenskonstruktionen im Prosawerk Monika Marons.* Würzburg: Königshausen & Neumann, 2002.

Bond, Greg. "On the Misery of Nature and the Nature of Misery: W. G. Sebald's Landscapes." In *W. G. Sebald: A Critical Companion*, ed. J. J. Long and Anne Whitehead. Edinburgh: Edinburgh UP, 2004. 31–44.

Bopp, Petra. "Fremde im Visier. Private Fotografien von Wehrmachtssoldaten." In *Mit der Kamera bewaffnet: Krieg und Fotografie,* ed. Anton Holzer. Marburg: Jonas, 2003. 97–117.

———. "Wo sind die Augenzeugen, wo ihre Fotos?" In *Eine Ausstellung und ihre Folgen: Zur Rezeption der Ausstellung Vernichtungskrieg. Verbrechen der Wehrmacht 1941 bis 1944*, ed. Hamburger Institut für Sozialforschung. Hamburg: Hamburger Edition, 1999. 198–229.

Braese, Stephan. "Überlieferungen." *Beiheft zur Zeitschrift für deutsche Philologie. Deutsch-jüdische Literatur: Die Generation nach der Shoah*, ed. Sander L. Gilman and Hartmut Steinecke. Berlin: Erich Schmidt Verlag, 2002. 9–16.

Branston, Gill. *Cinema and Cultural Modernity.* Buckingham, Philadelphia: Open UP, 2000.

Brecht, Bertolt. "Fragen eines lesenden Arbeiters." In *Gedichte 2: Sammlungen 1938–1956, Werke, Große kommentierte Berliner und Frankfurter Ausgabe*, vol. 12, ed. Werner Hecht, Jan Knopf, Werner Mittenzwei, Klaus-Detlev Müller. Berlin. Weimar: Aufbau; Frankfurt am Main: Suhrkamp, 1988, 29.

Brinker-Gabler, Gisela. "Exile, Immigrant, Re/Unified: Writing (East) Postunification Identity in Germany." In *Writing New Identities: Gender, Nation, and Immigration in Contemporary Europe*, ed. Gisela Brinker-Gabler and Sidonie Smith. Minneapolis: U of Minnesota P, 1997. 264–92.

Broder, Henryk. *A Jew in the New Germany*. Trans. Sander L. Gilman and Lilian M. Friedberg. Urbana: U of Illinois P, 2004.

———. "Zur Demokratie angetreten — ein Volk macht Dienst nach Vorschrift." In Lea Fleischmann, *Dies ist nicht mein Land: Eine Jüdin verläßt die Bundesrepublik*. Frankfurt am Main, Hoffmann & Campe, 1980. 251–72.

Brooks, Peter. *The Melodramatic Imagination: Balzac, Henry James, Melodrama, and the Mode of Excess*. New York: Columbia UP, 1984.

Broszat, Martin. "Resistenz und Widerstand." In *Bayern in der NS-Zeit*, vol. 4, ed. Martin Broszat and Elke Fröhlich. Munich: Oldenbourg, 1983. 691–709.

Brussig, Thomas. *Helden wie wir*. Berlin: Volk & Welt, 1996.

Bubis, Ignatz. "Rede des Präsidenten des Zentralrats der Juden in Deutschland am 9. November 1998 in der Synagoge Rykerstrase in Berlin." In *Die Walser-Bubis-Debatte, Eine Dokumentation*, ed. Frank Schirrmacher. Frankfurt am Main: Suhrkamp, 1999. 106–13.

Bücken, Hajo, and Dieter Rex. *Die wilden Fünfziger*. Reichelsheim: Edition XXL, 2001.

Bundesamt für Verfassungsschutz, *Rechtsextremismus in der Bundesrepublik Deutschland — Ein Lagebild*. Cologne: September 1996.

Buttlar, Horst v. "'Neue Rechte' in Deutschland: Braune in Nadelstreifen." *Der Spiegel*, 10 October 2003.

Campt, Ina M. "Afro-German Cultural Identity and the Politics of Positionality: Contests and Contexts in the Formation of a German Ethnic Identity." *New German Critique* 58 (1993): 109–26.

Canetti, Elias. *Die Stimmen von Marrakesch*. Munich: Hanser, 1967.

Caruth, Cathy. *Unclaimed Experience: Trauma, Narrative, and History*. Baltimore, London: Johns Hopkins UP, 1996.

Celan, Paul. "Einem, der vor der Tür stand." In *Gedichte in zwei Bänden*. Frankfurt am Main: Suhrkamp, 1978. 142–43.

Charmley, John. *Churchill, The End of Glory: A Political Biography*. London: Hodder & Stoughton, 1993.

Chaumont, Jean-Michel. "Geschichtliche Verantwortung und menschliche Würde bei Jean Améry." In *Über Jean Améry*, ed. Irene Heidelberger-Leonard. Heidelberg: Carl Winter, 1990. 29–47.

Connerton, Paul. *How Societies Remember*. Cambridge: Cambridge UP, 1989.

Cornils, Ingo. "Long Memories: The German Student Movement in Recent Fiction." *German Life and Letters* 56 (2003): 89–101.

Cosgrove, Mary. "Melancholy Competitions: W. G. Sebald Reads Günter Grass and Wolfgang Hildesheimer." *German Life and Letters* 59/2 (2006), special issue: *Memory Contests*, eds. Anne Fuchs and Mary Cosgrove, 217–32.

Cosgrove, Mary, and Anne Fuchs. "Introduction." *German Life & Letters* 59/2 (2006), special issue: *Memory Contests*, ed. Anne Fuchs and Mary Cosgrove, 3–10.

Ceuppens, Jan. "Seeing Things: Spectres and Angels in W. G. Sebald's Prose Fiction." In *W. G. Sebald: A Critical Companion*, ed. J. J. Long and Anne Whitehead. Edinburgh: Edinburgh UP, 2004. 190–202.

Daniels, Patsy J. *The Voice of the Oppressed in the Language of the Oppressor: A Discussion of Selected Postcolonial Literature from Ireland, Africa, and America*. New York, London: Routledge, 2001.

David, Maya Khemlani, ed. *Methodological and Analytical Issues in Language Maintenance and Language Shift Studies*. Frankfurt am Main, Bern, Berlin: Lang, 2002.

De Benoist, Alain. "Netzwerke funktionieren wie Viren." *Junge Freiheit*, 13 September 2002.

Deleuze, Gilles, and Felix Guattari. *Kafka: Toward a Minor Literature*. Minneapolis: U of Minnesota P, 1986.

Delius, Friedrich Christian. *Mein Jahr als Mörder*. Berlin: Rowohlt, 2004.

Denneler, Iris. *Von Namen und Dingen: Erkundungen zur Rolle des Ich in der Literatur*. Würzburg: Königshausen & Neumann, 2001.

Derrida, Jacques. *De la grammatologie*. Paris: Minuit, 1967.

———. "Shibboleth: For Paul Celan." In *Word Traces: Readings of Paul Celan*, ed. Aris Fioretos. Baltimore: Johns Hopkins UP, 1994. 3–72.

Detering, Heinrich. "Grosse Literatur für kleine Zeiten: Ein Meisterwerk: W. G. Sebalds *Die Ausgewanderten*." *Frankfurter Allgemeine Zeitung*, 17 November 1992, reprinted in *W. G. Sebald*, ed. Franz Loquai. Eggingen: Isele, 1997. 82–87.

Deutsch, Eva, and Brigitte Schwaiger. *Die Galizianerin*. Reinbeck: Rowohlt, 1982.

Dilthey, Wilhelm. "Über das Studium der Geschichte der Wissenschaften vom Menschen, der Geschichte und dem Staat." In *Die geistige Welt, Einleitung in die Philosophie des Lebens. Erste Hälfte: Abhandlungen zur Grundlegung der Geisteswissenschaften*. In *Gesammelte Schriften V*, ed. Georg Misch. Leipzig, Berlin: B. G. Teubner, 1924. 31–73.

Diner, Dan. "The Destruction of Narrativity: The Holocaust in Historical Discourse." In *Catastrophe and Meaning: The Holocaust and the Twentieth Century*, ed. Moishe Postone and Eric Santner. Chicago: U of Chicago P, 2003. 67–80.

———. "Negative Symbiose: Deutsche und Juden nach Auschwitz." *Babylon: Beiträge zur jüdischen Gegenwart* 1/9 (1988): 9–20.

———. "Negative Symbiose — Deutsche und Juden nach Auschwitz." In *Jüdisches Leben in Deutschland seit 1945*, ed. Micha Brumlik, et al. Frankfurt am Main: Athenäum, 1988. 243–57.

Dische, Irene. "Eine Jüdin für Charles Allen." In *Fromme Lügen*. Trans. Otto Bayer und Monika Elwenspoek. Reinbeck: Rowohlt, 1994. 7–74.

Dischereit, Esther. *Als mir mein Golem öffnete: Gedichte*. Passau: Karl Sturz, 1996.

———. *Merryn*. Frankfurt am Main: Suhrkamp, 1992.

Dischereit, Esther. "Nachwort." In Gertrud Kolmar. *Die jüdische Mutter.* Frankfurt am Main: Suhrkamp, 2003. 195–215.

Döblin, Alfred. *Als ich wiederkam: Schriften zu Leben und Werk.* Olten: Walter, 1986.

Dresden, Sem. *Persecution, Extermination, Literature.* Toronto: U of Toronto P, 1995.

Dubiel, Helmut. *Niemand ist frei von der Geschichte: Die nationalsozialistische Herrschaft in den Debatten des Deutschen Bundestages.* Munich: Carl Hanser, 1999.

Durzak, Manfred. "Laokoons Söhne. Zur Sprachproblematik im Exil." *Akzente* 21 (1974): 53–63.

Duttlinger, Carolin. "Traumatic Photographs: Remembrance and the Technical Media in W. G. Sebald's *Austerlitz.*" In *W. G. Sebald: A Critical Companion,* ed. J. J. Long and Anne Whitehead. Edinburgh: Edinburgh UP, 2004. 155–71.

Dye, Elizabeth. " 'Weil die Geschichte nicht aufhört': Günter Grass's *Im Krebsgang.*" *German Life and Letters* 57 (2004): 472–87.

Eakin, John Paul. *Fictions in Autobiography: Studies in the Art of Self-Invention.* Princeton: Princeton UP, 1985.

Edvardson, Cordelia. *Gebranntes Kind sucht das Feuer.* Munich: Hanser, 1986.

Eigler, Fredericke. "Engendering Cultural Memory in Selected Post-Wende Literary Texts of the 1990s." *German Quarterly* 74/4 (2001): 392–406.

———. "Nostalgisches und kritisches Erinnern am Beispiel von Martin Walsers *Ein springender Brunnen* und Monika Marons *Pawels Briefe.*" In *Monika Maron in Perspective: Dialogische Einblicke in zeitgeschichtliche, intertextuelle und rezeptionsbezogene Aspekte ihres Werkes,* ed. Elke Gilson. Amsterdam: Rodopi, 2002. 157–80.

Emde, Helga. "I Too Am German — An Afro-German Perspective." In *Who is German? Historical and Modern Perspectives on Africans in Germany,* ed. Leroy T. Hopkins. Washington: American Institute for Contemporary German Studies, 1999. 33–42.

Escure, Genevive, ed. *Creoles, Contact, and Language Change: Linguistics and Social Implications.* Amsterdam: Benjamins, 2004.

Eshel, Amir. "Vom eigenen Gewissen: Die Walser-Bubis-Debatte und der Ort des Nationalsozialismus im Selbstbild der Bundesrepublik." *Deutsche Vierteljahresschrift für Literaturwissenschaft und Geistesgeschichte* 2 (2000): 333–60.

Fichte, Johann Gottlieb. *Reden an die deutsche Nation 1807/1808.* Hamburg: Meiner, 1978.

Fishman, Joshua A. "Language Maintenance and Language Shift as a Field of Inquiry." *Linguistics* 9 (1964): 32–70.

Fleischmann, Lea. *Dies ist nicht mein Land: Eine Jüdin verläßt die Bundesrepublik.* Hamburg, Hoffmann & Campe, 1980.

Fleischmann, Lea. *Ich bin Israelin: Erfahrungen in einem orientalischen Land.* Hamburg: Hoffmann & Campe, 1982.

Fludernik, Monika, ed. *Hybridity and Postcolonialism: Twentieth-Century Indian Literature.* Tübingen: Stauffenburg, 1998.

Forte, Dieter. "Menschen werden zu Herdentieren." *Der Spiegel,* 5 April 1999, 220–23.

Foster, Leonard W. *The Poets Tongues: Multilingualism in Literature.* London: Cambridge UP, 1970.

Foucault, Michel. *Discipline and Punish: The Birth of the Prison,* trans. Alan Sheridan. Harmondsworth: Allen Lane, 1977.

Frei, Norbert, ed. *Adenauer's Germany and the Nazi Past: The Politics of Amnesty and Integration.* New York: Columbia UP, 2002.

———. *Hitlers Eliten nach 1945.* Munich: dtv, 2003.

———. *1945 und wir. Das Dritte Reich im Bewußtsein der Deutschen.* Munich: Beck, 2005.

Freud, Sigmund. "Über die Deckerinnerung." In *Gesammelte Werke,* vol. 1, ed. Anna Freud, et al., Frankfurt am Main: Fischer, 1999. 529–54.

Friedländer, Saul, ed. *Probing the Limits of Representation: Nazism and the Final Solution.* Cambridge, MA, London: Harvard UP, 1992.

Friedrich, Jörg. *Der Brand: Deutschland im Bombenkrieg 1940–1945.* Munich: Propyläen, 2002.

Frings, Ute. "Bilder der Erinnerung." *Frankfurter Rundschau,* 14 April 2000.

Fritzsche, Peter. "The Case of Modern Memory." *The Journal of Modern History* 73 (2001): 87–117.

———. "Volkstümliche Erinnerung und deutsche Identität nach dem Zweiten Weltkrieg." In *Verletztes Gedächtnis: Erinnerungskultur und Zeitgeschichte im Konflikt,* ed. Konrad H. Jarausch and Martin Sabrow. Frankfurt am Main: Campus, 2002. 75–97.

———. "Where Did All the Nazis Go? Reflections on Collaboration and Resistance." *Tel Aviver Jahrbuch für deutsche Geschichte* 23 (1994): 191–214.

Fuchs, Anne. "The Deeper Nature of My German: Mother Tongue, Subjectivity, and the Voice of the Other in Elias Canettis Autobiography." In *A Companion to the Works of Elias Canetti,* ed. Dagmar C. G. Lorenz. Rochester, NY: Camden House, 2004. 45–60.

———. *Die Schmerzensspuren der Geschichte: Zur Poetik der Erinnerung in W. G. Sebalds Prosa.* Cologne, Weimar, Vienna: Böhlau, 2004.

———. "Towards an Ethics of Remembering: The Walser-Bubis Debate and the Other of Discourse." *German Quarterly* 75.3 (2002): 235–47.

———. "Trauma or History? The End of World War II in Margret Boveri's Tage des Überlebens," in *Schreiben gegen Krieg und Gewalt: Ingeborg Bachmann und die deutschsprachige Literatur,* ed. Dirk Goettsche, Franziska Meyer et al. Krieg und Literatur X. Göttingen: V&R unipress, 2006. 103–18.

Fulbrook, Mary. "Re-presenting the Nation: History and Identity in East and West Germany." In *Representing the German Nation: History and Identity in Twentieth-Century Germany*, ed. Mary Fulbrook and Martin Swales. Manchester: Manchester UP, 2000. 172–92.

Funke, Hajo. *Paranoia und Politik: Rechtsextremismus in der Berliner Republik*. Berlin: Schiler Verlag, 2002.

Gardner, Robert C. *Social Psychology and Second Language Learning: The Role of Attitudes and Motivation*. London: Arnold, 1985.

Garrett, Peter, Nikolas Coupland, and Angie Williams. *Investigating Language Attitudes: Social Meanings of Dialect, Ethnicity and Performance*. Cardiff: U of Wales P, 2003.

Gelbin, Cathy S. *An Indelible Seal: Race, Hybridity and Identity in Elisabeth Langgässer's Writings*. Essen: Blaue Eule, 2001.

———. "Die jüdische Thematik im (multi)kulturellen Diskurs der Bundesrepublik." In *AufBrüche: Kulturelle Produktionen von Migrantinnen, Schwarzen und jüdischen Frauen in Deutschland*, ed. Cathy S. Gelbin, et al. Königstein/Ts.: Ulrike Helmer Verlag, 1999. 87–111.

———. "The Monster Returns: Golem Figures in the Writings of Benjamin Stein, Esther Dischereit and Doron Rabinovici." In *Jewish Writing in Austria and Germany Today*, ed. Hilary Herzog, Todd Herzog, and Benjamin Lapp. New York: Berghahn, forthcoming.

Gellner, Ernest. *The Psychoanalytic Movement or the Coming of Unreason*. London: Paladin/Grafton, 1985.

Gesenius, Wilhelm. *Hebräisches und aramäisches Handwörterbuch über das Alte Testament*. Berlin: Springer-Verlag, 1962.

Gessenharter, Wolfgang. *Kippt die Republik? Die Neue Rechte und ihre Unterstützung durch Politik und Medien*. Munich: Knaur, 1994.

Gessler, Philipp. "Die andere Wehrmachtsausstellung." *Tageszeitung*, 2 April 2000.

Geyer, Michael. "The Place of Second World War in German Memory and History." *New German Critique* 71 (1997): 20.

Gilman, Sander L. *Difference and Pathology: Stereotypes of Sexuality, Race, and Madness*. Ithaca, NY: Cornell UP, 1985.

———. *Jewish Self-Hatred: Anti-Semitism and the Hidden Language of the Jews*. Baltimore: Johns Hopkins UP, 1986.

———. *Jurek Becker: Die Biographie*. Berlin: Ullstein, 2002.

———. "Salome, Syphilis, Sara Bernhardt and the Modern Jewess." *German Quarterly* 66 (1993): 195–211.

Gilson, Elke. "Nur wenige kurze Augenblicke, die sicher sind: Zur konstruktivistisch inspirierten Darstellung des Erinnerns und Vergessens in Monika Marons Familiengeschichte Pawels Briefe." *Colloquia Germanica* 33/3 (2000): 275–88.

Glaeser, Ernst. *The Last Civilian*. Trans. Gwenda David and Eric Mosbacher. New York: Robert M. McBridge, 1935.

Glaser, Hermann. "Kultur und Identitäten." *Aus Politik und Zeitgeschichte* 50 (2001): 3–5.

Goertz, Karein. "Borderless and Brazen: Ethnicity Redefined by Afro-German and Turkish German Poets." *The Comparatist* 21 (1997): 68–91.

Goldschmidt, Georges-Arthur. *Die Absonderung: Erzählung.* Zurich: Ammann, 1991.

———. *La fort interrompue. Récit.* Paris: Seuil, 1991.

———. *La traverse des fleuves: Autobiographie.* Paris: Seuil, 1999.

———. *Quand Freud voit la mer: Freud et la langue allemande.* Paris: Buchet/Chastel, 1988.

———. *Über die Flüsse: Autobiographie.* Zurich: Ammann, 2001.

———. "Une chaise deux dossiers/Ein Stuhl mit zwei Lehnen." Trans. Michael von Killisch-Horn, *Sirene* 4/8 (1991): 68–99.

———. "Vorwort zur deutschen Ausgabe." In *Als Freud das Meer sah: Freud und die deutsche Sprache.* Trans. Brigitte Groe. Zurich: Ammann, 1999. 11.

Goldschmidt, Georges-Arthur, and Hans-Ulrich Treichel. "Jeder Schriftsteller ist zweisprachig. Ein Gespräch." *Sprache im technischen Zeitalter* 32/131 (1994): 273–85.

Gove, Antonina Filonov. "Multilingualism and Ranges of Tone in Nabokovs Bend Sinister." *Slavic Review* 32 (1973): 79–90.

Graham, Elaine. *Representations of the Post/human: Monsters, Aliens and Others in Popular Culture.* Manchester: Manchester UP, 2002.

Grass, Günter. *Im Krebsgang.* Göttingen: Steidel, 2002.

Greenblatt, Stephen. *Shakespearian Negotiations: The Circulation of Social Energy in Renaissance.* Oxford: Clarendon, 1988.

Greiner, Bernhard, ed. *Placeless Topographies: Jewish Perspectives on the Literature of Exile.* Tübingen: Niemeyer, 2003.

Greiner-Mai, Herbert, ed. "Introduction." In *Hölderlins Werke in zwei Bänden,* vol. 1. Berlin & Weimar: Aufbau-Verlag, 1968. 5–34.

Grimm, Wilhelm. *Volk ohne Raum.* Munich: Langen, 1932.

Grimwood, Marita. "Postmemorial Positions: Reading and Writing after the Holocaust in Anne Michaelss Fugitive Pieces." *Canadian Jewish Studies* 11 (2003): 111–30.

Günter, Manuela. *Überleben schreiben: Zur Autobiographik der Shoah.* Würzburg: Königshausen & Neumann, 2002.

Habermas, Jürgen. *The New Conservatism: Cultural Criticism and the Historians' Debate,* ed. and trans. Sherry Weber Nicholson. Cambridge: Polity Press, 1989.

Hage, Volker. "Feuer vom Himmel." *Der Spiegel,* 12 January 1998, 138–41.

———. "Gespräch mit W. G. Sebald." *Akzente. Zeitschrift für Literatur* 1 (2003): 35–50.

———. *Zeugen der Zerstörung: Die Literaten und der Luftkrieg.* Frankfurt am Main: Fischer, 2003.

Hageböck, Michael. "Endzeit." In *Wir 89er*, ed. Roland Bubik. Frankfurt am Main, Berlin, 1995. 145–62.

Hahn, Ulla. *Unscharfe Bilder: Roman*. Munich: dtv, 2005.

Hake, Sabine. *German National Cinema*. London, New York: Routledge 2002.

Halbwachs, Maurice. *On Collective Memory*. Ed. and trans. Lewis A. Coser. Chicago: U of Chicago P, 1992.

Hall, Katharina. "Jewish Memory in Exile: The Relation of W. G. Sebald's *Die Ausgewanderten* to the Tradition of the Yizkor Books." In *Jews in German Literature since 1945: German-Jewish Literature?*, ed. Pol O'Dochartaigh. Amsterdam: Rodopi, 2000. 152–64.

Hall, Stuart. "Who Needs 'Identity.'" In *Questions of Cultural Identity*, ed. Stuart Hall and Paul Du Gay. London: Sage, 1996. 1–17.

Hamburger Institut für Sozialforschung, ed. *Verbrechen der Wehrmacht: Dimensionen des Vernichtungskrieges 1941–1944*. (DVD) Hamburg: Hamburger Edition, 2004.

Hamilton, Peter, and Roger Hargreaves. *The Creation of Identity in Nineteenth Century Photography*. Aldershot and Burlington: Lund Humphries, 2001.

Haraway, Donna. "A Manifesto for Cyborgs: Science, Technology, and Socialist Feminism in the 1980s." In *Coming to Terms*, ed. Elizabeth Weed. New York: Routledge, 1985. 149–81.

Harig, Ludwig. *Also Ordnung ist das ganze Leben*. Munich, Vienna: Hanser, 1986.

———. *Und wenn sie nicht gestorben sind: Aus meinem Leben*. Munich, Vienna: Hanser, 2002.

———. *Wehe dem, der aus der Reihe tanzt*. Munich, Vienna: Hanser, 1990.

———. *Wer mit den Wölfen heult, wird Wolf*. Munich, Vienna: Hanser, 1996.

Harlan, Veit. *Jud Süß*. Berlin: UFA, 1940.

Harris, Stefanie. "The Return of the Dead: Memory and Photography in W. G. Sebald's *Die Ausgewanderten*." *German Quarterly* 74.4 (2001): 370–92.

Härtling, Peter. *Nachgetragene Liebe*. Darmstadt: Luchterhand, 1980.

Heer, Hannes, and Klaus Naumann, eds. *Vernichtungskrieg: Verbrechen der Wehrmacht 1941 bis 1944*. Hamburg: Hamburger Edition, 1996. English: *War of Extermination: The German Military in World War II 1941–1944*. Oxford: Berghahn, 2000.

Hegel, Georg Wilhelm Friedrich. "Herrschaft und Knechtschaft." In *Phänomenologie des Geistes*. Hamburg: Felix Meiner, 1952. 146–50.

Heidelberger-Leonard, Irene. "Jean Amérys Selbstverständnis als Jude." In *Über Jean Améry*, ed. Irene Heidelberger-Leonard. Heidelberg: Carl Winter, 1990. 17–27.

Heinrichs, Hans-Jürgen. "Die Überquerung der Flüsse: Das autobiographische Schreiben von Jorge Semprun und Georges-Arthur Goldschmidt." *Merkur* 54/6 (2000): 487–99.

Herf, Jeffrey. *Divided Memory: The Nazi Past in the Two Germanys*. Cambridge, MA: Harvard UP, 1997.

Heschel, Susannah. "Konfigurationen des Patriarchats, des Judentums und des Nazismus im deutschen feministischen Denken." In *Der feministische "Sündenfall"? Antisemitische Vorurteile in der Frauenbewegung,* ed. Johanna Gehmader, Susanne Heine, Susanne Heschel, Charlotte Kohn-Ley, and Ilse Korotin. Vienna: Picus, 1994. 160–208.

Hesse, Klaus, and Philipp Springer, eds. *Vor aller Augen: Fotodokumente des nationalsozialistischen Terrors in der Provinz.* Essen: Klartext, 2002.

Hettche, Thomas. *Der Fall Arbogast.* Cologne: Dumont, 2001.

Hirsch, Marianne. *Family Frames: Photography, Narrative and Postmemory.* Cambridge, MA, London: Harvard UP, 1997.

———. "Projected Memory: Holocaust Photographs in Personal and Public Fantasy." In *Acts of Memory: Cultural Recall in the Present,* ed. Mieke Bal, Jonathan Crewe, and Leo Spitzer. Hanover, London: UP of New England, 1999. 3–23.

———. "Surviving Images: Holocaust Photographs and the Work of Postmemory." In *Visual Culture and the Holocaust,* ed. Barbie Zelizer. London: Athlone, 2001. 215–46.

Hobsbawm, Eric, and Terence Ranger, eds. *The Invention of Tradition.* Cambridge: Cambridge UP, 1983.

———. *On History.* London: Weidenfels & Nicolson, 1997.

Hoffmann, Christhard. "Zum Begriff der Akkulturation." In *Handbuch der deutschsprachigen Emigration 1933–1945,* ed. Claus-Dieter Krohn. Darmstadt: Primus, 1998. 117–28.

Hoffmann-Curtius, Kathrin. "Trophäen und Amulette. Die Fotografien von Wehrmachts- und SS-Verbrechen in den Brieftaschen der Soldaten." *Fotogeschichte* 78 (2000): 63–76.

Holdenried, Michaela. "Das Ende der Aufrichtigkeit? Zum Wandel autobiographischer Dispositive am Beispiel von Georges-Arthur Goldschmidt." *Archiv für das Studium der neueren Sprachen und Literaturen* 149 (1997): 1–18.

Holz, Harald. "Die Tragik der deutschen Geschichte." *Criticon* 135 (1993): 39.

Honigmann, Barbara. *Roman von einem Kinde.* Darmstadt: Luchterhand, 1986.

———. *Soharas Reise.* Berlin: Rowohlt, 1996.

Honold, Alexander. "'Verlorene Generation': Die Suggestivität eines Deutungsmusters zwischen Fin de siècle und Erstem Weltkrieg." In Sigrid Weigel, Ohad Parnes, Ulrike Vedder, and Stefan Willer, eds. *Generation: Zur Genealogie des Konzepts — Konzepte von Genealogie.* Munich: Fink, 2005. 31–56.

Horkheimer, Max. *Dialektik der Aufklärung: Philosophische Fragmente.* Frankfurt am Main: Fischer, 1979.

Horn, Andrés. "Ästhetische Funktion der Sprachmischung in der Literatur." *Arcadia* 16 (1981): 225–41.

Hügel-Marshall, Ika. *Daheim unterwegs: Ein deutsches Leben.* Berlin: Orlanda Frauenverlag, 1998.

Hüppauf, Bernd. "Der entleerte Blick hinter der Kamera." In *Vernich-tungskrieg*, ed. Heer and Naumann, 504–27.

Huyssen, Andreas. "On Rewritings and New Beginnings: W. G. Sebald and the Literature about the Luftkrieg." *Zeitschrift für Literaturwissenschaft und Linguistik* 31 (2001): 72–90.

"Immer von ihrem Gewissen geführt. Interview mit Oberst Kleyser." *Junge Freiheit*, 20 July 2001.

Im toten Winkel: Hitlers Sekretärin. Directed by André Heller & Othmar Schmiderer. Dor Film, 2002.

Jahn, Peter, and Ulrike Schmiegelt, eds. *Fotofeldpost: Geknipste Kriegserlebnisse 1939–45.* Berlin: Elefanten 2000.

Janna, Simonetta. "Sprachpuzzle und Selbstfindung: Delius *Der Sonntag, an dem ich Weltmeister wurde.*" In *F. C. Delius: Studien über sein literarisches Werk*, ed. Manfred Durzak. Tübingen: Stauffenberg, 1997. 163–80.

Jaschke, Hans-Gerd. "Nationalismus und Ethnopluralismus. Zum Wieder-aufleben von Ideen der 'Konservativen Revolution.'" *Aus Politik und Zeit-geschichte* 3/4 (1993): 3–10.

Jaspers, Karl. *The Question of German Guilt.* Trans. E. B. Ashton. New York: Dial Press, 1948.

———. *Die Schuldfrage.* Heidelberg: L. Schneider, 1946.

Jeutter, Ralf. "'Am Rand der Finsternis': the Jewish Experience in the Context of W. G. Sebald's Prose." In *Jews in German Literature since 1945: German-Jewish Literature?*, ed. Pol O'Dochartaigh. Amsterdam; Rodopi, 2000. 165–77.

Jünger, Ernst. *In Stahlgewittern.* Stuttgart: Klett-Cotta, 1978.

———. *Strahlungen I.* Stuttgart: Klett-Cotta, 1988.

Jürgs, Michael, and Freimut Duve, eds. *Stoppt die Gewalt: Stimmen gegen den Ausländerhaß.* Hamburg, Zurich: Luchterhand, 1992.

Kaes, Anton. "German Cultural History and the Study of Film: Ten Theses and a Postscript." *New German Critique* 65 (1995): 47–58.

Kafka, Franz. "Die Verwandlung." In *Sämtliche Erzählungen.* Frankfurt am Main: Fischer, 1995. 56–99.

Kastner, Jörg. *Wenn der Golem erwacht.* Bern: Scherz Verlag, 2000.

Kellerhoff, Sven Felix. "Heile Kriegswelt." *Berliner Morgenpost*, 30 March 2000.

Kieselsteine. Script Nadja Seelich, dir. Lukas Stepanik. Filmverleih Hans Peter Hofmann, Vienna, 1982.

Kinder, Hermann. *Der Schleiftrog.* Zurich: Diogenes, 1977.

Klebes, Martin. "Infinite Journey: From Kafka to Sebald." In *W. G. Sebald: A Critical Companion*, ed. J. J. Long and Anne Whitehead. Edinburgh: Edin-burgh UP, 2004. 123–39.

Kleinert, Andreas. *Schimanski: Das Geheimnis des Golem.* Germany, 2003.

Klemperer, Victor. *I Will Bear Witness, 1933–1941.* New York: Random House, 1998.

Klemperer, Victor. *Ich will Zeugnis ablegen bis zum letzten: Tagebücher 1942–1945.* Berlin: Aufbau-Verlag, 1995.

Klötzer, Sylvia. "Wir haben so lange nach vorne gelebt: Erinnerung und Identität: Flugasche und Pawels Briefe." In *Monika Maron in Perspective: Dialogische Einblicke in zeitgeschichtliche, intertextuelle und rezeptionsbezogene Aspekte ihres Werkes,* ed. Elke Gilson. Amsterdam: Rodopi, 2002. 35–56.

Kluge, Alexander. *Neue Geschichten: Hefte 1–18, Unheimlichkeit der Zeit.* Frankfurt am Main: Suhrkamp, 1977.

Klüger, Ruth. "Die Ödnis des entlarvten Landes: Antisemitismus im Werk jüdisch-österreichischer Autoren." In *Katastrophen: Über deutsche Literatur.* Göttingen: Wallstein, 1994. 59–82.

———. "Wanderer zwischen falschen Leben." *Text + Kritik* 158 (2003), *W. G. Sebald,* 95–102.

———. *Weiter leben.* Göttingen: Wallstein, 1992.

Koenen, Gerd. *Das rote Jahrzehnt: Unsere kleine deutsche Kulturrevolution.* Cologne: Kiepenheuer & Witsch, 2001.

Koepnick, Lutz. "Honour Your German Master: History, Memory, and Identity in Joseph Vilsmaier's Comedian Harmonists (1997)." In *Light Motives: German Popular Film in Perspective,* ed. Randall Halle and Margaret McCarthy. Detroit: Wayne State UP, 2003. 349–75.

———. "Reframing the Past: Heritage Cinema and Holocaust in the 1990s." *New German Critique* 87 (2002): 47–82.

Köhler, Lotte, and Hans Saner, eds. *Hannah Arendt: Karl Jaspers Briefwechsel 1926–1969.* Munich, Zurich: Piper, 2001. 88–93.

Köpke, Wulf. "Die Wirkung des Exils auf Sprache und Stil. Ein Vorschlag zur Forschung." *Exilforschung* 3 (1985): 225–37.

Koshar, Rudy. *Germany's Transient Pasts: Preservation and National Memory in the Twentieth Century.* Chapel Hill: U of North Carolina P, 1998.

Koslowski, Timo. "Thomas Hettche." In *Kritisches Lexikon der Gegenwartsliteratur,* ed. Heinz Ludwig Arnold. Munich: Edition Text + Kritik, 2002. 4–8.

Kracauer, Siegfried. *Theorie des Film: Die Errettung der äußeren Wirklichkeit,* trans. Friedrich Walter and Ruth Zellschan. Frankfurt am Main: Suhrkamp, 1964.

———. *Theory of Film: The Redemption of Physical Reality.* New York: Oxford UP, 1960.

Kracht, Annette. *Migration und kindliche Zweisprachigkeit: Interdisziplinarität und Professionalität sprachpädagogischer und sprachbehindertenpädagogischer Praxis.* Münster: Waxmann, 2000.

Krebs, Pierre. "Eine Epoche in der Krise." *Elemente,* Hauptausgabe, 1990. 8–19.

Krohn, Claus-Dieter, ed. *Handbuch der deutschsprachigen Emigration 1933–1945.* Darmstadt: Primus, 1998.

Lacan, Jacques. "Le stade du miroir comme formateur de la fonction du Je." *Écrits.* Paris: Éditions du Seuil, 1966. 93–100.

LaCapra, Dominick. *Writing History, Writing Trauma.* Baltimore, London: Johns Hopkins UP, 2001.

Lagrou, Pieter. *The Legacy of Nazi Occupation: Patriotic Memory and National Recovery in Western Europe, 1945–1965.* New York: Cambridge UP, 2000.

Lalvani, Suren. *Photography, Vision, and the Production of Modern Bodies.* Albany: SUNY Press, 1996.

Lamping, Dieter. "Linguistische Metamorphosen. Aspekte des Sprachwechsels in der Exilliteratur." In *Germanistik und Komparatistik: DFG-Symposion 1993,* ed. Hendrik Birus. Stuttgart: Metzler, 1995. 528–40.

———. *Von Kafka bis Celan: Jüdischer Diskurs in der deutschen Literatur des 20. Jahrhunderts.* Göttingen: Vandenhoek & Ruprecht, 1998.

Lander, Jeanette. *Jahrhundert der Herren.* Berlin: Aufbau, 1993.

———. *Die Töchter.* Frankfurt am Main: Insel, 1976.

Lange, Hartmut. "Existenz und Moderne: Über Selbsterkenntnis als Solidarität." In *Die selbstbewußte Nation,* ed. Schwilk and Schacht, 432–43.

Langer, Lawrence L. *Holocaust Testimonies: The Ruins of Memory.* New Haven: Yale UP, 1991.

Langgässer, Elisabeth. *Märkische Argonautenfahrt.* Hamburg: Claassen, 1950.

Langthaler, Hilde. *Golem Now.* Vienna: Triton, 2000.

Lüdi, Georges, and Bernard Py. *Tre bilingue.* Bern: Lang, 2003.

Lenk, Kurt. "Ideengeschichtliche Dispositionen rechtsextremen Denkens." *Aus Politik und Zeitgeschichte* 9/10 (1998): 13–19.

Leone, Massimo. "Textual Wanderings: A Vertiginous Reading of W. G. Sebald." In *W. G. Sebald: A Critical Companion,* ed. J. J. Long and Anne Whitehead. Edinburgh: Edinburgh UP, 2004. 89–101.

Leopold, Werner F. *Speech Development of a Bilingual Child: A Linguists Record.* Evanston, IL: Northwestern UP, 1939–1949.

Lethen, Helmut. "Der Text der Historiografie und der Wunsch nach einer physikalischen Spur: Das Problem der Fotografie in den beiden Wehrmachtsaustellungen." *Zeitgeschichte* 29 (2002): 76–86.

———. *Verhaltenslehre der Kälte: Lebensversuche zwischen den Kriegen.* Frankfurt am Main: Suhrkamp 1994.

Leupold, Dagmar. *Nach den Kriegen.* Munich: Beck, 2004.

Levin, Judith, and Daniel Uzel. "Ordinary Men, Extraordinary Photos." *Yad Vashem Studies* 26 (1998): 265–93.

Lind, Jakov. *Eine Seele aus Holz.* Darmstadt: Luchterhand, 1962.

Lionnet, Françoise. *Autobiographical Voices: Race, Gender, Self-Portraiture.* Ithaca, London: Cornell UP, 1989.

———. "*Métissage,* Emancipation, and Textuality." In *Life/Lines: Theorizing Women's Autobiography,* ed. Bella Brodzki and Celeste Schenck. Ithaca, London: Cornell UP, 1988. 260–78.

Löffler, Sigrid. "'Melancholie ist eine Form des Widerstands': Über das Satur-nische bei W. G. Sebald und seine Aufhebung in der Schrift." *Text + Kritik* 158 (2003), *W. G. Sebald*, 103–11.

———. "Wildes Denken: Gespräch mit W. G. Sebald." In *W. G. Sebald*, ed. Franz Loquai. Eggingen: Edition Isele, 1997. 35–37.

Long, J. J. "History, Narrative and Photography in W. G. Sebald's *Die Ausge-wanderten.*" *The Modern Language Review* 98 (2003): 117–37.

Lorde, Audre. *A Burst of Light: Essays by Audre Lorde.* Ithaca, NY: Firebrand Books, 1988.

———. "Foreword to the English Language Edition." In *Showing Our Colors: Afro-German Women Speak Out*, ed. May Opitz, Katharina Oguntoye, and Dagmar Schultz, trans. Anne V. Adams. Amherst: U of Massachusetts P, 1992. vii–xiv.

———. *The Collected Poems of Audre Lorde.* New York, London: Norton, 1997.

Lorenz, Dagmar C. G. "Hoffentlich werde ich taugen: Zu Situation und Kon-text von Brigitte Schwaiger/Eva Deutsch *Die Galizianerin.*" *Yearbook of Women in German* 6 (1991): 1–25.

———. "Transcending the Boundaries of Space and Culture: The Figures of the Maharal and the Golem after the Shoah — Friedrich Torberg's *Golems Wiederkehr*, Leo Perutz's *Nachts unter der steinernen Brücke*, Frank Zwill-inger's *Maharal*, and Nelly Sachs's *Eli: Ein Mysterienspiel vom Leiden Israels.*" In *Transforming the Center, Eroding the Margins: Essays on Ethnic and Cul-tural Boundaries in German-Speaking Countries*, ed. Dagmar C. G. Lorenz and Renate S. Posthofen. Columbia, SC: Camden House, 1998. 285–302.

Madsen, Deborah L., ed. *Beyond the Borders: American Literature and Post-Colonial Theory.* London: Pluto Press, 2003.

Malkmus, Bernhard. "'All of Them Signs and Characters from the Type-Case of Forgotten Things': Intermedia Configurations of History in W. G. Sebald." In *Memory Traces: 1989 and the Question of German Cultural Iden-tity*, ed. Silke Arnold-de-Simine. Oxford, Bern, Berlin: Lang, 2005. 211–44.

Mann, Thomas. "Warum ich nicht nach Deutschland zurückkehre." In *Essays 6: Meine Zeit 1945–1955*, ed. Hermann Kurze and Stephan Stachorski. Frankfurt am Main: Fischer, 1977. 33–45.

Mannheim, Karl. "Das Problem der Generationen." In *Wissenssoziologie*, ed. Kurt H. Wolff (Soziologische Texte 28). Berlin, Neuwied: Luchterhand, 1964. 509–65.

Marcus, Laura. *Auto/biographical Discourses: Criticism, Theory, Practice.* Man-chester: Manchester UP, 1994.

Marcuse, Herbert. *Eros and Civilization. A Philosophical Enquiry into Freud.* Boston: Beacon Press, 1956.

Maron, Monika. *Pawels Briefe.* Frankfurt am Main: Fischer, 1999.

———. *Quer über die Gleise: Essays, Artikel, Zwischenrufe.* Frankfurt am Main: Fischer, 2000.

———. *Stille Zeile sechs.* Frankfurt am Main: Fischer, 2001.

Massaquoi, Hans J. "*Neger, Neger, Schornsteinfeger!*" *Meine Kindheit in Deutschland*. Bern, Munich, Vienna: Scherz, 1999. In English: *Destined to Witness: Growing up Black in Nazi Germany*. New York: William Morrow, 1999.

Mauelshagen, Claudia. *Der Schatten des Vaters: Deutschsprachige Väterliteratur der siebziger und achtziger Jahre*. Bern, Frankfurt am Main: Lang, 1995.

McCulloh, Mark R. *Understanding W. G. Sebald*. Columbia, SC: U of South Carolina P, 2003.

McHale, Brian. *Postmodernist Fiction*. London, New York: Routledge, 1987.

Mechtersheimer, Alfred. "Nation und Internationalismus: Über nationales Selbstbewußtsein als Bedingung des Friedens." In *Die selbstbewußte Nation*, ed. Schwilk and Schacht, 345–63.

Meckel, Christoph. *Suchbild: Meine Mutter*. Munich, Vienna: Hanser, 2002.

———. *Suchbild: Über meinen Vater*. Frankfurt am Main: Fischer, 1983.

Meier-Bergfeld, Peter. "Deutschland und Österreich." In *Die selbstbewußte Nation*, ed. Schwilk and Schacht, 195–226.

Meinecke, Friedrich. *Die deutsche Katastrophe: Betrachtungen und Erinnerungen*. Wiesbaden: Brockhaus, 1946.

Menasse, Robert. *Selige Zeiten, Brüchige Welt*. Frankfurt am Main: Suhrkamp, 1994.

———. *Sinnliche Gewissheit*. Frankfurt am Main: Suhrkamp, 1996.

———. *Die Vertreibung aus der Hölle*. Frankfurt am Main: Suhrkamp, 1993.

Mitgutsch, Anna. *Abschied von Jerusalem*. Berlin: Rowohlt, 1995.

———. *In fremden Städten*. Munich: dtv, 1994.

Mitscherlich, Alexander, and Margarete Mitscherlich. *The Inability to Mourn: Principles in Collective Behavior*. Trans. Beverley R. Placzek. New York: Grove Press, 1975 [1967].

Moeller, Robert G. *War Stories: The Search for a Usable Past in the Federal Republic of Germany*. Berkeley: U of California P, 2001.

Mohler, Armin. *Liberalenbeschimpfung*. Essen: Heitz & Höffkes, 1990.

Mommsen, Hans. "Der Widerstand gegen Hitler und die deutsche Gesellschaft." In *Der Widerstand gegen den Nationalsozialismus: Die deutsche Gesellschaft und der Widerstand gegen Hitler*, ed. Jürgen Schmädeke and Peter Steinbach. Munich: R. Piper, 1985. 3–24.

Mondada, Lorenza, and Simona Pekarek Doehler, eds. *Plurilinguisme — Mehrsprachigkeit — Plurilingualism: Enjeux identitaires, socio-culturels et éducatifs*. Tübingen: Francke, 2003.

Morgan, Peter. "The Sign of Saturn: Melancholy, Homelessness and Apocalypse in W. G. Sebald's Prose Narratives." *German Life and Letters* 58 (2005): 75–92.

Müller, Jan-Werner. *Another Country: German Intellectuals, Unification and National Identity*. New Haven and London: Yale UP, 2000. 129–30.

Münster, Clemens. "Zum Aufbau der geistigen Bildung." *Frankfurter Hefte: Zeitschrift für Kultur und Politik* 8 (1946): 703–14.

Naumann, Klaus. *Der Krieg als Text: Das Jahr 1945 im kulturellen Gedächtnis der Presse.* Hamburg: Hamburger Edition, 1998.

Nelde, Peter H., ed. *Mehrsprachigkeit, Minderheiten und Sprachwandel/Multilingualism, Minorities and Language Change.* St. Augustin: Asgard, 2004.

Neumann, Peter Horst. *Zur Lyrik Paul Celans: Eine Einführung.* Göttingen: Vandenhoek & Ruprecht, 1990.

Niven, Bill. *Facing the Nazi Past: United Germany and the Legacy of the Third Reich.* London, New York: Routledge, 2002.

Nombuso, Sithebe. "Ost- oder Westdeutschland, für mich ist das kein großer Unterschied." In *Entfernte Verbindungen: Rassismus, Antisemitismus, Klassenunterdrückung,* ed. Ika Hügel, Chris Lange, May Ayim, Ilona Bubeck, Gülsen Aktas, Dagmar Schultz. Berlin: Orlanda Frauenverlag, 1993. 224–32.

Nora, Pierre. "Generation." In *Realms of Memory: Rethinking the French Past: Vol. 1: Conflicts and Divisions.* Trans. Arthur Goldhammer. New York: Columbia UP, 1996. 499–531.

———. *Zwischen Gedächtnis und Geschichte.* Trans. Wolfgang Kaiser. Frankfurt: Fischer, 1998.

Novick, Peter. *The Holocaust in American Life.* New York: Houghton Mifflin, 1999.

Oguntoye, Katharina. *Eine Afro-Deutsche Geschichte: Zur Lebenssituation von Afrikanern und Afro-Deutschen von 1884 bis 1950.* Berlin: Hoho Verlag, 1997.

Oguntoye, Katharina, May Opitz, and Dagmar Schultz, eds. *Farbe bekennen: Afro-deutsche Frauen auf den Spuren ihrer Geschichte.* Berlin: Orlanda Frauenverlag, 1986.

Pache, Ilona, and Regina-Maria Dackweiler. "An Interview with Audre Lorde (1987)." In *Conversations with Audre Lorde,* ed. Joan Wylie Hall. Jackson: U of Mississippi P, 2004, 164–70.

Opitz, May, Katharina Oguntoye, and Dagmar Schultz, eds. *Our Colors: Afro-German Women Speak Out.* Trans. Anne V. Adams. Amherst: U of Massachusetts P, 1992.

Pascal, Roy. *Design and Truth in Autobiography.* London: Routledge, 1960.

Paver, Chloe E. M. *Narrative and Fantasy in the Post-War German Novel.* Oxford: Clarendon Press, 1999.

———. *Refractions of the Third Reich in German and Austrian Fiction and Film.* Oxford: Oxford UP, forthcoming.

Pelevin, Victor. *Omon Ra.* Trans. Andrew Bromfield. London: Harbord, 1994.

Perry, Joe. "The Madonna of Stalingrad: The (Christmas) Past and West German National Identity after World War II." *Radical History Review* 83 (2002): 7–27.

Petz, Ernst. *Kafka der Golem und Fußball und Prag: 1 phantastischer Roman.* Vienna: Aarachne, 1998.

Pfahl-Traughber, Armin. *"Konservative Revolution" und "Neue Rechte": echtextremistische Intellektuelle gegen den demokratischen Verfassungsstaat.* Opladen: Leske und Budrich, 1998.

Plessens, Elisabeth. *Mitteilung an den Adel.* Zurich, Cologne: Benzinger, 1976.

Plowman, Andrew. "Escaping the Autobiographical Trap? Monika Maron, the Stasi and *Pawels Briefe.*" In *German Writers and the Politics of Culture: Dealing with the Stasi,* ed. Paul Cooke and Andrew Plowman. Basingstoke: Palgrave, 2003. 227–42.

———. "History, Identity and the Writer: Helga Königsdorf and Monika Maron since 1990." In *Legacies and Identity: East and West German Responses to Unification,* ed. Martin Kane. Oxford: Peter Lang, 2002. 81–96.

———. "Was will ich als Westdeutscher erzählen?: The Old West and Globalisation in Recent German Prose." In *German Literature and The Age of Globalisation,* ed. Stuart Taberner. Birmingham: Birmingham UP, forthcoming.

———. "Westalgie? Nostalgia for the Old Federal Republic in Recent German Prose." *Seminar* 40 (2004): 1–14.

Porsch, Donald C. *Die Zweisprachigkeit während des primären Spracherwerbs.* Tübingen: Narr, 1983.

Pott, Gudrun Patricia. "Die Flegeljahre der Republik. Der Aufstieg aus dem Nichts." *Der Spiegel,* 18 May 1999, 148–50.

Rabinovici, Doron. *Credo und Credit.* Frankfurt am Main: Suhrkamp, 2001.

———. *Instanzen der Ohnmacht: Wien 1938–1945. Der Weg zum Judenrat.* Frankfurt: Jüdischer Verlag, 2000.

———. *Ohnehin.* Frankfurt: Suhrkamp, 2004.

———. "Der richtige Riecher." In *Papirnik.* Frankfurt am Main: Suhrkamp, 1994. 7–18, 60–73.

———. *Suche nach M.* Frankfurt: Suhrkamp, 1997.

Rector, Martin. "Frühe Absonderung, später Abschied. Adoleszenz und Faschismus in den autobiographischen Erzählungen von Georges-Arthur Goldschmidt und Peter Weiss." *Peter Weiss Jahrbuch* 4 (1995): 122–39.

Regener, Susanne. *Fotografische Erfassung: Zur Geschichte medialer Konstruktionen des Kriminellen.* Munich: Fink, 1999.

Rehmann, Ruth. *Der Mann auf der Kanzel: Fragen an einen Vater.* Munich, Vienna, 1979.

Reichel, Peter. *Erfundene Erinnerung: Weltkrieg und Judenmord in Film und Theater.* Munich: Hanser, 2004.

Reifarth, Dieter, and Viktoria Schmidt-Linsenhoff. "Die Kamera der Täter." In *Vernichtungskrieg,* ed. Heer and Naumann, 475–503.

Rensmann, Lars. "Four Wings of the Intellectual New Right" (unpublished manuscript), 2003.

Robertson, Ritchie. *Kafka: Judaism, Politics, and Literature.* Oxford: Oxford UP, 1985.

Rohrmoser, Günter. *Deutschlands Tragödie.* Munich: Olzog, 2002.

Ronjat, Julet. *Le développement du langage observé chez un enfant bilingue.* Paris: Champion, 1913.

Rosenstone, Robert A. "The Historical Film: Looking at the Past in a Postliterate Age." In *The Historical Film: History and Memory in Media,* ed. Marcia Landy. London: Athlone Press, 2001. 50–66.

Rosenthal, Gabriele, ed. *Der Holocaust im Leben von drei Generationen: Familien von Überlebenden der Shoah und von Nazi-Tätern.* Gießen: Psychosozial Verlag, 1997.

Rossino, Alexander B. "Eastern Europe through German Eyes. Soldiers' Photographs 1939–42." *History of Photography* 23 (1999): 313–21.

Rühle, Lothar. "Ein Patriarch vom Rhein. Der Kanzler Konrad Adenauer." *Der Spiegel,* 18 May 1999, 110–15.

Sachs, Nelly. "Golem Tod." In *Das Leiden Israels: Eli: In den Wohnungen des Todes: Sternverdunkelung.* Frankfurt am Main: Edition Suhrkamp, 1996. 196.

Said, Edward. W. "Traveling Theory." In *The World, the Text and the Critic.* London: Vintage, 1991. 226–47.

Sander, Helke. "Telefongespräch mit einem Freund." In *Die Geschichten der drei Damen K.* Munich: dtv, 1991. 104–14.

Schacht, Ulrich. "Stigma und Sorge: Über deutsche Identität nach Auschwitz." In *Die selbstbewußte Nation,* ed. Schwilk and Schacht, 57–68.

Schaffrath, Michael. "Wir sind wieder wer: Die wachsende Bedeutung der Sportkultur." In *Die Kultur der 50er Jahre,* ed. Werner Faulstich. Munich: Wilhelm Fink, 2002. 145–57.

Schedel, Susanne. *"Wer weiß, wie es vor Zeiten wirklich gewesen ist?" Textbeziehungen als Mittel der Geschichtsschreibung bei W. G. Sebald.* Würzburg: Königshausen & Neumann, 2004.

Scheil, Stefan. "Argumentation mit der Brechstange." *Junge Freiheit,* 11 April 2003.

Schelsky, Helmut. "Gesellschaftlicher Wandel." In *Auf der Suche nach Wirklichkeit: Gesammelte Aufsätze.* Düsseldorf, Cologne: Diedrichs, 1965. 337–51.

Schildt, Axel. *Ankunft im Westen: Ein Essay zur Erfolgsgeschichte der Bundesrepublik.* Frankfurt am Main: Fischer, 1999.

———. *Moderne Zeiten: Freizeit, Massenmedien und Zeitgeist in der Bundesrepublik der 50er Jahre.* Hamburg: Christians, 1995.

Schildt, Axel, and Arnold Sywottek. "Reconstruction and Modernization: West German Social History during the 1950s." In *West Germany under Reconstruction,* ed. Robert G. Moeller. Ann Arbor: U of Michigan P, 1997. 413–43.

Schindel, Robert. *Born-Where.* Trans. Michael Roloff. Riverside: Ariadne Press, 1995.

Schindel, Robert. *Gebürtig*. Frankfurt am Main: Suhrkamp, 1994.

Schlant, Ernestine. *The Language of Silence: West German Literature and the Holocaust*. New York, London: Routledge, 1999.

Schleiermacher, Friedrich. "Über die verschiedenen Methoden des Übersetzens." In *Das Problem des Übersetzens*, ed. Hans Joachim Strig. Darmstadt: Wissenschaftliche Buchgesellschaft, 1963. 38–70.

Schlösser, Manfred, and Hans-Rolf Ropertz, eds. *An den Wind geschrieben*. Darmstadt: Agora, 1960.

Schmeling, Manfred, and Monika Schmitz-Emans, eds. *Multilinguale Literatur im 20. Jahrhundert*. Würzburg: Königshausen & Neumann, 2002.

Schmiegelt, Ulrike. "Macht euch um mich keine Sorgen. . . ." In *Fotofeldpost: Geknipste Kriegserlebnisse 1939–45*, ed. Peter Jahn und Ulrike Schmiegelt. Berlin: Elefanten 2000. 23–31.

Schmitt, Carl. *Ex Captivitate Salus: Erfahrungen der Zeit 1945/47*. Berlin: Duncker & Humblot, 1950.

Schneider, Peter. *Vati*. Darmstadt: Luchterhand, 1987.

Schneider, Stefan. "Frühkindliche Mehrsprachigkeit aus sprachwissenschaftlicher Sicht." In *Vielerlei Zungen: Mehrsprachigkeit + Spracherwerb + Pädagogik + Psychologie + Literatur + Medien*, ed. Allan James. Klagenfurt: Drava, 2003. 11–48.

Scholem, Gershom. *Von der mystischen Gestalt der Gottheit: Studien zu Grundbegriffen der Kabbala*. Frankfurt am Main: Suhrkamp, 1977.

———. *Zur Kabbala und ihrer Symbolik*. Frankfurt am Main: Suhrkamp, 1973.

Schönhuber, Franz. "Endzeit." *Nation und Europa*, January 1997, 9–12.

Schornstheimer, Michael. *Die leuchtenden Augen der Frontsoldaten: Nationalsozialismus und Krieg in den Illustriertenromanen der fünfziger Jahre*. Berlin: Metropol, 1995.

Schulte, Christian. "Die Naturgeschichte der Zerstörung. W. G. Sebalds Thesen zu Luftkrieg und Literatur." *Text + Kritik* 158 (2003), *W. G. Sebald*, 82–94.

Schwarz, Egon. "Austria, Quite a Normal Nation." *New German Critique* 93/3 (2004): 175–91.

Schwilk, Heimo, and Ulrich Schacht, eds. *Die selbstbewußte Nation: "Anschwellender Bocksgesang" und andere Beiträge zu einer deutschen Debatte*. Berlin: Ullstein, 1994.

Sebald, W. G. "Against the Irreversible: On Jean Améry." Trans. Anthea Bell. In *On the Natural History of Destruction*. London: Hamish Hamilton, 2003. 147–71.

———. *Die Ausgewanderten. Vier lange Erzählungen*. Frankfurt am Main: Fischer, 1994.

———. *Austerlitz*. Munich, Vienna: Carl Hanser, 2001.

———. *Austerlitz*. Trans. Anthea Bell. London: Hamish Hamilton, 2003.

Sebald, W. G. *Die Beschreibung des Unglücks: Zur österreichischen Literatur von Stifter bis Handke.* Salzburg, Vienna: Residenz, 1985.

———. *Campo Santo.* Ed. Sven Meyer. Munich, Vienna: Carl Hanser, 2003.

———. *The Emigrants.* Trans. Michael Hulse. London: The Harvill Press, 1996.

———. "Jean Améry und Primo Levi." In *Über Jean Améry,* ed. Irene Heidelberger-Leonard. Heidelberg: Carl Winter, 1990. 115–23.

———. "Konstruktionen der Trauer: Günter Grass und Wolfgang Hildesheimer." *Der Deutschunterricht* 35 (1983): 32–46.

———. *Logis in einem Landhaus: Über Gottfried Keller, Johann Peter Hebel, Robert Walser und andere.* Munich: Carl Hanser, 1998.

———. *Luftkrieg und Literatur: Mit einem Essay über Alfred Andersch.* Munich, Vienna: Hanser, 1999.

———. "Mit den Augen des Nachtvogels: Über Jean Améry." In *Campo Santo,* ed. Sven Meyer. Munich, Vienna: Carl Hanser, 2003. 149–70.

———. *On the Natural History of Destruction.* Trans. Anthea Bell. London: Hamish Hamilton, 2003.

———. "Der Schriftsteller Alfred Andersch." In *Luftkrieg und Literatur,* 113–47.

———. *Schwindel. Gefühle.* Frankfurt am Main: Eichborn, 1990.

———. *Unheimliche Heimat: Essays zur österreichischen Literatur.* Frankfurt am Main: Fischer, 1994.

———. "Verlorenes Land: Jean Améry und Österreich." In *Unheimliche Heimat: Essays zur österreichischen Literatur.* Frankfurt am Main: Fischer, 1994. 131–44.

———. *Vertigo.* Trans. Michael Hulse. London: The Harvill Press, 1999.

———. "Die Zerknirschung des Herzens: Über Erinnerung und Grausamkeit im Werk von Peter Weiss." *Orbis litterarum* 41 (1986): 265–78.

———. "Zwischen Geschichte und Naturgeschichte. Versuch über die literarische Beschreibung totaler Zerstörung." *Orbis litterarum* 37 (1982): 345–66. Reprint in *Campo Santo,* 69–100.

Seebacher-Brandt, Brigitte. "Norm und Normalität: Über die Liebe zum eigenen Land." In *Die selbstbewußte Nation,* ed. Schwilk and Schacht, 43–56.

Sephocle, Marilyn. "Black Germans and Their Compatriots." In *The African-German Experience,* ed. Carol Aisha Blackshire-Belay. London: Praeger, 1996. 13–27.

Seydel, Heinz, ed. *Welch Wort in die Kälte gerufen.* Berlin: Verlag der Nation, 1968.

Shedletzky, Itta. "Eine deutsch-jüdische Stimme sucht Gehör: Zu Esther Dischereits Romanen, Hörspielen und Gedichten." In *In der Sprache der Täter: Neue Lektüren deutschsprachiger Nachkriegs- und Gegenwartsliteratur,* ed. Stephan Braese. Opladen: Westdeutscher Verlag, 1998. 199–225.

Silverman, Kaja. *The Threshold of the Visible World*. London: Routledge, 1996.

Simmel, Georg. "Die Ruine." In *Philosophische Kultur: Über das Abenteuer, die Geschlechter und die Krise der Moderne*. Berlin: Klaus Wagenbach, 1998. 118–24.

Spengler, Oswald. *Der Untergang des Abendlandes*. Munich: Beck, 1922.

Stein, Benjamin. *Das Alphabet des Juda Liva*. Munich: dtv, 1998.

Steinbach, Peter. "Der Widerstand als Thema der politischen Zeitgeschichte." In *Bekenntnis, Widerstand, Martyrium: Von Barmen 1934 bis Plötzensee 1944*, ed. Gerhard Besier and Gerhard Ringshausen. Göttingen: Vandenhoeck & Ruprecht, 1986. 11–74.

Stoehr, Irene. "Machtergriffen? Deutsche Frauenbewegung 1933." *Courage* 2 (1983): 24–32.

Strauß, Botho. "Anschwellender Bocksgesang." *Der Spiegel*, 8 February 1993.

———. *Beginnlosigkeit: Reflexionen über Fleck und Linie*. Munich: dtv, 2nd ed. 1997.

———. *Die Fehler des Kopisten*. Munich, Vienna: Hanser, 1997.

———. *Der Untenstehende auf Zehenspitzen*. Munich, Vienna: Carl Hanser, 2004.

Swales, Martin. "Theoretical Reflections on the Work of W. G. Sebald." In *W. G. Sebald: A Critical Companion*, ed. J. J. Long and Anne Whitehead. Edinburgh: Edinburgh UP, 2004. 23–28.

Sywottek, Arnold. "Wege in 50er Jahre." In *Modernisierung im Wiederaufbau: Die westdeutsche Gesellschaft der 50er Jahre*, ed. Axel Schildt and Arnold Sywottek. Bonn: Dietz, 1993. 19–39.

Taberner, Stuart. *German Literature of the 1990s and Beyond: Normalization and the Berlin Republic*. Rochester, NY: Camden House, 2005.

———. "Philo-Semitism in Recent German Film: *Aimée und Jaguar, Rosenstraße* and *Das Wunder von Bern*," *German Life and Letters* 58:3 (2005): 357–72.

Thiam, Awa. *Speak Out, Black Sisters: Feminism and Oppression in Black Africa*. Trans. Dorothy S. Blair. London: Pluto Press, 1986.

Timm, Uwe. *Am Beispiel meines Bruders*. Cologne: Kiepenheuer & Witsch, 2003.

———. *In My Brothers Shadow*. Trans. Anthea Bell. London: Bloomsbury, 2005.

———. *Rot*. Cologne: Kiepenheuer & Witsch, 2001.

Toteberg, Michael, ed. *Good Bye Lenin. Ein Film von Wolfgang Becker, Drehbuch von Bernd Lichtenberg, Co-Autor Wolfgang Becker*. Berlin: Schwarzkopf & Schwarzkopf, 2003.

Tracy, Rosemarie. "Vom Ganzen und seinen Teilen. Überlegungen zum doppelten Erstspracherwerb." *Sprache und Kognition* 15/1–2 (1996): 70–92.

Ulbrich, Stefan. "Es entsteht eine neue Kultur." *Junge Freiheit*, 7 October 1992, 24.

Utsch, Susanne. "Vergnügen und Qual des englisch-Schreibens: An Approach to the Literary Language Shift of Klaus Mann." In *Die Alchemie des Exils:*

Exil als schöpferischer Impuls, ed. Helga Schreckenberger. Vienna: edition präsens, 2005.

Vad, Erich. "Eine ganze Generation unter Generalverdacht." *Junge Freiheit*, 11 January 2002.

Venohr, Wolfgang. "Vor 50 Jahren." *Junge Freiheit* 1/2, January/February, 1992.

Vertlib, Vladimir. *Abschiebung*. Salzburg: Otto Möller, 1995.

———. *Das besondere Gedächtnis der Rosa Masur*. Munich: dtv, 2001.

———. " 'Jude, wie interessant' — 'A Jew, How Interesting!' " In *Juden in Salzburg*, ed. Helga Embacher. Salzburg: Anton Pustet, 2002. 104–11.

———. *Zwischenstationen*. Vienna: Deutike, 1999.

Vesper, Bernward. *Die Reise*. Jassa: März-Verlag, 1977.

Vogt, Jochen. "Er fehlte, er fehlte, er hat gefehlt: Ein Rückblick auf die sogenannten Väterbücher." In *Deutsche Nachkriegsliteratur und der Holocaust*, ed. Stephan Braese, Holger Gehle, Doron Kiesel, Hanno Lowey. Frankfurt am Main, New York: Campus, 1998. 385–99.

Walser, Martin. "Erfahrungen beim Verfassen einer Sonntagsrede." In *Die Walser-Bubis-Debatte. Eine Dokumentation*, ed. Frank Schirrmacher. Frankfurt am Main: Suhrkamp, 1999. 7–29.

Wandruszka, Mario. *Interlinguistik: Umrisse einer neuen Sprachwissenschaft*. Munich: Piper, 1971.

———. *Die Mehrsprachigkeit des Menschen*. Munich: Piper, 1979.

Webber, Andrew. *The Doppelgänger: Double Visions in German Literature*. Oxford: Clarendon Press, 1996.

Weber, Markus R. "Die fantastische befragt die pedantische Genauigkeit: Zu den Abbildungen in W. G. Sebalds Werken." *Text + Kritik* 58 (2003): 63–74.

Weigel, Sigrid. "Generation as a Symbolic Form: On the Genealogical Discourse of Memory since 1945." *The Germanic Review* 77 (2002): 264–77.

———. "Télescopage im Unbewußten: Zum Verhältnis von Trauma, Geschichtsbegriff und Literatur." In Elisabeth Bronfen, Birgit Erdle, and Sigrid Weigel, eds. *Trauma zwischen Psychoanalyse und kulturellen Deutungsmustern*. Cologne: Böhlau, 1999. 51–76.

Weigel, Sigrid, Ohad Parmes, Ulrike Vedder, and Stefan Willer, eds. *Generation: Zur Genealogie des Konzepts — Konzepte von Genealogie*. Munich: Fink, 2005.

Weiler, Gerda. *Ich verwerfe im Lande die Kriege: Auf den Spuren des Matriarchats im Alten Testament*. Munich: Verlag Frauenoffensive, 1984.

Weinreich, Uriel. *Languages in Contact: Findings and Problems*. The Hague: Mouton, 1953.

Weißmann, Karlheinz. *Alles was recht(s) ist: Ideen, Köpfe und Perspektiven der politischen Rechten*. Graz, Stuttgart: Leopold Stocker, 2000.

———. *Rückruf in die Geschichte*. Frankfurt am Main, Berlin: Ullstein, 1992.

Welzer, Harald. "Der Holocaust im deutschen Familiengedächtnis." In *Verbrechen erinnern: Die Auseinandersetzung mit Holocaust und Völkermord*, ed. Volkhard Knigge and Norbert Frei. Munich: Beck, 2002. 342–58.

———. "Schön unscharf: Über die Konjunktur der Familien- und Generationenromane." *Mittelweg* 36.1 (2004): 53–65.

Welzer, Harald, Sabine Moller, and Karoline Tschugnall, eds. *"Opa war kein Nazi." Nationalsozialismus und Holocaust im Familiengedächtnis*. Frankfurt am Main: Fischer Verlag, 2002.

Wenders, Wim. *"That's Entertainment: Hitler."* In *Emotion Pictures: Essays und Filmkritiken*. Frankfurt: Verlag der Autoren, 1986.

Willer, Stefan. *Poetik der Etymologie: Texturen sprachlichen Wissens in der Romantik*. Berlin: Akademie, 2003.

Wilms, Wilfried. "Taboo and Repression in W. G. Sebald's On the Natural History of Destruction." In *W. G. Sebald: A Critical Companion*, ed. J. J. Long and Anne Whitehead. Edinburgh: Edinburgh UP, 2004. 175–89.

Winkler, Willi. "Dumm debattiert sich's besser." *Süddeutsche Zeitung*, 30 March 2000, 23.

Wirner, Stefan. "Dresden geht in sich." *Jungle World* 6 (9 February 2005): 5.

Wouk, Herman. *War and Remembrance*. ABC Circle Films, 1988.

Wylie, Hal, ed. *Multiculturalism and Hybridity in African Literatures*. Trenton, NJ: Africa World Press, 2000.

Yakut, Atilla. *Cultural Linguistics and Bilingualism: A Bibliography*. Frankfurt am Main: Landeck, 1994.

Zilkosky, John. "Sebald's Uncanny Travels: The Impossibility of Getting Lost." In *W. G. Sebald: A Critical Companion*, ed. J. J. Long and Anne Whitehead. Edinburgh: Edinburgh UP, 2004. 102–20.

Zipes, Jack. "The Contemporary German Fascination for Things Jewish: Towards a Jewish Minority Culture." In *Reemerging Jewish Culture in Germany: Life and Literature since 1989*, ed. Sander Gilman and Karen Remmler. New York, London: New York UP, 1994. 15–46.

Zitelmann, Rainer. "Position und Begriff." In *Die selbstbewußte Nation*, eds. Schwilk and Schacht, 163–81.

Editors and Contributors

ELIZABETH BOA is Emeritus Professor of German at the University of Nottingham, UK. She has published *Critical Strategies: German Fiction in the Twentieth Century* (London, 1972; co-author J. H. Reid), *The Sexual Circus: Wedekind's Theatre of Subversion* (Oxford, 1987), *Kafka: Gender, Class, Race in the Letters and Fictions* (Oxford, 1996) and *Heimat — A German Dream: Regional Loyalties and National Identity in German Culture 1890–1990* (Oxford, 2000; co-author Rachel Palfreyman) as well as numerous articles on German literature from the eighteenth century to the present day. She is co-editor with Janet Wharton of *Women and the Wende: Social Effects and Cultural Reflections of the German Unification Process* (German Monitor 31, 1994) and, with Heike Bartel, of *Anne Duden: A Revolution of Words* (German Monitor 56, 2003).

MARY COSGROVE is Lecturer in German at the School of Literatures, Languages and Cultures, University of Edinburgh. Her teaching and research interests include twentieth-century German-Jewish literature, post-1945 and contemporary German literature, contemporary German memory debates, Holocaust historiography and memory. She has published on writers such as Albert Drach, W. G. Sebald, Wolfgang Hildesheimer, and Günter Grass. Her dissertation, *Grotesque Ambivalence: Mourning and Melancholy in the Prose Work of Albert Drach* (Niemeyer, 2004) explores memory discourses in the writing of the Austro-Jewish Holocaust survivor, Albert Drach. Recently she has co-edited (with Anne Fuchs) a special issue on German memory contests (*German Life & Letters* 59/2 [2006]). Her current project focuses on melancholy and history in the post-1945 German novel.

MATTHIAS FIEDLER is currently DAAD-Lektor at University College Dublin. He studied Germanistik, History, and Anthropology at the University of Göttingen and has recently published his Ph.D. thesis on German Africa discourses in the eighteenth and nineteenth centuries, *Zwischen Abenteuer, Wissenschaft und Kolonialismus. Der deutsche Afrikadiskurs im 18. und 19. Jahrhundert* (2005). His current research interests include memory contests in contemporary German literature and European film.

PETER FRITZSCHE is Professor of History at the University of Illinois at Urbana-Champaign and the author of numerous books including *Reading Berlin 1900* (Cambridge, 1996) and *Stranded in the Present: Modern Time and the Melancholy of History* (Cambridge, 2004).

ANNE FUCHS is Professor of Modern German Literature and Culture at University College Dublin. She is author of *Dramaturgie des Narrentums: Das Komische in der Prosa Robert Walsers* (1993), *A Space of Anxiety: Dislocation and Abjection in Modern German-Jewish Literature* (1999), and *Die Schmerzensspuren der Geschichte: Zur Poetik der Erinnerung in der Prosa W. G. Sebalds* (2004). Her most recent articles focus on cultural memory in modern German literature. Co-editorships include *Ghetto Writing: Traditional and Eastern Jewry in German-Jewish Ghetto Writing from Heine to Hilsenrath* (with Florian Krobb, 1999), *Cultural Memory: Essays on European Literature and History* (with Edric Caldicott, 2003), *Sentimente, Gefühle Empfindungen: Zur Geschichte und Literatur des Affektiven von 1770 bis heute* (with Sabine Strümper-Krobb, 2003) and a special issue on German memory contests (*German Life & Letters* 59/2 [2006], with Mary Cosgrove).

CATHY S. GELBIN has held posts in Jewish Studies at the universities of Potsdam and Sussex and has been Lecturer in German Studies at the University of Manchester since 2000. Her research and teaching focus on constructions of Jews and gender in nineteenth- and twentieth-century German culture. Select publications include *An Indelible Seal: Race, Hybridity and Identity in Elisabeth Langgaesser's Writings* (2001), *Auf-Brüche: Kulturelle Produktionen von Migrantinnen, Schwarzen und jüdischen Frauen in Deutschland* (1999; co-editor), and *Archiv der Erinnerung: Interviews mit Überlebenden der Shoah: Videographierte Lebenserzählungen und ihre Interpretationen* (Potsdam, 1998; co-editor).

GEORG GROTE is College Lecturer in the School of Languages, Literatures and Film in University College Dublin. His research areas include Western European history with special focus on historical and contemporary collective organization of peoples through nationalism and regionalism. Recent publications on Irish cultural nationalism and the South Tyrol issue in the twentieth century include: *Anglo-Irish Theatre and the Formation of a Nationalist Political Culture between 1890 and 1930* (Mellen, 2003) and "Gehen oder Bleiben? — Die Identitätskrise der deutschsprachigen Südtiroler 1939–1943" (*Modern Austrian Literature* 37, No. 1/2, 2004).

J. J. LONG is Professor of German at the University of Durham. He is author of *The Novels of Thomas Bernhard* (Camden House, 2001), and co-editor of *W. G. Sebald: A Critical Companion* (Edinburgh, 2004). He has published widely on twentieth-century literature, including articles on

Wyndham Lewis, Wolfgang Hildesheimer, Heinrich Böll, Hans Lebert, Gerhard Fritsch, and Dieter Kühn. His current research concerns W. G. Sebald and the relationship between German writers and photography.

DAGMAR C. G. LORENZ is Professor of Germanic Studies at the University of Illinois at Chicago. She researches on Austrian and nineteenth- and twentieth-century German and German-Jewish literary and cultural issues and Holocaust studies, with an emphasis on history and social thought and minority discourses. Recent publications include *Keepers of the Motherland: German Texts by Jewish Women Writers* (1997) and *Verfolgung bis zum Massenmord: Diskurse zum Holocaust in deutscher Sprache* (1992). She was editor of *German Quarterly*. She has edited volumes including *Contemporary Jewish Writing in Austria* (1999), *A Companion to the Works of Arthur Schnitzler* (Camden House, 2003), and most recently *A Companion to the Works of Elias Canetti* (Camden House, 2004).

JENNIFER E. MICHAELS is Samuel R. and Marie-Louise Rosenthal Professor of Humanities and Professor of German at Grinnell College in Iowa. She received her M.A. degree in German from Edinburgh University and her M.A. and Ph.D. in German from McGill University in Montreal. She has published four books and numerous articles about twentieth-century German and Austrian literature and culture, her main teaching and research interest.

CHLOE E. M. PAVER is Senior Lecturer in German at the University of Exeter. She is the author of *Narrative and Fantasy in the Postwar German Novel* (Oxford UP, 1999) and of *Refractions of the Third Reich in German and Austrian Fiction and Film* (Oxford UP, forthcoming). Currently the holder of a Humboldt Fellowship at the University of Konstanz, she is conducting a study of recent historical exhibitions about the Third Reich, which builds on the essay published in this volume.

ANDREW PLOWMAN teaches German language, literature, and film at the University of Liverpool. His research interests include the student movement of 1968, autobiography, and contemporary literature. His most recent publications have looked at the way the West German past is represented in recent German literature.

STEFAN WILLER is Wissenschaftlicher Mitarbeiter at the Center for Literary Research, Berlin. His main research interests are the concepts of "the generation" and "legacy" in literature and cultural history from the eighteenth to the twentieth century; literary research and the history of knowledge; and reader theory and philology. His publications include *Botho Strauß zur Einführung* (Junius, 2000); *Poetik der Etymologie: Texturen sprachlichen*

Wissens in der Romantik (Akademie, 2003); and *Generation: Zur Genealogie des Konzepts — Konzepte von Genealogie* (Fink, 2005; co-editor).

ROGER WOODS is Professor of German at the University of Nottingham (UK). His research focuses on the conservative revolution in the Weimar Republic, East German intellectuals before and after unification, and autobiography in twentieth-century Germany. Recent publications include *Nation ohne Selbstbewußtsein: Von der Konservativen Revolution zur Neuen Rechten* (2001). Professor Woods has just completed a full-length study of the New Right: *The Fractured Mind: The New Right in Germany as Culture and Politics.*

Index

Printed in the United States
95979LV00002B/1-18/A

9 781571 133243